BLUE HELMETS : A ~~REVIEW OF UN~~ P9-DWY-213

DATE DUE

~~JA 8 '93~~			
~~FE 26 '93~~			
~~MY 7 '93~~			
~~UE 22 '95~~			
MY 24 '96			
~~NY 27 '99~~			
~~JE 8 '00~~			
~~JE 9 '05~~			
AP 18 '05			

DEMCO 38-296

The Blue Helmets
A Review of United Nations Peace-keeping

The Blue Helmets

A Review
of United Nations
Peace-keeping

Second edition

United Nations

Note

This second edition of *The Blue Helmets* has been compiled in response to a request by the General Assembly at its Forty-fourth Session in 1989. It contains a comprehensive account of the peace-keeping operations of the United Nations from their inception in 1948 up to June 1990. It represents an attempt to make available in easily accessible form the main facts about these operations. It is intended to be a work of reference for general use and is not a formal report of the United Nations.

ISBN: 92-1-100444-6

UNITED NATIONS PUBLICATION
Sales No.: E.90.I.18

Published by the United Nations Department of Public Information
DPI/1065—40500—August 1990—21M

United Nations peace-keeping operations 1948–90

1948–	**UNTSO**
	United Nations Truce Supervision Organization
1949–	**UNMOGIP**
	United Nations Military Observer Group in India and Pakistan
1956–67	**UNEF I**
	First United Nations Emergency Force
1958	**UNOGIL**
	United Nations Observation Group in Lebanon
1960–64	**ONUC**
	United Nations Operation in the Congo
1962–63	**UNTEA/UNSF**
	United Nations Temporary Executive Authority and United Nations Security Force in West New Guinea (West Irian)
1963–64	**UNYOM**
	United Nations Yemen Observation Mission
1964–	**UNFICYP**
	United Nations Peace-keeping Force in Cyprus
1965–66	**DOMREP**
	Representative of the Secretary-General in the Dominican Republic
1965–66	**UNIPOM**
	United Nations India–Pakistan Observation Mission
1973–79	**UNEF II**
	Second United Nations Emergency Force
1974–	**UNDOF**
	United Nations Disengagement Observer Force
1978–	**UNIFIL**
	United Nations Interim Force in Lebanon
1988–90	**UNGOMAP**
	United Nations Good Offices Mission in Afghanistan and Pakistan

1988– **UNIIMOG**
United Nations Iran-Iraq Military Observer Group

1989– **UNAVEM**
United Nations Angola Verification Mission

1989–90 **UNTAG**
United Nations Transition Assistance Group in Namibia

1989– **ONUCA**
United Nations Observer Group in Central America

Contents

Part V The Congo...213

Foreword   by the Secretary-General

In 1988 and 1989 the United Nations Security Council set up five new peace-keeping operations. This doubled, in two years, the number of operations in the field, a striking increase when it is remembered that only thirteen such operations had been established during the previous 40 years. In September 1988, the Norwegian Nobel Committee awarded the Nobel Peace Prize to the peace-keeping forces of the United Nations.

These events have been hailed as a renaissance of peace-keeping, the innovative technique of conflict control and resolution which the United Nations has developed over the years. The late 1980s have certainly seen a much greater readiness on the part of the Member States to make use of this technique. There has also been wider recognition of the contribution which it can make to the maintenance of international peace and security.

As I stated in 1985 in my Foreword to the first edition of this book (see page xix), peace-keeping evolved as a technique for controlling dangerous regional conflicts at a time when relations between the most powerful nations were not such as to permit the Security Council to function fully in the manner envisaged in the Charter. Now, only five years later, the world has witnessed a dramatic improvement in the ability of the Council's members—both permanent and non-permanent—to work together to help control and resolve regional conflicts. Rather than leading to activation of the Charter provisions for the use of force by the Security Council, the new political climate has permitted greater and more effective use of the United Nations' armoury of non-violent means of controlling and resolving conflicts.

Peace-keeping, being based on consent and co-operation, is one of those means. It is most effective when used in close conjunction with others of them, especially the peace-making efforts of the Secretary-General which are, themselves, often undertaken in close consultation with the Security Council. Peace-keeping involves the deployment of military personnel by the United Nations—but not to fight or threaten anyone. On the contrary, their function is to use their international status and military skills, in many different ways, to help the parties control and eventually resolve their conflicts.

In this second edition of *The Blue Helmets*, the text of the first edition has been revised and updated as necessary and five new chapters have been added to describe the five operations set up in 1988 and 1989.

It will be noted that most of the new operations follow a familiar pattern, with the United Nations military personnel being used to monitor or verify compliance by various parties with agreements which they have entered into. But the functions of UNTAG in Namibia extended far beyond what could be called traditional peace-keeping. Like UNTAG, two other operations described in this book, ONUC in the Congo (as it then was) and UNTEA/UNSF in West Irian, assumed a wide range of non-military duties and included large civilian components. But UNTAG broke new ground—in monitoring the local police force, in supervising and controlling an election conducted by the *de facto* authority in the territory, above all in promoting and shaping a process of rapid political change. In so doing, UNTAG acquired experience which will be of great value if the Security Council decides to set up further such operations in the future. At least two of those which are currently at the planning stage could fall into this category.

If UNTAG broke new ground, its experience also underlined again the conditions which have to be filled if a peace-keeping operation is to succeed—a clear and practicable mandate, the consent and co-operation of the parties, the support of the Security Council, and prompt provision of the necessary funds. Since the first edition of this book was published, much concern has been expressed about the cost of peace-keeping. It *is* an expensive activity; in 1989 the peace-keeping budget was almost as great as the Organization's regular budget. But it is inexpensive by comparison with the alternative: the annual cost of the observer group which monitors the cease-fire between Iran and Iraq is less than the value of the crude oil carried in only two supertankers.

I hope that the international community will continue to use the peace-keeping technique and that the next edition of this book will again describe new operations. Even more I hope that the existing operations will have been terminated as a result of the settlement of the conflicts to which they relate. For a peace-keeping operation is intended to be an interim arrangement; it should, ultimately, contribute to a just and lasting solution to the conflict concerned.

If the Security Council decides to set up further peace-keeping operations, the Secretariat will be ready. So, too, I know, will be the Member States, now numbering more than half the United Nations membership, who have contributed military or civilian personnel to peace-keeping operations. The last word belongs to them, for without their readiness to make their citizens available for United Nations service, often in difficult and sometimes in dangerous places, peace-keeping would not be possible. These men and women have carried out their important tasks in a manner reflecting credit on themselves and on their countries. We all owe them a large debt of gratitude.

July 1990

Javier Pérez de Cuéllar

Foreword to the First Edition

Like many political institutions, the United Nations has been faced, virtually throughout its existence, with a deep gulf between theory and practice, between the principles and objectives of the Charter and the political realities of our time. The effort to bridge this gulf has been the main theme of the first forty years of the United Nations.

Nowhere has the gulf between theory and practice been so evident as in the primary function of the United Nations, the maintenance of international peace and security. The Charter's provisions for this purpose, based primarily on the activity of the Security Council and the unanimity of its permanent members, have never yet been permitted to function fully. Being unable to exercise the magisterial but relatively simple powers prescribed in the Charter, the Council has had, time and again, to fall back on less well-defined measures—good offices, conciliation, mediation and delegation of responsibility to the Secretary-General.

Of these less well-defined measures, the form of conflict control which is now known as peace-keeping is perhaps the most original and most ambitious. Peace-keeping is a technique not mentioned, let alone described, in the Charter. In fact it is in many ways a reversal of the use of military personnel foreseen in the Charter. It has been developed for situations where there is no formal determination of aggression. Its practitioners have no enemies, are not there to win, and can use force only in self-defence. Its effectiveness depends on voluntary co-operation.

It may seem strange that the United Nations has turned to various forms of this technique no less than 13 times and that peace-keeping is widely regarded as one of the Organization's most successful innovations. The reason presumably lies in the nature of international relations in our time. There are now many conflicts which neither side can hope to win but in which peaceful settlement remains elusive. Peace-keeping offers a dignified and inexpensive escape from such situations. In the present relationship of the most powerful nations, it is usually impossible for the Security Council to reach more drastic decisions for putting an end to threats to or breaches of the peace.

In a time of nuclear armament, it is more than ever important that regional conflicts in sensitive areas should be kept out of the sphere of possible great-Power nuclear confrontation. In this context, peace-keeping operations are one important means of conflict control, working, as they usually do, in partnership with the efforts of the Security Council and the Secretary-General to gain time and to promote just and peaceful settlements of international disputes. It is worth noting that peace-keeping operations tend to be established for conflict control in particularly sensitive areas of the world where the danger of escalation is high.

I believe that this novel but still fragile creation is an important addition to the armoury of peace in the nuclear age. I hope that the lessons of the past will contribute to a strengthening and wider employment of the peace-keeping technique in the future. In the particular international conditions of our time, I believe that the institution and technique of United Nations peace-keeping is an indispensable, and potentially highly effective, weapon in the struggle for world peace.

October 1985

Javier Pérez de Cuéllar

Part I **An overview**

The Charter

A holding action

Characteristics

Peace-keeping and peace-making

The operations

An overview

The Charter

The first of the purposes of the United Nations listed in its Charter is "To maintain international peace and security, and to that end: to take effective collective measures for the prevention and removal of threats to the peace, and for the suppression of acts of aggression or other breaches of the peace, and to bring about by peaceful means, and in conformity with the principles of justice and international law, adjustment or settlement of international disputes or situations which might lead to a breach of the peace".

Concrete measures to be taken by the United Nations Security Council, the principal organ which was vested with the primary responsibility for the maintenance of international peace and security, to achieve this purpose are set out in Chapters VI and VII of the Charter. Chapter VI provides that international disputes "likely to endanger the maintenance of international peace and security" can be brought to the attention of the Security Council or the General Assembly. The Security Council is expressly mandated to call on the parties to settle their disputes by peaceful means, to recommend appropriate procedures or methods of adjustment and, in addition, to recommend actual terms of a settlement. The action of the Security Council in this context is limited to making recommendations; essentially, the peaceful settlement of international disputes must be achieved by the parties themselves, acting on a voluntary basis to carry out the decisions of the Council in accordance with the Charter.

If the Security Council determines that a threat to the peace, breach of the peace or act of aggression exists, the Council may use the broad powers given it in Chapter VII of the Charter. In order to prevent an aggravation of the situation, the Security Council may call upon the parties concerned to comply with such provisional measures as it deems necessary or desirable. Next, it may decide, under Article 41, what measures not involving the use of armed force are to be employed by the Members of the United Nations, including the complete or partial interruption of economic relations, communications, and the severance of diplomatic relations. Should the Security Council consider such measures inadequate, it may take, under Article 42, "such action by air, sea and land forces as may be necessary to maintain or restore international peace and security". For this purpose, all Members of the United Nations undertake to make available to the Security Council, on its call and in accordance with special agreements, the necessary armed forces, assistance and facilities. Plans for the application of armed force are to be made by the Security Council with the assistance of a Military Staff Committee.

The measures outlined in Articles 41 and 42 constitute the core of the system of collective security envisaged by the Charter. A basic feature of this system is the determining role assigned to China, France, the Union of Soviet Socialist Republics, the United Kingdom of Great Britain and Northern Ireland and the United States of America. These Powers are permanent members of the Security Council and can block any of its substantive decisions by their veto. They also control the activities of the Military Staff Committee, which is made up exclusively of their military representatives. Consequently, the United Nations collective security system, and especially its key provision concerning the use of armed force, can work only if there is full agreement and co-operation among the permanent members.

A holding action

During most of the United Nations' history this condition has not been met. The evolution of international relations after the Second World War quickly brought to the fore differences which existed among the Member States, and in particular the five permanent members of the Security Council, and these inevitably affected the functioning of the Organization. New conflicts arose, particularly during the process of decolonization, and many could not be resolved by peaceful means. A way had to be found to stop hostilities and to control conflicts so that they would not develop into broader conflagrations. Out of that need, United Nations peace-keeping operations evolved as, essentially, holding actions. There was not, and still is not, any particular theory or doctrine behind them. They were born of necessity, largely improvised, a practical response to a problem requiring action. The term "peace-keeping operation" did not gain currency until much later.

As the United Nations practice has evolved over the years, a peace-keeping operation has come to be defined as an operation involving military personnel, but without enforcement powers, undertaken by the United Nations to help maintain or restore international peace and security in areas of conflict. These operations are voluntary and are based on consent and co-operation. While they involve the use of military personnel, they achieve their objectives not by force of arms, thus contrasting them with the "enforcement action" of the United Nations under Article 42.

Peace-keeping operations have been most commonly employed to supervise and help maintain cease-fires, to assist in troop withdrawals, and to provide a buffer between opposing forces. However, peace-keeping operations are flexible instruments of policy and have been adapted to a variety of uses, including helping to implement the final settlement of a conflict.

Peace-keeping operations are never purely military. They have always included civilian personnel to carry out essential political or administrative functions, sometimes on a very large scale, as, for instance, in the Congo operation or in the independence process in Namibia. In both those operations, and in several others, civilian police have also played an important role. During the resurgence of peace-keeping that has taken place in the later 1980s, with five new operations being established in two years and others under active planning, the expectation has developed that the peace-keeping operations of the future, like that in Namibia, may well be closely integrated civilian/military undertakings with overall responsibility in the field being entrusted to a civilian rather than a military officer.

It is difficult to subsume all these various operations under any one clause of the Charter. It is clear that they fall short of the provisions of Chapter VII described above, which deal with enforcement. At the same time they go beyond purely diplomatic means or those described in Chapter VI of the Charter. As former Secretary-General Dag Hammarskjöld put it, peace-keeping might be put in a new Chapter "Six and a Half". Initially, questions were raised about the legality of the United Nations' use of military personnel in a manner not specifically provided for in the Charter. In recent years, however, something close to consensus has developed that these operations can be considered as having a basis, apart from the principle of consent, in the broad powers conferred by the Charter upon the United Nations and especially the Security Council.

Characteristics

In practice, there has evolved a broad degree of consensus on the essential characteristics of peace-keeping operations and on the conditions that must be met if they are to succeed.

The first of these essential characteristics is that peace-keeping operations are set up only with the consent of the parties to the conflict in question. Their consent is required not only for the operation's establishment but also, in broad terms, for the way in which it will carry out its mandate. The parties are also consulted about the countries which will contribute troops to the operation. It is a key principle that the operation must not interfere in the internal affairs of the host countries and must not in any way favour one party against another. This requirement of impartiality is fundamental, not only on grounds of principle but also to ensure that the operation is effective. A United Nations operation cannot take sides without becoming a part of the conflict which it has been set up to control or resolve. For their part, the parties to the conflict are expected to provide continuing support to the operation by allowing it the freedom of movement and other facilities which it needs to carry out its task. This co-operation is essential. The peace-keepers have no rights of enforcement and their use of force is limited to self-defence, as a last resort. This means that if a party chooses not to co-operate, it can effectively defy a peace-keeping operation.

In line with the Security Council's primary responsibility for the maintenance of international peace and security, peace-keeping operations have mainly been established by the Council (though two were, exceptionally, authorized by the General Assembly). This means that no operation can be established without a broad consensus within the international community that it is the right thing to do. It is the Security Council's responsibility to ensure that the operation is given a mandate which is clear, accepted by the parties concerned and practicable in the situation existing on the ground. Also essential is the continuing support of the Security Council, which may be asked by the Secretary-General to intervene if one or other of the parties fails to provide the necessary support and co-operation. If the mandate is unclear or ambiguous, the operation is likely to face recurrent difficulties and its activities may become controversial, with the consequent risk that it may lose the necessary support of the Security Council or the necessary agreement of one of the parties concerned. Nevertheless, there have been times when the mandate of a peace-keeping operation has not been as clear as could have been wished, e.g., when the Security Council has decided that the primary requirement of international peace and security requires the creation of an operation even if it is clear from the outset that the operation will not easily achieve the objectives given to it.

The military personnel who serve in peace-keeping operations are provided by Member States on a voluntary basis. Once so provided, they pass under the command of the Secretary-General in all operational matters, as the Secretary-General is responsible for the direction of the operation and is required to report thereon at regular intervals to the Security Council. Those who serve in military observer missions are almost invariably unarmed. Those who serve in peace-keeping forces are equipped with light defensive weapons but are not authorized to use force except in self-defence. This right is exercised only sparingly because of the obvious danger that if a United Nations force uses its weapons its impartiality is, however unfairly, called in question. This requirement sometimes demands exceptional restraint on the part of soldiers serving in United Nations peace-keeping forces.

Finally, it is essential that the operation should have a sound financial basis. The financing of peace-keeping has been one of its most controversial and least satisfactory aspects. Almost all operations are now financed by obligatory contributions levied on Member States. If the Member States do not pay their contributions promptly and in full, the Secretary-General lacks the financial resources needed to reimburse to the troop-contributing Governments the sums due to them. This means, in effect, that those Governments have to pay an unfairly high share of the cost of the operation in question, in addition to sending their soldiers to serve in unpredictable and sometimes dangerous situations.

Peace-keeping and peace-making

Peace-keeping operations have usually been mounted only after hostilities have already broken out. However, the Charter of the United Nations aims at a system of international relations wherein the use of force as a means of foreign policy is eliminated altogether. Consequently, the Charter deals at length with the peaceful settlement of disputes. This may be achieved by various means, including multilateral diplomatic efforts within the framework of the Security Council, bilateral efforts of Member States, or through the good offices of the Secretary-General. These approaches to peace-making are by no means mutually exclusive. On the contrary, the Organization has been most successful when co-ordinated efforts were undertaken at all levels.

In recent years, there has been a marked increase in the demand for the Secretary-General's good offices, with a view to helping the parties to a conflict to compose their differences. In responding to these demands, the Secretary-General has usually been able to rely on a formal request of the Security Council or the General Assembly. In some cases, peace-keeping operations were established as a direct result of agreements reached through his and others' diplomatic efforts, and in some cases—West Irian and Namibia are the best examples—as part of complex arrangements for the final and, in the end, peaceful settlement of the conflict.

Peace-keeping operations are intended to be provisional and thus temporary measures. They can never, alone, resolve a conflict. Their tasks are essentially two: to stop or contain hostilities and thus help create conditions in which peace-making can prosper; or to supervise the implementation of an interim or final settlement which has been negotiated by the peace-makers. Ideally, peace-keeping should move in step with peace-making in a combined effort leading to the peaceful resolution of a conflict. In practice this ideal cannot always be attained. Sometimes it is less difficult to keep a cease-fire in being than to negotiate away the causes of the original conflict. In such cases it is right for the Security Council to ask itself from time to time whether the peace-keeping operation has "become part of the problem" by protecting the parties from the consequences of their negotiating stands. But it should not be assumed that longevity means that a peace-keeping operation has failed; on the contrary, longevity may be a measure of its success in preventing a recurrence of hostilities in spite of the intractability of the conflict between the parties.

The operations

United Nations peace-keeping operations can be divided into broad categories: observer missions, which consist largely of officers who are almost invariably unarmed; and peace-keeping forces, which consist of lightly armed infantry units, with the necessary logistic support elements. These categories are not, however, watertight. Observer missions are sometimes reinforced by infantry and/or logistic units, usually for a specific purpose and a brief period of time. Peace-keeping forces are often assisted in their work by unarmed military observers.

The first use of military personnel by the United Nations was in 1947, in two United Nations bodies: the Consular Commission in Indonesia and the Special Committee on the Balkans. Since the small officer groups worked as members of the national delegations comprising those bodies, and were not under the Secretary-General's authority, they cannot be considered as United Nations peace-keeping operations as the term has come to be used.

The international force in Korea was not a United Nations peace-keeping operation in the current sense of the term since the enforcement action was not carried out by the Organization, was not based on the consent of the parties, and involved the use of force.

The first peace-keeping operation established by the United Nations was an observer mission, the United Nations Truce Supervision Organization (UNTSO), which was set up in Palestine in June 1948. Later observer missions were: the United Nations Military Observer Group in India and Pakistan (UNMOGIP) in 1949, the United Nations Observation Group in Lebanon (UNOGIL) in 1958, the United Nations Yemen Observation Mission (UNYOM) in 1963, the United Nations India-Pakistan Observation Mission (UNIPOM) in 1965, the Mission of the Representative of the Secretary-General in the Dominican Republic (DOMREP) in the same year, the United Nations Good Offices Mission in Afghanistan and Pakistan (UNGOMAP) in 1988, the United Nations Iran-Iraq Military Observer Group (UNIIMOG) also in 1988, the United Nations Angola Verification Mission (UNAVEM) in 1989 and the United Nations Observer Group in Central America (ONUCA) in 1990. Of these, UNTSO, UNMOGIP, UNIIMOG, UNAVEM and ONUCA are still in operation.

There have been, in all, eight peace-keeping forces. The first was the United Nations Emergency Force (UNEF I), which was in operation in the Egypt–Israel sector from November 1956 until May 1967. The United Nations Operation in the Congo (ONUC) was deployed in the Republic of the Congo (now Zaire) from July 1960 until June 1964. The United Nations Security Force in West Irian (UNSF) was in operation from its establishment in September 1962 until April 1963. The second United Nations Emergency Force (UNEF II) functioned between Egypt and Israel from October 1973 until July 1979. The United Nations Transition Assistance Group (UNTAG) was deployed in Namibia from March 1989 until March 1990. The other three forces, which are still in operation, are the United Nations Peace-keeping Force in Cyprus (UNFICYP), established in March 1964; the United Nations Disengagement Observer Force (UNDOF) established in the Syrian Golan Heights in May 1974; and the United Nations Interim Force in Lebanon (UNIFIL), established in March 1978.

Part II **The Arab–Israeli conflict**

General review

UN Truce Supervision Organization

First UN Emergency Force

Second UN Emergency Force

UN Disengagement Observer Force

UN Interim Force in Lebanon

Chapter I **General review**

No other international issue is more complex and more potentially dangerous for the maintenance of international peace and security than the Arab-Israeli conflict in the Middle East. No other issue has claimed more of the Organization's time and attention. It is also the issue out of which the concept of United Nations peace-keeping evolved. The first such operation, in the form of an observer mission, was created in the Middle East in 1948; the first of the United Nations peace-keeping forces was also created in the Middle East, in 1956.

The Arab-Israeli conflict has its origin in the problem of Palestine which arose from the conflicting claims of the Arab and Jewish communities over the future status of that territory. In 1947 Palestine was a Territory administered by the United Kingdom under a Mandate from the League of Nations, with a population of about 2 million, two thirds of whom were Arabs and one third, Jews. Both communities laid claims to the control of the entire Territory after the United Kingdom Mandate ended. Unable to find a solution acceptable to both communities, the British Government brought the matter before the General Assembly in April 1947. A Special Committee appointed by the Assembly to make recommendations for the future status of Palestine proposed in a majority plan the partition of the Territory into an Arab State and a Jewish State, with an international régime for Jerusalem. The partition plan was adopted by the Assembly in November. A United Nations Palestine Commission was to carry out its recommendations, with the assistance of the Security Council. The plan was not accepted by the Palestinian Arabs and Arab States, and the Commission's efforts were inconclusive.

As the impasse continued, violent fighting broke out in Palestine, and the Security Council on 23 April 1948 established a Truce Commission for Palestine, composed of the consular representatives of Belgium, France and the United States, to supervise a cease-fire the Council had called for. The Assembly on 14 May decided to appoint a United Nations Mediator for Palestine who would promote a peaceful adjustment of the future situation of Palestine. On the same day, the United Kingdom relinquished its Mandate over Palestine, and the Jewish Agency proclaimed the State of Israel (which became a United Nations Member a year later, on 11 May 1949) on the territory allotted under the partition plan. The next day, the Palestinian Arabs, assisted by Arab States, opened hostilities against Israel. The war

13

ended with a truce, called for by the Security Council, which was to be supervised by the United Nations Mediator with the assistance of military observers. The first United Nations peace-keeping operation, the United Nations Truce Supervision Organization (UNTSO), came into being as a consequence.

Since 1948, there have been six full-fledged wars directly connected with the Arab–Israeli conflict, and five United Nations peace-keeping operations have been established in the region. Of these, three are still active—the overall UNTSO operation, an observer force on the Golan Heights and a peace-keeping force in southern Lebanon. The other two operations, now discontinued, were the first and second United Nations Emergency Forces, both in the Egypt–Israel sector.

Chapter II   United Nations Truce Supervision Organization

A. Introduction

The first peace-keeping operation in the Middle East was the United Nations Truce Supervision Organization (UNTSO), which continues to operate in the Middle East. It initially came into being during the Arab-Israeli war of 1948 to supervise the truce called for in Palestine by the Security Council. In 1949 its military observers (UNMOs) remained to supervise the Armistice Agreements between Israel and its Arab neighbours which were for many years the main basis of the uneasy truce in the whole area. UNTSO's activities have been and still are spread over territory within five States, and therefore it has relations with five host countries (Egypt, Israel, Jordan, Lebanon, Syrian Arab Republic).

Following the wars of 1956, 1967 and 1973, the functions of the observers changed in the light of changing circumstances, but they remained in the area, acting as go-betweens for the hostile parties and as the means by which isolated incidents could be contained and prevented from escalating into major conflicts.

UNTSO personnel have also been available at short notice to form the nucleus of other peace-keeping operations and have remained to assist those operations. The availability of the UNMOs for almost immediate deployment after the Security Council had acted to create a new operation has been an enormous contributory factor to the success of those operations. Rapid deployment of United Nations peace-keepers has been essential to the success of many operations, since their actual presence has been the initial deterrent to renewed fighting.

In the Middle East, groups of UNMOs are today attached to the peace-keeping forces in the area: the United Nations Disengagement Observer Force (UNDOF) in the Golan Heights and the United Nations Interim Force in Lebanon (UNIFIL). A group remains in Sinai to maintain a United Nations presence in that peninsula. There is also a group of observers in Beirut, Lebanon, and a liaison office in Amman.

This body of experienced and highly trained staff officers and its communications system were invaluable in setting up the First

15

United Nations Emergency Force (UNEF I) at short notice during the time of the Suez crisis, as well as for the United Nations Operation in the Congo (ONUC) in 1960, the United Nations Observation Group in Lebanon (UNOGIL) during the crisis of 1958, the United Nations Yemen Observation Mission (UNYOM) in 1963, the Second United Nations Emergency Force (UNEF II) in Sinai in 1973, the United Nations Disengagement Observer Force (UNDOF) the following year, the United Nations Interim Force in Lebanon (UNIFIL) in 1978, and the United Nations Good Offices Mission in Afghanistan and Pakistan (UNGOMAP) and the United Nations Iran-Iraq Military Observer Group (UNIIMOG) in 1988.

At the present time, the following countries provide military observers to UNTSO: Argentina, Australia, Austria, Belgium, Canada, Chile, China, Denmark, Finland, France, Ireland, Italy, the Netherlands, New Zealand, Norway, Sweden, Switzerland, the USSR and the United States. UNTSO's authorized strength in 1990 was 298 observers.

B. Supervision of the truce

The first observer group

In early May 1948, the Truce Commission established by the Security Council the previous month brought to the Council's attention the need for control-personnel for effective supervision of the cease-fire which the Council had called for when it created the Commission. As the situation worsened, the Commission, on 21 May, formally asked the Council to send military observers to assist it.

On 29 May, the Security Council called for a four-week cessation of all acts of armed force and non-introduction of fighting personnel or war material into Palestine and Arab countries involved in the fighting. The Council decided that the Mediator (Count Folke Bernadotte, of Sweden), in concert with the Truce Commission, should supervise the truce and be provided with a sufficient number of military observers for that purpose. Resolution 50(1948) formed the basis of what would become UNTSO.

After intensive discussions in the area, the Mediator reported a truce agreement, which went into effect on 11 June 1948.* Ralph J. Bunche, the then Personal Representative of the Secretary-General, was instrumental, with the Mediator, in putting into effect the arrangements for the group of military observers. These arrangements had to be made without previous guidelines and implemented

---

* A/648, S/829.

within a period of less than two weeks between the adoption of the Council's resolution and the effective truce.

The question of the nationality of the observers was resolved by the Mediator's requesting 21 observers each from the States members of the Truce Commission (Belgium, France and the United States), with a further five senior staff officers coming from his own country (Sweden), to act as his personal representatives in supervising the truce. The Mediator appointed one of them, Lieutenant-General Count Thord Bonde, as his Chief of Staff. The United States supplied 10 auxiliary technical personnel such as aircraft pilots and radio operators. The Secretary-General made available 51 guards, recruited from the Secretariat's security force at Headquarters, to assist the military observers.

While these arrangements were being made, the beginnings of what were to become different positions on the question of authority became discernible. The Soviet Union made known its view that the selection of military observers should be decided by the Security Council, and expressed the hope that Soviet observers would be appointed. This view was not supported by the Council.

Administratively, the observers remained under their respective army establishments, receiving their normal remunerations from their Governments but getting a daily subsistence allowance from the United Nations, which also met extra expenses resulting from the mission. National uniforms were worn with a United Nations armband. (The distinctive blue beret with United Nations badge was not used until November 1956.) During their assignments with the Organization, the observers were to take orders only from the United Nations authorities. The parties to the conflict were required to co-operate with the observers, to whom the Convention on the Privileges and Immunities of the United Nations applied, and ensure their safety and freedom of movement.

The first group of 36 observers arrived in Cairo between 11 and 14 June and were immediately deployed in Palestine and some of the Arab countries. The number of observers was subsequently increased to 93—31 from each of the States members of the Truce Commission. Their activities, under the general control of the Secretary-General, were directed in the field by the Chief of Staff on behalf of the Mediator. For political and practical reasons, the Mediator clearly separated the truce operation from his mediation mission, with Haifa becoming the temporary headquarters for the former and the island of Rhodes remaining the base for the latter. Close liaison was maintained between the Commission, which supervised the truce in

Jerusalem, and the Mediator, who supervised the remainder of the operations area. The functions of the observers and the operating procedures were laid down by the Mediator in consultation with the Secretary-General.

Method of operation

These observers were, and remain today, unarmed. They operated then, as they still do, with the consent of the parties and were dependent on the co-operation of the parties for their effectiveness. Thus they had no power to prevent a violation of the truce or to enforce any decisions. There was no element of enforcement in their functioning, although their very presence was something of a deterrent to violations of the truce and, acting on the basis of United Nations resolutions, they exercised a degree of moral suasion. In the case of any complaint or incident where they could not achieve a settlement between the parties on the spot, their only recourse was to report the matter to their supervisors and ultimately to the Mediator; in turn, at his discretion, he could report to the Secretary-General and, through him, to the Security Council. Complaints from local civilians or from troops of the parties concerned were dealt with by observers on the spot, those from military commanders by an area commander or the Chief of Staff, and those from Governments by the Mediator himself. In cases requiring investigation, the inquiries were carried out by observers at the scene whenever possible.

The four-week truce expired on 9 July 1948. While the provisional Government of Israel accepted the Mediator's proposal for an extension, the Arab Governments did not. As soon as the truce expired, large-scale fighting erupted again between Arab and Israeli forces. On 15 July, in response to an appeal by the Mediator, the Security Council ordered a cease-fire, with a clear threat of applying the enforcement procedures of Chapter VII of the Charter if necessary (resolution 54(1948)). The Mediator set the time for commencement of the cease-fire at 1500 GMT on 18 July. Both parties complied with the Council's cease-fire order and all fighting stopped by the appointed time.

The second group

Since the new truce was of indefinite duration and was to remain in force until a peaceful adjustment of the situation in Palestine was reached, a more elaborate system of truce supervision was required. As the observers for the first truce and their equipment had already left the area, the new operation had to be created and equipped from scratch. However, profiting from the experience gained earlier, the Mediator was able to set up a larger and more effective operation in a relatively short time.

The Mediator requested the Governments of Belgium, France and the United States each to place at his disposal 100 observers for the supervision of the truce. By 1 August 1948, 137 of those observers had arrived in the mission area. Subsequently, a total of 682 observers and auxiliary technical personnel was requested by the Mediator, of which 572 were actually provided. Major-General Aage Lundström of the Swedish Air Force was appointed Chief of Staff, and he and nine other Swedish officers formed the Mediator's personal staff. The headquarters of the operation remained in Haifa and the general principles and rules devised for the first truce continued to apply. However, the deployment of observers underwent important changes. Observers were now divided into a number of groups assigned to each Arab army and each Israeli army group. One group was assigned to Jerusalem, one to cover the coast and ports of the truce area, one to control convoys between Tel Aviv and Jerusalem and, later, an additional group was set up to cover airports in the truce area. The Chief of Staff was assisted by a Central Truce Supervision Board, presided over by him and consisting of a senior officer from each member of the Truce Commission, together with the Chief of Staff's political adviser, who was a member of the United Nations Secretariat.

On 17 September 1948, the Mediator was assassinated in Jerusalem by Jewish terrorists belonging to the Lehi Organization, also known as the Stern Gang. Ralph Bunche took over the Mediator's duties and was appointed Acting Mediator. Increased tension led to renewed fighting in October in Jerusalem, the Negev and, to a lesser extent, the Lebanese sector. The Security Council adopted a series of decisions and resolutions to restore the cease-fire and strengthen the observation operation.

The decisions and resolutions of the Security Council between October and December 1948 were the following: on 19 October, a call for an immediate and effective cease-fire in the Negev, to be followed by negotiations through United Nations intermediaries to settle outstanding problems in the area; also on 19 October, a call to the Governments and authorities concerned to grant United Nations observers freedom of movement and access in their areas of operation, to ensure their safety and to co-operate fully with them in their conduct of investigations into incidents; on 4 November, a call to Governments concerned to withdraw their troops to the positions they had occupied on 14 October and to establish truce lines and such neutral or demilitarized zones as desirable; and, on 16 November, a request to the parties to seek agreement directly or through the Acting Mediator with a view to the immediate establishment of an armistice.

Acting Mediator's efforts

With the full support of the Security Council and the General Assembly, the Acting Mediator resumed his mediating efforts, concentrating first on arranging indirect negotiations between Egypt and Israel. But his efforts were momentarily interrupted in late December, when hostilities erupted again between Egyptian and Israeli forces in southern Palestine.

Upon receipt of the Acting Mediator's report on this subject, the Security Council adopted another resolution on 29 December (resolution 66(1948)), by which it called upon the Governments concerned to order an immediate cease-fire and to facilitate the complete supervision of the truce by United Nations observers. An effective cease-fire was established by the Acting Mediator soon afterwards.

c. General Armistice Agreements

Four General Armistice Agreements

The Acting Mediator's efforts led to the conclusion of four General Armistice Agreements between Israel and the four neighbouring Arab States—Egypt, Jordan, Lebanon and Syria—in early 1949. On 11 August 1949, the Security Council assigned new functions to UNTSO in line with these Agreements (resolution 73(1949)). The role of Mediator was ended. While the resolution made no reference to the Truce Commission, this body had become inactive since the armistice and had in fact been abolished, although the Council took no formal decision to that effect.

With the termination of the role of the Mediator, UNTSO became an autonomous operation, officially a subsidiary organ of the Council, with the Chief of Staff assuming command. Its method of operation was radically altered, since its main responsibility now was to assist the parties in supervising the application and observance of the General Armistice Agreements.

UNTSO's main responsibilities related to the work of the Mixed Armistice Commissions (MACs) set up by the Armistice Agreements. The Egypt–Israel General Armistice Agreement provided for a MAC of seven members, three from each side and the Chief of Staff (or a senior officer designated by him) as Chairman. The Commission was empowered to employ observers which, if they were to be United Nations military observers, would remain under UNTSO command. The other General Armistice Agreements were similar, except that the respective MACs were composed of five members, two from each party and the Chairman.

Structural changes

The Chief of Staff, as commander of the operation, re-ported to the Secretary-General and was responsible to him. Although the title of Chief of Staff was no longer fully suitable, it was maintained since it was specifically mentioned in the Armistice Agreements and also in Security Council resolution 73(1949). Until 1951, the Chief of Staff had, administratively, the same status as the observers. This was changed in that year when he was given an appointment as a senior official of the United Nations Secretariat with the grade of Principal Director (later Assistant Secretary-General). This arrangement, which greatly strengthened the control of the Secretary-General over UNTSO, was applied to the heads of subsequent peace-keeping operations.

Demilitarized zones

In two cases, armistice arrangements included the establishment of demilitarized zones. One of these zones was established in the El Auja area on the Israeli side of the Armistice Demarcation Line between Egypt and Israel. The Egypt–Israel General Armistice Agreement provided that both Egyptian and Israeli armed forces should be totally excluded from the demilitarized zone and that the Chairman of the Egypt–Israel Mixed Armistice Commission and the observers attached to the Commission should be responsible for ensuring the full implementation of this provision. The Israel–Syria Armistice Agreement contained similar provisions concerning the demilitarized zone established near Lake Tiberias. In this case, the Chairman of the Israel–Syria Mixed Armistice Commission was also empowered to authorize the return of civilians to villages and settlements in the demilitarized zone and the employment of limited numbers of locally recruited civilian police in the zone for internal security purposes.

Mixed Armistice Commissions

The main task of the Commissions was the investigation and examination of the claims or complaints presented by the parties relating to the application and observance of the Armistice Agreements. These claims or complaints concerned, mainly, firing across the Armistice Demarcation Line, crossing of the Line by persons or animals, overflights on the wrong side of the Line, the presence of troops or equipment in demilitarized zones or defensive areas and illegal cultivation contrary to agreements. Occasionally, the Commissions also gave attention to special problems of common interest to the parties.

The observers assigned to each Commission carried out the investigations of complaints submitted to the Commission. They assisted in the handing over of people who had crossed the Armistice Demarcation Line, as well as the handing over of animals and property, and they witnessed the work done by the parties under anti-malaria, anti-rabies and anti-locust agreements. They also participated in rescue and search missions when such missions were undertaken by UNTSO at the request of one of the parties. The Chief of Staff was given special responsibilities for the protection of Mount Scopus, in Jerusalem.

Cease-fire supervision

In addition to its functions relating to the General Armistice Agreements, UNTSO had the responsibility of observing and maintaining the cease-fire, ordered by the Security Council in its resolution 54(1948), which continued to be in force. When an outbreak of violence threatened, the Chief of Staff of UNTSO would, on his own initiative, seek to prevent it by appealing to the parties for restraint, and when a firing incident actually occurred, he would arrange for an immediate cease-fire. In serious cases, the Chief of Staff could bring the matter to the attention of the Security Council through the Secretary-General.

Government House, UNTSO headquarters

On 25 May 1949, the headquarters of UNTSO was transferred from Haifa to Government House in Jerusalem. Government House had been the seat of the British Mandatory Administration during the Mandate period. On the departure of the British authorities from Palestine, and at their request, the International Committee of the Red Cross took over Government House in trust for any successor administration and, during the early fighting in Jerusalem, it established a neutral zone in the area where the building and its grounds were located. On 7 October 1948, following renewed fighting, during which the status of the neutral zone was violated by both Israeli and Jordanian forces, the International Committee transferred Government House and the surrounding grounds to United Nations protection. Both States parties were informed of these arrangements and did not raise any objections.

The cease-fire agreement of 30 November 1948 for the Jerusalem area left intact Government House and the neutral zone. The General Armistice Agreement concluded between Israel and Jordan on 3 April 1949 provided that in the Jerusalem sector the Armistice Demarcation Lines should correspond to the lines defined in the cease-fire agreement of 30 November 1948, and therefore the status of the Government House area and the neutral zone remained unaltered. Shortly after the conclusion of the Armistice Agreement, Government House became the headquarters of the United Nations Truce Supervision Organization.

On 5 June 1967, after fighting broke out in Jerusalem, Israeli forces occupied Government House and escorted UNTSO staff out of its premises. The Secretary-General at United Nations Headquarters and the Chief of Staff in Jerusalem repeatedly pressed the Israeli authorities for the return of Government House to UNTSO. After lengthy negotiations, the Israeli Government agreed on 22 August 1967 to return Government House and most of its surrounding grounds.* The headquarters of UNTSO was immediately re-established at Government House and has remained there until today.

Commission headquarters

The reorganization of UNTSO after August 1949 was geared to the activities of the four Mixed Armistice Commissions. Each Commission had a headquarters and such ancillary installa-

* S/7930/Add.29.

tions as it decided to establish. The headquarters of the Israel-Jordan Mixed Armistice Commission was set up in the neutral zone in Jerusalem. The Israel–Lebanon Mixed Armistice Commission (ILMAC) was headquartered in Beirut with a substation located at Naqoura near the Armistice Demarcation Line. The Israel–Syria Mixed Armistice Commission (ISMAC) was established in Damascus with a control centre at Tiberias on the Israeli side of the Armistice Demarcation Line. Finally, the Egypt–Israel Mixed Armistice Commission (EIMAC) was established in the demilitarized zone of El Auja and was later transferred to Gaza.

Implementation of the Armistice Agreements

The 1949 General Armistice Agreements were meant to be temporary arrangements to be followed by the conclusion of peace treaties. But that was not to be. Two major obstacles appeared soon after the signing of the Armistice Agreements. Israel, for security reasons, refused to let the many Palestinian Arab refugees who had fled their homes during the hostilities return to the areas it controlled, and the Arabs continued to refuse to recognize the existence of Israel and to enter into peace negotiations with it. Thus, the basic issues remained unresolved.

Because of constant disagreement between the parties, the Chief of Staff and the UNTSO observers assigned to the Commissions came to play an increasingly important role. In each Commission, sensitive issues were often deadlocked and resolutions had to be decided by the casting vote of the Chairman. Most investigations into incidents and violations of the Armistice Agreements were carried out by UNTSO observers alone, since the military representatives of the parties could not work with each other. To smooth over difficulties and avert incidents, UNTSO personnel often had to exercise good offices or act as mediators. But, however active and important their functions were, the ultimate responsibility for the observance and application of the provisions of the Armistice Agreements rested with the parties themselves, and without their co-operation and goodwill the Agreements steadily eroded.

Egypt–Israel Mixed Armistice Commission

The difficulties encountered in the implementation of the General Armistice Agreements and the relationships between the parties varied from one Mixed Armistice Commission to another.

The most difficult Commission was the Egypt–Israel Mixed Armistice Commission. From the start, Egypt strongly protested against Israel's expulsion of thousands of Palestinians to the Gaza Strip. The matter was brought before the Security Council, which, in its resolution 89(1950) of 17 November 1950, requested EIMAC to give urgent attention to the Egyptian complaint and reminded both Egypt and Israel, as Member States of the United Nations, of their obligations under the Charter to settle their outstanding differences. But despite the Council's decision, the problem remained unresolved. In 1951 Egypt decided to impose restrictions on the passage of international commercial shipping and goods destined for Israel through the Suez Canal. Despite the request contained in Security Council resolution 95(1951) of 1 September 1951, Egypt maintained these restrictions, and indeed extended them to the Strait of Tiran in 1953. By early 1955, Palestinian *fedayeen* undertook, with increasing frequency, commando raids into Israeli territory which were followed by harsh retaliation from Israel. In reaction to the establishment of Egyptian military positions in the El Quseima–Abu Aweigila area, near the border, the Israeli forces occupied the demilitarized zone of El Auja on 21 September 1956 and, shortly thereafter, the Commission became paralysed as Israel prevented the Egyptian delegates to the Commission from entering the area.

Following the outbreak of the October 1956 war, Israel denounced the Armistice Agreement with Egypt. After that, the Israeli Government refused to take part in EIMAC. The Secretary-General did not accept this unilateral denunciation as valid, and consequently UNTSO continued to maintain the machinery of the Mixed Armistice Commission. The Commission's headquarters was transferred from El Auja to the town of Gaza in Egyptian-controlled territory. The Commission continued to examine complaints submitted by Egypt, and UNTSO observers continued to conduct patrols on the Egyptian side of the Armistice Demarcation Line. But without Israel's co-operation, these activities were largely symbolic and the real peace-keeping functions were carried out by the United Nations Emergency Force (UNEF I), which was established in the wake of the war and with which UNTSO co-operated closely *(see following chapter)*.

Eleven years later, when UNEF I was withdrawn at the request of the Egyptian Government, the Secretary-General pointed out in his report of 19 May 1967 to the Security Council* that EIMAC remained in existence and could, as it had done prior to the establishment of UNEF, provide a limited form of United Nations presence

---

* S/7896.

in the area. With this in view, the number of observers assigned to the Commission was brought up from 6 to 20 towards the end of May and their patrol activities along the Armistice Demarcation Line were markedly increased. The Government of Israel, while maintaining its position on the Armistice Agreement, raised no objection to this action, and the additional observers sent from Jerusalem to Gaza passed through the Israeli check-point on the coastal road without difficulty. But this emergency measure was not enough and, soon after the withdrawal of UNEF, war erupted again between Israel and Arab States.

Israel–Syria Mixed Armistice Commission

Great difficulties were also experienced by the Israel–Syria Mixed Armistice Commission. Two of the most frequent disputes concerned the cultivation by Israeli farmersof disputed lands in the demilitarized zone and the activities of Israeli patrols and fishermen on the eastern side of Lake Tiberias next to the Armistice Demarcation Line. These Israeli activities were considered to be illegal by the Syrians and often led to intense exchanges of fire between Israeli and Syrian forces. In addition, there was the unending cycle of violence marked by Palestinian commando raids and Israeli reprisals in the border areas.

In order to ease the situation, the Chief of Staff of UNTSO decided, with the agreement of the parties, to establish in the 1950s a number of observation posts along the Armistice Demarcation Line. These served to reduce tension to some extent in the sensitive areas, but incidents nevertheless continued to occur frequently. On 19 January 1956, after a particularly violent Israeli attack against Syrian forces, the Security Council adopted resolution 111(1956), by which it condemned the attack and called once again on the parties to implement the General Armistice Agreement and to respect the Armistice Demarcation Line and the demilitarized zone. But, despite the call of the Security Council, the situation was not improved. As of 14 October 1966, there were 35,485 Israeli complaints and 30,600 Syrian complaints pending before the Commission. The Commission was completely paralysed by the large number of complaints and constant disputes between the parties. It held its last regular meeting in 1951 and its last emergency meeting in February 1960. From 1966 onwards, relations between Israel and Syria deteriorated sharply. At the beginning of 1967, the Secretary-General succeeded in arranging a series of "extraordinary emergency meetings" of the Commission in order to discuss the cultivation problem in the demilitarized zone which at the time had led to many incidents. But these meetings ended in failure, and on 7 April a serious incident occurred during which Israeli aircraft attacked Damascus itself and shot down six Syrian aircraft. This incident marked the beginning of a new escalation which eventually led to the June 1967 war.

Israel-Jordan Mixed Armistice Commission

The Israel-Jordan Armistice Agreement was subject to different pressures. The West Bank and the Old City of Jerusalem formed part of the Holy Land and were of special importance. They contained large numbers of Palestinian Arabs, many of whom were uprooted and displaced from the area held by Israel. A narrow strip of neutral zone supervised by the United Nations separated the Israeli and Jordanian sectors of the Holy City. The Armistice Agreement created two enclaves: an Israeli enclave on Mount Scopus in Jerusalem and a Jordanian enclave in Latrun on the road from Jerusalem to Tel Aviv. The West Bank was a staging area for the activities of Palestinian *fedayeen*. These factors led to many disputes and problems, which often resulted in exchanges of fire across the Line between the two opposing armies. Despite the difficulties, the Commission continued to meet in emergency sessions until June 1967, and sub-committee meetings were held regularly, on a weekly basis, in an effort to resolve outstanding problems.

Israel–Lebanon Mixed Armistice Commission

Unlike the other Commissions, that for Israel–Lebanon functioned smoothly and often effectively from 1949 until 1967. The main difficulties arose in connection with the activities of Palestinian commandos. However, the Lebanese authorities acted firmly to stop or contain those activities and there were few incidents along the Armistice Demarcation Line. Problems of common concern were discussed and resolved in regular meetings of the Commission, which functioned until the June 1967 war, when Israel denounced the Armistice Agreement with Lebanon as it did the others, although no hostilities took place along the Israel–Lebanon Armistice Demarcation Line.

Observer strength

As for the personnel involved, in 1948 there were 572 observers and auxiliary technical personnel, but with the entry into force of the General Armistice Agreements, UNTSO's observer strength was reduced to between 30 and 140 according to prevailing circumstances. It had 128 observers at the outbreak of the June 1967 war.

D. Cease-fire observation operations, 1967–1973

Background

UNTSO played a crucial role in helping to bring the June 1967 war to an end.

The war started in the early morning of 5 June between Israeli and Egyptian forces and quickly spread to the Jordanian and Syrian fronts. On 6 June, the Security Council adopted resolution 233(1967), calling upon the Governments concerned to take forthwith, as a first step, all measures for an immediate cease-fire. As hostilities continued, the Council met again on 7 June and, by resolution 234(1967), demanded that the Governments concerned should discontinue all military activities at 2000 hours GMT on the same day. Fighting stopped on the Egyptian and Jordanian fronts on 8 June, but it went on unabated between the Israeli and Syrian forces on the Golan Heights. On 9 June, the Security Council adopted resolution 235(1967), by which it confirmed its previous resolutions for an immediate cease-fire, demanded that hostilities should cease forthwith and requested the Secretary-General "to make immediate contacts with the Governments of Israel and Syria to arrange immediate compliance with the above-mentioned resolutions, and to report to the Security Council not later than two hours from now".

On instructions from the Secretary-General, the Chief of Staff of UNTSO, Lieutenant-General Odd Bull of Norway, contacted the Israeli and Syrian authorities on 10 June and proposed to them, as a practical arrangement for implementing the cease-fire demanded by the Security Council, that both sides cease all firing and movement forward at 1630 hours GMT on the same day. He also proposed that the observers, accompanied by liaison officers of each side, be deployed along the front lines as soon as possible in order to observe the implementation of the cease-fire. Those proposals were accepted by both sides and the UNMOs were deployed accordingly in the combat area in the early morning of 11 June.

Israel–Syria sector

On the following days, UNTSO observers demarcated the cease-fire lines on each side. The two cease-fire lines, which included a buffer zone approximately one to three miles wide, were agreed to by the two sides in indirect negotiations conducted by the observers. In signing the map demarcating the cease-fire lines, the Syrian representative stressed that the lines were a purely practical arrangement for the specific purpose of facilitating the observation of the cease-fire by the United Nations and should not affect or prejudice the claims and positions of the Syrian Government.

With the demarcation of the cease-fire lines, UNTSO set up a number of observation posts on each side of the buffer zone. There were, by the end of 1967, seven observation posts on the Israeli side and nine on the Syrian side. Those on the Syrian side were under the control of the headquarters of ISMAC in Damascus and those on the Israeli side reported to the Control Centre at Tiberias. General direction was assumed by the Chief of Staff of UNTSO. The observers, all of whom were drawn from the existing establishment of UNTSO, performed their duties by manning the observation posts and by conducting patrols along the lines as necessary. The two parties were notified by the Chief of Staff of UNTSO that all firings, movements forward of the cease-fire line on each side and overflights would be considered as breaches of the cease-fire.

Arrangements made by the Chief of Staff were endorsed by the Security Council, which, in resolution 236(1967) of 11 June 1967: affirmed that its demand for a cease-fire and discontinuance of all military activities included a prohibition of any forward military movements subsequent to the cease-fire; called for the prompt return to the cease-fire positions of any troops which might have moved forward subsequent to 1630 hours GMT on 10 June 1967; and called for "full co-operation with the Chief of Staff of the United Nations Truce Supervision Organization and the observers in implementing the cease-fire, including freedom of movement and adequate communications facilities".

After the adoption of the resolution, the observers submitted regularly to the Security Council, through the Secretary-General, reports on the cease-fire situation in the Israel–Syria sector. These arrangements continued until the October 1973 war.

Suez Canal area

When the cease-fire went into effect in the Egypt–Israel sector on 8 June 1967, no observation machinery was set up in that area. At that time, the Israeli forces had reached the eastern bank of the Suez Canal, except for a small area around Port Fuad on the northern tip of the Canal. The situation in the Suez Canal sector was generally quiet during the last part of June but, from early July on, tension began to rise. On 8 July, heavy fighting broke out between Egyptian and Israeli forces at various locations along the Canal, with each side accusing the other of violations of the cease-fire. When the Security Council met on that day, the Secretary-General expressed regret that he was unable to provide the Council with information about the new outbreak of fighting since no United Nations observers were stationed in the area. In this connection, he indicated that as early as 4 July he had decided to take the initiative towards a possible alleviation of this situation and had undertaken exploratory talks with the representatives of Egypt and Israel about the stationing of United Nations military observers in the Canal sector.

On 9 July, the Security Council approved a consensus statement in accordance with which the Secretary-General requested the Chief of Staff of UNTSO to work out with the Governments of Egypt* and Israel, as speedily as possible, the necessary arrangements to station observers in the Suez Canal sector. Two days later, having received the agreement of both parties, the Secretary-General instructed the Chief of Staff to work out with the local authorities of both sides a plan for the actual stationing of military observers.

The Chief of Staff proceeded in much the same way as for the observation operation on the Golan Heights. The problem of demarcation of the cease-fire lines was much simpler in this case since, except for the Port Fuad area, the Suez Canal itself constituted a natural buffer zone. The observers made an attempt to demarcate a line of separation in the Port Fuad area, but no agreement could be reached. This question, therefore, remained a subject of

* Documents of these years refer to Egypt as the United Arab Republic. Egypt and Syria, separate Members of the United Nations since 1945, joined together in February 1958 to form the United Arab Republic. In September 1961, the Syrian Arab Republic resumed its status as an independent State and its separate membership in the United Nations. Egypt retained the title of the United Arab Republic, reverting to the name of Egypt, or Arab Republic of Egypt, in 1971. For convenience, the title of Egypt is used in this book wherever possible.

controversy, but because of the marshy terrain in the area there were few incidents.

The observation operation began on 17 July when seven observation posts were established along the Canal. This number was eventually increased to 15: eight on the eastern side of the Canal under the Control Centre at Qantara and seven on the western side under the Control Centre at Ismailia. At the beginning, military observers drawn from the existing UNTSO establishment were assigned to the Suez Canal. However, the nationalities of the observers gave rise to some difficulty, as certain countries were not acceptable to Israel, and others not acceptable to Egypt. Finally, after lengthy discussions, agreements were reached on six countries from which observers might be drawn: Austria, Burma (now Myanmar), Chile, Finland, France and Sweden. The original observers were then replaced by 90 new observers from those six countries.

The main task of the observers was to observe and report on breaches of the cease-fire, including firings, overflights and movements forward which, in this case, meant movement of boats and craft in the Canal. An understanding was reached on 27 July whereby the two parties agreed to stop all military activities in the Suez Canal, including the movement in or into the Canal of boats or craft for one month, it being understood that the Canal authorities would continue to revictual and secure the safety of the 15 ships stranded in the Canal. This agreement was later extended indefinitely.*

With these arrangements, the situation in the Suez Canal sector became stabilized and, although there were occasional exchanges of fire, the cease-fire generally held. This lull lasted until early 1969, when fighting suddenly broke out again. From that time until August 1970, there were intense exchanges of artillery fire across the Canal between the Egyptian and Israeli positions every day, with occasional air strikes by one side or the other. This period of fighting, which lasted nearly 20 months, was known as the "war of attrition". It was full-fledged warfare except that the positions of the opposing armies did not move forward. During the entire period of hostilities, the Secretary-General reported in detail to the Security Council on all the developments monitored by the observers, and appealed on several occasions for an end to the hostilities, but his efforts were inconclusive. Egypt stated that it refused to continue to observe the cease-fire, which it regarded as in effect perpetuating the Israeli occupation of its sovereign territory, while Israel asserted that it would observe the cease-fire only if the other side were willing to do so. Neither side brought the matter before the Security Council and,

* S/8053/Add.1,2.

largely because of the opposing positions taken by two of the permanent members, the Council did not attempt to take it up.

The fighting came to an end on 7 August 1970 under a proposal initiated by the United States Government. Under the proposal, Egypt, Israel and Jordan agreed to designate representatives to discussions to be held under the auspices of the Special Representative of the Secretary-General for the Middle East, Ambassador Gunnar V. Jarring, of Sweden.* In order to facilitate the Special Representative's task of promoting agreement in accordance with Security Council resolution 242(1967) of 22 November 1967 (containing general principles for a Middle East settlement), they undertook strictly to observe the cease-fire resolutions of the Security Council as from 7 August. On that day, fighting stopped in the Suez Canal sector and the situation there remained quiet until 6 October 1973, when hostilities once again broke out between Egyptian and Israeli forces.

Israel-Jordan sector

No cease-fire observation was established in the Israel-Jordan sector. At the end of the June 1967 war, Israeli forces had occupied the entire West Bank up to the Jordan River. The situation in that sector was generally quiet until the end of 1967 but there was increasing tension in 1968 and 1969, mainly because of the activities of Palestinian commandos operating from the east side of the Jordan Valley and retaliatory action by the Israeli forces. The Secretary-General sounded out the Israeli and Jordanian authorities about the possibility of stationing United Nations observers in the Jordan Valley but could not secure an agreement. On several occasions, the Security Council met to consider serious incidents in the Israel-Jordan sector, and the Secretary-General drew attention to the fact that in the absence of agreements from the parties or of a decision by the Security Council, it was not possible to establish a machinery for the observation of the cease-fire in the sector.

The situation in the Israel-Jordan sector, however, became much quieter after September 1970, when the bulk of the Palestinian armed elements moved to Lebanon.

Israel-Lebanon sector

During the June 1967 war, no fighting took place between Israel and Lebanon, and the Armistice Demarcation Line between the two countries remained intact. Nevertheless, the Israeli

* S/9902.

Government denounced the Armistice Agreement with Lebanon after the war, as it did the other Armistice Agreements, on the grounds that during the hostilities Lebanese authorities had claimed that they were at war with Israel. The Lebanese Government, however, denied this and insisted on the continued validity of the Agreement. Since the Secretary-General held the view that the Armistice Agreement could not be denounced unilaterally, UNTSO continued to maintain the headquarters of ILMAC at Beirut, as well as a substation at Naqoura in southern Lebanon. But the Commission had few activities and the number of observers assigned to it was considerably reduced.

Following the 1967 war, the Palestinian population in Lebanon markedly increased with the influx of a sizeable number of displaced persons from the occupied West Bank and Gaza, and the Palestine Liberation Army stepped up its training activities in the country, especially in the south. As a result, anti-Israeli raids by Palestinian commandos from Lebanon and reprisals by Israeli forces became more frequent. The situation deteriorated further following the departure of Palestinian armed elements in 1970 from Jordan to Lebanon.

In early 1972, tension heightened in the Israel–Lebanon sector as a result of increasing activities by Palestinian commandos based in southern Lebanon and severe reprisal attacks by Israeli forces. On 29 March, the Permanent Representative of Lebanon to the United Nations submitted the following request to the Security Council:

> "The Lebanese Government, because of repeated Israeli aggression against Lebanon and because the work of the Lebanon-Israel Mixed Armistice Commission has been paralysed since 1967, wishes the Security Council to take necessary action to strengthen the United Nations machinery in the Lebanese–Israeli sector by increasing the number of observers, on the basis of the Armistice Agreement of 1949."*

On 30 March, the members of the Security Council decided that the request of the Lebanese Government should be met, and asked the Secretary-General to make the necessary arrangements to this effect. In a memorandum dated 4 April,† the Secretary-General informed the Council that, following consultations with the Lebanese authorities, the Chief of Staff of UNTSO had recommended the establishment of three observation posts on the Lebanese side of the Armistice Demarcation Line, together with an increase in the number of observers assigned to the Armistice Commission from the existing seven to 21. On 19 April 1972, the members of the Security Council, in informal consultations, agreed with the proposed plans.

The cease-fire observation operation in the Israel–Lebanon sector commenced on 24 April 1972 with the establishment of the three

* S/10611, annex. † *Ibid.*

proposed observation posts, all on Lebanese territory. Two additional observation posts were later set up and the total observer strength was increased to 34. Those observers, who were all drawn from the existing establishment of UNTSO, manned the five observation posts and conducted patrols along the Armistice Demarcation Line as necessary. Their responsibility was to observe and report on violations of the Demarcation Line.

Unlike the previous cease-fire observer operations, the one in Lebanon was established without the agreement of Israel. However, Israel did not seek to obstruct the operation, and the additional observers and their equipment which were transferred from Jerusalem to southern Lebanon passed through the Israeli border check-point without hindrance.

From April 1972 until the Israeli invasion of Lebanon in March 1978, the observers assigned to the Israel–Lebanon sector reported regularly to the Security Council, through the Secretary-General, on the situation along the Armistice Demarcation Line. These reports dealt mainly with violations of the Line by the Israeli forces, since no such violations were committed by the Lebanese forces. The Israeli violations included firings across the Line, overflights and the establishment of some six positions on the Lebanese side of the Line.

Maintenance of the armistice supervision machinery

Having already denounced the Armistice Agreement with Egypt in 1956, Israel denounced the other three agreements after the war of 1967. The Secretary-General did not accept this act as valid for reasons that he explained in the introduction to his annual report to the General Assembly as follows:

" . . .there has been no indication either in the General Assembly or in the Security Council that the validity and applicability of the Armistice Agreements have been changed as a result of the recent hostilities or of the war of 1956; each Agreement, in fact, contains a provision that it will remain in force 'until a peaceful settlement between the parties is achieved'. Nor has the Security Council or the General Assembly taken any steps to change the pertinent resolutions of either organ relating to the Armistice Agreements or to the earlier cease-fire demands. The Agreements provide that by mutual consent the signatories can revise or suspend them. There is no provision in them for unilateral termination of their application. This has been the United Nations position all along and will continue to be the position until a competent organ decides otherwise."*

The machinery for the supervision of the Armistice Agreements has accordingly been maintained. The Chiefs of the UNTSO

* A/6701/Add.1.

observers in Beirut, Damascus and Amman are the nominal Chairmen of the Israel–Lebanon, Israel–Syria and Israel–Hashemite Kingdom of Jordan Mixed Armistice Commissions, respectively. The headquarters of the Egypt–Israel Mixed Armistice Commission in Gaza was closed in July 1967 and the officer in charge of the observers in that sector was assigned the nominal function of Chairman of the Commission until 1979, when Egypt and Israel concluded a peace treaty.

E. Activities since 1973

Egypt–Israel sector

Cease-fire observation in the Suez Canal sector was terminated shortly after the outbreak of the October 1973 war, at the request of the Egyptian Government. On 6 October, in a surprise attack, Egyptian forces crossed the Canal and soon advanced beyond the UNTSO observation posts on the eastern bank of the Canal, while, in a co-ordinated move, Syrian troops simultaneously attacked the Israeli positions on the Golan Heights. The first days of the war were marked by heavy air and ground activity, which was fully reported to the Security Council by the Secretary-General on the basis of information received from the observers. In the course of the hostilities, two United Nations observers were killed.

On 8 October, the Egyptian Permanent Representative informed the Secretary-General that, since the United Nations observers were now behind the Egyptian lines, which put them in physical danger and made their presence unnecessary, the Government of Egypt requested the Secretary-General to take measures for their transfer to Cairo for their security. The Secretary-General immediately brought this request to the attention of the Security Council, which agreed that it should be acceded to. By 9 October, all the United Nations observation posts on both sides of the Canal were closed and the observers were withdrawn to the Cairo area.

Following the closure of the observation posts, the United Nations no longer had direct information on the hostilities between Egypt and Israel which were raging in the western part of the Sinai.

Assistance to UNEF II

The October 1973 war and its aftermath are described in greater detail in the chapter below on the Second United Nations Emergency Force (UNEF II). As far as UNTSO is concerned, Security Council resolution 340(1973) of 25 October 1973 provided for an increase in the number of UNTSO observers in the Egypt–Israel sector and gave them the task of assisting and co-operating with UNEF II in the fulfilment of that Force's mandate. During the initial phase, the observers manned certain check-points and observation posts in the area controlled by UNEF II. They also assisted in exchanges of prisoners of war and undertook searches for bodies of soldiers killed during the hostilities. In addition, some observers were assigned as staff officers at UNEF II headquarters. After the conclusion of the disengagement agreement of January 1974, they conducted patrols in the buffer zone established in the Sinai and carried out inspections of the area of limitation of forces and armament on both sides of the buffer zone. While the observers remained administratively attached to UNTSO, they were placed under the operational control of the Commander of UNEF II.

At the end of October 1973, additional observers (3 from Sweden and 10 from Finland), were provided at the request of the Secretary-General to strengthen the observer group in the Egypt–Israel sector. Thus the total strength of UNTSO was increased to 225 observers, from 16 countries. In November 1973, the Governments of the United States and of the Soviet Union, in a joint approach to the Secretary-General, offered to make available observers from their countries for service with UNTSO. The Soviet Union would provide 36 observers and the United States 28—who, with the 8 Americans already assigned to the mission, would bring the number of United States observers also to 36. The Secretary-General accepted these offers with the informal concurrence of the Security Council.

Observer Group Egypt

In July 1979, the mandate of UNEF II lapsed. On 24 July 1979, the Secretary-General, after consultations held by the Security Council, issued a statement in which he indicated that, in view of the fact that the withdrawal of UNEF was without prejudice to the continued presence of the UNTSO observers in the area, he intended to make, in accordance with existing decisions of the Security Council, the necessary arrangements to ensure the further functioning of UNTSO.

In accordance with the above statement and with the agreement of the Egyptian Government, UNTSO has continued to maintain a presence in the area. Its observers in the Egypt–Israel sector are organized as Observer Group Egypt (OGE), with a strength of 55 (June 1990). OGE operates six outposts in the Sinai and an outpost at Ismailia and conducts patrols in most parts of the Sinai, except for an area under the Multinational Force and Observers (MFO), an operation set up outside the United Nations in 1982 to supervise the implementation of the peace treaty between Egypt and Israel. OGE headquarters in Cairo maintains liaison for UNTSO with the Egyptian authorities.

Israel–Syria sector

During the October 1973 war, the central part of the buffer zone established by UNTSO on the Golan Heights was the scene of fierce fighting. In the first days of the war, Syrian forces attacked and overran several Israeli positions along the cease-fire lines. However, by 11 October, the Israeli troops had counter-attacked and in turn crossed over to the eastern side of the buffer zone on either side of the Quneitra–Damascus road. As the battle developed, some of the United Nations observation posts had to be evacuated, but others continued to operate.

When the cease-fire called for by the Security Council took effect on 25 October 1973, Israeli forces had occupied a pocket around the village of Saassa on the eastern side of the buffer zone, some 40 kilometres west of Damascus. The United Nations observers set up temporary observation posts around that pocket, and with these changes, the cease-fire observation operation was resumed.

Assistance to UNDOF

UNTSO's cease-fire observation in the Israel–Syria sector was discontinued on 31 May 1974 when the United Nations Disengagement Observer Force was established (*see chapter V*) and the 90 United Nations observers assigned to the Israel–Syria sector were detailed to UNDOF as an integral part of the Force. Operating out of Tiberias and Damascus, they manned observation posts located near the area of operation and in the vicinity of the lines on both sides, and they conducted the fortnightly inspections of the areas of limitation in armaments and forces provided for under the disengagement agreement of 1974. In 1979, the observers detailed to assist UNDOF were formed into Observer Group Golan (OGG), which has continued to carry out the tasks described above, under the supervision and operational control of the UNDOF commander.

Under the terms of the protocol to the disengagement agreement, the personnel of UNDOF must come from Members of the United Nations that are not permanent members of the Security Council. Observers from those countries assigned to the Israel–Syria sector are not therefore involved in the supervision of the disengagement agreement. They form a separate unit, the Observer Detachment Damascus (ODD), which performs support functions for OGG.

The UNTSO establishment in the Israel–Syria sector is currently (June 1990) the largest in the mission area. It comprises altogether 138 military observers: 96 in OGG, 35 in ODD and 7 assigned to staff positions in the UNDOF headquarters.

Israel–Jordan sector

During the war of 1973, the Israel–Jordan sector remained quiet. UNTSO has continued to maintain a small liaison office in Amman, which is staffed by two military observers. The chief of the office is also the designated chairman of the Israel–Hashemite Kingdom of Jordan Mixed Armistice Commission.

Israel–Lebanon sector

The UNTSO operation in the Israel–Lebanon sector experienced severe difficulties following the outbreak of civil war in Lebanon in 1975. Since the UNTSO observers were not armed, their security had to be ensured by the host Government. When the five observation posts were set up along the Armistice Demarcation Line in 1972, the Lebanese army established a check-point next to each of them. At the beginning of the civil war, the Lebanese army disintegrated and the United Nations observers manning the posts were left on their own in an increasingly dangerous situation. The Secretary-General had three choices at the time: suspend the operation, arm the observers for their protection, or ask them to continue to operate as before in spite of the changed conditions. After careful consideration and consultation with the contributing countries, the last-mentioned solution was adopted. On a number of occasions, observers' vehicles were hijacked and their observation posts broken into by one faction or another. But there were few serious incidents and, on the whole, the fighting factions respected the status of the United Nations observers.

Assistance to UNIFIL

When the Security Council established the United Nations Interim Force in Lebanon in March 1978 (see chapter VI), UNTSO's cease-fire observation in the Israel–Lebanon sector was discontinued and the observers were assigned to assist UNIFIL in the fulfilment of its tasks. It was stipulated, however, that the military observers of UNTSO would continue to function on the Armistice Demarcation Line after the termination of the mandate of UNIFIL.*

The observers assigned to assist UNIFIL were formed into Observer Group Lebanon (OGL) and were placed under the operational control of the commander of UNIFIL. They manned observation posts, conducted patrols and carried out liaison duties with parties active in and around the UNIFIL area of operation. They also performed staff duties at UNIFIL headquarters, especially in the early days of the Force. The headquarters of ILMAC in Beirut did not become part of OGL, but it functioned as a liaison office for UNIFIL until that Force established its own liaison office in Beirut.

At present, OGL comprises 65 military observers. They continue to man the five observation posts along the Lebanese side of the Armistice Demarcation Line and operate four mobile teams in parts of the UNIFIL area of operation, including those that are under Israeli control and where UNIFIL units are not deployed.

Despite UNIFIL's presence, southern Lebanon has remained the most hazardous assignment for the UNTSO observers. They have often been caught in cross-fire and one died as a result of a mine explosion in January 1988. While the various parties and groups have generally continued to respect the international status of the unarmed observers, some of them have been threatened on account of their nationality. On 17 February 1988, the Chief of OGL, Lieutenant Colonel William R. Higgins (United States), was kidnapped south of Tyre by unknown persons. Strenuous efforts were made to establish his whereabouts and obtain his release, but on 30 July 1989, the group which claimed to be holding him announced that they had killed him. It has so far proved impossible to establish his fate with certainty.

---

* S/12611.

Observer Group Beirut

In June 1982, Israeli forces invaded Lebanon again and soon reached Beirut, where the Palestine Liberation Organization (PLO) had its headquarters and where many PLO fighters had concentrated. The PLO called for the deployment of UNIFIL in the Beirut area, but this was strongly opposed by Israel. Various proposals for the establishment of a United Nations military observer group in and around Beirut were examined by the Security Council in June and July, but no agreement could be reached. On 1 August, after Israel's forces had entered West Beirut, the Security Council authorized the Secretary-General to deploy immediately, on the request of the Government of Lebanon, United Nations observers to monitor the situation in and around Beirut. The Secretary-General instructed UNTSO to make the necessary arrangements in consultation with the parties concerned. When the Israeli reply was delayed, the Secretary-General immediately set up observation machinery in the Beirut area in territory controlled by the Lebanese Government. The 10 observers assigned to ILMAC were constituted as the Observer Group Beirut (OGB) and took up their new duties on 3 August. The same day, the Israeli forces resumed their advance on West Beirut. Their unwillingness to co-operate with UNTSO prevented the reinforcement of OGB, as the observers could not reach Beirut without passing through Israeli check-points.

In the mean time, the United States worked out arrangements for the evacuation of the PLO fighters under the supervision of a multinational force (MNF), not connected with the United Nations. This operation was completed on 1 September and the MNF was withdrawn.

On 14 September, Bashir Gemayel, the President-elect of Lebanon, was assassinated. The next morning the Israeli forces returned in strength to West Beirut. On the afternoon of 17 September, units of the Christian militia of which Gemayel had been the leader entered the Sabra and Shatila refugee camps in the southern suburbs of Beirut and killed a large number of Palestinian refugees. In the early hours of 19 September, by resolution 521(1982), the Security Council condemned the massacre and authorized the Secretary-General to increase the number of observers in and around Beirut from 10 to 50. The Council also requested the Secretary-General to initiate urgent consultations on additional steps which the Council might take, including the possible deployment of United Nations forces.

On 20 September, the Secretary-General was able to inform the Security Council that the additional observers were on their way to Beirut. He also reported that about 2,000 men from UNIFIL could be sent to Beirut, if required.* However, on 24 September, the MNF returned to Beirut. It remained there until 1984.

The UNTSO observers in Beirut performed their duties by means of observation posts and mobile patrols. Their task was to monitor the situation in and around Beirut, with emphasis on developments involving Israelis and Palestinians. Following the withdrawal of the Israeli forces from the Beirut area in September 1983, the tasks of the Observer Group were reduced and its strength gradually brought down to the former level. At present, the eight observers assigned to OGB perform liaison functions for UNTSO. The chief of OGB is also the designated chairman of ILMAC.

Financial aspects

Since its establishment in 1948, UNTSO has been financed from the regular budget of the United Nations. Its costs are therefore assessed as part of each biennial programme budget. As of 31 December 1989, UNTSO's total expenditures since its inception amounted to approximately $310.5 million. For the biennium 1990–1991, the resources approved by the General Assembly for UNTSO's budget were $47.4 million.

Assistance to other operations

The military officers assigned as United Nations observers to UNTSO have frequently been drawn on as a reserve of experienced personnel, especially in setting up new peace-keeping operations. Able to move at extremely short notice, they have given valuable service in the initial phases of all the peace-keeping operations in the Middle East, as well as the United Nations Operation in the Congo in 1960.

In addition, UNTSO contributed observers to two small military observer teams which were stationed in Tehran and Baghdad from 1984 to 1988 to monitor the moratorium arranged by the Secretary-General on military attacks against civilian centres during the conflict between Iran and Iraq.† Military officers seconded from UNTSO, as well as from UNDOF and UNIFIL, served in the United Nations Good Offices Mission in Afghanistan and Pakistan for that operation's duration (*see chapter XIV*). ‡

* S/15408.   † S/16627.   ‡ S/20230.

UNTSO observers participated in a technical mission to Angola in 1987, following a complaint by its Government against aggression by South Africa.* UNTSO provided the officers for the technical mission, led by its Chief of Staff, and advance parties dispatched to Iran and Iraq to prepare for the deployment of the United Nations Iran-Iraq Military Observer Group in 1988 (*see chapter XV*).† The Chief of Staff of UNTSO also led the preliminary fact-finding mission on Cambodia to gather technical information for the Paris Conference on Cambodia in August 1989.‡

* S/19359.   † S/20093.   ‡ A/44/670.

Chapter III **First United Nations Emergency Force**

A. Creation

Background

In October 1956, the United Nations faced a major crisis. The 1949 General Armistice Agreement between Egypt and Israel—concluded under the auspices of and supervised by the United Nations—collapsed when Israel and two major Powers occupied large portions of Egyptian territory. The Organization reacted to the crisis with speed and firmness and, to overcome it, conceived a new form of peace-keeping and set up its first peace-keeping force. This historic development was made possible mainly through the vision, resourcefulness and determination of Secretary-General Dag Hammarskjöld and Lester Pearson, who was at the time Secretary for External Affairs of Canada.

Since the summer of 1955, relations between Egypt and Israel had been steadily deteriorating, despite the efforts of the Chief of Staff of UNTSO and the Secretary-General himself. Palestinian *fedayeen*, with the support of the Egyptian Government, had been launching frequent raids against Israel from their bases in Gaza, and these had been followed by increasingly strong reprisal attacks by Israeli armed forces. The decision taken by Egypt in the early 1950s to restrict Israeli shipping through the Suez Canal and the Strait of Tiran at the entrance to the Gulf of Aqaba, in contravention of a decision of the Security Council, remained a controversial and destabilizing issue. In the heightening tension, the control of armaments—which the Tripartite Declaration of France, the United Kingdom and the United States, of May 1950, had sought to achieve in the Middle East—had broken down, and Egypt and Israel were engaging in an intense arms race, with the East and the West supplying sophisticated weapons and equipment to the opposing sides.

On 19 July 1956, the United States Government decided to withdraw its financial aid for the Aswan Dam project on the Nile River. President Gamal Abdel Nasser announced the nationalization of the Suez Canal Company a week later and declared that Canal dues would be used to finance the Aswan project.

On 23 September 1956, the Governments of France and the United Kingdom requested the President of the Security Council to convene the Council to consider the "situation created by the unilateral action of the Egyptian Government in bringing to an end the system of international operation of the Suez Canal, which was confirmed and completed by the Suez Canal Convention of 1888".* On the following day, Egypt countered with a request that the Security Council consider "actions against Egypt by some Powers, particularly France and the United Kingdom, which constitute a danger to international peace and security and are serious violations of the Charter of the United Nations".†

The Security Council first met on 26 September to consider both items. At the same time, private negotiations were being carried out between the Foreign Ministers of the three countries with the good offices of the Secretary-General. By 12 October, Hammarskjöld was able to work out six principles on which there seemed to be general agreement. These principles were incorporated in a draft resolution which the Security Council unanimously adopted on the next day. This became resolution 118(1956), by which the Security Council "agrees that any settlement of the Suez question should meet the following requirements:

"(1) There should be free and open transit through the Canal without discrimination, overt or covert—this covers both political and technical aspects;

"(2) The sovereignty of Egypt should be respected;

"(3) The operation of the Canal should be insulated from the politics of any country;

"(4) The manner of fixing tolls and charges should be decided by agreement between Egypt and the users;

"(5) A fair proportion of the dues should be allotted to development;

"(6) In case of disputes, unresolved affairs between the Suez Canal Company and the Egyptian Government should be settled by arbitration with suitable terms of reference and suitable provisions for the payment of sums found to be due."

Following the adoption of this resolution, Hammarskjöld announced that he would pursue his efforts to promote an agreement based on the principles laid down by the Security Council. However, a new situation developed in late October 1956, when Israel, in cooperation with the British and French Governments, launched an all-out attack on Egypt.

The Israeli forces crossed the border on the morning of 29 October, advancing in three columns towards El Arish, Ismailia and the

* S/3654.   † S/3656.

Mitla Pass. In the early hours of 30 October, the Chief of Staff of UNTSO, Major-General E. L. M. Burns, of Canada, called for a cease-fire and requested Israel to pull its forces back to its side of the border. In the afternoon of the same day, the British and French Governments addressed a joint ultimatum to Egypt and Israel calling on both sides to cease hostilities within 12 hours and to withdraw their forces to a distance of 10 miles on each side of the Suez Canal. They also requested Egypt to allow Anglo-French forces to be stationed temporarily on the Canal at Port Said, Ismailia and Suez for the purpose of separating the belligerents and ensuring the safety of shipping. The ultimatum was accepted by Israel whose troops in any case were still far from the Suez Canal, but it was rejected by Egypt. On 31 October, France and the United Kingdom launched an air attack against targets in Egypt, which was followed shortly by a landing of their troops near Port Said at the northern end of the Canal.

General Assembly's first emergency special session

The Security Council held a meeting on 30 October at the request of the United States, which submitted a draft resolution calling upon Israel immediately to withdraw its armed forces behind the established armistice lines.* It was not adopted because of British and French vetoes. A similar draft resolution† sponsored by the Soviet Union was also rejected. The matter was then transferred to the General Assembly, on a proposal by Yugoslavia, in accordance with the procedure provided by Assembly resolution 377(V) of 3 November 1950 entitled "Uniting for peace". Thus, the first emergency special session of the General Assembly called under that resolution was convened on 1 November 1956.

In the early hours of the next day, the General Assembly adopted, on the proposal of the United States, resolution 997(ES-I), calling for an immediate cease-fire, the withdrawal of all forces behind the armistice lines and the reopening of the Canal. The Secretary-General was requested to observe and report promptly on compliance to the Security Council and to the General Assembly, for such further action as those bodies might deem appropriate in accordance with the United Nations Charter.

The resolution was adopted by 64 votes to 5, with 6 abstentions. The dissenters were Australia and New Zealand, in addition to France, Israel and the United Kingdom. In explaining Canada's abstention, Lester Pearson stated that the resolution did not provide for, along with the cease-fire and a withdrawal of troops, any steps

---

* S/3710.   † S/3713/Rev.1.

to be taken by the United Nations for a peace settlement, without which a cease-fire would be only of a temporary nature at best.

Before the session, Pearson had had extensive discussions with Hammarskjöld and he felt that it might be necessary to establish some sort of United Nations police force to help resolve the crisis. Pearson submitted to the General Assembly, when it reconvened the next morning, a draft resolution on the establishment of an emergency international United Nations force.

Enabling resolutions of the United Nations Force

The Canadian proposal was adopted by the General Assembly on the same morning and became resolution 998(ES-I) of 4 November 1956, by which the Assembly:

> "*Requests,* as a matter of priority, the Secretary-General to submit to it within forty-eight hours a plan for the setting up, with the consent of the nations concerned, of an emergency international United Nations Force to secure and supervise the cessation of hostilities in accordance with all the terms of the aforementioned resolution [997(ES-I)]."

The voting was 57 to none, with 19 abstentions. Egypt, France, Israel, the United Kingdom and the Soviet Union and Eastern European States were among the abstainers.

At the same meeting, the General Assembly also adopted resolution 999(ES-I), by which it reaffirmed resolution 997(ES-I) and authorized the Secretary-General immediately to arrange with the parties concerned for the implementation of the cease-fire and the halting of the movement of military forces and arms into the area.

On the same day, the Secretary-General submitted his first report on the plan for an emergency international United Nations Force,* in which he recommended certain preliminary steps, including the immediate setting up of a United Nations Command. All his recommendations were endorsed by the General Assembly and included in resolution 1000(ES-I) adopted on 5 November 1956, by which the Assembly:

- Established a United Nations Command for an emergency international Force to secure and supervise the cessation of hostilities in accordance with all the terms of General Assembly resolution 997(ES-I) of 2 November 1956;
- Appointed, on an emergency basis, the Chief of Staff of UNTSO, Major-General (later Lieutenant-General) E. L. M. Burns, as Chief of the Command;
- Authorized the Chief of the Command immediately to recruit, from the observer corps of UNTSO, a limited number of officers who were to be nationals of countries other than those having permanent membership in the Security Council, and further authorized him, in consulta-

* A/3289.

tion with the Secretary-General, to undertake the recruitment directly, from various Member States other than the permanent members of the Security Council, of the additional number of officers needed;
  – Invited the Secretary-General to take such administrative measures as might be necessary for prompt execution of the actions envisaged.

The resolution was adopted by 57 votes to none, with 19 abstentions. As with resolution 998(ES-I), Egypt, France, Israel, the United Kingdom, the Soviet Union and Eastern European States abstained.

Concept and guiding principles

On 6 November, the Secretary-General submitted to the General Assembly his second and final report on the plan for an emergency United Nations Force.* In this report, Hammarskjöld defined the concept of the new Force and certain guiding principles for its organization and functioning. The main points:

(a) At the outset, Hammarskjöld observed, an emergency international United Nations Force could be developed on the basis of three concepts. In the first place, it could be set up on the basis of principles reflected in the constitution of the United Nations itself. This would mean that its chief responsible officer should be appointed by the United Nations itself and in his functions should be responsible ultimately to the General Assembly and/or the Security Council. His authority should be so defined as to make him fully independent of the policies of any one nation and his relations to the Secretary-General should correspond to those of the Chief of Staff of UNTSO. A second possibility would be for the United Nations to charge a country, or a group of countries, with the responsibility to provide independently for an international Force serving for the purposes determined by the United Nations. In this approach, which was followed in the case of the Unified Command in Korea, it would obviously be impossible to achieve the same independence in relation to national policies as would be established through the first concept. Finally, as a third possibility, an international Force might be set up in agreement among a group of nations, later to be brought into an appropriate relationship to the United Nations. This approach was open to the same reservation as the second concept and possibly others. Hammarskjöld noted that in deciding on 5 November 1956 to establish a United Nations Command, on an emergency basis, the General Assembly had chosen the first type of international force.

(b) Hammarskjöld set out certain guiding principles for the organization and functioning of the Force:

* A/3302.

- The decision taken by the General Assembly on the United Nations Command recognized the independence of the Chief of Command and established the principle that the Force should be recruited from Member States other than the permanent members of the Security Council. In this context, the Secretary-General observed that the question of the composition of the staff and contingents should not be subject to agreement by the parties involved since such a requirement would be difficult to reconcile with the development of the international Force along the course already being followed by the General Assembly.
- The terms of reference of the Force were to secure and supervise the cessation of hostilities in accordance with all the terms of the General Assembly's resolution 997(ES-I) of 2 November 1956. It followed from its terms of reference that there was no intent in the establishment of the Force to influence the military balance in the current conflict, and thereby the political balance affecting efforts to settle the conflict. The Force should be of a temporary nature, the length of its assignment being determined by the needs arising out of the current conflict.

(c)   Guidelines on the functions to be performed were outlined:

- The General Assembly's resolution of 2 November 1956 urged that "all parties now involved in hostilities in the area agree to an immediate cease-fire and, as part thereof, halt the movement of military forces and arms into the area", and further urged the parties to the Armistice Agreements promptly to withdraw all forces behind the armistice lines, to desist from raids against those lines into neighbouring territories and to observe scrupulously the provisions of the Agreements. These two provisions combined indicated that the functions of the United Nations Force would be, when a cease-fire was established, to enter Egyptian territory with the consent of the Egyptian Government, in order to help maintain quiet during and after the withdrawal of non-Egyptian forces and to secure compliance with the other terms established in the resolution.
- The Force obviously should have no rights other than those necessary for the execution of its functions, in co-operation with local authorities. It would be more than an observer corps, but in no way a military force temporarily controlling the territory in which it was stationed; nor should the Force have functions exceeding those necessary to secure peaceful conditions, on the assumption that the parties to the conflict would take all necessary steps for compliance with the recommendations of the General Assembly. Its functions could, on this basis, be assumed to cover an area extending roughly from the Suez Canal to the Armistice Demarcation Lines established in the Armistice Agreement between Egypt and Israel.

(d)   The Secretary-General indicated that the question as to how the Force should be financed required further study. A basic rule, which could be applied provisionally, would be that a State providing a unit would be responsible for all costs of equipment and salaries, while all other costs should be financed by the United Nations outside its normal budget. It was obviously impossible to make any estimate of the costs without knowledge of the size of the Force and the length of its assignment. The only practical course therefore would be for the General Assembly to vote on a general authorization for those costs on the basis of general principles such as those suggested in the report.

(e)   The Secretary-General stated that, because of the time factor, he could discuss the question of participation in the Force with only a limited number of Member Governments. The reaction so far led him to believe that it should be possible to meet quickly at least the most basic need for personnel. It was his hope that broader participation would be possible as soon as a plan was approved so that a more definite judgement might be possible concerning the implications of participation. Noting that several matters had to be left open because of the lack of time and the need for further study, the Secretary-General suggested that those matters be submitted to exploration by a small committee of the General Assembly. Such a committee might also serve as an advisory committee to the Secretary-General for questions relating to the operation.

Advisory Committee

After considering the report of the Secretary-General, the General Assembly adopted, on 7 November, resolution 1001 (ES-I)—approving the guiding principles for the organization and functioning of the emergency international United Nations Force as expounded in the Secretary-General's report; concurring in the definition of the functions of the Force in the report; and approving provisionally the basic rule concerning the financing of the Force laid down in that report. The Assembly established an Advisory Committee composed of Brazil, Canada, Ceylon (now Sri Lanka), Colombia, India, Norway and Pakistan. It requested the Committee, whose Chairman was the Secretary-General, to undertake the development of those aspects of the planning for the Force and its operation not already dealt with by the General Assembly and which did not fall within the area of the direct responsibility of the Chief of Command. It authorized the Secretary-General to issue all regulations and instructions essential to the effective functioning of the Force, following consultation with the Committee, and to take all other necessary administrative and executive action. The Committee was to continue to assist the Secretary-General in his responsibilities, and it could request the convening of the General Assembly if necessary. Finally, the Assembly requested all Member States to afford assistance as necessary to the United Nations Command in the performance of its functions, including arrangements for passage to and from the area involved.

This resolution, which, with resolution 998(ES-I) of 4 November, formed the basis for the establishment of the United Nations Emergency Force, was adopted by 64 votes to none, with 12 abstentions. France and the United Kingdom voted this time with the majority. Egypt and Israel remained with the abstainers, together with South Africa and the Soviet Union and Eastern European States. The representatives of France and the United Kingdom indicated that the resolution was acceptable to their Governments because it provided, as they had urged, for an effective international Force in the area. In explaining his abstention, the representative of the Soviet Union stated that the establishment of the Force under General Assembly resolution 1000(ES-I) and the plan for its implementation in resolution 1001(ES-I) were contrary to the Charter, and that the only reason for abstaining rather than voting against the proposal lay in the hope of preventing any further extension of the aggression against Egypt.

Further General Assembly resolutions

On the same day, 7 November, the General Assembly also adopted resolution 1002(ES-I), by which it called once again upon Israel immediately to withdraw all its forces behind the armistice lines, and upon France and the United Kingdom immediately to withdraw all their forces from Egyptian territory.

The voting was 65 to 1, with 10 abstentions. Israel cast the lone negative vote. France and the United Kingdom abstained, together with Australia, Belgium, Laos, Luxembourg, the Netherlands, New Zealand, Portugal and South Africa. The representatives of France and the United Kingdom indicated that an immediate withdrawal of their forces could lead to a power vacuum between Egyptian and Israeli forces and that withdrawal could only be effected subsequent to proof of the effective operation of UNEF.

The first emergency special session of the General Assembly ended on 10 November 1956. Before closing the session, the Assembly adopted resolution 1003(ES-I), by which it decided to refer the matter to its eleventh regular session which was then about to convene.

During the first emergency special session, the General Assembly had adopted a total of seven resolutions. By these resolutions, the Assembly gave the Secretary-General the authority and support he required to bring about the cessation of hostilities in Egypt and the withdrawal of foreign troops from Egyptian territory with the assistance of a new type of peace-keeping machinery, the United Nations peace-keeping force. The idea of such a force, which was to have such an impact on the work of the United Nations for the maintenance of international peace and security, came initially from Lester Pearson. Dag Hammarskjöld, through his untiring efforts and extraordinary diplomatic and administrative skill, made it a practical reality.

Initial stages of UNEF

The United Nations Emergency Force was the key element in the United Nations efforts to resolve the crisis arising from the military action of the Israeli and Anglo-French forces against Egypt. It was a pre-condition for securing the cease-fire and a pre-condition for bringing about the withdrawal of the invading forces. Therefore, a priority objective of the Secretary-General, after the adoption of the enabling resolutions, was to assemble a usable Force and land it in Egypt as rapidly as possible.

The establishment of this first peace-keeping Force in United Nations history was a task of great complexity. The concept had no real precedent. The nearest parallel was UNTSO, which also had peace-keeping functions but was a much simpler operation and did not provide much help as regards the many organizational and operational problems involved.

Immediately after the Assembly authorized the Force, the Chief of Command, General Burns, who was in Jerusalem at the time, selected a group of UNTSO observers who began planning the organization of the new Force. Hammarskjöld approached the Governments of the potential participating countries to obtain the required military personnel. He also initiated negotiations with the Egyptian Government to secure its agreement as the host country for the entry and stationing of the Force in Egypt.

Negotiations with the Egyptian Government

A key principle governing the stationing and functioning of UNEF, and later of all other peace-keeping forces, was the consent of the host Government. Since it was not an enforcement action under Chapter VII of the Charter, UNEF could enter and operate in Egypt only with the consent of the Egyptian Government. This principle was clearly stated by the General Assembly in adopting resolution 1001(ES-I) of 7 November 1956 concerning the establishment of UNEF.

Immediately after the adoption of that resolution, Hammarskjöld instructed General Burns to approach the Egyptian authorities in Cairo in order to prepare the ground for the prompt implementation of the resolution. The Government of Egypt had already accepted the terms of resolution 1000(ES-I) on the establishment of a United Nations Command, and this was considered by the Secretary-General as an acceptance in principle of the Force itself.

However, before consenting to the arrival of the Force on its territory, Egypt wished to have certain points in the Assembly resolution clarified. In particular, it wanted to know in clearer terms the functions of the Force, especially in regard to whether, when the Force reached the Armistice Demarcation Line, the Governments concerned would agree to the areas to be occupied by it, how long the Force would stay, whether it was supposed to have functions in the Suez Canal area apart from observing the withdrawal of the Anglo-French forces and whether it would stay in the Canal area after the Anglo-French withdrawal.

Firm assurance was given to the Egyptian authorities that cooperation with the United Nations would not infringe Egyptian sovereignty, detract from Egypt's power freely to negotiate a settlement on the Suez Canal or submit Egypt to any control from the outside. The Secretary-General impressed upon those authorities that the Force provided a guarantee for the withdrawal of foreign forces from Egypt and that, since it would come only with Egypt's consent, it could not stay or operate in Egypt if that consent were withdrawn.

On the basis of the General Assembly's resolutions as interpreted by the Secretary-General, the Government of Egypt gave its consent on 14 November to the arrival of UNEF in Egypt, and the first transport of UNEF troops took place on the next day.

While the exchange of views that had taken place was considered sufficient as a basis for the sending of the first units of UNEF to Egypt, the Secretary-General felt that a firmer foundation had to be laid for the presence and functioning of the Force in Egypt and for the continued co-operation with the Egyptian authorities. He also considered it essential to discuss personally with the Egyptian authorities, at the highest level, various questions which flowed from the decision to send the Force to Egypt, including the selection of national contingents.

Hammarskjöld therefore visited Cairo from 16 to 18 November. During this visit, he reached agreement with the Egyptian Government on the composition of the Force. President Nasser had first opposed the inclusion of the Canadian, Danish and Norwegian units because they belonged to the North Atlantic Treaty Organization (NATO) and because, in his view, Canada and the United Kingdom were too congeneric. But on the insistence of Hammarskjöld, this opposition was withdrawn. The basic discussions centred on the stationing and functioning of the Force.

The good faith agreement

On this essential matter, a "good faith agreement" was worked out and included in an aide-mémoire which served as the basis for the stationing of UNEF in Egypt. It noted that the Assembly, by resolution 1001(ES-I), had approved the principle that the Force could not be requested "to be stationed or operate on the territory of a given country without the consent of the Government of that country".* It then went on to say:

> The Government of Egypt and the Secretary-General of the United Nations have stated their understanding on the basic points for the presence and functioning of UNEF as follows:
> 1. The Government of Egypt declares that, when exercising its sovereign rights on any matter concerning the presence and functioning of UNEF, it will be guided, in good faith, by its acceptance of General Assembly resolution 1000(ES-I) of 5 November 1956.
> 2. The United Nations takes note of this declaration of the Government of Egypt and declares that the activities of UNEF will be guided, in good faith, by the task established for the Force in the aforementioned resolutions; in particular, the United Nations, understanding this to correspond to the wishes of the Government of Egypt, reaffirms its willingness to maintain UNEF until its task is completed.
> 3. The Government of Egypt and the Secretary-General declare that it is their intention to proceed forthwith, in the light of points 1 and 2 above, to explore jointly concrete aspects of the functioning of UNEF, including its stationing and the question of its lines of communication and supply; the Government of Egypt, confirming its intention to facilitate the functioning of UNEF, and the United Nations are agreed to expedite in co-operation the implementation of guiding principles arrived at as a result of that joint exploration on the basis of the resolutions of the General Assembly.†

The Secretary-General brought this aide-mémoire to the attention of the General Assembly in a report of 20 November 1956.‡ In so doing, he stated that ". . .The aide-mémoire, if noted with approval by the General Assembly, with the concurrence of Egypt, would establish an understanding between the United Nations and Egypt on which the co-operation could be developed and necessary agreements on various details be elaborated." No objection was raised by the Assembly in this connection.

---

* *Ibid.*   † A/3375, annex.   ‡ A/3375.

Other Hammarskjöld/Nasser memoranda and agreements

In addition to the good faith agreement, two other memoranda were agreed upon between Hammarskjöld and President Nasser. One of them set out the understanding that the area to be occupied by UNEF after the Israeli withdrawal would be subject to agreement and that the Force would have no function in the Port Said and the Suez Canal areas after the withdrawal of the Anglo-French troops. UNEF could not stay or operate in Egypt unless Egypt continued its consent. The other memorandum specifically separated the question of the reopening of the Suez Canal from the functions of UNEF. Hammarskjöld brought these memoranda to the attention of the Advisory Committee.

With these agreements, UNEF was set up. Subsequent discussions were continued between the Secretariat and the Egyptian authorities to work out more detailed and comprehensive arrangements on the status of the Force in Egypt. These arrangements were set out in a letter dated 8 February 1957 from the Secretary-General to the Minister for Foreign Affairs of Egypt and were accepted by the latter in his reply of the same date to the Secretary-General.* This exchange of letters constituted the agreement on the status of the United Nations Emergency Force in Egypt which the General Assembly noted with approval in its resolution 1126(XI) of 22 February 1957.

Status of the Force agreement

The status of the Force agreement covered a wide range of problems, including the premises of the Force and the use of the United Nations flag, freedom of movement, privileges and immunities of the Force, civil and criminal jurisdiction and settlement of disputes or claims. Two of the key provisions concerned freedom of movement and criminal jurisdiction. Members of the Force were to enjoy full freedom of movement in the performance of their duties. They were to be subject to the exclusive jurisdiction of their respective national Governments in respect of any criminal offences which they might commit in Egypt.

The agreement on the status of UNEF was the first document of this kind. It provided a pattern which was followed for the subsequent peace-keeping forces in the Congo and Cyprus. No agreements of this kind could be worked out for later forces for various political reasons but the status of the Force agreement for UNEF has

* A/3526.

been used as a precedent to deal with various problems arising from the operations of UNEF II, UNDOF and UNIFIL.

Negotiations with the participating countries

The principles of consent applied not only to the host Government but also to the participating countries. In accordance with the principles approved by the General Assembly, the Force was to be composed of national contingents accepted for service by the Secretary-General from among those voluntarily offered by Member States. Troops from the permanent members of the Security Council or from any country which, for geographical and other reasons, might have a special interest in the conflict would be excluded. In selecting the contingents, the Secretary-General had to take due account of the views of the host Government and such other factors as their suitability in terms of the needs of the Force, their size and availability, the extent to which they would be self-contained, the undesirability of too great a variation in ordnance and basic equipment, the problem of transportation and the goal of balanced composition.

The size of the Force was to be determined by the Commander in consultation with the Secretary-General and in the light of the functions to be performed. The original estimate by the Force Commander of the manpower needs to perform those tasks was the equivalent of two combat brigades, or about 6,000 men. It was decided that the national contingents should be sufficiently large to be relatively self-contained and that the Force should have adequate support units, including a light air-unit. From the point of view of balance, it was desirable that the differences in the size of the units should not be so great as to lead to excessive dependence on any one State.

The Secretary-General sought certain assurances from the participating countries. He pointed out that the effective functioning of UNEF required that some continuity of service of the participating units should be assured in order to enable the Force Commander to plan his operations. He also insisted that the Commander of each national contingent should take orders exclusively from the Force Commander and should be in a position to exercise the necessary disciplinary authority with the members of his contingent.

The arrangements between the United Nations and the contributing countries were expanded and set out in formal agreements in the form of an exchange of letters between the Secretary-General and the respective participating Governments.

By 5 November 1956, Canada, Colombia, Denmark, Finland, Norway, Pakistan and Sweden had replied affirmatively. In the following days, Afghanistan, Brazil, Burma (now Myanmar), Ceylon (now Sri Lanka), Chile, Czechoslovakia, Ecuador, Ethiopia, India, Indonesia, Iran, Laos, New Zealand, Peru, the Philippines, Romania and Yugoslavia also offered to provide contingents. In addition, the United States Government informed the Secretary-General that it was prepared to help as regards airlifts, shipping, transport and supplies. Italy agreed to place at the disposal of the United Nations the facilities of Capodichino Airport at Naples for the assembly and transit of UNEF personnel and equipment and to help in the airlift of personnel and equipment from Italy to Egypt. The Swiss Government, a non-member State, offered to defray part of the cost of Swissair charter planes.

UNEF's composition

In consultation with the Force Commander and after discussions with the Government of Egypt, Hammarskjöld accepted contingents from 10 countries: Brazil, Canada, Colombia, Denmark, Finland, India, Indonesia, Norway, Sweden and Yugoslavia. The offers of assistance from the United States, Italy and Switzerland were also accepted. With the agreement of Egypt, an air base at Abu Suweir near Ismailia was used as the central depot for the early contingents.

The extent of the area to be covered by UNEF called for highly mobile reconnaissance. This need was met by Yugoslavia, which provided a complete reconnaissance battalion. Canada later supplied a fully equipped, light-armoured squadron. Supporting units were obtained and assigned with the same urgency as those engaged in patrolling. The Indian contingent was given responsibility for the supply depot and the service institute; Canada and India provided units for transport, the Provost Marshal and signals; Norway and Canada covered the medical needs. The Canadian contingent was also made responsible for the ordnance depot and workshop, the base post office, engineering, the dental unit, movement control and air support.

General Burns and his group of UNTSO military observers arrived in Cairo on 12 November 1956 and set up a temporary headquarters there. The first UNEF units, composed of Colombians, Danes and Norwegians, flew to Egypt on 15 and 16 November. They were followed by other contingents. The target strength of about 6,000 men was reached in February 1957 after the Brazilian battalion had arrived at Port Said by sea. With the appointment of staff officers selected from the participating countries, the UNTSO military observers returned to their normal duties in Jerusalem.

The Governments of Indonesia and Finland, which had agreed to participate in the Force only for a limited period, withdrew their contingents in September and December 1957, respectively. The Colombian Government withdrew its contingent in December 1958. The other contingents continued to serve with UNEF until the withdrawal of the Force in 1967. The deployment and assignment of the contingents were changed from time to time according to the requirements of the operation.

The strength of the Force remained at the authorized level of about 6,000 until the end of 1957. In the following years, it was gradually reduced because the situation in the area of operation remained quiet and also because of financial difficulties. There were 5,341 all ranks with the Force in 1960, 5,102 in 1963, 4,581 in 1965 and 3,959 in 1966. In November 1965, a survey team was sent to the area to examine the possibility of further reductions. In accordance with its recommendations, the strength was further brought down to 3,378 at the time the Force began its withdrawal in May 1967.

UNEF's organization

The United Nations Emergency Force, established by the General Assembly, was a subsidiary organ of the Assembly under Article 22 of the Charter. It was directed by the Secretary-General under the general authority of the General Assembly.

The Secretary-General was authorized to issue all regulations and instructions which might be essential to the effective functioning of the Force and to take all other necessary administrative and executive actions. To assist him in these matters, Hammarskjöld set up an informal military group at Headquarters composed of military representatives of participating countries and headed by his military adviser—Major-General I. A. E. Martola of Finland, during the formative period. The Secretary-General was also assisted by the Advisory Committee established under Assembly resolution 1001(ES-I).

The command of the Force was assumed in the field by the Force Commander (originally designated as the Chief of Command), who was appointed by the General Assembly on the recommendation of

the Secretary-General. The Commander was operationally responsible for the performance of all functions assigned to the Force by
the United Nations and for the deployment and assignment of the
troops placed at the disposal of the Force. He had direct authority
for the operation of the Force and also was responsible for the provision of facilities, supplies and auxiliary services. He reported to
the Secretary-General and was responsible to him. He was normally
a general officer seconded by a Member State at the request of the
Secretary-General, and during his assignment with the United Nations received an appointment as a senior official of the United Nations Secretariat with the rank of Assistant Secretary-General (Under-
Secretary during Dag Hammarskjöld's time).

The Force Commander was authorized to appoint the officers
of his command in consultation with the Secretary-General. In selecting the officers, the Commander was required to give due consideration to the goal of a balanced composition and to the importance of
contributions made by the participating countries. The national contingents were under the command of the contingent commanders,
who were appointed by their respective Governments. These contingents remained part of their respective national armed forces but,
during their assignment to UNEF, they owed international allegiance
and were placed under the operational control of the United Nations.
This control was exercised through the contingent commanders, who
received their instructions from the Force Commander. Changes in
contingent commanders were made by the Governments of participating countries in consultation with the Force Commander.

The officers and soldiers of each contingent continued to wear
their national uniforms but with United Nations insignia. The blue
beret and helmet were created by Hammarskjöld during the formative days of UNEF.

Responsibility for disciplinary action in national contingents
rested with the contingent commanders. Reports concerning
disciplinary action were communicated to the Force Commander,
who might consult with the contingent commanders and, if necessary,
with the authorities of the participating Governments concerned.

Military police were provided by the Force Commander for all
camps, establishments and other premises occupied by the Force
and for such areas where the Force was deployed in the performance
of its functions. Elsewhere, UNEF military police might be employed
in so far as such employment was necessary to maintain discipline
and order among members of the Force, subject to arrangements

with the authorities of the host country and in liaison with those authorities.

B. Cease-fire and withdrawal of foreign forces

Establishment of the cease-fire

The first objective of Secretary-General Hammarskjöld was to secure a cease-fire in accordance with the call of the General Assembly contained in resolution 997(ES-I) of 2 November 1956.

During the meeting at which this resolution was adopted, the representative of Israel stated that his Government agreed to an immediate cease-fire, provided that a similar answer was forthcoming from Egypt. On the same day, the Egyptian Government informed the Secretary-General that it would accept the call for a cease-fire on the condition that military actions against Egypt were stopped. The Secretary-General immediately notified Israel, France and the United Kingdom of Egypt's position and called upon all four parties to bring hostilities to an end.*

On 4 November, Hammarskjöld requested all four parties concerned to bring to a halt all hostile military action by 2400 hours GMT on the same day. In identical messages addressed to the Governments of France and the United Kingdom,† he pointed out that in the light of the replies received from Egypt and Israel, it was obvious that the positions of France and the United Kingdom would determine whether or not it would be possible to achieve a cease-fire between Egypt and Israel. He urged the two Governments to give him a definitive acceptance on his cease-fire call at the earliest possible moment. On 5 November, France and the United Kingdom informed the Secretary-General that as soon as the Governments of Egypt and Israel signified acceptance of, and the United Nations endorsed a plan for, an international Force with the prescribed functions, they would cease all military action. ‡

Later in the day, the British representative announced that a cease-fire had been ordered at Port Said. Orders had also been given to cease all bombing forthwith throughout Egypt, and other forms of air action would be limited to the support of any necessary operation in the Canal area. Also on the same day, Egypt accepted the

* A/3287.   † *Ibid.*   ‡ A/3294 and A/3293.

Secretary-General's request for a cease-fire without any attached conditions and Israel informed the Secretary-General that in the light of Egypt's declaration, it confirmed its readiness to agree to a cease-fire.

In an aide-mémoire dated 5 November,* the Secretary-General informed France and the United Kingdom that, since on that date the General Assembly had taken a decisive step towards setting up the international Force by establishing a United Nations Command, and since Egypt and Israel had agreed, without conditions, to a cease-fire, the conditions for a general cease-fire would seem to be established.

In their replies of 6 November,† the two Governments announced that their forces were being ordered to cease fire at midnight GMT on the same day, pending confirmation that Egypt and Israel had accepted an unconditional cease-fire and that there would be a United Nations Force competent to secure and supervise the attainment of the objectives of resolution 997(ES-I). The Secretary-General promptly informed Egypt and Israel that the cease-fire would become effective at midnight. He noted that the Assembly had not made the cease-fire dependent on the creation or the functioning of UNEF, since its call for a cease-fire and its decision to establish the Force were in separate resolutions.

The cease-fire was established at midnight GMT on 7/8 November and, except for isolated incidents, generally held.

Withdrawal of the Anglo-French force

At the same time as the Secretary-General was taking urgent steps to set up the new Force, he was pressing France and the United Kingdom for an early withdrawal of their forces from the Port Said area.

The two Governments told him that their troops would be withdrawn as soon as the proposed United Nations Force was in a position to assume effectively the tasks assigned to it and, in particular, to ensure that hostilities would not be resumed in the area.

Hammarskjöld therefore endeavoured to move the first units of UNEF to Egypt and build up its strength as rapidly as he could. But the establishment of this first United Nations peace-keeping force was not an easy job, and it took time to obtain the required units from the various contributing countries, transport them to the area of operations and make them fully operational. The first units from the Colombian, Danish and Norwegian contingents arrived in the area on

* A/3310.   † A/3306 and A/3307.

15 and 16 November and were immediately deployed in the Suez Canal area.

On 24 November, the General Assembly adopted resolution 1120(XI), by which it noted with regret that two thirds of the French forces and all of the British forces remained in Egypt, and it reiterated its call to the British and French Governments for the immediate withdrawal of their forces.

In messages dated 3 December,* the British and French Governments noted that an effective United Nations Force was currently arriving in Egypt, that the Secretary-General had accepted the responsibility for organizing the task of clearing the Suez Canal as expeditiously as possible, that free and secure transit would be re-established through the Canal when it was cleared and that the Secretary-General would promote as quickly as possible negotiations with regard to the future régime of the Canal on the basis of the six requirements set out in the Security Council's resolution 118(1956) of 13 October 1956. The two Governments confirmed their decision to continue the withdrawal of their forces from the Port Said area without delay.

The Secretary-General immediately instructed General Burns to get in touch with the Anglo-French Commander and work out with him arrangements for the complete withdrawal of the Anglo-French forces without delay, ensuring that UNEF would be in a position to assume its responsibilities in the Port Said area by the middle of December.†

On 22 December, the withdrawal of the Anglo-French forces was completed and UNEF took over the Port Said area.

Initial withdrawal of the Israeli forces:
November 1956–mid-January 1957

The negotiations undertaken by Hammarskjöld to achieve the withdrawal of the Anglo-French forces required nearly two months; those regarding the withdrawal of Israeli forces took much longer. By resolution 997(ES-I) of 2 November 1956, the General Assembly had urged the parties to the Armistice Agreements promptly to withdraw all forces behind the armistice lines, to desist from raids across those lines into neighbouring territory and to observe scrupulously the Armistice Agreements. In resolution 1002(ES-I) of 7 November, the Assembly, after noting its decision to establish a United Nations Command for an international force, called

* A/3415.   † *Ibid.*

once again upon Israel immediately to withdraw its forces behind the armistice lines.

On 7 November, the Prime Minister of Israel, David Ben Gurion, in a statement to the Israeli Knesset (Parliament), stated that the armistice lines between Egypt and Israel had no validity and that "on no account will Israel agree to the stationing of a foreign force, no matter how called, in her territory, or in any of the areas occupied by her". On hearing of this statement, the Secretary-General immediately wrote to the Minister for Foreign Affairs of Israel, Golda Meir, to inform her that this position was in violation of the resolutions of the General Assembly and, if maintained, would seriously complicate the task of giving effect to those resolutions.

On 21 November,* in reply to queries by the Secretary-General, the Government of Israel stated that there had already been a withdrawal of its forces for varying distances along the entire Egyptian frontier. It reiterated its position regarding the withdrawal of the Israeli forces and indicated that the satisfactory arrangements it sought were such as would ensure Israel's security against the recurrence of the threat or danger of attack and against acts of belligerency by land or sea. Noting that it had not yet had an opportunity to discuss the question of satisfactory arrangements to be made with the United Nations in connection with UNEF, it stated that it was awaiting information on the proposed size, location and stationing arrangements of the Force and on the methods proposed for the discharge of its functions as laid down in the General Assembly's resolutions of 2, 5 and 7 November. It was also awaiting a clarification by Egypt on its policy and intention with respect to belligerency or peace with Israel which must influence Israel's dispositions on matters affecting its security.

At a meeting held on 24 November, the General Assembly adopted resolution 1120(XI) by which, after noting that the Israeli forces had not yet been withdrawn behind the armistice lines, reiterated its call to Israel to comply forthwith with its resolution. On the same day, the representative of Israel informed the Secretary-General† that the equivalent of two infantry brigades had been withdrawn from Egyptian territory into Israel.

In a letter dated 1 December,‡ the representative of Israel advised the Secretary-General that on the morning of 3 December, Israeli forces would be removed from a wide belt of territory (about 50 kilometres) in proximity to the Suez Canal along its entire length. Elements of UNEF immediately entered the evacuated area, although progress in this process was slowed down because of minefields and

* A/3384, annex 2.   † A/3389/Add.1   ‡ A/3410.

destroyed roads. On 11 December, Israel announced that it was ready to effect further withdrawal of troops in the Sinai peninsula in order to enable UNEF to extend its occupation eastward.

General Burns met with General Moshe Dayan, the Israeli Commander, on the morning of 16 December. They agreed on specific arrangements for a first phase of withdrawal, and UNEF troops moved forward to within five kilometres of new Israeli positions.

Regarding further withdrawals, General Dayan informed the UNEF Commander that, according to his instructions, the Israeli forces were to withdraw from the remainder of the Sinai at an approximate rate of 25 kilometres each week during the next four weeks. This plan was considered by General Burns to be inadequate. Consequently, at his request, a new withdrawal proposal was submitted by the Israeli Government on 21 December. The new proposal envisaged that the remaining Israeli withdrawal would take place in two phases. The second phase would involve a full Israeli withdrawal behind the armistice lines at an unstated date.

In accordance with this proposal, a further withdrawal of Israeli forces took place on 7 and 8 January 1957 to a north-south line roughly following meridian 33 degrees, 44 minutes, leaving no Israeli forces west of El Arish. On 15 January, the Israeli forces withdrew eastward another 25 to 30 kilometres, except in the area of Sharm el Sheikh. This phase involved the entry into El Arish and St. Catherine's Monastery of the United Nations Emergency Force, which had closely followed the withdrawing Israeli troops.

Sharm el Sheikh and the Gaza Strip

A day earlier, on 14 January, the Government of Israel had informed the Secretary-General that by 22 January the Sinai Desert would be entirely evacuated by Israeli forces with the exception of the Sharm el Sheikh area, that is "the strip on the western coast of the Gulf of Aqaba which at present ensures freedom of navigation in the Strait of Tiran and in the Gulf". Reporting on this matter to the General Assembly,* the Secretary-General stated that under the terms of the Assembly's resolution, the Israeli forces should be withdrawn also from that area.

In this connection, he observed that the international significance of the Gulf of Aqaba might be considered to justify the right of innocent passage through the Strait of Tiran and the Gulf in accordance with recognized rules of international law. He did not consider that a discussion of the various aspects of this matter and its possible rela-

* A/3500.

tion to the action requested in the General Assembly on the Middle East crisis fell within the mandate established for him in resolution 999(ES-I) of 4 November. Like the cease-fire, withdrawal was a preliminary and essential phase in the process through which a viable basis might be laid for peaceful conditions in the area. The General Assembly, in giving high priority to the cease-fire and withdrawal, in no way disregarded all the other aims which must be achieved in order to create more satisfactory conditions than those prevailing during the period preceding the crisis. The basic function of UNEF, which was to help maintain quiet, gave the Force great value as a background for efforts towards resolving such pending problems, although it was not in itself a means to that end.

On 19 January 1957, the General Assembly adopted resolution 1123(XI) by which, after recalling its resolutions of 2, 4, 7 and 24 November 1956, requested the Secretary-General "to continue his efforts for securing the complete withdrawal of Israel in pursuance of the above-mentioned resolutions, and to report on such completion to the General Assembly, within five days".

In pursuance of that resolution, Hammarskjöld held further discussions with Israeli representatives on 20 and 23 January. On 23 January, Israel presented its views in an aide-mémoire on the Israeli position on the Sharm el Sheikh area and the Gaza Strip.* Its position on each of the two areas was:

(a) For the Sharm el Sheikh area, Israel's aim was the simultaneous reconciliation of two objectives: the withdrawal of Israeli forces from that area and the guaranteeing of permanent freedom of navigation by the prevention of belligerence. In this matter, Egyptian compliance with the decision of the Security Council—resolution 95(1951) of 1 September 1951—had a legal and chronological priority over Israel's duty to fulfil recommendations in which Egypt had an interest. Accordingly, Israel formally requested the Secretary-General to ascertain Egypt's intentions with respect to the Council's 1951 resolution concerning the Suez Canal.

(b) For the Gaza Strip, Israel, after questioning the legality of the Egyptian occupation of Gaza from 1948 to 1956 and criticizing its actions during this period, proposed a plan under which the Israeli military forces would be withdrawn but an Israeli civilian administration would remain to deal with security and administrative matters; the United Nations Emergency Force would not enter and be deployed in the Gaza area, but Israel would co-operate with the United Nations Relief and Works Agency for Palestine Refugees in the Near East regarding the care and maintenance of the refugees

* A/3511.

in the area. In this connection, Israel was ready to work out with the United Nations a suitable relationship with respect to the Gaza Strip.

The position of the Secretary-General was set out in his report of 24 January 1957:*

- In connection with the question of Israeli withdrawal from the Sharm el Sheikh area, attention had been directed to the situation in the Strait of Tiran and the Gulf of Aqaba. This problem was of longer duration and was not directly related to the current crisis. It followed from principles guiding the United Nations that the Israeli military action and its consequences should not be elements influencing the solution of this problem. The Secretary-General concluded that upon the withdrawal of the Israeli forces, UNEF would have to follow them inthe same way as it had in other parts of the Sinai, its movements being determined by its duties in respect of the cease-fire and the withdrawal. In accordance with the general legal principles recognized as decisive for the deployment of the Force, UNEF should not be used in such a way as to prejudice the solution of the controversial questions involved.

- Regarding the status of Gaza, the United Nations could not recognize a change of the *de facto* situation created under the Armistice Agreement, by which the administration and security in the Strip were left in the hands of Egypt, unless the change was brought about through settlement between the parties. Nor could it lend its assistance to the maintenance of a *de facto* situation contrary to the one created by the Agreement. These considerations excluded the United Nations from accepting Israeli control over the area even if it were of a non-military character. Deployment of UNEF in Gaza under the resolutions of the General Assembly would have to be on the same basis as its deployment along the Armistice Demarcation Line and in the Sinai peninsula. Any broader function for it in that area, in view of the terms of the Armistice Agreement and a recognized principle of international law, would require the consent of Egypt.

Second withdrawal of Israeli forces: February 1957

On 2 February 1957, the General Assembly, after receiving the Secretary-General's report, adopted two resolutions.

By resolution 1124(XI), it deplored the failure of Israel to complete its withdrawal behind the Armistice Demarcation Line and called upon it to do so without delay. By resolution 1125(XI), the

* A/3512.

Assembly, recognizing that withdrawal by Israel must be followed by action which would assure progress towards the creation of peaceful conditions, called upon Egypt and Israel scrupulously to observe the provisions of the 1949 General Armistice Agreement and considered that "after full withdrawal of Israel from the Sharm el Sheikh and the Gaza areas, the scrupulous maintenance of the Armistice Agreement requires the placing of the United Nations Emergency Force on the Egyptian-Israel Armistice Demarcation Line and the implementation of other measures as proposed in the Secretary-General's report, with due regard to the considerations set out therein with a view to assist in achieving situations conducive to the maintenance of peaceful conditions in the area". The General Assembly further requested the Secretary-General, in consultation with the parties concerned, to take steps to carry out these measures and to report to it as appropriate.

On 4 February, the Secretary-General met with the representative of Israel to discuss implementation of the Assembly's resolutions. Israel presented to him an aide-mémoire in which it raised two points. First, it requested the Secretary-General to ask the Government of Egypt whether Egypt agreed "to the mutual and full abstention from belligerent acts, by land, air and sea, on withdrawal of Israeli troops". Secondly, Israel sought clarification as to whether "immediately on the withdrawal of Israeli forces from the Sharm el Sheikh area, units of the United Nations Emergency Force will be stationed along the western shore of the Gulf of Aqaba in order to act as a restraint against hostile acts, and will remain so deployed until another effective means is agreed upon between the parties concerned for ensuring permanent freedom of navigation and the absence of belligerent acts in the Strait of Tiran and the Gulf of Aqaba".*

During the same meeting, the Secretary-General asked whether, with regard to Gaza, it was understood by the Government of Israel that the withdrawal had to cover elements of civilian administration as well as military troops. Hammarskjöld considered a clarification on this point to be a prerequisite to further consideration of the Israeli aide-mémoire. There was, in his view, an unavoidable connection between Israel's willingness to comply fully with General Assembly resolution 1124(XI) as concerned the Gaza Strip and what might be done towards maintaining quiet in the Sharm el Sheikh area, and it was unrealistic to assume that the latter question could be solved while Israel remained in Gaza.

With regard to the second point raised by Israel, the Secretary-General noted that the debate in the General Assembly and the re-

* A/3527, annex I.

port on which it was based made it clear that the stationing of the United Nations Emergency Force at Sharm el Sheikh would require Egyptian consent. In the light of this implication of Israel's question, the Secretary-General considered it important, as a basis for his consideration of the aide-mémoire, to learn whether Israel itself consented in principle to the stationing of UNEF units on its territory in implementation of the functions established for the Force by the Assembly's resolutions and, in particular, its resolution 1125(XI) where it was indicated that the Force should be placed on the Egyptian-Israeli Armistice Demarcation Line.

This meeting was followed by an exchange of communications between the Secretary-General and the representative of Israel, and a meeting between them was held on 10 February. But these were all inconclusive, as each side wanted to receive the clarifications it had sought before replying to the questions addressed to it. In this connection, the Secretary-General stated that the fact that Israel had not found it possible to clarify elements decisive for the consideration of its requests had complicated the efforts to achieve implementation of the Assembly's resolutions.

In reporting on this matter to the General Assembly on 11 February,* the Secretary-General commented that the relationship between resolution 1124(XI) on withdrawal and resolution 1125(XI) on measures to be carried out after withdrawal afforded the possibility of informal explorations of the whole field covered by these two resolutions, preparatory to negotiations. Later, the results of such explorations might be used in the negotiations through a constructive combination of measures, representing for the two countries parallel progress towards the peaceful conditions sought. However, such explorations could not be permitted to invert the sequence between withdrawal and other measures, nor to disrupt the evolution of negotiations towards their goal. Progress towards peaceful conditions, following the general policy suggested in the last report of the Secretary-General, on which General Assembly resolution 1125(XI) was based, had to be achieved gradually.

Final withdrawal of Israeli forces: March 1957

In concluding his report, the Secretary-General stated that, in the situation now facing the United Nations, the General Assembly, as a matter of priority, might wish to indicate how it wished him to proceed with further steps to carry out its decisions.

* A/3527.

The Assembly did not adopt any further resolution on this matter after the Secretary-General's report, but the Israeli Government eventually softened its position on the withdrawal from the Gaza Strip, although it maintained its denunciation of the 1949 General Armistice Agreement with Egypt and continued to oppose the stationing of the United Nations Emergency Force on its side of the Armistice Demarcation Line.

On 1 March, the Foreign Minister of Israel announced in the General Assembly the decision of her Government to act in compliance with the request contained in Assembly resolution 1124(XI) to withdraw behind the Armistice Demarcation Line.

The same day, the Secretary-General instructed the Commander of UNEF as a matter of utmost urgency to arrange for a meeting with the Commander-in-Chief of the Israeli forces in order to agree with him on arrangements for the complete and unconditional withdrawal of Israel in accordance with the Assembly's decision.

On 4 March, the declaration of 1 March was confirmed by the Israeli Government. The same day, General Burns met at Lydda with General Dayan. Technical arrangements were agreed upon for the withdrawal of the Israeli forces and the entry of UNEF troops into the Gaza Strip during the hours of curfew on the night of 6/7 March. Agreement was also reached for a similar takeover of the Sharm el Sheikh area on 8 March.

On 6 March, General Burns reported that UNEF troops were in position in all camps and centres of population in the Gaza Strip. The operation was carried out according to plan and without incident. By 0400 hours GMT, all Israelis had withdrawn from the Strip with the exception of an Israeli troop unit at Rafah Camp. By agreement, that last Israeli element was to be withdrawn at 1600 hours GMT on 8 March and full withdrawal from the Sharm el Sheikh area would be effected at the same time. These withdrawals took place as agreed and thus the Secretary-General was able to report to the General Assembly on 8 March 1957 full compliance with its resolution 1124(XI) of 2 February 1957.

C. **UNEF deployment**

Deployment along the Armistice Demarcation Line

In its resolution 1125(XI), on measures to be taken after the withdrawal of the Israeli forces from Egyptian territory, the

General Assembly called upon the Governments of Egypt and Israel to observe scrupulously the provisions of the 1949 General Armistice Agreement and considered that, after full withdrawal of Israel from the Sharm el Sheikh and Gaza areas, "the scrupulous maintenance of the Armistice Agreement requires the placing of the United Nations Emergency Force on the Egyptian-Israel Armistice Demarcation Line".

On 11 February 1957,* the Secretary-General reported to the Assembly that Egypt had reaffirmed its intent to observe fully the provisions of the Armistice Agreement to which it was a party, on the assumption that observance would be reciprocal. The Secretary-General drew attention to the desire expressed by Egypt to see an end to all raids and incursions across the Armistice Line in both directions, with effective assistance from United Nations auxiliary organs to that effect.

Israel maintained its denunciation of the Armistice Agreement. In a letter of 25 January,† the representative of Israel had stated that "Israel does not claim that the absence of an armistice agreement means the existence of a state of war with Egypt, even though Egypt insisted on the existence of a state of war even when the Agreement was in existence. Israel is prepared to confirm its position on this by signing immediately with Egypt an agreement of non-belligerency and mutual non-aggression, but the Agreement, violated and broken, is beyond repair".

The Secretary-General did not accept Israel's denunciation as valid, as there was no provision in the 1949 Agreement for unilateral termination of its application. Consequently, the machinery for the supervision of the Armistice Agreement was maintained by UNTSO (*see chapter II above*).

In his report of 8 March 1957, ‡ the Secretary-General informed the General Assembly that arrangements would be made through which, without any change in the legal structure or status of UNTSO, its functions in the Gaza area would be placed under the operational control of UNEF. Close co-operation between the two United Nations peace-keeping operations was maintained.

Regarding the placing of UNEF along the Armistice Demarcation Line, the Secretary-General interpreted this as requiring the deployment of the Force on both sides of the Line. The Egyptian Government had consented to the deployment of UNEF on its territory along the Line as well as in the Sharm el Sheikh area on the basis of the "good faith agreement" set out in the aide-mémoire of November 1956 (*see above*). At the beginning of February 1957, the

* *Ibid.* † A/3527, annex V. ‡ A/3568.

Secretary-General had sought clarification from Israel as to whether, as a question of principle, it agreed to the stationing of UNEF units on its side of the Armistice Demarcation Line. No clarification was obtained and, in a letter dated 6 February to the representative of Israel,* the Secretary-General said he assumed that, at least for the present, Israel's reply to this question was essentially negative. In view of the Israeli position, UNEF could be deployed only on the Egyptian side.

As of 8 March 1957, UNEF was deployed along the western side of the Armistice Demarcation Line along the Gaza Strip, along the international frontier between the Sinai and Israel, as well as in the Sharm el Sheikh area.

Phases of deployment and activities

UNEF began operating in Egypt on 12 November 1956, when the Force Commander and a group of military observers detached from UNTSO set up a temporary headquarters in Cairo. It was withdrawn ten-and-a-half years later, on 18 May 1967, at the request of the Egyptian Government. The operation of the Force during this period may be divided into four phases: the first phase, which extended from mid-November to late December 1956, was centred on the withdrawal of the Anglo-French forces from the Port Said area. The second, from that time to early March 1957, concerned the withdrawal of the Israeli forces from the Sinai peninsula, except the Gaza Strip and the Sharm el Sheikh area. The third, in March, related to those areas. The fourth and last phase, which began with the deployment of UNEF along the borders between Egypt and Israel, covered a period of more than 10 years from March 1957 until May 1967, during which time the Force effectively maintained peace in those sensitive areas.

First phase: Suez Canal area (November-December 1956)

When UNEF became operational in mid-November 1956, the cease-fire had been achieved and was generally holding. The Anglo-French forces were occupying the Port Said area including Port Fuad in the northern end of the Suez Canal. The Israeli forces were deployed east of the Canal about 10 kilometres from it. The Secretary-General was actively negotiating with the three Governments concerned and pressing for the early withdrawal of their forces from Egyptian soil.

* A/3527, annex III.

The objectives of UNEF were to supervise the cessation of hostilities and to assist in the withdrawal process once agreement was reached on this matter. Shortly after its arrival in Egypt, UNEF was interposed between the Anglo-French and the Egyptian forces, occupying a buffer zone. All incidents involving the cease-fire were reported to the proper authorities, who were urged to prevent recurrences. No provisions had been made for the establishment of joint machinery whereby incidents could be examined and discussed. UNEF's role was limited to investigating, reporting and, if warranted, protesting to the relevant authorities.

By arrangements with the Anglo-French forces, units of UNEF entered Port Said and Port Fuad and took responsibility for maintaining law and order in certain areas, in co-operation with the local authorities. The Force also undertook guard duty of some vulnerable installations and other points.

In the period of transition, when the Anglo-French forces were preparing to leave and during the withdrawal process, UNEF undertook certain essential administrative functions such as security and the protection of public and private property, with the co-operation of the Governor and the Police Inspector in Port Said. With the sanction of the local authorities, UNEF personnel also performed administrative functions with respect to public services, utilities and arrangements for the provisioning of the local population with foodstuffs, and exercised limited powers of detention. All administrative and policing responsibilities were turned over to the Egyptian authorities the day following the Anglo-French evacuation.

Other tasks of the Force included clearing minefields in the Suez Canal area and arranging for exchanges of prisoners and detainees between the Egyptian Government and the Anglo-French command. In the last stage of the withdrawal of the Anglo-French troops from Port Said and Port Fuad, UNEF units were stationed around the final perimeter of the zone occupied by the withdrawing forces, thus preventing clashes between them and the Egyptian troops.

Second phase: Sinai peninsula (December 1956–March 1957)

After the withdrawal of the Anglo-French forces, UNEF concentrated its efforts on maintaining the cease-fire between the Egyptian and Israeli forces and on arranging for Israeli withdrawal from Egyptian territory.

The Israeli forces withdrew from the Sinai peninsula, with the exception of the Gaza and the Sharm el Sheikh areas, in three stages:

on 3 December 1956, on 7 and 8 January 1957 and from 15 to 22 January 1957.

On the whole, the functions performed by UNEF in the Sinai were similar to those undertaken in the Canal area. The Force was interposed between the Egyptian and Israeli forces in a temporary buffer zone from 3 December onwards, moving eastbound as the Israeli forces withdrew, and in accordance with pre-arranged procedures.

During the successive stages of the Israeli withdrawal, UNEF temporarily undertook some local civic responsibilities, including security functions in a few inhabited areas, handing over such responsibilities to the Egyptian civilian authorities as soon as they returned to their posts. The Force also arranged and carried out exchanges of prisoners of war between Egypt and Israel and discharged certain investigatory functions. It cleared minefields in the Sinai and repaired portions of damaged roads and tracks crossing the peninsula.

Third phase: Gaza Strip and Sharm el Sheikh (March 1957)

After 22 January 1957, Israel held on to the last two areas it still occupied. The persistent negotiations to ensure withdrawal are described above. The withdrawal from the Gaza Strip took place on 6 and 7 March 1957 and that from the Sharm el Sheikh area from 8 to 12 March.

In accordance with the arrangements agreed to by the Egyptian Government, a UNEF detachment was stationed in Sharm el Sheikh following the withdrawal of the Israeli forces. This detachment maintained an observation post and kept the Strait of Tiran under constant watch.

In the Gaza Strip, two local conditions were of special concern to UNEF as it moved into the area. It was across the Armistice Demarcation Line along the Strip that the greatest number of infiltrations and raids had occurred during past years and there were in the area a large number of Palestinian Arab refugees, who were being assisted by UNRWA.

UNEF units entered the Gaza Strip on 6 March as the withdrawal of Israeli forces began. As a first step, arrangements were made between the Force Commander and the Israeli authorities for the United Nations to assume its responsibilities in the Strip as the Israeli troops and civil administrators withdrew.

On 7 March, General Burns notified the population of Gaza that UNEF, acting in fulfilment of its functions as determined by the

General Assembly and with the consent of the Government of Egypt, was being deployed in the area for the purpose of maintaining quiet during and after the withdrawal of the Israeli forces. He also announced that until further arrangements were made, UNEF had assumed responsibility for civil affairs in the area and that UNRWA would continue to provide food and other services as in the past.

The involvement of UNEF in civil administration was of a purely temporary nature, pending the re-establishment of local civilian authority. In this connection, UNEF co-operated closely with UNRWA in meeting the needs of the local population. The operation of the Force during this initial period was greatly facilitated by the presence in Gaza of an important branch of UNRWA and by the fact that the Egypt-Israel Mixed Armistice Commission had its headquarters in Gaza and made available to the Force its personnel and its communications facilities.

Final phase: deployment along the borders (March 1957–May 1967)

After the completion of the withdrawal of all foreign forces from Egyptian territory, the main objective of UNEF was to supervise the cessation of hostilities between Egypt and Israel. Its basic functions were to act as an informal buffer between the Egyptian and Israeli forces along the Armistice Demarcation Line (ADL) and the international frontier in order to avoid incidents, prevent illegal crossings of the Line by civilians of either side for whatever purposes, and to observe and report on all violations of the Line whether on land, sea or in the air.

To perform these functions, UNEF troops were deployed on the western side of the ADL and the international frontier, covering a distance of 273 kilometres. The Sinai coast from the northern end of the Gulf of Aqaba to the Strait of Tiran, a further distance of 187 kilometres, was kept under observation by UNEF air reconnaissance. As indicated earlier, a UNEF detachment was stationed at Sharm el Sheikh near the Strait of Tiran.

By day, the entire length of the ADL (about 59 kilometres) was kept under observation by some 72 intervisible observation posts. Each post was manned during daylight hours; by night, the sentries were withdrawn and replaced by patrols of five to seven men each. The patrols moved on foot, covering the length of the ADL on an average of three rounds each night and giving particular attention to roads likely to be used by infiltrators. Platoon camps were set up to the rear of the posts, each holding a reserve detachment available to go to the aid of an observation post or patrol should the need arise. Telephone communications by day and a system of flare signals, supplemented by wireless, at night ensured a speedy response to calls for help.

Along the international frontier, rough terrain and scattered minefields restricted the access roads for potential infiltrators, who tended to confine their activities to certain areas. These sensitive areas were covered by a system of patrols. Eight outposts were established along the frontier. Motor patrols from these outposts covered the areas between the outposts and certain tracks. In addition to ground observers, the entire length of the international frontier was also patrolled by air reconnaissance planes on a daily basis, later reduced to three times a week. Any suspicious activity seen from the air could be checked by ground patrols dispatched from the outposts.

To prevent infiltration and incidents, UNEF secured the co-operation of the Egyptian authorities. The inhabitants of Gaza were officially informed that the Government of Egypt, as a matter of policy, was opposed to infiltration across the Armistice Demarcation Line. They were notified that they were forbidden to approach the ADL within 50 to 100 metres by day and 500 metres by night. The police in Gaza were instructed to take effective measures to find persons responsible for laying mines and for other incidents and to prevent recurrences. The local Palestinian police also co-operated with UNEF in preventing infiltrations. UNEF was authorized to apprehend infiltrators and persons approaching the ADL in suspicious circumstances. In practice, this applied to a zone extending up to 500 metres from the line. The persons so apprehended were interrogated by UNEF and then were handed over to the local police.

In the performance of their duties, UNEF soldiers were not authorized to use force except in self-defence. They were never to take the initiative in the use of force, but could respond with fire to an armed attack upon them, even though this might result from a refusal on their part to obey an order from the attacking party not to resist. UNEF maintained close liaison with the two parties, particularly with the Egyptian authorities as representatives of the host Government.

UNEF enjoyed full freedom of movement in the Gaza Strip and between the Sinai posts, UNEF headquarters and the units deployed along the Armistice Demarcation Line. This included freedom of flight over the Sinai peninsula and the Gaza Strip for UNEF aircraft, as well as the manning of the Gaza airport by UNEF.

The deployment of UNEF along the ADL raised a question of the respective responsibilities of the Force and UNTSO. As indicated earlier, Israel denounced the General Armistice Agreement with Egypt in early November 1956, but the United Nations did not accept this unilateral action. Therefore, the Chairman of the Egypt-Israel Mixed Armistice Commission and the UNTSO military observers had remained at their posts throughout the Israeli occupation of the Gaza Strip and afterwards. Upon the withdrawal of the Israeli forces, the Secretary-General, as a practical arrangement and without any change in the legal status of the Mixed Armistice Commission, placed the UNTSO personnel assigned to EIMAC under the operational control of the Commander of UNEF. In view of its position with respect to the General Armistice Agreement, the Government of Israel lodged its complaints of violations of the ADL only with UNEF, but the Force maintained that official investigations of incidents should be carried out through the Armistice Commission. In practice, problems arising between Israel and the United Nations relating to matters covered by the General Armistice Agreement were resolved in a practical way, with UNEF taking over some of the duties previously performed by UNTSO.

The activities carried out by UNEF following its deployment along the Armistice Demarcation Line and the international frontier, and the methods followed in this connection, remained virtually unchanged until the withdrawal of the Force in May 1967. Its area of operations, which had been one of the most disturbed areas in the Middle East, became remarkably quiet. Incidents, such as crossings of the ADL/international frontier, firing across the Line and air violations, naturally continued to occur, but they were relatively infrequent and generally of a minor nature. Virtually uninterrupted peace prevailed in the area, thanks to the presence and activities of UNEF.

UNEF withdrawal, 1967

While quiet prevailed along the Egyptian-Israeli borders after November 1956, there was continued tension in other sectors of the Middle East, particularly on the Israel-Jordan and Israel-Syria fronts. After the creation, in 1964, of the Palestine Liberation Organization and its main group, El Fatah, there appeared to be a new level of organization and training of Palestinian commandos. Palestinian raids against Israel, conducted mainly from Jordanian and Syrian territory, became a regular occurrence, and the Israeli forces reacted with increasingly violent retaliation. There was a marked contrast between the quiet along the Egyptian border and the confrontation situation in other sectors.

In early 1967, tension between Israel and Syria again reached a critical level, mainly because of disputes over cultivation rights in the demilitarized zone near Lake Tiberias. For years, Syria complained that Israelis were illegally seizing lands belonging to Arab Palestinians in the demilitarized zone, and the cultivation of disputed land had led to frequent firing incidents between Israeli and Syrian forces. Efforts within the Mixed Armistice Commission failed. On 7 April 1967, an exchange of fire across disputed farmland led to heavy shelling of Israeli villages by Syrian artillery and intensive air attacks by Israel against Syrian targets—the most serious clash since 1956. The incidents of 7 April were followed by a heightening of tension in the entire region, despite appeals by Secretary-General U Thant for restraint, and the moderating efforts of UNTSO.

In the evening of 16 May, the UNEF Commander received a request from the Egyptian Commander-in-Chief of the armed forces for withdrawal of "all UN troops which installed OP's (observation posts) along our borders".* The General who handed the message to the Force Commander told him that UNEF must order immediate withdrawal from El Sabha and Sharm el Sheikh, commanding the Strait of Tiran and therefore access to the Red Sea and southern Israel. The UNEF Commander replied that he did not have authority to do that. The Secretary-General, on being informed, gave instructions to the Commander to "be firm in maintaining UNEF positions while being as understanding and as diplomatic as possible in your relations with local UAR (United Arab Republic) officials". While the Secretary-General sought clarifications from Cairo, Egyptian troops moved onto UNEF's line, occupying some United Nations posts.

The Secretary-General met with members of the UNEF Advisory Committee and told them of the events in the field, making it known that if a formal request for UNEF's withdrawal came from the Egyptian Government he would have to comply. He pointed out that the Force was on Egyptian territory only with the consent of the Government and could not remain there without it. He also consulted members of the Security Council. The various meetings held by the Secretary-General showed that within the United Nations there was a deep division among the membership of the Advisory Committee and the Security Council on the course of action to be followed. After consulting the Advisory Committee, the Secretary-General informed the representative of Egypt that while he did not question in any sense Egypt's authority to deploy its troops as it saw fit on its own territory,

* A/6669 and A/6730.

the deployment of Egyptian troops in areas where UNEF troops were stationed might have very serious implications for UNEF and its continued presence in the area.

In the mean time, the Egyptian Foreign Minister in Cairo summoned representatives of nations with troops in UNEF to inform them that UNEF had terminated its tasks in Egypt and the Gaza Strip and must depart forthwith. The Governments of India and Yugoslavia decided that, whatever the decision of the Secretary-General, they would withdraw their contingents from UNEF. The same day, 18 May, Egyptian soldiers prevented UNEF troops from entering their posts.

While these activities were taking place, the Secretary-General raised with the Israeli Government the question of stationing UNEF on the Israeli side of the Line, thus maintaining the buffer, but this was declared entirely unacceptable to Israel. Shortly thereafter, the Permanent Representative of Egypt delivered a message to the Secretary-General stating his Government's decision to terminate UNEF's presence in the territory of Egypt and the Gaza Strip and requesting steps for withdrawal as soon as possible. The Secretary-General informed contributing countries he would report to the General Assembly and the Security Council about the events, stating it was up to Member countries to decide whether the competent organs should or could take up the matter and pursue it accordingly. He then informed Egypt that the request would be complied with, while indicating his serious misgivings. UNEF's Commander was instructed to take the necessary action for withdrawal to begin on 19 May and end in the last days of June.

During two tense days from 16 to 18 May 1967, the Secretary-General did all he could to persuade Egypt not to request the withdrawal of UNEF and to persuade Israel to accept the Force on its side of the border. But neither Government agreed to co-operate. In such circumstances, U Thant could have brought the matter before the Security Council by invoking Article 99 of the Charter, but he chose not to do so because he knew that with the United States and the Soviet Union firmly on opposing sides of the question, no action could be taken by the Council.

The fundamental fact is that United Nations peace-keeping operations are based on the principle of consent. To maintain UNEF in Egypt against the will of the Egyptian Government, even if it had been possible to do so, which was not the case, would have created a dangerous precedent which would have deterred potential host Governments from accepting future United Nations peace-keeping operations on their soil.

In the case of UNEF, its withdrawal would not have, in itself, necessarily led to war in the area. Following an appeal by the Secretary-General, the Government of Israel made it known to U Thant that it would exercise restraint but would consider a resumption of terrorist activities along the borders, or the closure of the Strait of Tiran to Israeli shipping, as *casus belli*. Immediately after the withdrawal of UNEF, U Thant increased the number of UNTSO observers of the Egypt-Israel Mixed Armistice Commission to provide a United Nations presence along the Armistice Demarcation Line, and he arranged to visit Cairo on 22 May to discuss with the Egyptian Government possible security arrangements along the Egyptian-Israeli borders. However, just before he arrived in Cairo, President Nasser announced the closure of the Strait of Tiran. With this decision the die was cast, and, on 5 June, full-fledged war erupted.

Some UNEF units which were awaiting repatriation were caught up in the fighting in Gaza, and 15 United Nations troops were killed. All military personnel had gone by 13 June, except for the Force Commander and a small group of staff officers who left on 17 June.

UNEF is a telling example of the importance of United Nations peace-keeping forces and their limitations. Its establishment in October 1956 put an end to a destructive war and, for more than 10 years, it effectively maintained peace in one of the most sensitive areas of the Middle East. But in the absence of a complementary peace-making effort, the root cause of the conflict between Egypt and Israel remained unresolved. Moreover, because Israel refused to accept UNEF on its territory, the Force had to be deployed only on the Egyptian side of the border, and thus its functioning was entirely contingent upon the consent of Egypt as the host country. Once that consent was withdrawn, its operation could no longer be maintained.

Chapter IV **Second United Nations Emergency Force**

A. **Background**

The situation in the Suez Canal sector and on the Golan Heights from June 1967 until October 1973 is described in the chapter on UNTSO, which had set up cease-fire observation operations in those areas *(see chapter II above).*

On 6 October 1973, in a surprise move, Egyptian forces crossed the Canal and soon advanced beyond the UNTSO observation posts on its eastern bank, while, in a co-ordinated move, Syrian troops simultaneously attacked the Israeli positions on the Golan Heights. By 9 October, following a request by Egypt acceded to by the Security Council, United Nations observation posts on both sides of the Canal were closed and the observers withdrawn.

The Security Council met from 8 to 12 October to consider the conflict and the overall situation, but, because of the opposing positions of the major Powers, could not reach a decision. Meanwhile war raged on. By 21 October, the situation had become critical; an Israeli armoured column had crossed the Canal where it was engaging Egyptian forces, and the Egyptian Third Army on the east bank was about to be cut off. The Soviet Union and the United States jointly requested an urgent meeting of the Security Council. On 22 October, the Council, on a proposal submitted jointly by the two major Powers, adopted resolution 338(1973) which called for a cease-fire and a start to implementing resolution 242(1967). The cease-fire call was confirmed in a further resolution [339(1973)] on 23 October, and the Secretary-General was requested to dispatch United Nations observers immediately.

Fighting continued, however, and President Anwar Sadat of Egypt issued direct appeals to the Soviet Union and the United States, requesting them to send American and Soviet troops to the area to enforce the cease-fire. The United States Government was opposed to the request, but the USSR agreed. The two major Powers, in disagreement after their joint cease-fire initiative, were suddenly on a collision course, each threatening military action. It was probably the most dangerous situation confronting the world since the Cuban missile crisis of October 1962.

At the request of Egypt, the Security Council was convened again on 24 October. The non-aligned members of the Council, in close co-operation with the Secretary-General, worked out a resolution calling for an increase in UNTSO observers in the area and the establishment of a new United Nations peace-keeping force, which became the second United Nations Emergency Force (UNEF II). The establishment and dispatch of the new peace-keeping operation effectively brought the crisis to an end.

Establishment

On 25 October 1973, on a proposal by Guinea, India, Indonesia, Kenya, Panama, Peru, the Sudan and Yugoslavia, the Security Council adopted resolution 340(1973), by which it demanded that an immediate and complete cease-fire be observed and that the parties return to the positions occupied by them at 1650 hours GMT on 22 October 1973. The Council also requested the Secretary-General, as an immediate step, to increase the number of United Nations military observers on both sides, and decided to set up immediately under its authority a United Nations Emergency Force to be composed of personnel drawn from United Nations Member States except the permanent members of the Security Council. It requested the Secretary-General to report within 24 hours on the steps taken to that effect.

Immediately after the adoption of the resolution, the Secretary-General addressed a letter to the President of the Security Council,* indicating that he would deliver the requested report within the time-limit set by the Council. In the mean time, as an urgent measure and in order that the Emergency Force might reach the area of conflict as soon as possible, he proposed to arrange for units of the Austrian, Finnish and Swedish contingents serving with the United Nations Peace-keeping Force in Cyprus (UNFICYP) to proceed immediately to Egypt. He also proposed to appoint Major-General (later Lieutenant-General) Ensio P. H. Siilasvuo, of Finland, the Chief of Staff of UNTSO, as interim Commander of the new Force and to ask him to set up a provisional headquarters in Cairo with personnel from UNTSO.

The Secretary-General requested the Council President to let him know urgently whether the proposal was acceptable to the members of the Council, adding that the proposed steps would be without prejudice to the more detailed and comprehensive report on the Emergency Force which he would submit to the Council on the next day. The President, after informally consulting the members of the Council, conveyed the Council's agreement to the Secretary-

* S/11049.

General on the same evening. This procedure would henceforth be used frequently by the Secretary-General to get the Security Council's consent when measures needed to be taken.

Guidelines for UNEF II

The Secretary-General's report requested by the Council set forth proposals regarding the guidelines for the functioning of the Force as well as a plan of action for the initial stages of the operation.*

The proposed principles and guidelines for the Emergency Force were as follows:

(a)   Three essential conditions must be met for the Force to be effective. First, it must have at all times the full confidence and backing of the Security Council. Secondly, it must operate with the full co-operation of the parties concerned. Thirdly, it must be able to function as an integrated and efficient military unit.

(b)   The Force would be under the command of the United Nations, vested in the Secretary-General, under the authority of the Security Council. The command in the field would be exercised by a Force Commander appointed by the Secretary-General with the Council's consent. The Commander would be responsible to the Secretary-General. The Secretary-General would keep the Security Council fully informed of developments relating to the functioning of the Force. All matters which could affect the nature or the continued effective functioning of the Force would be referred to the Council for its decision.

(c)   The Force must enjoy the freedom of movement and communication and other facilities necessary for the performance of its tasks. The Force and its personnel should be granted all relevant privileges and immunities provided for by the Convention on the Privileges and Immunities of the United Nations. The Force should operate at all times separately from the armed forces of the parties concerned. Consequently, separate quarters and, wherever desirable and feasible, buffer zones would have to be arranged with the co-operation of the parties. Appropriate agreements on the status of the Force would also have to be concluded with the parties.

(d)   The Force would be composed of a number of contingents to be provided by selected countries, upon the request of the Secretary-General. The contingents would be selected in consultation with the Security Council and with the parties concerned, bear-

* S/11052/Rev.1.

ing in mind the accepted principle of equitable geographical representation.

(e)   The Force would be provided with weapons of a defensive character only. It would not use force except in self-defence. Self-defence would include resistance to attempts by forceful means to prevent it from discharging its duties under the Security Council's mandate. The Force would proceed on the assumption that the parties to the conflict would take all the necessary steps for compliance with the Council's decisions.

(f)   In performing its functions, the Force would act with complete impartiality and would avoid actions which could prejudice the rights, claims or positions of the parties concerned.

(g)   The costs of the Force would be considered as expenses of the Organization to be borne by the Members, as apportioned by the General Assembly.

In the same report, the Secretary-General set forth certain urgent steps to be taken. In order that UNEF II might fulfil the responsibilities entrusted to it, it was considered necessary that the Force should have a total strength in the order of 7,000. The Force would initially be stationed in the area for a period of six months, subject to extension.

The Secretary-General engaged in the necessary consultations with a number of Governments, in addition to Austria, Finland and Sweden, regarding provision of contingents of suitable size for the Force at the earliest possible time. In addition to his requests to countries to provide contingents for the Force, the Secretary-General proposed to seek logistic support as necessary from a number of other countries, which might include the permanent members of the Security Council.

Finally, the Secretary-General stated that, while there were many unknown factors, the best possible preliminary estimate of cost, based upon past experience and practice, was approximately $30 million for the Force for a six-month period.

This report was approved by the Security Council on 27 October (resolution 341(1973)). In accordance with the Secretary-General's recommendations, the Council set up the new Force—for an initial period of six months, subject to extension.

Composition and strength of the Force

UNEF II had already begun its operations on the basis of interim arrangements approved by the Security Council. On the morning of

26 October, General Siilasvuo and his group of UNTSO military observers set up temporary headquarters in Cairo using UNTSO's liaison office. During the same afternoon, advance elements of Austrian, Finnish and Swedish troops arrived from Cyprus and were immediately deployed along the front line. They were joined a few days later by an Irish company. The four contingents were quickly reinforced, and their presence and activities effectively defused a highly explosive situation.

Having taken these emergency measures, the Secretary-General had now to secure other contingents and build up the Force to its authorized level of 7,000 all ranks. In accordance with the guidelines approved by the Security Council, the Force was to be composed of contingents from countries selected by the Secretary-General, in consultation with the parties and the Security Council, bearing in mind the principle of equitable geographical representation.

The question of the composition of the Force gave rise to some difficulties during the consultations with the Security Council. In view of the need to set up a working force without delay, the Secretary-General wanted to secure contingents from countries that could provide the required troops at short notice. In particular, he had planned to ask Canada to supply the logistics component, since it was, aside from the major Powers, one of the few countries which could readily do so. But the Soviet Union insisted that a Warsaw Pact country should be included in the new Force if a North Atlantic Treaty Organization member was. After a lengthy debate held in closed session, the Security Council decided that the Secretary-General should consult with Ghana (African regional group), Indonesia and Nepal (Asian regional group), Panama and Peru (Latin American regional group), Poland (Eastern European regional group) and Canada (Western European and other States group)—the two last-mentioned having particular responsibility for logistic support.

In accordance with this decision, the Secretary-General held urgent consultations with the various Governments concerned with a view to obtaining the required personnel and equipment and working out acceptable administrative and financial arrangements. As a result of these contacts, in addition to Austria, Finland, Ireland and Sweden, whose troops had already arrived, Canada, Ghana, Indonesia, Nepal, Panama, Peru, Poland and Senegal were asked to provide contingents.

The Secretary-General had planned to set a ceiling of 600 for each contingent. However, in view of the complexity of the logistical problems and the decision of the Security Council to divide responsibilities in this regard between Canada and Poland, whose respective military establishments were differently organized and had different equipment and weapons, the strength of the logistical support elements had to be considerably increased.

The strength of the Canadian and Polish logistics components and the division of responsibilities between them were the subject of lengthy negotiations between the military representatives of those two countries and experts from the Secretariat. After more than two weeks of such discussions, an understanding was reached.* The logistics support system was to be composed of a Polish road transport unit including a maintenance element, and a Canadian service unit consisting of a supply company, a maintenance company, a movement control unit and a postal detachment. In addition, Canada would provide an aviation unit and Poland a medical unit subject to the availability of a suitable building. The Canadian contingent would have a total strength of about 1,000 and the Polish contingent about 800.

While these negotiations were going on, General Siilasvuo was pressing for the early arrival of the logistics units. He indicated that because of the difficulty of getting local supplies, it was important that the logistics facilities be set up before the arrival of additional contingents. In the light of this recommendation, it was decided that the Austrian, Finnish, Irish and Swedish units which had arrived in the area at the beginning of the operation should be brought up to battalion strength as soon as possible, and operate with vehicles, stores and equipment borrowed from UNFICYP and from UNTSO.

By mid-November, advance parties of the Canadian and Polish contingents had arrived in the area and they were soon followed by the main bodies of those contingents. By the end of November, the logistics components were well established and the other contingents of UNEF II began to arrive in the area at a steady rate. By 20 February 1974, the strength of UNEF II had reached the authorized level of 7,000 (actually, 6,973). It included contingents from 12 countries: Austria (604), Canada (1,097), Finland (637), Ghana (499), Indonesia (550), Ireland (271), Nepal (571), Panama (406), Peru (497), Poland (822), Senegal (399), Sweden (620).

From February until May 1974, the strength of UNEF II was slightly decreased (to 6,645), mainly because of some reduction of the Finnish, Peruvian and Swedish contingents. In May, the Irish contingent was withdrawn at the request of its Government. Following the adoption of Security Council resolution 350(1974) of 31 May 1974 on the establishment of the United Nations Disengagement Observer Force (UNDOF), and the approval by the Council of interim arrange-

* S/11056/Add.6, annex.

ments proposed by the Secretary-General to give effect to that resolution, the Austrian and Peruvian contingents and elements of the Canadian and Polish logistics contingents (approximately 1,050 troops in all) were transferred from UNEF II to UNDOF in Syria. As a result, the total strength of UNEF II decreased to 5,079 in June 1974. It was brought up to 5,527 at the end of July with the arrival of additional Canadian and Polish personnel.

The Nepalese contingent was withdrawn beginning in August 1974 and the Panamanian contingent in November 1974. The total strength of UNEF II, with contingents from seven countries, was progressively reduced to 3,987 by October 1975.

On 17 October 1975,* the Secretary-General reported to the Security Council that, owing to the more extensive responsibilities entrusted to UNEF II under an Agreement between Egypt and Israel signed at Geneva on 4 September 1975 and the large increase in the areas of operation, additional military personnel would be needed to enable the Force to execute its new functions adequately. He proposed accordingly to reinforce each non-logistic contingent by one company (an increase of some 750 all ranks) and the Polish and Canadian logistics contingents by 50 and 36 men, respectively. He also proposed to reinforce the air unit by additional aircraft and helicopters. In accordance with the Secretary-General's request, Finland, Ghana, Indonesia and Sweden each agreed to supply an additional rifle company while Canada and Poland provided additional personnel for logistic support. After consulting the Security Council in May 1976,† the Secretary-General accepted the offer of the Government of Australia to supply four helicopters with their crews and support personnel (45 men) to UNEF II.

The Senegalese contingent was withdrawn in May and June 1976. In a report of 18 October 1976, ‡ the Secretary-General noted that in view of the satisfactory results in operational arrangements in the current circumstances, and in the interest of economy, there was for the time being no intention to provide for the replacement of the Senegalese contingent unless a change in the situation should make it necessary. Upon the withdrawal of the Senegalese contingent, the total strength of UNEF II was reduced to 4,174. It remained more or less at that level during the next three years. At the time of its withdrawal in July 1979, UNEF II had 4,031 personnel, and its various contingents were: Australia (46), Canada (844), Finland (522), Ghana (595), Indonesia (510), Poland (923), Sweden (591). Of this total, 99 all ranks were assigned to UNEF II headquarters. The international civilian supporting staff of that headquarters numbered 160. In addi-

* S/11849.   † S/12089.   ‡ S/12212.

tion to the above, UNEF II was assisted by 120 military observers from UNTSO.

Mandate renewals

The mandate of UNEF II which was originally approved for six months, until 24 April 1974, was subsequently renewed eight times. Each time, as the date of expiry of the mandate approached, the Secretary-General submitted a report to the Security Council on the activities of the Force during the period of the mandate. In each of those reports, the Secretary-General expressed the view that the continued presence of UNEF II in the area was essential, and he recommended, after consultations with the parties, that its mandate be extended for a further period. In each case, the Council took note of the Secretary-General's report and decided to extend the mandate of the Force accordingly. Thus the mandate of UNEF II was extended for six months in April 1974 (resolution 346(1974)), for another six months in October (resolution 362(1974)), for three months in April 1975 (resolution 368(1975)), another three months in July (resolution 371(1975)), and for one year in October 1975 (resolution 378(1975)), in October 1976 (resolution 396(1976)) and again in October 1977 (resolution 416(1977)). In October 1978, the mandate of UNEF II was extended a last time for nine months, until 24 July 1979 (resolution 438(1978)).

The discussions and decisions of the Security Council on the extension of the mandate naturally reflected the situation on the ground and the status of the negotiations undertaken for the disengagement of the forces in the area. Following the conclusion of the first disengagement agreement, in January 1974, both sides readily agreed to have the mandate extended for a further period of six months beyond 24 April 1974. But in April and July 1975, when negotiations aimed at the second disengagement of forces were deadlocked, Egypt declined to extend the mandate of the Force for more than three months and, in fact, consented to the extension in July 1975 only after a special appeal by the Security Council. In contrast, when the September 1975 disengagement agreement was finally concluded, both parties wanted the period of extension to be expanded to one year, and the Security Council so agreed. In October 1978, the Soviet Union, which was opposed to the Camp David accords concluded earlier that year, opposed a further extension for one year, and the Security Council finally settled for an extension period of nine months. In July 1979, after the signing of the peace treaty between Egypt and Israel, which had entered into force on 25 April 1979, the Council was unable to extend the mandate of UNEF II and decided to let it lapse.

In this connection, in his report to the Security Council of 19 July 1979,* the Secretary-General noted that the original context in which UNEF II had been created and in which it had previously functioned had basically changed during the past nine months. While the Governments of Egypt and Israel had both expressed themselves in favour of an extension of the mandate of UNEF II , the Soviet Union had expressed opposition to such a course. In this regard, the Secretary-General recalled that, according to the guidelines approved by the Security Council in October 1973, all matters which might affect the nature or the continued effective functioning of the Force would be referred to the Council for its decision. The Secretary-General added that whatever decisions the Council might reach, he would be ready to make the necessary arrangements.

The Security Council did not extend the mandate of UNEF II, which lapsed on 24 July 1979.

UNEF command

General Siilasvuo, who had commanded UNEF II on an interim basis during its initial period, was appointed UNEF Commander on 12 November 1973 by the Secretary-General, with the consent of the Security Council. In August 1975, he was assigned to the new post of Chief Co-ordinator of the United Nations Peace-keeping Missions in the Middle East and was replaced as UNEF Commander by Major-General (later Lieutenant-General) Bengt Liljestrand of Sweden, who held the post until 1 December 1976. Major-General Rais Abin of Indonesia, who became Acting Force Commander on that date, was appointed UNEF Commander on 1 January 1977 and held the post until the withdrawal of the Force in 1979.

Status of the Force

In accordance with established practice, the United Nations sought to work out an agreement on the status of the Force with Egypt as the host country and also with Israel as the other party concerned. The Office of Legal Affairs of the Secretariat engaged in negotiations to this end with both countries' Permanent Missions to the United Nations.

* S/13460.

While no special agreement* could be drawn up, it was agreed that as a practical arrangement the parties would be guided by the provision of the status of the Force agreement for UNEF I as well as by the Convention on the Privileges and Immunities of the United Nations.

With this understanding, the Force functioned smoothly and effectively. There were, of course, a number of organizational, operational and administrative problems. One of the main difficulties concerned the question of freedom of movement. The Israeli Government had opposed the inclusion in UNEF II of contingents from Ghana, Indonesia, Poland and Senegal on the grounds that these countries had no diplomatic relations with Israel, and it refused to extend to the personnel of their contingents freedom of movement in the areas it controlled.

The Secretary-General strongly protested against these restrictions for practical reasons and as a matter of principle. He took the position that UNEF II must function as an integrated and efficient military unit and that no differentiation should be made regarding the United Nations status of the various contingents. But despite his efforts and those of the Force Commander, the Israeli authorities maintained the restrictions, and the contingents affected had to be deployed within the United Nations buffer zones or in the Egyptian-controlled areas. The restrictions on the freedom of movement were also applied to Soviet observers attached to UNEF II.

B. **Activities of the Force**

The terms of reference of UNEF II were to supervise the implementation of Security Council resolution 340(1973), which demanded that an immediate and complete cease-fire be observed and that the parties return to the positions they had occupied at 1650 hours GMT on 22 October 1973. The Force would use its best efforts to prevent a recurrence of the fighting, and in the fulfilment of its tasks it would have the co-operation of the military observers of UNTSO. UNEF II was also to co-operate with the International Committee of the Red Cross in its humanitarian endeavours in the area.

These terms of reference,* which were approved by the Security Council on 27 October, remained unchanged during UNEF's entire mandate, but within this general framework the activities of the Force varied considerably over the years in the light of prevail-

* S/11052/Rev.1.

ing circumstances and of the agreements reached between the parties.

In the light of changing developments, the activities of UNEF II may be divided into four main phases.

First phase: October 1973–January 1974

Following the establishment of UNEF II, its immediate objective was to stop the fighting and prevent all movement forward of the troops on both sides. Urgent measures also had to be taken to provide Suez city and the Egyptian Third Army trapped on the east bank of the Canal with non-military supplies.

Troops from Austria, Finland, Sweden and, later, Ireland were dispatched to the front line as soon as they arrived. They interposed themselves whenever possible between the forward positions of the opposing forces. Observation posts and check-points were set up and patrols undertaken, with the assistance of UNTSO observers, in sensitive areas. These activities were carried out in close liaison with the parties concerned. With these measures, the situation was stabilized, the cease-fire was generally observed, and there were only a few incidents, which were resolved with the assistance of UNEF II.

A meeting between high-level military representatives of Egypt and Israel took place in the presence of UNEF representatives on 27 October 1973 at kilometre-marker 109 on the Cairo–Suez road to discuss the observance of the cease-fire demanded by the Security Council, as well as various humanitarian questions. At this meeting, preliminary arrangements were also agreed upon for the dispatch of non-military supplies to the town of Suez and the Egyptian Third Army. In accordance with these arrangements, convoys of lorries driven by UNEF II personnel were organized under the supervision of the Force and the International Committee of the Red Cross (ICRC) to bring supplies of a non-military nature through Israeli-held territory to Suez, and then to the Egyptian Third Army across the Canal.

These priority tasks having been met, UNEF II turned to the Security Council's demand for the return of the forces of both parties to the positions they had occupied on 22 October 1973. More meetings were held at kilometre-marker 109 to discuss this matter, together with possible mutual disengagement and the establishment of buffer zones to be manned by UNEF II.

In the mean time, the United States Secretary of State, Henry A. Kissinger, during visits to Egypt and Israel, succeeded in working out a preliminary agreement between the two countries for the implementation of Council resolutions 338(1973) and 339(1973). He transmitted it on 9 November* to Secretary-General Kurt Waldheim, who immediately instructed General Siilasvuo to take the necessary measures and to make available his good offices, as appropriate, for carrying out the terms of that agreement. On 11 November, at kilometre-marker 101 on the Cairo–Suez road, the new site for meetings, the agreement was signed by Major-General Mohamed El-Gamasy for Egypt and by Major-General Aharon Yaariv for Israel. It was also signed by General Siilasvuo on behalf of the United Nations.

The agreement, which was to enter into force immediately, contained the following six points:

1 Egypt and Israel agreed to observe scrupulously the cease-fire called for by the Security Council;
2 both sides agreed that discussions between them would begin immediately to settle the question of the return to the 22 October positions;
3 the town of Suez would receive daily supplies of food, water and medicine and all wounded civilians in the town would be evacuated;
4 there would be no impediment to the movement of non-military supplies to the east bank;
5 the Israeli check-points on the Cairo–Suez road would be replaced by United Nations check-points; and
6 as soon as the United Nations check-points were established on that road, there would be an exchange of all prisoners of war, including wounded.

Immediately after the signing of this agreement, the parties started discussions under the auspices of General Siilasvuo on the modalities of its implementation. These discussions continued sporadically until January 1974. Except for the provision on the return to the 22 October positions, the agreement was implemented without much difficulty.

On the morning of 15 November, the Israeli personnel at the check-points on the Cairo–Suez road were replaced by UNEF II personnel. Convoys of non-military supplies plied smoothly to and from Suez. As these convoys had to be driven by UNEF II personnel, some 100 military drivers were supplied by the Governments of Austria, Finland and Sweden at very short notice at the request of the Secretary-General. The exchange of prisoners of war took place in

* S/11091 and S/11056/Add.3, annex.

mid-November with aircraft made available without cost by the Swiss Government to the International Committee of the Red Cross.

But the most important clause, which concerned the return to the 22 October positions and the separation of the opposing forces under United Nations auspices, remained unresolved despite General Siilasvuo's efforts. On 29 November, Egypt broke off the negotiations, a decision which inevitably created a heightening of tension in the area. However, thanks to the presence of UNEF II, the cease-fire continued to hold.

Until mid-November, the operations were carried out by the Austrian, Finnish, Irish and Swedish battalions. After that date, the Canadian and Polish logistics components started to arrive. These were followed by other contingents. By mid-January 1974, 10 contingents were at hand. These contingents were deployed as follows:*

- The Swedish battalion had established its headquarters in Ismailia and was deployed in the northern sector, both east and west of the Suez Canal, north of the town. The battalion provided the Force Reserve and drivers for the UNEF II convoys carrying non-military supplies to the Egyptian troops on the east bank of the Canal.

- The Austrian battalion had its headquarters in Ismailia and was deployed south of that town, west of the Canal. The battalion also provided drivers for the UNEF II convoys.

- The Finnish battalion had its headquarters in Suez city, and was deployed south of the Cairo–Suez road, including the Suez city and Adabiya areas. The battalion supervised the UNEF II convoys, as well as the supply convoys for Suez city.

- The Irish battalion, with headquarters in Rabah, was deployed in the northern sector east of the Suez Canal in the Qantara area.

- The Peruvian battalion, with headquarters in Rabah, was carrying out reconnaissance of its future positions, which would be located in the central sector east of the Suez Canal, south of the Irish battalion's area of responsibility.

- The Panamanian battalion, also with headquarters in Rabah, was carrying out reconnaissance of its future positions, which would be located in the southern sector east of the Suez Canal, south of the Peruvian battalion's area of responsibility.

- The Indonesian battalion was to be deployed west of the Canal with base camp at Ismailia.

* S/11056/Add.7.

- The Senegalese battalion had not yet arrived except for an advance party which was carrying out reconnaissance for future operational assignment.
- The Canadian logistic support unit, with base camp in Cairo, provided supply, maintenance, communications and postal services throughout the mission area.
- The Polish logistic support unit, with base camp in Cairo, provided drivers for UNEF II transport and was carrying out reconnaissance in preparation for the establishment of the UNEF II field hospital.

The headquarters of UNEF II, with an international staff on which the various contributing countries were represented, remained in Cairo.

Second phase: January 1974–October 1975

While the negotiations at kilometre-marker 101 for the return to the 22 October positions were dragging on, the United States and the Soviet Union initiated a joint effort to promote the implementation of Security Council resolution 338(1973), which called for negotiations to start between the parties concerned under appropriate auspices aimed at establishing a just and durable peace in the Middle East. This effort resulted in the convening of the Peace Conference on the Middle East at Geneva on 21 December 1973 under the auspices of the United Nations and the co-chairmanship of the two Powers. The Secretary-General was asked to serve as the convener of the Conference and to preside at the opening phase which would be held at the Foreign Minister level. The Governments of Egypt, Israel and Jordan accepted to attend, but Syria refused and the Palestine Liberation Organization (PLO) was not invited.

The Conference, which discussed the disengagement of forces in the Egypt-Israel sector, as well as a comprehensive settlement of the Middle East problem, was inconclusive and adjourned on 22 December 1973 after three meetings. Before adjourning, it decided to continue to work through the setting up of a Military Working Group, which would start discussing forthwith the question of disengagement of forces. The Working Group was composed of the military representatives of Egypt and Israel and the Commander of UNEF II as Chairman.

During the first half of January 1974, the United States Secretary of State undertook a new mediation effort. In negotiating separately with the Governments of Egypt and Israel, in what was known as his "shuttle diplomacy", he worked out an agreement on the disengagement and separation of their military forces. This agreement was signed on 18 January 1974 by the military representatives of Egypt and Israel, and by General Siilasvuo as witness, within the framework of the Military Working Group of the Geneva Peace Conference at a meeting held at kilometre-marker 101 on the Cairo–Suez road. The agreement provided for the deployment of Egyptian forces on the eastern side of the Canal, west of a line designated on the map annexed to the agreement (the line ran parallel to the Canal, about 10 kilometres east of it), the deployment of Israeli forces east of another line, the establishment of a zone of disengagement manned by UNEF II, and areas of limited forces and armament on both sides of that zone.

In subsequent meetings held at kilometre-marker 101 under the chairmanship of General Siilasvuo, the military representatives of Egypt and Israel worked out a detailed procedure for the implementation of the agreement.

In accordance with this procedure, the disengagement operation began on 25 January. The operation proceeded by phases. At each phase, Israeli forces withdrew from a designated area after handing it over to UNEF II, and UNEF II held that area for a few hours before turning it over to the Egyptian forces. During the entire disengagement process, UNEF II interposed between the forces of the two sides by establishing temporary buffer zones. UNEF II was also responsible for the survey and marking of the lines of disengagement, which was carried out by UNTSO military observers under UNEF II supervision, with the assistance of Egyptian and Israeli army surveyors for their respective sides. The whole operation was carried out smoothly according to plan and was completed by 4 March 1974.*

After the completion of the operation, most non-logistic contingents were deployed in or near the newly established zone of disengagement. By mid-March, UNEF II had a total strength of 6,814 all ranks. The various contingents were deployed as follows:†

- The Irish battalion had its base camp at Rabah. It manned eight outposts in the zone of disengagement from the Mediterranean Sea to a line immediately south of Qantara.
- The Peruvian battalion had its base camp at Rabah. It manned 10 outposts in the zone of disengagement, in a sector from the southern limit of the Irish battalion to a line directly east of Ismailia.

* S/11056/Add.13.   † S/11056/Add.14.

- The Swedish battalion had its base camp at Ismailia. It manned 14 outposts in the zone of disengagement, in a sector from the southern limit of the Peruvian battalion to a line east of Déversoir.
- The Indonesian battalion had its base camp at Ismailia. It manned 14 outposts in the zone of disengagement, in a sector from the southern limit of the Swedish battalion to a line east of Kabrit.
- The Senegalese battalion had its base camp at Suez city. It manned 12 outposts in the zone of disengagement, in a sector from the southern limit of the Indonesian battalion to a line east of a point 10 kilometres north of Suez.
- The Finnish battalion had its base camp at Suez city. It manned 15 outposts in the zone of disengagement, in a sector from the southern limit of the Senegalese battalion to the Gulf of Suez.

The headquarters of UNEF II was moved to Ismailia in August 1974.

As a result of this disengagement, the situation in the Egypt-Israel sector became much more stable. The main task of UNEF II was the manning and control of the zone of disengagement and, to do this, it established static check-points and observation posts and conducted mobile patrols. It also carried out, with the assistance of UNTSO observers, weekly and later bi-weekly inspections of the areas of limited forces and armament (30 kilometre zone), as well as inspections of other areas agreed by the parties. The Force Commander continued the practice of separate meetings with the military authorities of Egypt and Israel concerning the implementation of the Force's terms of reference and the inspections carried out by UNEF II, and he continued to lend his assistance and good offices in cases where one of the parties raised questions concerning the observance of the agreed limitations of forces and armament.

In addition, UNEF II continued to co-operate with the International Committee of the Red Cross on humanitarian matters. It played an important part in assisting in exchanges of prisoners of war and the transfer of civilians from one side to the other. UNEF II also undertook an operation, which was completed in July 1974, for the search for the remains of soldiers killed during the October 1973 war.

In view of the quiet that prevailed in the area, it was possible to reduce gradually the strength of UNEF II. The Irish Government decided to withdraw its troops in May 1974. In June, following the establishment of the United Nations Disengagement Observer Force on the Golan Heights, the Security Council decided, upon the recommendation of the Secretary-General, to transfer the Austrian and Peruvian contingents and elements of the Canadian and Polish logistics components to the new UNDOF. The Nepalese contingent, which had been made available to the United Nations for six months only, was repatriated in August and September 1974. Finally, the Panamanian contingent was withdrawn in November 1974. As a result of these and later developments, the total strength of UNEF II decreased to 5,079 in June 1974, 4,029 in April 1975 and 3,987 in October 1975.

Third phase: November 1975–May 1979

In September 1975, the United States Secretary of State, through further indirect negotiations, succeeded in obtaining the agreement of Egypt and Israel for a second disengagement of their forces in the Sinai. The new agreement* provided for the redeployment of Israeli forces east of lines designated in a map annexed to the agreement, the redeployment of the Egyptian forces westwards and the establishment of buffer zones controlled by UNEF II. It also provided that there would be no military forces in the southern areas of Ras Sudr and Abu Rudais. On both sides of the buffer zones, two areas of limited forces and armament were to be set up where the number of military personnel should be limited to 8,000 and the armament to 75 tanks and 72 artillery pieces, including heavy mortars.

Finally, the agreement set up a joint commission, under the aegis of the United Nations Chief Co-ordinator of the United Nations Peacekeeping Missions in the Middle East, to consider any problems arising from the agreement and to assist UNEF II in the execution of its mandate. Attached to the agreement was a United States plan to establish an early warning system in the area of the Giddi and Mitla Passes, consisting of three watch stations set up by the United States and of two surveillance stations, one operated by Egyptian personnel and the other by Israeli personnel.

The Secretary-General submitted reports to the Security Council on this matter in September 1975.† He advised the Council that the new agreement between Egypt and Israel had been initialled by the parties on 1 September and would be signed by them at Geneva on 4 September. Following the signing, the representatives of Egypt and Israel were, within five days, to begin preparation of a detailed protocol for the implementation of the basic agreement in the Military Working Group of the Geneva Peace Conference on the Middle East. In accordance with previous practice, the Secretary-General

---

* S/11818/Add.1.   † S/11818 and Add.1-4.

instructed General Siilasvuo, the Chief Co-ordinator, who had presided at the previous meetings of the Military Working Group, to proceed to Geneva so as to be available in the same capacity for the forthcoming meetings of the Working Group.

The Working Group, meeting under the chairmanship of General Siilasvuo, reached agreement on the protocol of the agreement, which was signed on 22 September by the representatives of the two parties and by General Siilasvuo as witness. The protocol set out a detailed procedure for the implementation of the agreement.

The responsibilities entrusted to UNEF II under the agreement of 4 September and its protocol were much more extensive than those it had had previously, and its area of operations was much larger. The Force's first task was to mark on the ground the new lines of disengagement. To carry out this work, a group of surveyors was supplied by Sweden, at the request of the Secretary-General. Work began in October 1975 and was completed in January 1976, in accordance with the timetable set out in the protocol.

In November 1975, UNEF II began its assistance to the parties for the redeployment of their forces. The first phase of the redeployment took place in the southern area and was completed on 1 December 1975. During that period, UNEF II, through the Chief Coordinator, supervised the transfer of the oilfields and installations in the area. The second phase of the redeployment, which took place in the northern area, began on 12 January 1976 and was completed on 22 February. The Force monitored the redeployment of the forces of the two parties by providing buffer times for the transfer of evacuated areas to Egyptian control, occupying temporary buffer zones and manning temporary observation posts. The Force acted as a secure channel of communication and contact between the parties throughout the redeployment process.

After the completion of the redeployment operation, UNEF II carried out the long-term functions specified in the protocol. In the southern area, its task was to assure that no military or paramilitary forces of any kind, military fortifications or military installations were in the area. To perform that task, it established check-points and observation posts in accordance with the protocol and conducted patrols throughout the area, including air patrols. It also ensured the control of buffer zones in the southern area and, to this effect, it maintained permanent check-points along the buffer-zone lines. It also supervised the use of common road sections by the parties in accordance with arrangements agreed to by them and it provided escorts in those sections when necessary.

The functions of UNEF II in the buffer zone in the northern area were carried out by means of a system of check-points, observation posts and patrols by land. In the early-warning-system area, which was located in the buffer zone, UNEF II provided escorts, as required, to and from the United States watch stations and the Egyptian and Israeli surveillance stations. The Force was also entrusted with the task of ensuring the maintenance of the agreed limitations of forces and armament within the areas specified in the agreement and, to this effect, it conducted bi-weekly inspections. Those inspections were carried out by UNTSO military observers under UNEF supervision, accompanied by liaison officers of the respective parties.

The joint commission established by the disengagement agreement met in the buffer zone under the chairmanship of the United Nations Chief Co-ordinator as occasion required. The Force received a number of complaints from both parties alleging violations by the other side. Those complaints were taken up with the party concerned by the Force Commander or the Chief Co-ordinator and, in some instances, were referred to the joint commission.

The Force maintained close contact with representatives of the International Committee of the Red Cross in its humanitarian endeavours and extended its assistance in providing facilities for family reunions and student exchanges, which took place at an agreed site in the buffer zone.

All these tasks were carried out efficiently. There were few incidents and problems and, whenever they occurred, they were resolved without difficulty with the co-operation of the parties concerned.

Fourth phase: May–July 1979

The peace treaty concluded in March 1979 between Egypt and Israel as a result of negotiations conducted under the auspices of the United States, and which entered into force on 25 April, had a direct bearing on the termination of UNEF II and affected its activities during the final period.

The treaty provided that, upon completion of a phased Israeli withdrawal over three years, security arrangements on both sides of the Egyptian-Israeli border would be made with the assistance of United Nations forces and observers. Article VI stipulated that "the parties will request the United Nations to provide forces and observers to supervise the implementation of the security arrangements". The United Nations forces and observers would have been asked to perform a variety of duties, including the operation of check-points, reconnaissance patrols and observation posts along the boundaries of and within the demilitarized zone, and ensuring freedom of navigation through the Strait of Tiran. United Nations forces would also have been stationed in certain areas adjoining the demilitarized zone on the Egyptian side, and United Nations observers would have patrolled a specified area on the Israeli side of the international boundary. In an annex to the treaty, the United States undertook to organize a multinational force of equivalent strength if the United Nations were unable to monitor the forces as envisaged by the treaty.

The intention of the parties was to have UNEF II perform these tasks. However, there was strong opposition to the treaty from the PLO and many Arab States, and opposition by the Soviet Union in the Security Council. As previously stated, the Security Council decided to allow the mandate of the Force to lapse on 24 July 1979.

On 25 May 1979, in pursuance of the relevant provisions of the peace treaty, the Israeli forces withdrew from the northern Sinai to the east of El Arish and the Egyptians took over control of that area. UNEF II was not involved in this move except by permitting access of Egyptian personnel to the buffer zone and the areas of limited forces and armament and by providing escorts to the parties within these areas as the Israeli withdrawal was being carried out. During this process, UNEF II withdrew from the northern part of the buffer zone, which was handed over to the Egyptian authorities. Except in areas of the Sinai controlled by Egyptian forces, UNEF II continued to function as previously. In particular, it continued to provide a physical separation of the areas of limited forces and armament. It also provided escorts to authorized non–United Nations visitors and to personnel of the parties travelling to and from the early-warning-system stations.

After the mandate of UNEF II lapsed in July 1979, the various contingents were rapidly repatriated, except for a Swedish guard unit and limited groups of the Canadian and Polish logistics contingents which remained in the area to assist in the winding up of the Force.

Chapter V

United Nations Disengagement Observer Force

A. Background and establishment

Background

At the end of the October 1973 war, while tranquillity was restored on the Egyptian front with the deployment of the second United Nations Emergency Force (UNEF II), no new peace-keeping force was established on the Syrian front in the Golan Heights. There, fighting subsided following the cease-fire call contained in Security Council resolution 338(1973) of 22 October 1973. By that time, the Israeli forces had crossed the 1967 cease-fire lines and occupied a salient up to and including the village of Saassa on the Quneitra–Damascus road. United Nations military observers set up temporary observation posts around that salient and, with these changes, the cease-fire observation operation in the Israel–Syria sector was resumed.

However, tension remained high in the area. There was a continuous pattern of incidents in and around the buffer zone supervised by the United Nations military observers. These involved artillery, mortar and automatic-weapon fire, and overflights by Israeli and Syrian aircraft. Frequent complaints of cease-fire violations were submitted by the two parties, although cease-fires proposed from time to time by the United Nations observers resulted in temporary cessation of firing. From early March 1974 until the end of May, the situation in the sector became increasingly unstable, and firing—involving use of artillery, tanks and rockets—intensified. Against this background, the United States Secretary of State undertook a diplomatic mission, which resulted in the conclusion of an Agreement on Disengagement between Israeli and Syrian Forces in May 1974.

Agreement on disengagement of forces

The Secretary-General, who was kept informed of these developments, reported to the Security Council on 29 May* that the signing of the Agreement would take place on 31 May 1974 in the Egyptian-Israeli Military Working Group of the Geneva Peace

---

* S/11302.

Conference on the Middle East. He also informed the Council that he had instructed Lieutenant-General Ensio P. H. Siilasvuo, the Commander of UNEF, to be available for the signing of the Agreement, under the aegis of the United Nations.

On 30 May, the Secretary-General transmitted to the Security Council the text of the Agreement as well as the Protocol to that Agreement which dealt with the establishment of the United Nations Disengagement Observer Force (UNDOF).*

Under the terms of the Agreement, Israel and Syria were scrupulously to observe the cease-fire on land, sea and in the air, and refrain from all military actions against each other from the time of the signing of the document, in implementation of Security Council resolution 338(1973). It further provided that the two military forces would be separated in accordance with agreed principles, which called for the establishment of an area of separation and of two equal areas of limitation of armament and forces on both sides of the area. The detailed plan for the disengagement of forces would be worked out by the military representatives of Israel and Syria in the Military Working Group. They were to begin their work 24 hours after the signing of the Agreement and complete it within five days. Disengagement was to begin within 24 hours thereafter and be completed not later than 20 days after it had begun. The provisions of the Agreement concerning the cease-fire and the separation of forces were to be inspected by UNDOF personnel. All wounded prisoners of war were to be repatriated within 24 hours after signature of the Agreement, and all other prisoners upon completion of the work of the Military Working Group. The bodies of all dead soldiers held by either side would be returned for burial within 10 days. The final paragraph of the Agreement stated that it was not a peace agreement, but that it was a step towards a just and durable peace on the basis of Security Council resolution 338(1973).

Protocol on UNDOF

According to the Protocol to the Agreement, Israel and Syria agreed that the function of UNDOF would be to maintain the cease-fire, to see that it was strictly observed, and to supervise the Agreement and Protocol with regard to the areas of separation and limitation. In carrying out its mission, the Force was to comply with generally applicable Syrian laws and regulations and not hamper the functioning of local civil administration. It was to enjoy the freedom of movement and communication necessary for its mission and be pro-

* S/11302/Add.1, annexes I and II.

vided with personal weapons of a defensive character to be used only in self-defence.

The strength of UNDOF was set at 1,250 men, to be selected by the Secretary-General, in consultation with the parties, from Member States of the United Nations which were not permanent members of the Security Council.

In transmitting the documents, the Secretary-General, noting that the Protocol called for the creation of a United Nations Disengagement Observer Force, indicated that he would take the necessary steps in accordance with the Protocol's provisions, if the Security Council should so decide. He intended that the proposed Force would be drawn, at least initially, from United Nations military personnel already in the area.

Establishment of UNDOF

On 30 May 1974,* the representative of the United States requested an urgent meeting of the Security Council to consider the situation in the Middle East, in particular the disengagement of Israeli and Syrian forces. At the meeting, the Secretary-General drew attention to his reports on this matter and said that, were the Council so to decide, he would set up UNDOF on the basis of the same general principles which had governed the establishment of UNEF II.

On 31 May, the Agreement on Disengagement and the Protocol were signed at Geneva by the military representatives of Israel and Syria. Later on the same day, the Security Council adopted resolution 350(1974) by which it decided to set up UNDOF immediately, under its authority, and requested the Secretary-General to take the necessary steps.

The Force was established for an initial period of six months, subject to renewal by the Security Council. The Secretary-General was asked to keep the Council fully informed of further developments.

Secretary-General's proposal

After the adoption of the resolution, the Secretary-General presented his proposals for interim arrangements. He suggested that initially UNDOF should comprise the Austrian and Peruvian contingents from UNEF II, supported by logistical elements from Canada and Poland, also to be drawn from UNEF II, and by UNTSO military observers who were already deployed in the area (except

* S/11304.

those from permanent member countries of the Security Council). The Secretary-General also proposed to appoint, as interim Commander, Brigadier-General Gonzalo Briceño Zevallos of Peru, who was at the time commanding the northern brigade of UNEF II. The interim Commander was to be assisted by staff officers drawn from UNEF and UNTSO. The Security Council agreed to the Secretary-General's proposals.

Military Working Group

The Military Working Group met in Geneva from 31 May 1974 until 5 June under the chairmanship of General Siilasvuo to work out practical arrangements for the disengagement of forces.*

Military representatives of the Syrian Arab Republic joined the Group, and the representatives of the Soviet Union and the United States, as co-chairmen of the Geneva Peace Conference, also participated in the meetings.

Full agreement was reached on a disengagement plan, with a timetable for the withdrawal of Israeli forces from the areas east of the 1967 cease-fire line, as well as from Quneitra and Rafid, and the demilitarization of an area west of Quneitra. A map showing the different phases of disengagement was signed at the final meeting on 5 June.

In the negotiations in the Military Working Group, the two parties also agreed that both sides would repatriate all prisoners of war by 6 June, and that they would co-operate with the International Committee of the Red Cross in carrying out its mandate, including the exchange of bodies, which was also to be completed by 6 June. They would make available all information and maps of minefields in their respective areas and the areas to be handed over by them.

UNDOF beginnings

On 3 June 1974, the Secretary-General, having obtained the agreement of the Government of Peru, appointed General Briceño as interim Commander of UNDOF. General Briceño arrived in Damascus from Cairo on the same day and immediately established a provisional headquarters in the premises of the Israel–Syria Mixed Armistice Commission, assuming command over the 90 UNTSO observers detailed to UNDOF.

* S/11302/Add.2.

Later the same day, advance parties of the Austrian and Peruvian contingents arrived in the mission area. They were joined on the following days by the remainder of the two contingents and the Canadian and Polish logistic elements. Some logistic support was given by UNEF.

By 16 June, the strength of UNDOF was brought to 1,218 all ranks, near its authorized level of 1,250.

Extension of the mandate

The initial six-month mandate of UNDOF expired on 30 November 1974. Since then, the mandate has been repeatedly extended by the Security Council upon the recommendation of the Secretary-General and with the agreement of the two parties concerned.

In November 1975, Syria was reluctant to agree to a further extension because no progress had been made in the settlement of the wider Middle East problem. The Secretary-General met with President Hafez Al Assad in Damascus that month and, after extensive discussions, the President gave his agreement for the renewal of the UNDOF mandate for another period of six months, to be combined with a specific provision that the Security Council would convene, in January 1976, to hold a substantive debate on the Middle East problem, including the Palestine question, with the participation of representatives of the Palestine Liberation Organization.*

Extending the UNDOF mandate for a further six months, the Security Council, in resolution 381(1975) of 30 November 1975, decided to reconvene on 12 January 1976 to continue the debate on the Middle East problem, taking into account all relevant United Nations resolutions.

In May 1976, the Secretary-General again had to travel to Damascus to secure the agreement of the Syrian Government for a further extension. However, from November 1976 onwards, the two parties readily gave their agreement for further extensions. On each occasion since that date, the Security Council, in renewing UNDOF's mandate for further six-month periods, called on the parties concerned to implement resolution 338(1973) and requested the Secretary-General to submit at the end of the extension period a report on the measures taken to implement that resolution. In connection with the adoption of the resolutions on the renewal of the mandate, the President of the Security Council made a complementary statement on each occasion endorsing the view of the Secretary-

* S/11883/Add.1.

General that, despite the prevailing quiet in the Israel–Syria sector, the situation in the Middle East as a whole would remain unstable and potentially dangerous unless real progress could be made towards a just and lasting settlement of the Middle East problem in all its aspects.

On 14 December 1981, the Israeli Government decided to apply Israeli law in the occupied Golan Heights. Syria strongly protested against this decision, and both the Security Council and the General Assembly declared that it was null and void. The Israeli decision, however, has not affected the operation of UNDOF in any significant way.

Organization of UNDOF

The organization of UNDOF is similar to that of UNEF II. The Force is under the exclusive command and control of the United Nations at all times. The Force Commander is appointed by the Secretary-General with the consent of the Security Council and is responsible to him. Following General Briceño, who was interim Commander until 15 December 1974, the command of UNDOF was assumed by Colonel (later Major-General) Hannes Philipp, of Austria (December 1974–April 1979), Colonel (later Major-General) Günther G. Greindl, also of Austria (until February 1981), Major-General Erkki R. Kaira, of Finland (until June 1982), Major-General Carl-Gustav Stahl, of Sweden (until May 1985), Major-General Gustav Hägglund, of Finland (until May 1986), Major-General Gustaf Welin, of Sweden (until September 1988) and Major-General Adolf Radauer, of Austria (since September 1988).

UNDOF was originally composed of the Austrian and Peruvian contingents and the Canadian and Polish logistic elements transferred from UNEF II. The Peruvian contingent was withdrawn in July 1975 and replaced by an Iranian contingent in August of that year. This contingent was in turn withdrawn in March 1979 and replaced by a Finnish contingent.

UNDOF in June 1990 was composed of contingents from Austria, Canada, Finland and Poland. A number of observers, detailed from UNTSO, who are not nationals of permanent members of the Security Council, are included in UNDOF as an integral part of the Force. In addition, UNTSO observers assigned to the Israel–Syria Mixed Armistice Commission may assist UNDOF as occasion requires.

UNDOF strength

Within two weeks of its establishment, the total strength of UNDOF was brought to near its authorized level of about 1,250. From that time until August 1979—except for a brief period from March to August 1979 when the strength of the Force was temporarily below the authorized level as a result of the withdrawal of the Iranian battalion—the strength of UNDOF remained around that figure. In August 1979,* the Secretary-General informed the Security Council that, as a result of the withdrawal of UNEF II, which had hitherto provided third-line logistic support to UNDOF, it had become necessary to strengthen the existing Canadian and Polish logistic units. The Security Council agreed to the proposed increase to 1,450. Following consultations with the parties, the strength of UNDOF was gradually brought up to 1,331 in May 1985. As of June 1990 the strength and composition of UNDOF was as follows: Austria (535); Canada (229); Finland (412); Poland (156); seven UNTSO observers were also assigned to the Force. In addition, UNTSO observers assigned to the Israel–Syria Mixed Armistice Commission assist UNDOF as necessary.

Financial aspects

From its inception UNDOF has been financed from the amounts appropriated for UNEF II, for which the establishment of a special account had been authorized by General Assembly resolution 3101(XXVIII) of 11 December 1973. In accordance with this resolution, the costs of UNEF II were levied upon all Member States. In its resolution 3211 B (XXIX) of 29 November 1974, the General Assembly requested the Secretary-General to continue to maintain the special account, to which appropriations for both Forces were now credited. Following the termination of UNEF II in July 1979, the account remained open for UNDOF.

In mid-1990 the annual cost of UNDOF was running at approximately $39.4 million. Contributions outstanding to the account as of 30 June 1990 amounted to $30.3 million, or 6.4 per cent of the sums levied on Member States since the beginning of the mission.

* S/13479.

B. Activities of UNDOF

Initial deployment

Following the signing of the Agreement on Disengagement, all firings ceased in the Israel–Syria sector as of 1109 hours GMT on 31 May 1974. This was confirmed by the United Nations military observers stationed in the sector. These observers, who were later incorporated into UNDOF, continued to man selected observation posts and patrol bases along the cease-fire line while the newly arrived contingents of UNDOF began deployment in the area. The Austrian and Peruvian infantry battalions set up positions between the Israeli and Syrian forces, the former in the Saassa area and the latter from Quneitra south along the cease-fire lines.

Disengagement operation

The disengagement operation began on 14 June and proceeded apace until 27 June. In accordance with the agreed plan, the operation was carried out in four phases.

During the first phase, the Israeli forces handed over to UNDOF an area of some 270 square kilometres (about 28 square kilometres in the Saassa area and about 243 square kilometres east of Lake Tiberias) in the afternoon of 14 June. The next morning, the Syrian forces commenced deploying in that area while UNDOF established a new buffer zone west of the evacuated area.

The same procedure was followed for the second phase, which took place on 18 and 19 June and covered an area of some 374 square kilometres (about 214 square kilometres east of Lake Tiberias and about 160 square kilometres north and north-west of the Saassa area), and for the third phase, which took place on 23 June and involved an area of about 132 square kilometres east and north of Quneitra.

The fourth phase took place on 24 and 25 June. During that phase, the Israeli forces evacuated the area of separation, which was taken over by UNDOF. On 25 June, after UNDOF completed its deployment, Syrian civilian administration was established in the area of separation. On 26 June, UNDOF observers inspected the areas of limited forces and armament (in the 10-kilometre zones) on each side of the area of separation. The next day they proceeded with the inspection of the 20- and 25-kilometre zones, thus completing the implementation of the disengagement operation.

The disengagement process was marred by a serious incident during its last phase. Early on the morning of 25 June, four Austrian soldiers were killed and another wounded when their vehicle ran over a land-mine on the slopes of Mount Hermon in the area of separation. From 25 to 27 June, at the request of the Syrian Government and on the basis of an agreement reached with the Israeli authorities through UNDOF headquarters, a body of 500 Syrian soldiers equipped with mine-clearing tanks carried out mine-clearing operations at various locations in the area of separation, under the close supervision of UNDOF observers.

Supervision of the Agreement

Following the completion of the disengagement operation, UNDOF undertook the delineation and marking of the lines bounding the area of separation. This task, which was carried out with the co-operation and assistance of the Israeli and Syrian forces on their respective sides, proceeded smoothly and was completed in early July 1974.

After the delineation of the area of separation, UNDOF set up a series of check-points and observation posts within that area. In addition, two base camps were established, one on the east side of the area of separation and the other on the west side. At the same time, UNDOF headquarters, which remained in Damascus, was moved from the office of the Israel–Syria Mixed Armistice Commission to a building made available by the Syrian Government. The Quneitra communication relay station, which had been set up by UNTSO, was placed under the control of UNDOF. These arrangements have remained essentially unchanged.

UNDOF headquarters maintains close liaison with both sides through their senior military representatives. At the local level, the commanders of the UNDOF units maintain liaison with one side or the other through liaison officers designated by the parties.

The Austrian battalion and the Polish logistic unit are currently in a base camp near Wadi Faouar, eight kilometres east of the area of separation, while the Finnish battalion and the Canadian logistic unit share a base camp near the village of Ziouani, west of that area. As of June 1990, the Austrian battalion manned 19 positions and seven outposts; the Finnish battalion, 16 positions and six outposts—the former in the area north of the Damascus–Quneitra road and the latter south of that road. The UNTSO military observers assigned to the Israel–Syria sector, who operate out of Damascus on the Syrian side and

Tiberias on the Israeli side, manned 11 observation posts near the area of separation.

The main function of UNDOF is to supervise the area of separation to make sure that there are no military forces within it. This is carried out by means of static positions and observation posts which are manned 24 hours a day, and by foot and mobile patrols operating along predetermined routes by day and night. Temporary outposts and additional patrols may be set up from time to time as occasion requires.

In accordance with the terms of the Agreement on Disengagement, UNDOF conducts fortnightly inspections of the area of limitation of armament and forces. These inspections, which cover the 10-, 20- and 25-kilometre zones on each side of the area of separation, are carried out by United Nations military observers with the assistance of liaison officers from the parties, who accompany the inspection teams on their respective sides.

These inspections have generally proceeded smoothly with the co-operation of the parties concerned, although on both sides restrictions are regularly placed on the movement of the inspection teams in some localities. The findings of the inspection teams are communicated to the two parties but are not made public. When one party complains about the other party's violation of the agreement on the limitation of armament and forces, the Force Commander will try to resolve the matter through his good offices. So far, no serious problems have arisen in this connection.

Humanitarian activities

In addition to its normal peace-keeping functions, UNDOF has carried out activities of a humanitarian nature as occasion requires. At the request of the parties, UNDOF has from time to time exercised its good offices in arranging for the transfer of released prisoners and the bodies of war dead between Israel and Syria. It has assisted the International Committee of the Red Cross (ICRC) by providing it with facilities for the hand-over of prisoners and bodies, for the exchange of parcels and mail across the area of separation, and for the transit of Druze students from the occupied Golan to attend school in Syria. Of particular note was the assistance extended to ICRC on 28 June 1984 when 297 prisoners of war, 16 civilians and the remains of 77 persons were exchanged between Israel and Syria. In 1976, UNDOF worked out arrangements, with the co-operation of the two parties, for periodic reunions of Druze families living on different sides of the area of separation. Those family reunions took place every fortnight in the village of Majdel Chams in the area of separation, under the supervision of UNDOF, until February 1982, when they had to be discontinued because of the controversy arising from Israel's decision in December 1981 to apply Israeli law to the occupied Golan Heights.

Incidents and casualties

During the initial period, there were a number of serious incidents. Besides the four Austrian soldiers killed and another wounded in a mine incident on 25 June 1974, another mine explosion occurred on 20 April 1977 in which an Austrian officer was killed and an Iranian officer was wounded. Despite the mine-clearing operations undertaken by the Syrian forces in 1974, there were still many unexploded mines in and near the area of separation. The engineers of the Polish logistic unit continue to search for and defuse unexploded mines, shells and bombs in and near the area.

On 9 August 1974, a United Nations aircraft, flying from Ismailia to Damascus in the established air corridor, crashed as a result of anti-aircraft fire, north-east of the Syrian village of Ad Dimas. All nine Canadians aboard were killed.

In November 1975, there was a shooting incident in which two Syrian shepherds were killed by an Israeli patrol. There were also alleged crossings of the area of separation, resulting in one case in the death of three Israeli citizens. In November 1977, two members of the Iranian battalion came under fire from the Israeli side and both were wounded.

Whenever such incidents occur, UNDOF seeks to resolve the situation by negotiation and appropriate corrective measures. The incidents have not seriously affected the operations of the Force.

Current situation

Since November 1977, there have been no major incidents. The main problems in the area arise from the presence of Syrian shepherds grazing their flocks near the western edge of the area of separation. They sometimes cross the line, either in ignorance or because there are good grazing lands on the other side. A number of shepherds have been killed as a result of detonating mines in the area of separation.

Problems arise for UNDOF as a result of the restrictions placed upon its troops by one party or the other. Because, until 1990, Poland had no diplomatic relations with Israel, the Israeli forces restricted the movement of the Polish forces on the Israeli side of the area of separation. The Force Commander, fully supported by the Secretary-General, protested against these restrictions on the grounds that UNDOF is an integrated unit and all its elements must enjoy freedom of movement on an equal basis. Following the establishment of diplomatic relations between Israel and Poland, it is expected that this problem will now be resolved.

As noted above, restrictions are regularly placed by both sides on the movement of the UNDOF inspection teams, which are not allowed to visit certain localities when inspecting the area of limitation of armament and forces. These restrictions are invariably protested by the Force Commander.

On the whole, however, UNDOF encounters no serious difficulties that would affect its smooth functioning. In his periodic reports on the activities of the Force, the Secretary-General has been able to report that the situation in the Israel–Syria sector has remained quiet and that UNDOF has continued to perform its functions effectively with the co-operation of the parties.

Chapter VI

United Nations Interim Force in Lebanon

A. Background and establishment

Background

Although the Lebanese civil war which had broken out in April 1975 officially ended in October 1976—after the election of President Elias Sarkis, the constitution of a new central Government and the establishment of an Arab Deterrent Force—fighting did not completely stop in southern Lebanon. When Syrian troops of the Deterrent Force deployed towards the south, the Israeli Government threatened to take stern counter-measures if they should advance beyond an imaginary east-west red line, extending south of the Zahrani River. Whether because of this threat or for some other reasons, the Syrian forces stopped short of the red line. The authority of the central Government was not restored in the south. Sporadic fighting continued in that area between the Christian militias, which were assisted by Israel, and the armed elements of the Lebanese National Movement, a loose association of a variety of Moslem and leftist parties, supported by the armed forces of the Palestine Liberation Organization (PLO). The PLO was the dominant force in southern Lebanon at the time and had established many bases in the area. From these it launched commando raids against Israel which were followed by intensive Israeli retaliation.

On 11 March 1978, a commando raid, for which the PLO claimed responsibility, took place in Israel near Tel Aviv and, according to Israeli sources, resulted in 37 deaths and 76 wounded among the Israeli population.* In retaliation, Israeli forces invaded Lebanon on the night of 14/15 March, and in a few days occupied the entire region south of the Litani River except for the city of Tyre and its surrounding area.

Establishment of UNIFIL

On 15 March, the Lebanese Government submitted a strong protest to the Security Council against the Israeli invasion.†

---

* S/12598. † S/12600.

It stated that it was not responsible for the presence of Palestinian bases in southern Lebanon and had no connection with the Palestinian commando operation. It said it had exerted tremendous efforts with the Palestinians and the Arab States in order to keep matters under control, but Israeli objections regarding the entry of the Arab Deterrent Force to the south had prevented the accomplishment of Lebanon's desire to bring the border area under control. The Security Council met on 17 March 1978 and on the following days to consider the Lebanese complaint.

On 19 March, on a proposal by the United States, the Security Council adopted resolution 425(1978), by which it called for strict respect for the territorial integrity, sovereignty and political independence of Lebanon within its internationally recognized boundaries. It called upon Israel immediately to cease its military action against Lebanese territorial integrity and withdraw forthwith its forces from all Lebanese territory. It also decided, "in the light of the request of the Government of Lebanon, to establish immediately under its authority a United Nations interim force for southern Lebanon for the purpose of confirming the withdrawal of Israeli forces, restoring international peace and security and assisting the Government of Lebanon in ensuring the return of its effective authority in the area, the force to be composed of personnel drawn from Member States". The Council requested the Secretary-General to submit a report to the Council within 24 hours on the implementation of the resolution.

Terms of reference and guidelines

On the same afternoon, the Secretary-General submitted a report to the Security Council in which he set out the terms of reference of the new Force, to be called the United Nations Interim Force in Lebanon (UNIFIL), the guidelines for the Force and a plan of action for its speedy establishment.*

The Force was to confirm the withdrawal of Israeli forces, restore international peace and security, and assist the Government of Lebanon in ensuring the return of its effective authority in the area. It would establish and maintain itself in an area of operation to be defined in the light of those tasks, and would use its best efforts to prevent the recurrence of fighting and to ensure that its area of operation would not be utilized for hostile activities of any kind. In the fulfilment of its tasks, the Force would have the co-operation of the military observers of the United Nations Truce Supervision Organization (see chapter II above), who would continue to function on the

* S/12611.

Armistice Demarcation Line (ADL) after the termination of UNIFIL's mandate.

In the first stage, the Force would confirm the withdrawal of the Israeli forces from Lebanese territory to the international border. Once this was achieved, it would establish and maintain an area of operation to be defined in consultation with the parties concerned. It would supervise the cessation of hostilities, ensure the peaceful character of the area of operation, control movement and take all measures deemed necessary to assure the effective restoration of Lebanese sovereignty. The Secretary-General also indicated that, with a view to facilitating UNIFIL's tasks, it might be necessary to work out arrangements with Israel and Lebanon as a preliminary measure for the implementation of the Security Council resolution, and it was assumed that both parties would give their full co-operation to UNIFIL in this regard.

Particular emphasis was placed on the principles of non-use of force and non-intervention in the internal affairs of the host country. UNIFIL would not use force except in self-defence, which would include resistance to attempts by forcible means to prevent it from discharging its duties under the Council's mandate. Like any other United Nations peace-keeping operation, UNIFIL could not and should not take on responsibilities which fell under the Government of the country in which it was operating. Those responsibilities should be exercised by the competent Lebanese authorities.

In working out the terms of reference of UNIFIL, the Secretary-General had wanted to define more clearly the area of operation of the Force and its relationship with the PLO. But he could not do so, as the discussions he held with the member States of the Security Council and with other Governments concerned revealed a profound disagreement among them on both subjects. As will be seen later, these two questions weighed heavily on the operations of UNIFIL.

The guidelines proposed by the Secretary-General were essentially the same as those applied to UNEF II and UNDOF (*see chapters IV and V above*). Important decisions on the organization of UNIFIL, such as the appointment of the Force Commander or the selection of contingents, would be taken by the Secretary-General, but he would need to consult the Security Council and obtain its consent. All matters which might affect the nature or the continued effective functioning of the Force would be referred to the Council for its decision.

The Secretary-General said that Lieutenant-General Ensio P.H. Siilasvuo, Chief Co-ordinator of the United Nations Peace-keeping

Missions in the Middle East, would be instructed to contact immediately the Governments of Israel and Lebanon for the purpose of reaching agreement on the modalities of the withdrawal of the Israeli forces and the establishment of a United Nations area of operation. Major-General (later Lieutenant-General) E.A. Erskine, of Ghana, the Chief of Staff of UNTSO, would be appointed immediately as interim Commander and, pending the arrival of the first contingents of the Force, would perform his tasks with the assistance of a group of UNTSO military observers. At the same time, urgent measures would be taken for the early arrival in the area of contingents of the Force. The Secretary-General proposed that the Force have a total strength of the order of 4,000 and that it be stationed initially in the area for six months. The best possible preliminary cost estimate was approximately $68 million for a Force of 4,000 all ranks for that period. As with UNEF II and UNDOF, the costs of UNIFIL were to be considered as expenses of the Organization to be borne by Member States as apportioned by the General Assembly.

By resolution 426(1978) of 19 March 1978, the Council approved the Secretary-General's report and decided that UNIFIL should be established for an initial period of six months, subject to extension.

Beginnings of the Force

While the members of the Security Council, in close consultation with the Secretary-General, were discussing the establishment of UNIFIL, the situation in southern Lebanon remained extremely tense and volatile. Israeli forces had occupied most of southern Lebanon up to the Litani River, but the PLO troops regrouped with much of their equipment in the Tyre pocket and in their strongholds north of the Litani, particularly Nabatiyah and Château de Beaufort. Intense exchanges of fire continued between the opposing forces.

The Secretary-General's two immediate objectives were to set up the new Force and deploy it along the front lines as soon as possible, and to initiate negotiations on the withdrawal of the Israeli forces.

General Erskine, who had been appointed as interim Commander of UNIFIL on 19 March, immediately set up temporary headquarters at Naqoura in southern Lebanon, in the premises of the UNTSO out-station, with the 45 military observers who were already in the area. These were soon reinforced by 19 additional observers of UNTSO. In order to make UNIFIL operational without delay, the Secretary-General transferred some military personnel from the two existing peace-keeping forces in the Middle East, after obtaining the concurrence of the Governments concerned. One reinforced company from the Iranian contingent of UNDOF and another from the Swedish contingent of UNEF were temporarily assigned to the new Force, together with a movement control detachment and a signal detachment of the Canadian logistic unit of UNEF.

Meanwhile, urgent action had to be taken to seek and obtain 4,000 troops for the Force. France, Nepal and Norway had already offered to provide contingents. On 21 March, after securing the agreement of the Council, the Secretary-General accepted the offers of the three Governments. Later, in response to an appeal by the Secretary-General, Nigeria and Senegal each agreed to provide an infantry battalion.

The first French troops arrived in Beirut on 23 March; the Norwegian contingent came a week later and the Nepalese by mid-April. With the Canadian, Iranian and Swedish units already in the area, the strength of UNIFIL reached 1,800 all ranks by 8 April, 2,502 by 17 April and 4,016 by the beginning of May.

Strength of the Force

On 1 May 1978,* shortly after the Israeli withdrawal began, the Secretary-General recommended that the total strength of the Force should be brought to 6,000. He also indicated that the Governments of Fiji, Iran and Ireland were prepared to make available a battalion each for service with UNIFIL. By resolution 427(1978) of 3 May 1978, the Security Council approved the Secretary-General's recommendation. The three new battalions arrived in the mission area during the first days of June. The Swedish and Iranian companies that had been temporarily detached from UNEF and UNDOF returned to their parent units.

As of mid-June 1978, the strength of the Force was 6,100. The contingents were: Infantry battalions—Fiji (500), France (703), Iran (514), Ireland (665), Nepal (642), Nigeria (669), Norway (723), Senegal (634); Logistic units—Canada (102), France (541), Norway (207). In addition, 42 military observers of UNTSO assisted UNIFIL in the performance of its tasks, having been organized on 1 April 1978 as Observer Group Lebanon (OGL), under the operational control of the Force Commander of UNIFIL.

From June 1978 until June 1981, the strength of UNIFIL varied between 5,750 and 6,100, according to the movements of the various contingents. The Canadian logistic detachments were returned to UNEF

---

* S/12675.

in October 1978. At the request of their Governments, the Iranian battalion was withdrawn beginning in January 1979 and the French infantry battalion in March 1979. The last was replaced by a Dutch battalion, which arrived in the mission area by early March; a Ghanaian contingent joined UNIFIL in September 1979.

The strength of UNIFIL was further increased to about 7,000 in early 1982 on the recommendation of the Secretary-General (resolution 501(1982) of 25 February 1982). In response to a request of the Secretary-General, the French Government agreed to provide a new infantry battalion of about 600 all ranks and the Ghanaian and Irish Governments agreed to increase their battalions. These changes brought the strength of UNIFIL to 6,945 at the beginning of June 1982. The composition of the Force at that date was: Infantry battalions—Fiji (628), France (595), Ghana (557), Ireland (671), Nepal (432), Netherlands (810), Nigeria (696), Norway (660), Senegal (561); Headquarters camp command—Ghana (140), Ireland (51); Logistic units—France (775), Italy (34), Norway (191), Sweden (144).

Following the second Israeli invasion of Lebanon, in June 1982, the strength and composition of UNIFIL underwent important changes. In September 1982, at the request of the French Government, 482 officers and men of the French infantry battalion were temporarily released from UNIFIL to their national authorities, which incorporated them in the French contingent of the multinational force in Beirut. The Nepalese battalion was withdrawn by 18 November 1982 and replaced by a Finnish battalion. Two companies of the Nigerian battalion were repatriated without replacement in November 1982 and the remainder in January 1983. In October 1983, the Netherlands decided to reduce its contingent from 810 to 150. In February 1984, the French unit withdrawn in 1982 was returned to UNIFIL. In October 1984, the Senegalese contingent was withdrawn and was replaced by a Nepalese battalion which arrived in the area in January-February 1985. In October 1985, the Netherlands contingent was withdrawn, its positions being taken over by the Fijian and Nepalese battalions, the latter increased by an additional infantry company.

In December 1986, the bulk of the infantry and part of the logistic battalions provided by France were withdrawn. The latter was replaced by a Swedish logistic battalion, while the Finnish, Ghanaian and Nepalese contingents were increased and assumed the tasks of the French infantry battalion. The remaining elements of the French logistic battalion and one infantry company formed a French composite battalion, responsible for logistic functions and the protection of the UNIFIL headquarters. Following a substantive redeployment of the Force, the entire French composite battalion was stationed at the Naqoura Camp. At the same time, a composite mechanized company, which now consists of elements of the Fijian, Finnish, Ghanaian, Irish, Nepalese, Norwegian and Swedish battalions, was established as a separate unit called the Force Mobile Reserve. The unit, stationed near the headquarters of the Fijian battalion, is available for quick deployment to trouble spots throughout the UNIFIL area of operation.

The strength of UNIFIL as at 30 June 1990 stood at 5,854, composed as follows: Fiji (725), Finland (542), France (499), Ghana (891), Ireland (749), Italy (52), Nepal (851), Norway (897), Sweden (648).

The Force is supported by approximately 250 international staff members of the United Nations Secretariat and about 400 local Lebanese staff.

Force Commanders

General Erskine, who acted as interim Commander at the outset of the operation, was appointed Force Commander on 12 April 1978. On 14 February 1981 he was reappointed Chief of Staff of UNTSO and was succeeded at UNIFIL by Lieutenant-General William Callaghan, of Ireland. On 1 June 1986 the command of UNIFIL was assumed by Lieutenant-General Gustav Hägglund, of Finland, who returned to his national service in June 1988. Since 1 July 1988 Lieutenant-General Lars-Eric Wahlgren, of Sweden, has commanded the Force.

During the initial stages of UNIFIL, General Siilasvuo, the Chief Co-ordinator of the United Nations Peace-keeping Missions in the Middle East, played a leading role in the negotiations with the Israeli authorities concerning the withdrawal of the Israeli forces from Lebanon. After the termination of UNEF II, the post of Chief Co-ordinator was discontinued in 1979.

B. UNIFIL activities: March–April 1978

Negotiating problems

Like all United Nations peace-keeping forces, UNIFIL has no enforcement power and requires the co-operation of the parties concerned to fulfil its tasks. Resolution 425(1978) mentioned only

Israel and Lebanon. Immediately after the adoption of the resolution, the Secretary-General sought and obtained an undertaking from both of those countries to co-operate with UNIFIL.

To obtain the co-operation of the PLO, the Secretary-General on 27 March issued an appeal to all the parties concerned, including the PLO, for a general cease-fire.* This was followed up with a meeting between Mr. Yasser Arafat, Chairman of the Executive Committee of the PLO, and General Erskine, the Force Commander, during which a pledge of co-operation with UNIFIL was secured from the PLO.

Another complication arose from the presence and activities in southern Lebanon of various Lebanese armed elements not controlled by the central Government. UNIFIL could not officially negotiate with these armed elements, although they were very much a part of the problem, some of them having sided with the PLO and others with Israel. The Lebanese National Movement (LNM), a loose association of Lebanese Moslem and leftist parties, allied with the PLO, and the armed elements of the two groups operated under a joint command. When difficulties arose with the armed elements, UNIFIL generally endeavoured to resolve them in negotiations with the PLO leadership.

On the opposite side, UNIFIL had to contend with Lebanese *de facto* forces, which were composed mainly of Christian militias led by Major Saad Haddad, a renegade officer of the Lebanese National Army. When UNIFIL encountered problems with the *de facto* forces, it sought the co-operation and assistance of the Israeli authorities, since these forces were armed, trained and supplied by Israel and, by all evidence, closely controlled by it.

Problems concerning the area of operation

A second major difficulty encountered by UNIFIL arose from the lack of a clear definition of its area of operation. Security Council resolution 425(1978), which was the result of a compromise, was vague on this point. It indicated only that UNIFIL would operate in southern Lebanon and that one of its tasks was to confirm withdrawal of the Israeli forces to the international border. In his report on the implementation of the resolution,† which had to take into account the views of the various members of the Security Council, the Secretary-General was unable to propose a clearer definition and merely stated that UNIFIL would set up an area of operation in consultation with the parties. But the parties had very different percep-

* S/12620/Add.1.   † S/12611.

tions of the tasks of UNIFIL and no agreement could be reached on a definition of its area of operation. This difficulty gravely hampered UNIFIL's work from the very start.

First deployment

On 20 March 1978, General Erskine established temporary headquarters in Naqoura. At the same time, General Siilasvuo initiated negotiations with the Israeli authorities in Jerusalem to secure their agreement to withdraw their troops from Lebanon without delay. Pending the withdrawal, plans were made to deploy the UNIFIL troops in a strip of land immediately south of the Litani River and, in particular, to assume control of the Kasmiyah, Akiya and Khardala bridges, which were the three main crossing-points into southern Lebanon.

The Iranian and Swedish companies were instructed to proceed to the Akiya bridge in the central sector and the Khardala bridge in the eastern sector, respectively. Their movement to their destinations was initially delayed by the opposition of the Christian *de facto* forces which were deployed near those areas. However, this opposition was overcome through negotiations with the Israeli authorities, and the proposed deployment took place on 24 March and the following days. The Iranians established a position at the Akiya bridge and expanded their presence around it, while the Swedes were deployed at the Khardala bridge and in the area of Ibil as Saqy farther east. At the end of March, the Norwegian battalion had arrived and was deployed in the eastern sector and the Swedish company redeployed in the central/western sector.

The French battalion was sent to the Tyre region. The initial plan was for the French troops to deploy throughout the Tyre pocket and take control of the Kasmiyah bridge. But this was strongly opposed by the PLO on the grounds that the Israel Defence Forces (IDF) had not in fact occupied either the bridge or the city of Tyre during the fighting, and it became clear that it could not be achieved without heavy fighting and considerable casualties. In New York, the Arab representatives to the United Nations strongly supported the PLO's view that the Tyre pocket should not be included in UNIFIL's area of operation. In these conditions, the Secretary-General decided to delay the proposed deployment, pending negotiations with the PLO; in the event, such deployment was not pressed.

Meanwhile, the French battalion set up its headquarters in former Lebanese army barracks outside the city of Tyre. It established check-points around its headquarters and carried out patrolling activities along the front line, on the coastal road from Zahrani to Tyre and in the city of Tyre itself.

The UNTSO observers assigned to UNIFIL, namely Observer Group Lebanon, played an extremely useful role during this formative phase, since they were already familiar with local conditions. They continued to man the five observation posts established by UNTSO in 1972 along the Armistice Demarcation Line. Some observers served as staff officers at the Naqoura headquarters. Teams of two observers each were attached to the various contingents for liaison and other purposes. Other observers provided liaison with the Lebanese authorities, the Israeli forces, the PLO and various other armed groups in southern Lebanon. The office of the Israel-Lebanon Mixed Armistice Commission in Beirut ensured liaison between UNIFIL and the Lebanese Government.

Cease-fire

The situation in southern Lebanon remained volatile during the first days of UNIFIL. As previously mentioned, on 27 March 1978* the Secretary-General had issued an appeal to all the parties concerned to observe a general cease-fire. On 8 April,† General Erskine reported that the area had been generally quiet since then. However, considerable tension, with occasional exchanges of fire, continued in the Tyre area and the eastern sector, which was close to the main base of the Christian *de facto* forces in Marjayoun and the PLO stronghold of Château de Beaufort north of the Litani River. UNIFIL troops, which were deployed between the opposing forces in these two sensitive areas, endeavoured to maintain a precarious cease-fire, while the Secretary-General and General Siilasvuo continued to press the Israeli authorities to withdraw their troops from Lebanon without delay.

c. UNIFIL activities: April–June 1978

Initial withdrawal of Israeli forces

On 6 April 1978, the Chief of Staff of the Israel Defence Forces submitted to General Siilasvuo a plan for an initial withdrawal of the Israeli forces in two phases.‡ In a first phase, to take place on 11 April, the Israeli forces would withdraw from an area west of

* S/12620/Add.1. † S/12620/Add.2. ‡ *Ibid.*

Marjayoun. The Khardala bridge and a number of villages would be evacuated, but strategic villages such as El Khirba and Dayr Mimas would remain occupied. A second withdrawal would follow on 14 April and would cover a zone extending from a point on the Litani River two kilometres west of the Akiya bridge to a point about one kilometre west of Dayr Mimas. The area to be evacuated during the two first phases would cover about 110 square kilometres, or one tenth of the total occupied territory.

The next day,* the Secretary-General indicated that the Israeli plan was not satisfactory since Security Council resolution 425(1978) called for the withdrawal of Israeli forces without delay from the entire occupied Lebanese territory. The plan, however, was accepted on the understanding that a further withdrawal would be agreed upon at an early date. The proposed withdrawal took place as scheduled without incident. All the positions evacuated by the Israeli forces were handed over to UNIFIL troops.

Further negotiations between General Siilasvuo and the Israeli authorities led to a third phase of the Israeli withdrawal, which took place on 30 April.† This withdrawal was more extensive and covered an area of about 550 square kilometres. As in the previous withdrawals, the positions evacuated by the Israeli forces were taken over by UNIFIL troops without incident.

Following the third phase of the Israeli withdrawal, UNIFIL was deployed in two separate zones south of the Litani River within an area of about 650 square kilometres, or approximately 45 per cent of the territory occupied by Israel. The western zone had an area of about 600 square kilometres and the eastern zone about 50 square kilometres. Between the two zones, there was a gap some 15 kilometres wide just south of Château de Beaufort. In this gap, UNIFIL was able to maintain only four isolated positions, including one at the Khardala bridge.

Pending further withdrawals of the Israeli forces, UNIFIL acted to consolidate its control of the area in which it was deployed. Its main objectives were to supervise and monitor the cease-fire and to ensure that no unauthorized armed personnel entered its area. To this end, observation posts and check-points were set up at various points of entry in its area of deployment, and frequent patrols were conducted throughout the area. All unauthorized armed and uniformed personnel were turned back at entry points and, if they were discovered within the area, UNIFIL troops endeavoured to disarm them and escort them out of its area.

---

* *Ibid.*   † S/12620/Add.4.

Problems after the initial Israeli withdrawal

Following the third phase of the Israeli withdrawal, UNIFIL was faced with two major problems. First, the Israeli Government was reluctant to relinquish the remaining area and the United Nations efforts to achieve further withdrawal met with increasing resistance. Secondly, PLO armed elements attempted to enter the area evacuated by the Israeli forces on the grounds that they had a legitimate right to do so under the terms of the Cairo agreement of 3 November 1969, concluded between Lebanon and the PLO, under the auspices of President Nasser of Egypt, which dealt with the presence of Palestinians in Lebanon.

The unco-operative attitude of certain PLO armed elements led to some serious clashes during the first days of May in the Tyre area. On 1 May, a group of armed elements attempted to infiltrate a UNIFIL position manned by French soldiers. When challenged, they opened fire on the French guards, who returned the fire in self-defence and killed two infiltrators. In the following days, French troops were ambushed at various locations and, during the ensuing exchanges of fire, three UNIFIL soldiers were killed and 14 wounded, including the Commander of the French battalion.*

Negotiations in the area

Strenuous negotiations were undertaken by the Secretary-General and his representatives in the field to prevent infiltration attempts by PLO armed elements and to avoid further incidents. Chairman Arafat confirmed that the PLO would co-operate with UNIFIL and that it would not initiate hostile acts against Israel from southern Lebanon, although it would continue its armed struggle from other areas. While the PLO's presence in southern Lebanon was a matter to be settled between itself and the Lebanese Government, the PLO would facilitate UNIFIL's tasks in response to the Secretary-General's appeal. In particular, the PLO would refrain from infiltrating armed elements into the UNIFIL area of operation. In exchange, Chairman Arafat insisted that the Palestinian armed elements who were already in the UNIFIL area of operation should be allowed to remain there. In order to secure the co-operation of the PLO, UNIFIL agreed to this condition, on the clear understanding that the limited number of armed elements allowed to remain in its area of operation would not be used for military purposes. The

* *Ibid.*

agreement involved about 140 armed elements belonging to various groups of the PLO, assembled in six positions.

The Secretary-General reported to the Security Council* that for humanitarian reasons, and as an *ad hoc* arrangement, UNIFIL had agreed to allow the delivery, under UNIFIL control, of certain non-military supplies—food, water and medicine—to limited Palestinian groups still in its area of operation. Strict instructions were given to the UNIFIL contingents concerned to keep a close watch over the six PLO positions.

Under the pressure of the United Nations, the Israeli Government announced its decision to withdraw its forces from the remaining occupied territory in Lebanon by 13 June 1978. The modalities for the withdrawal were to be determined between the Israeli authorities and Generals Siilasvuo and Erskine.

Following the announcement of this decision, intensive discussions were held between United Nations representatives and the Lebanese Government regarding the deployment of UNIFIL in the area to be evacuated and, in particular, regarding its relationship with the *de facto* forces under the command of Major Haddad. Pending full establishment of its authority in southern Lebanon, the Lebanese Government announced that it provisionally recognized Major Haddad as *de facto* commander of the Lebanese armed forces in his present area. The Lebanese army command would issue instructions to Major Haddad to facilitate UNIFIL's mission and deployment.†

UNIFIL also engaged in discussions with the Israeli authorities to work out practical arrangements for its deployment in the border area following the Israeli withdrawal. However, no common ground could be reached, and the instructions issued by the Lebanese Government to Major Haddad to facilitate UNIFIL's mission were totally ignored.

On 5 September 1978, Lebanon informed the Secretary-General that the commanders of the so-called "*de facto* Lebanese forces" were now to be considered as having no further authority whatsoever to act on behalf of the Lebanese Army, to negotiate with the United Nations, or to exercise any legal command in the area.‡

---

* S/12620/Add.5.   † S/12834.   ‡ S/12620/Add.5.

D. UNIFIL activities:
June 1978–July 1981

Last phase of the Israeli withdrawal

On 13 June 1978, General Erskine reported that the Israeli forces had withdrawn from southern Lebanon. This information was transmitted by the Secretary-General to the Security Council.* The manner in which the Israeli forces carried out the last phase of withdrawal, however, created major problems for UNIFIL. In contrast to the procedure followed during the previous three phases, the IDF on 13 June turned over most of its positions not to UNIFIL but to the *de facto* forces of Major Haddad, on the grounds that the IDF considered him a legitimate representative of the Lebanese Government. UNIFIL units were able to occupy only five positions evacuated by the Israeli forces on that day, because the *de facto* forces, which had been strongly armed by the Israelis, threatened to use force to oppose any attempts by UNIFIL to gain wider deployment.

In a letter dated 13 June,† Foreign Minister Moshe Dayan informed the Secretary-General that Israel had fulfilled its part in the implementation of Security Council resolution 425(1978). In his reply, ‡ the Secretary-General observed that the difficult task lying ahead for UNIFIL had not been facilitated by the decision of the Israeli Government not to turn over control of the evacuated area to UNIFIL. He added that he was making efforts to deal satisfactorily with the consequences of that development, in co-operation with the Lebanese Government.

Difficulties in deployment

In order to fulfil its mandate, UNIFIL had to be fully deployed in its entire area of operation, including the enclave controlled by the *de facto* forces of Major Haddad. The first objective of the Force after the events of 13 June 1978 was therefore to expand its deployment in the enclave. Pending realization of this objective, UNIFIL would continue to ensure that the area where it actually was deployed would not be used for hostile activities of any kind. It would endeavour to stop and contain infiltrations by the armed elements of the PLO and the Lebanese National Movement, as well as incursions and encroachments by the *de facto* forces or the Israeli forces.

* S/12620/Add.5   † S/12736.   ‡ S/12738.

It would also endeavour to maintain the cease-fire and prevent a resumption of hostilities in and around its area. At the same time, UNIFIL would exert all possible efforts to assist the Lebanese Government in restoring its authority and promote the return to normalcy in its area of deployment.

In these various fields of activity, UNIFIL encountered serious difficulties. No significant further deployment could be achieved in the enclave and, although hostile actions could, to a large extent, be contained in UNIFIL's area of deployment, there were frequent and destructive exchanges of fire between the opposing forces over and across its area until 24 July 1981, when cease-fire arrangements were worked out through a joint effort by the United States and the United Nations (*see below*).

The various objectives pursued by the Interim Force were closely interconnected, and set-backs in one inevitably affected the others.

Efforts towards further deployment in the enclave

Immediately after 13 June, the Secretary-General instructed General Siilasvuo and General Erskine to exert every effort, in close co-operation with the Lebanese Government, to achieve progressively wider deployment of UNIFIL in the enclave until the Force would ultimately be in a position effectively to discharge its mandate in its entire area of operation. He made it clear, however, that it remained his intention to utilize peaceful and diplomatic means to achieve this objective.

As a result of renewed efforts, UNIFIL was able to occupy 14 additional positions in the enclave in June and July and another five positions in September 1978. By that date, UNIFIL held a total of 24 positions in the enclave, in addition to its headquarters at Naqoura and the five posts previously established by UNTSO along the Armistice Demarcation Line. But no further deployment could be achieved.

In his report of 13 September 1978 to the Security Council,* and in subsequent reports, the Secretary-General pointed to the efforts made by him and his representatives to secure the full deployment of UNIFIL in its area of operation and the lack of progress in this regard. The Council repeatedly reaffirmed its determination to implement its resolutions on UNIFIL in the totality of the area of operation assigned to the Force, and called upon all the parties to extend

* S/12845.

the necessary co-operation to UNIFIL. The decisions of the Security Council remained unheeded.

This situation prevented UNIFIL from fulfilling an essential part of its mandate and made its other tasks considerably more difficult.

Prevention of infiltration by armed elements

Infiltration attempts resumed and increased soon after 13 June 1978. The inability of UNIFIL to take over the enclave from the pro-Israeli *de facto* forces undoubtedly contributed to the increase in infiltration attempts.

In order to prevent infiltration, UNIFIL, often assisted by Lebanese gendarmes, checked and inspected vehicles and personnel for military equipment and supplies at the check-points established at points of entry and along the main and secondary road networks in its area of deployment. Foot and motorized patrols were conducted day and night along key highways, in villages, as well as in remote wadis (ravines), and random night-time listening posts were established at selected localities to detect unauthorized armed movement.

After July 1979, UNIFIL's troops were redeployed in greater density along the perimeter of the UNIFIL area in order better to control infiltration, and a steady effort was made to improve its surveillance and detection capability. In particular, the number of night-vision binoculars and strong searchlights was increased, while the introduction of sophisticated ground surveillance radar provided the Force with an effective early warning system at medium range. Uniformed and armed personnel stopped at the check-points or caught by patrols were escorted out of the UNIFIL area.

The Palestinian or Lebanese armed elements stopped at check-points generally surrendered their weapons and left the UNIFIL area peacefully. In some cases, however, they reacted by firing at UNIFIL soldiers, who then had to return fire in self-defence. At other times, the infiltrators, after being turned back, would return with reinforcements to attack the UNIFIL position involved. In the most serious instances, armed elements retaliated by laying an ambush against UNIFIL personnel, not only at the scene of the original incident but also against UNIFIL positions or patrols elsewhere. UNIFIL tried to resolve all incidents by negotiation.

Given the difficulty of the terrain, the limited size of UNIFIL and its lack of enforcement power, it was virtually impossible to prevent all infiltration attempts. That difficulty was compounded by the existence of many arms caches in the UNIFIL area. Over the years, the PLO had set up a network of such caches throughout southern Lebanon. UNIFIL found and destroyed many of them, but many others remained.

Since UNIFIL did not want to impede the movement of innocent civilians, persons in civilian clothes could freely enter its area, provided that they had a valid identification card and did not carry weapons. It was relatively easy for PLO personnel and their Lebanese allies to pass through UNIFIL check-points unarmed and, once inside the area, get weapons from the caches. Armed elements could also infiltrate into the UNIFIL area with their weapons through uncharted trails and dirt tracks which could not be covered by UNIFIL check-points or observation posts. Inside the UNIFIL area, the PLO, and particularly the Lebanese National Movement, still had many sympathizers who voluntarily or under pressure gave the infiltrators shelter or other assistance. Despite its vigilance, UNIFIL could not detect and stop all such infiltrators.

In those conditions, the most effective way of stopping, or at least controlling infiltration was to secure the co-operation of the PLO. The PLO leadership did co-operate with UNIFIL to a significant degree. There were no infiltration attempts on a major scale and, when incidents involving infiltration occurred, the PLO leadership assisted UNIFIL in resolving them. But in a number of exceptional cases, the PLO was either unwilling or unable to help, and armed elements succeeded in infiltrating into the UNIFIL area and in setting up some additional positions inside it.

By July 1981, the number of Palestinian armed elements inside the UNIFIL area had increased to about 450, according to UNIFIL estimates, and they had established some 30 positions inside that area. There was, in particular, a concentration of armed element positions in the Jwayya area near the Tyre pocket. UNIFIL tried to have those positions removed by negotiations with the PLO at the highest level, but its efforts were inconclusive.

Nevertheless, UNIFIL did control infiltration by armed elements to an important degree. The number of such elements who succeeded in infiltrating the UNIFIL area was relatively limited, and most of those remained confined to the northern part of the area, well away from the frontier.

UNIFIL's records indicate that after its establishment in March 1978, there was only one major raid into northern Israel by PLO armed elements coming from its area. This happened on 6/7 April 1980, when five armed elements belonging to the Arab Liberation Front crossed the Armistice Demarcation Line and attacked the kibbutz of Misgav Am. To do this, they would have had to cross not only UNIFIL areas but also the enclave and the border. All five infiltrators and three Israeli civilians were killed.*

Harassment by *de facto* forces

The activities of the *de facto* forces under the command of Major Haddad also created serious difficulties for UNIFIL. No precise figures on the strength of those forces are available, but it is generally estimated that they numbered about 1,500 in June 1978. They were formed around a nucleus of some 700 former Christian soldiers of the Lebanese National Army, to which were added smaller groups of Christian phalangists from the north and locally recruited Christian and Shi'ite villagers. They were financed, trained, armed, uniformed and, by all evidence, controlled by the Israeli authorities.

The measures devised by UNIFIL to prevent infiltrations by the Palestinians and Lebanese leftist armed elements were also applied to the *de facto* forces, but there were few infiltrators from the enclave, and the main problems the United Nations encountered with these forces concerned their harassment of UNIFIL and the local population, and their attempts to encroach upon the UNIFIL area.

While making clear that full deployment in the enclave remained its main objective, UNIFIL concentrated its immediate efforts on preserving the installations it held there and on securing the freedom of movement it required for this purpose. With the assistance of the Israeli army, a *modus vivendi* was reached with the *de facto* forces whereby UNIFIL troops would enjoy freedom of movement on the main roads in the enclave five days a week in order to rotate personnel and resupply its installations. UNIFIL helicopters could fly over the enclave when necessary, but each overflight had to be cleared with Major Haddad's command on an *ad hoc* basis. However, even this limited freedom of movement was occasionally denied UNIFIL. When difficulties of one kind or another arose between UNIFIL and the *de facto* forces, Major Haddad would retaliate by closing the roads in the enclave to United Nations personnel and vehicles. This retaliatory measure would be taken either against UNIFIL as a whole or against specific contingents.

During periods of tension, some UNIFIL positions in the enclave, and particularly the five observation posts along the Armistice Demarcation Line, were at times completely isolated, and the United Nations personnel manning them subjected to severe harassment.

* S/13888.

In some cases, the observation posts were broken into by militiamen, their equipment stolen and the United Nations personnel threatened. On three occasions, the *de facto* forces attacked the UNIFIL head-quarters itself with mortar and artillery fire, causing casualties and considerable material damage.

In October 1978, at about the same time as the PLO intensified its attempts to infiltrate the UNIFIL area, the attitude of the *de facto* forces hardened further. These forces began to harass the local population in the UNIFIL area in various ways. A number of Shi'ite villages were subjected to occasional shelling from positions in the enclave, and the villagers were threatened with punitive measures if they continued to co-operate with UNIFIL. In a few instances, the *de facto* forces sent raiding parties into the UNIFIL area to abduct persons suspected of pro-PLO sentiments or to blow up their houses. This sort of pressure on the local population markedly increased after Major Haddad proclaimed the constitution of the so-called "State of Free Lebanon" in April 1979. UNIFIL strongly protested the harass-ment with the Israeli authorities. To deter attacks against villages in its area, it established additional positions in their vicinity.

From December 1978 onwards, the *de facto* forces made several attempts to set up positions within the UNIFIL area. These attempts were carried out by strongly armed groups, sometimes supported by tanks. Whenever this occurred, UNIFIL sent reinforcements to sur-round the raiding parties and, at the same time, tried by negotiation to have their positions removed, usually with the assistance of the Israeli army. In some cases, the raiding parties were persuaded to leave peacefully, but in others the negotiations were unsuccessful. Thus, five encroachment positions were established by the *de facto* forces between July 1979 and July 1980, all of which were located in strategic areas commanding views of important access roads.

To remove these positions, UNIFIL would have had to use force against the *de facto* forces and possibly the Israel Defence Forces, and casualties would have been heavy. In the circumstances, it was decided instead to seek a negotiated solution through the Israeli authorities. The Secretary-General raised this matter with the Israeli Government at the highest level but was told that Israel considered those positions important for its security and would not intervene to have them removed.

While, as a matter of principle and policy, UNIFIL sought to con-tain the actions of the *de facto* forces by negotiation, its troops were sometimes obliged to resist harassments and to use force in self-defence. Despite the restraint displayed by UNIFIL soldiers, violent incidents occurred in some cases.

On 24 April 1980, following an incident in which the *de facto* forces directed heavy shelling at UNIFIL headquarters, the Security Council adopted resolution 467(1980), by which it deplored all acts of hostilities against UNIFIL in or through its area of operation and condemned the deliberate shelling of the headquarters.

Israeli activities in and near the enclave

After 13 June 1978, the Israeli Government took the position that its forces had withdrawn from Lebanese territory in accordance with Security Council resolution 425(1978) and that henceforth it was no longer responsible for what happened in the enclave.

During the initial months, the presence of the Israel Defence Forces in the enclave appeared limited, but from November 1979 onwards, IDF activities increased. Israeli soldiers were frequently observed laying mines, manning check-points, transporting water and supplies and constructing new positions inside Lebanon in the border areas.

In late 1980,* UNIFIL reported an increasing number of encroachments by the IDF along the Armistice Demarcation Line. The original border-fence remained intact, but on the Lebanese side of it the IDF established new positions at selected points, laid minefields, fenced in strips of land and built dirt tracks and asphalt roads. At the same time, the presence of the IDF inside the enclave was greatly expanded. IDF gun and tank positions were established near Marjayoun, Major Haddad's headquarters, and along the coastal road. IDF personnel were sighted in various locations well inside the enclave. In the course of 1980, the IDF openly conducted military exercises near OP Khiam, a United Nations observation post north of the border.

On a number of occasions, the IDF carried out incursions into the UNIFIL area in search of PLO armed elements. UNIFIL took all possible measures to stop those incursions, and its efforts led at times to confrontations with IDF personnel, which were generally resolved by negotiation.

In addition to its activities in the enclave, the IDF frequently intruded into Lebanese air space and territorial waters. Its aircraft constantly flew over Lebanon for observation purposes and its patrol boats were often observed cruising near the Lebanese coast. The air and sea violations greatly increased after June 1980. During

* S/14295.

November 1980 alone, UNIFIL observed 312 air violations and 89 sea violations.

E. Hostile actions near the UNIFIL area

The UNIFIL area constituted an imperfect buffer between the opposing forces. As already described, the area was divided into two parts, with a gap of about 15 kilometres between them. In this gap, where the two opposing sides were separated only by the Litani River, UNIFIL was able to set up four positions, including one at the Khardala bridge, to provide at least a limited United Nations presence. But the gun positions of the PLO in its stronghold of Château de Beaufort north of the river, and those of the de facto forces in and around Marjayoun, reinforced in 1980 by IDF tanks and artillery, were not far apart. From its positions in the Tyre pocket and Château de Beaufort, the PLO's heavy artillery and rockets could easily reach villages and towns in northern Israel, including Nahariyya, Maalot, Metulla and Qiryat Shemona.

From March 1979 onwards, there were frequent exchanges of fire between the PLO and the de facto forces across the gap and over the UNIFIL area. When fighting intensified, the IDF would come to the support of the de facto forces and, in retaliation, PLO fighters would direct their heavy artillery and rockets at targets in northern Israel, which would in turn provoke violent reprisals by the IDF. Whenever PLO shelling resulted in Israeli casualties, and also after incidents inside Israel or Israeli-occupied territories for which the PLO claimed responsibility, the IDF would send its war-planes to launch massive attacks against PLO targets north of the UNIFIL area, sometimes as far as Beirut. In some cases, Israeli commandos were dispatched to destroy PLO installations.

Both the Israeli war-planes and the commandos would, as a rule, avoid the UNIFIL area by flying over the gap or taking the sea route. Since the armed forces engaged in the hostilities were located outside its area, UNIFIL could not take direct action to prevent or stop them. It did, however, endeavour to arrange cease-fires whenever possible, and brought the most serious cases to the attention of the Security Council.

Within one twelve-month period, there were two series of serious hostilities; one in August 1980 and the other in July 1981.

Hostilities of August 1980

During the evening of 18 August 1980, a heavy exchange of fire broke out between the IDF/*de facto* forces and PLO positions north of the Litani and continued with varying intensity for five days. According to UNIFIL observers,* the *de facto* forces fired approximately 2,460 rounds of artillery, mortar and tank fire, and the PLO armed elements about 300 rounds. On 19 and 20 August, Israeli war-planes attacked various PLO targets in the Château de Beaufort and Arnun areas.

On 19 August,† while the shelling and bombing were in progress, a group of about 200 IDF troops, transported by helicopter, carried out a commando raid to destroy PLO installations in and around the villages of Arnun and Kafr Tibnit. This operation was preceded by a buildup of IDF personnel and equipment throughout the enclave, where about 50 artillery pieces, 70 assorted vehicles and seven heavy helicopters were sighted by UNIFIL. According to Lebanese and Palestinian sources, the attacks resulted in at least 25 killed, including five Lebanese civilians, and 26 wounded, as well as very heavy destruction of houses and other property. The Israeli authorities indicated that the operation was intended to destroy PLO artillery and mortar nests which had shelled Israel's northern settlements and Major Haddad's enclave in southern Lebanon.

Hostilities of July 1981

The fighting which broke out in July 1981 was even more extensive. On 10 July, during an exchange of fire with the IDF/*de facto* forces' positions, PLO forces shelled the town of Qiryat Shemona in northern Israel with rockets, resulting, according to Israeli authorities, ‡ in the wounding of six civilians. On the same day,§ Israeli war-planes attacked PLO targets in Lebanon north of the UNIFIL area. The air attacks were followed by renewed exchanges of fire between the PLO armed elements' and the IDF and *de facto* forces' positions.

On 13 and 14 July, widespread Israeli air attacks continued and PLO armed elements again fired rockets into northern Israel, wounding, according to Israeli sources, two Israeli civilians in the coastal town of Nahariyya. The next day, there was a particularly heavy exchange of fire with a total of about 1,000 rounds of artillery, mortar and rockets fired by the two sides.

On 16 and 17 July, exchanges of fire intensified, with Israeli naval vessels joining in, while Israeli aircraft destroyed bridges on the Zahrani

* *Ibid.*   † S/14118.   ‡ S/14591.   § S/14789.

and Litani rivers and launched an intense attack on Beirut itself, causing heavy loss of life and damage to property. Exchanges of fire in all sectors, as well as Israeli air strikes and naval bombardments, continued on 18 and 19 July and, on a gradually declining scale, until 24 July.

During the period of intense violence in July, UNIFIL recorded the firing of some 7,500 rounds of artillery, mortar, tank and naval cannons by the IDF and the *de facto* forces, in addition to Israeli air strikes, and the firing of about 2,500 rounds of artillery, mortar and rockets by PLO armed elements. The total casualties during this period were six dead and 59 wounded on the Israeli side, immeasurably more among the Palestinians and Lebanese.

Security Council action

The Security Council met on 17 July 1981 at the request of the Lebanese Government. On the same day, the Council President issued an urgent appeal to the parties for restraint and an immediate end to all armed attacks.

On 21 July, the Council unanimously adopted resolution 490(1981), by which it called for an immediate cessation of all armed attacks and reaffirmed its commitment to the sovereignty, territorial integrity and independence of Lebanon within its internationally recognized boundaries.

July cease-fire

Following adoption of the resolution, parallel efforts undertaken by the United Nations and the United States Government led to the establishment of a *de facto* cease-fire on 24 July 1981.

On the morning of that day, Ambassador Philip Habib, the personal representative of the President of the United States, issued a statement in Jerusalem to the effect that, as of 1330 hours, 24 July 1981, all hostile military action between Lebanese and Israeli territory in either direction would cease.

The Secretary-General, who had been kept fully informed of the efforts of Ambassador Habib, immediately brought this statement to the attention of the Security Council.* He also reported to the Council that the Israeli Government had endorsed the statement, that the Lebanese Government had welcomed it, and that the PLO had assured him that it would observe the cease-fire called for by the Security Council.

* S/14613/Add.1.

The Commander of UNIFIL reported on 24 July that, as of 1320 hours local time, the area was quiet.

F. Efforts to restore the authority of the Lebanese Government in southern Lebanon

Civilian administration

After 13 June 1978, when it became apparent that Israeli control would continue in the enclave for an indefinite period, UNIFIL had to alter its original plan. While the Force would continue its efforts to assume control of the enclave through negotiations, it took action to help the Lebanese to deploy as many administrators and elements of the Lebanese army and the internal security forces (gendarmes) as possible in the area controlled by it.

Initially, UNIFIL's attention was focused on getting the Lebanese Government to send civilian administrative and technical personnel and elements of the Lebanese gendarmes to southern Lebanon. By late July 1978,* the Lebanese Government was represented south of the Litani River by a civilian administrator residing at Tyre, and by nearly 100 gendarmes based at Tyre and at three centres in the UNIFIL area. The gendarmes worked in close co-operation with UNIFIL. They assisted UNIFIL soldiers in the inspection of personnel and vehicles at check-points and, in many instances, served as interpreters and liaison officers with the local population. Civil offences reported to UNIFIL were handed over to the gendarmes for investigation.

UNIFIL carried out various humanitarian activities and rehabilitation programmes in close co-operation with the Lebanese authorities and the Co-ordinator of United Nations Assistance for the Reconstruction and Development of Lebanon. It took an active part in the execution of projects involving restoration of water, electricity and health services, distribution of supplementary food supplies and the rebuilding and repair of houses, schools and roads. The UNIFIL hospital maintained by the Swedish medical company in the Naqoura Camp and the medical facilities of its contingents were open to the local population, which used those services frequently.

* S/12845.

Army deployment, 1978

In the course of July 1978, extensive consultations were held between the Lebanese authorities and UNIFIL regarding the possibility of bringing Lebanese army units to the UNIFIL area of operation. Many obstacles had to be overcome. The de facto forces and the Israeli authorities were opposed to any move of the Lebanese army to the south. For different reasons, the PLO, which controlled the key coastal road from Sidon to Tyre, also opposed such a move.

The Lebanese National Army was still in the process of reconstruction and reorganization. Despite the difficulties involved, the Government of Lebanon decided to dispatch a task force of the Lebanese army to southern Lebanon on 31 July.* This task force, consisting of 700 men and equipment, was to travel to Tibnin through the Bekaa Valley, Kaoukaba, a village on the northern edge of the UNIFIL area, and Marjayoun, the headquarters of the de facto forces. The Secretary-General was informed of this decision on 25 July and an announcement was made by the Lebanese Government on the same day.

Following this announcement, UNIFIL contacted the Israeli authorities at various levels and requested their help to ensure that the de facto forces would not oppose the proposed move. The Israeli authorities refused to intervene on the grounds that it was a Lebanese internal affair.

The task force left the Beirut area in the early morning of 31 July and reached Kaoukaba a few hours later. On arrival, it was subjected to intense artillery and mortar fire by the de facto forces. Confronted with this hostile action, the task force stayed in Kaoukaba while the United Nations tried to negotiate agreement for its peaceful transit. But the Secretary-General and his representatives in the field failed to win the support of the Israeli authorities.

On the following days, the de facto forces continuously harassed the task force and fired more than 300 artillery rounds at it, killing one Lebanese soldier and wounding nine others. In August, the task force withdrew from Kaoukaba.

Army deployment, 1979

Following this attempt, UNIFIL engaged in new consultations with the Lebanese authorities in an effort to find alternative ways of bringing Lebanese army units into southern Lebanon.

* Ibid.

On 22 December 1978,* a joint working group of UNIFIL and Lebanese army officials was set up to work out a plan of action. On the proposal of the group, small teams of Lebanese army personnel were flown to southern Lebanon by UNIFIL helicopters and were assigned to various UNIFIL contingents to represent the Lebanese Government in their respective sectors.

In renewing the mandate of UNIFIL for a further period of five months, the Security Council, by resolution 444(1979) of 19 January 1979, invited the Lebanese Government to draw up, in consultation with the Secretary-General, a phased programme of activities to be carried out over the next three months to promote the restoration of its authority in southern Lebanon. The programme, as worked out by the Lebanese Government with the assistance of UNIFIL, set for its first phase four main objectives: (1) an increase of the Lebanese civilian administrative presence in the south; (2) the introduction of a battalion of the Lebanese National Army in the UNIFIL area; (3) the consolidation of the cease-fire in the area; and (4) further deployment of UNIFIL in the enclave.†

Within this programme, a Lebanese army battalion of 500 men was deployed in the UNIFIL area in April 1979. The *de facto* forces tried to prevent the deployment by subjecting UNIFIL headquarters and some of its positions to intense shelling from 15 to 18 April. These attacks caused casualties and heavy material damage, but UNIFIL stood firm, and the deployment of the Lebanese battalion proceeded as planned and was completed on 17 April. The Lebanese battalion, which was placed under the operational control of the Force Commander, set up its headquarters at Arzun in the Nigerian sector.

Army deployment, 1980–1981

In December 1980, the strength of the Lebanese battalion was increased to 617 men with the addition of some medical and engineering elements. Initially, the Lebanese battalion confined its activities to the immediate vicinity of Arzun, but, from early 1981 on, some of its units were gradually deployed in various UNIFIL sectors.

In June 1981,‡ a second Lebanese battalion was brought to the UNIFIL area, this time without incident, and raised the total strength of the Lebanese army presence in southern Lebanon to 1,350 all ranks. The new battalion included an engineering unit of 130, which assisted in various local projects, and a medical team of 10 assigned to the Tibnin hospital.

* S/13026.   † S/13258.   ‡ S/14537.

Efforts to reactivate the General Armistice Agreement

To promote the restoration of its authority and sovereignty in southern Lebanon, the Lebanese Government sought to reactivate the 1949 General Armistice Agreement between Israel and Lebanon and the Israel-Lebanon Mixed Armistice Commission (ILMAC) established under that Agreement.

In resolution 450(1979) of 14 June 1979, on a further extension of UNIFIL's mandate, the Security Council reaffirmed the validity of the General Armistice Agreement and called upon the parties to take the necessary steps to reactivate ILMAC. A plan of action, which the Secretary-General worked out in consultation with the Lebanese Government in September 1979,* set as the main long-term objective of the Force the restoration of the effective authority of the Lebanese Government in southern Lebanon up to the internationally recognized boundary, and the normalization of the area, including the reactivation of ILMAC in accordance with the 1949 Agreement.

In resolution 467(1980) of 24 April 1980, the Security Council requested the Secretary-General to convene a meeting of ILMAC, at an appropriate level, to agree on precise recommendations and further to reactivate the General Armistice Agreement conducive to the restoration of the sovereignty of Lebanon over all its territory up to the internationally recognized boundaries.

The Chief of Staff of UNTSO, General Erskine, who had been asked by the Secretary-General to follow up on that resolution, proposed on 18 November 1980 that a meeting preliminary to the convening of ILMAC be held at Naqoura on 1 December.† On 25 November, the Lebanese authorities agreed to the proposed meeting and insisted that it be attended by the Chairman of ILMAC. On 26 November, the Israeli authorities replied, stating that the Mixed Armistice Commission was no longer valid and that, as far as they were concerned, the proposed meeting could not be regarded as a preliminary meeting of ILMAC. They added, however, that this should not stand in the way of a meeting between Israeli and Lebanese representatives at the appropriate level, and they agreed to meet with the Lebanese representatives on the date and at the venue suggested by General Erskine.

The meeting took place at UNIFIL headquarters on 1 December 1980, ‡ under the chairmanship of the Chief of Staff of UNTSO. Israel and Lebanon were represented by senior military officers. Although the two sides disagreed on the validity of the General Armistice Agreement, they discussed the situation in southern Lebanon, par-

* S/13691.   † S/14295.   ‡ *Ibid.*

ticularly along the border. The Lebanese representative complained about the establishment of IDF positions in southern Lebanon and incursions by IDF personnel into Lebanese territory, while the Israeli representative asserted that Israel had no designs on Lebanon. Following this meeting, the UNTSO Chief of Staff kept in contact with both sides with a view to arranging another meeting in the near future, but no agreement could be reached.

G. Cease-fire: July 1981–April 1982

The cease-fire arrangements of 24 July 1981 were accepted by all the parties, and on that day all firing stopped (*see section E above*). UNIFIL kept close contact with the parties to ensure the maintenance of the cease-fire. Lieutenant-General William Callaghan, Commander of UNIFIL, obtained an undertaking from each of the parties that in the event of a breach of the cease-fire by the opposing side, the other side would exercise maximum restraint and, rather than take retaliatory action, would refer the matter to UNIFIL for resolution.

During the following days, however, the situation remained unstable because a dissident PLO group led by Mr. Ahmed Jebril continued to fire sporadically at targets in the enclave. General Callaghan strongly protested those violations of the cease-fire to the PLO command. Chairman Arafat replied that the firings were due to a misunderstanding and that the PLO was determined to observe strictly the cease-fire. On 27 July, following a meeting with Chairman Arafat, Mr. Jebril announced that his group would respect the cease-fire.

A second problem which threatened the cease-fire during the initial period arose from the continuing overflights of southern Lebanon by Israeli reconnaissance aircraft, which the PLO protested as violations of the cease-fire arrangements. In spite of approaches by the Commander of UNIFIL, Israel refused to stop such overflights on the grounds that they were not covered by the cease-fire arrangements. The Israeli overflights did not, however, provoke retaliatory action by the PLO.

The cease-fire held remarkably well until April 1982. For eight months the situation in southern Lebanon was quiet and there were no firings between the PLO and the IDF/*de facto* forces in the area.

With the restoration of the cease-fire in July 1981, the general situation in southern Lebanon had become much less tense. However, UNIFIL continued to experience serious difficulties with the armed elements of the PLO and the Lebanese National Movement on the one hand, and with the *de facto* forces of Major Haddad on the other. The armed elements continued their infiltration attempts after July 1981, though at a lower level. UNIFIL soldiers turned back 175 infiltrators in July 1981, 95 in August, 18 in September, 90 in October, 27 in November, 25 in December, 70 in January 1982, 27 in February, 98 in March, 69 in April and 27 in May. In a more serious development, PLO armed elements established additional positions in the UNIFIL area near the Tyre pocket. The Force immediately placed those positions under close surveillance to ensure that they would not be used for tactical or hostile purposes. At the same time, negotiations were undertaken with the PLO leadership to have them removed, but the talks were inconclusive.

Relations with the *de facto* forces also remained tense. Those forces continued to impose restrictions on UNIFIL's freedom of movement in the enclave. In the UNIFIL area of deployment, they not only continued to maintain four positions they had established, but set up a new one near the village of At Tiri, in the Irish sector.* The Force Commander sought the assistance of the Israeli authorities in this regard, stressing that the position was clearly provocative and might jeopardize the cease-fire. While the negotiations were in progress, the *de facto* forces harassed the UNIFIL headquarters at Naqoura and some of its positions in the enclave by cutting their supply lines. The harassments were eventually stopped with the help of the IDF, but the new position remained.

During this period of relative quiet, UNIFIL had to contend with a new problem in its area. In the later months, Amal, a Shi'ite political movement with a paramilitary organization, became more active in southern Lebanon, and there was mounting animosity between its followers and members of the pro-Palestinian Lebanese National Movement. Serious clashes broke out between the two groups in January and April 1982 in the Senegalese sector, and UNIFIL had to intervene to help restore law and order.

H. Israeli invasion: 1982–1985

Breakdown of the cease-fire

In early April 1982, tension markedly increased in southern Lebanon, not because of any violations of the cease-fire in the area but as a consequence of events elsewhere.

* S/14789.

On 3 April, an Israeli diplomat was assassinated in Paris and the Israeli Government held the PLO responsible, although responsibility was denied by that organization. On 13 April,* the Permanent Representative of Israel to the United Nations complained to the Security Council that, on the previous night, two PLO terrorists with large quantities of explosives had attempted to infiltrate into Israel from Jordanian territory. On 21 April, Israel launched massive air attacks against PLO targets in southern Lebanon. The PLO took no retaliatory action.

On the same day, the Secretary-General appealed for an immediate cessation of all hostile acts and urged all parties to exercise maximum restraint so that the cease-fire could be fully restored and maintained. On 22 April, the President of the Security Council issued a statement on behalf of the members of the Council in which he demanded an end to all armed attacks and warned against any recurrence of violations of the cease-fire, in accordance with Security Council resolution 490(1981) of 21 July 1981.

On 9 May 1982, Israeli aircraft again attacked PLO targets in several localities in Lebanon, causing many casualties. Following these attacks, PLO positions in the Tyre pocket fired rockets into northern Israel, for the first time since July 1981. The next day, the Lebanese Government strongly protested the Israeli air attacks as an act of aggression against Lebanon.† The Permanent Representative of Israel also addressed a letter to the President of the Council on that day in which he drew attention to recent terrorist attacks against civilians in Israel, for which Israel held the PLO responsible. ‡ Intense efforts were made by the United Nations, both at its New York Headquarters and in the field, to restore the cease-fire. There were no further incidents in the area in May, but the situation remained extremely volatile.

On the night of 3 June, the Israeli Ambassador to the United Kingdom was seriously wounded in London in a terrorist attack. Although the PLO disclaimed any responsibility for this assassination attempt, Israel launched on 4 June massive bombing raids against PLO targets in and around Beirut, causing heavy loss of life and destruction. Shortly after those attacks, intense exchanges of fire broke out between the PLO and the IDF/*de facto* forces' positions in southern Lebanon, over the UNIFIL area. The Israeli towns of Nahariyya, Qiryat Shemona and Metulla came under PLO artillery and rocket fire.

On the same afternoon, the Secretary-General urgently appealed to all concerned to desist from all hostile acts and to make

* S/14972. † S/15064. ‡ S/15066.

every effort to restore the cease-fire. Later that day, the President of the Security Council made a similar appeal on behalf of the members of the Council. Nevertheless, the exchanges of artillery fire continued unabated on 5 June in the same general areas. There were also intense Israeli air strikes in the vicinity of Beirut and Damur, and shelling by Israeli naval vessels in the Tyre area.

The Secretary-General, who was in continuous touch with the parties concerned, again made an urgent appeal on 5 June for a simultaneous cessation of hostilities at the earliest possible time. Later the same day, the Security Council met and unanimously adopted resolution 508(1982), by which it called upon all the parties to the conflict to cease immediately and simultaneously all military activities within Lebanon and across the Israeli-Lebanese border no later than 0600 hours local time on Sunday, 6 June.

Immediately after the adoption of that resolution, the Secretary-General instructed the Commander of UNIFIL to utilize every possibility of following up on the Council's resolution.* On the same evening, the PLO reaffirmed its commitment to stop all military operations across the Lebanese border, while reserving the right to respond to Israeli attacks. The Permanent Representative of Israel to the United Nations informed the Secretary-General that, while Israeli actions were taken in the exercise of its right of self-defence, the Council's resolution would be brought before the Israeli Cabinet. From 2300 hours local time on 5 June until 0600 hours the next morning, there were intermittent and relatively light exchanges of fire between the opposing sides, but shortly after 0600 hours, which was the cease-fire time set by the Security Council, Israeli forces launched intensive air attacks against various PLO targets in southern Lebanon.

Israeli invasion, June 1982

At 1030 hours local time on the morning of 6 June, General Callaghan met with Lieutenant-General Rafael Eitan, the Chief of Staff of the IDF, at Metulla in northern Israel.† General Callaghan's purpose was to discuss the implementation of Security Council resolution 508(1982), but instead he was told by General Eitan that the IDF planned to launch a military operation into Lebanon within half an hour, at 1100 hours local time. General Eitan also intimated that the Israeli forces would pass through or near UNIFIL positions and that he expected that UNIFIL would raise no physical difficulty to the advancing troops. General Callaghan pro-

* S/15194/Add.1   † *Ibid.*

tested in the strongest terms at this totally unacceptable course of action.

Immediately after the meeting, General Callaghan issued instructions to all UNIFIL units, in case of attack by one of the parties, to block advancing forces, take defensive measures and stay in their positions unless their safety was "seriously imperilled".

At 1100 hours local time, about two IDF mechanized divisions, with full air and naval support, crossed the border and entered the UNIFIL area. They advanced along three main axes: in the western sector, along the coastal road; in the central sector, towards At Tayyibah and the Akiya bridge; and in the eastern sector, through the Chouba–Chebaa area.

In accordance with their general instructions, UNIFIL troops took various measures to stop, or at least delay, the advance of the Israeli forces. On the coastal road leading to Tyre, Dutch soldiers planted obstacles before an advancing Israeli tank column and damaged one tank. During the encounter, Israeli tank barrels were trained on the Dutch soldiers while Israeli troops pushed aside the obstacles.

Other UNIFIL battalions also put up obstacles of various kinds, which were forcibly removed or bulldozed. A small Nepalese position guarding the Khardala bridge stood its ground for two days despite continued harassments and threats. Only after two days, on the morning of 8 June, could the Israeli tanks cross the bridge after partially destroying the Nepalese position.

Despite these efforts, the UNIFIL soldiers with their light defensive weapons could not withstand the massive Israeli invading forces, and the UNIFIL positions in the line of the invasion were bypassed or overrun within 24 hours. One Norwegian soldier was killed by shrapnel on 6 June.

On the morning of 6 June, the Security Council met again and unanimously adopted resolution 509(1982), by which it demanded that Israel withdraw all its military forces forthwith and unconditionally to the internationally recognized boundaries of Lebanon, and that all parties strictly observe the cease-fire.

On the evening of 7 June, Chairman Arafat informed the Secretary-General that the Lebanese-Palestinian joint command had decided to abide by the Security Council's resolution.* The Permanent Representative of Israel replied on behalf of his Government that the "Peace for Galilee" operation had been ordered because of the intolerable situation created by the presence in Lebanon of a large number of "terrorists" operating from that country and threatening the lives of the civilians of Galilee, and that any withdrawal of Israeli

---

* S/15178.

forces prior to the conclusion of concrete arrangements which would permanently and reliably preclude hostile action against Israel's citizens was inconceivable.*

UNIFIL's interim tasks

In commenting on the invasion in his report of 14 June 1982 to the Security Council,† the Secretary-General stated that UNIFIL, like all other United Nations peace-keeping operations, was based on certain fundamental principles, foremost of which was the non-use of force, except in self-defence. The Force was not meant to engage in combat to attain its goals; it had a strictly limited strength, armed only with light defensive weapons. It was for these reasons that certain essential conditions had been laid down at the time of the establishment of the Force. Those included, first, that it must function with the full co-operation of the parties concerned and, second, that it must have at all times the full confidence and backing of the Security Council. In this connection, it was a fundamental assumption that the parties would fully abide by the Council's decisions and that, in the event of non-compliance, the Council itself and those Member States in a position to bring their influence to bear would be able to act decisively to ensure respect for those decisions.

In the case of UNIFIL, those conditions were not met. Instead, UNIFIL had been faced with inadequate co-operation throughout its existence, culminating in an overwhelming use of force. Once the Israeli action commenced, it was evident that UNIFIL troops could, at best, maintain their positions and take defensive measures, seeking to impede and protest the advance.

The Israeli invasion of June 1982 radically altered the circumstances in which UNIFIL had been set up and under which it had functioned since March 1978. By 8 June, the UNIFIL area of operation had fallen under Israeli control and the Force had to operate behind the Israeli lines. Under those conditions, UNIFIL could no longer fulfil the tasks entrusted to it by the Security Council. Pending a Council decision on the Force's mandate, which was due to expire on 19 June 1982, the Secretary-General instructed General Callaghan, as an interim measure, to ensure that all UNIFIL troops and the UNTSO military observers attached to it continued to man their positions unless their safety was seriously imperilled, and to provide protection and humanitarian assistance to the local population to the extent possible. ‡

* *Ibid*   † S/15194/Add.2.   ‡ S/15194/Add.1.

These interim tasks were endorsed by the Security Council on 18 June, when it decided, by resolution 511(1982), to extend the mandate of UNIFIL for an interim period of two months. At the same time, the Council made clear that the Force's original terms of reference remained valid, and reaffirmed its call for the complete withdrawal of the Israeli forces from Lebanese territory.

In accordance with the instructions of the Secretary-General, UNIFIL remained deployed in its area of operation with only minor adjustments. Some positions considered as non-essential in the changed circumstances were closed down, while others were reinforced. UNTSO observers continued to man the five observation positions along the Armistice Demarcation Line and to maintain three teams outside the UNIFIL area—at Tyre, at Metulla in northern Israel and at Château de Beaufort north of the Litani River.

Much in the same way as they had done before the invasion, UNIFIL troops operated observation posts and check-points and conducted patrols in sensitive areas in order to prevent hostile actions and to do what they could to ensure the security and safety of the local population. They continued to prevent infiltrations and incursions into the UNIFIL area by armed irregulars. But they could not control the movement and actions of the Israeli forces or of the irregulars when they acted with those forces' direct support. In such cases, UNIFIL could only monitor their activities and report to the Secretary-General. In carrying out their functions, the UNIFIL troops co-operated closely with the local authorities and with the Lebanese gendarmes when they were available.

In addition, UNIFIL's efforts were devoted to humanitarian assistance. In co-operation with the United Nations Children's Fund (UNICEF) and the International Committee of the Red Cross, UNIFIL humanitarian teams distributed to needy local inhabitants food and water and other essential supplies. The UNIFIL hospital at Naqoura and the medical teams of the various national contingents dispensed medical care to the local population, including vaccination campaigns for Lebanese children. UNIFIL also assisted the local authorities with various community projects and with the repair of public buildings such as schools and local dispensaries. A French engineering unit did much to clear the area of mines, shells and explosive devices, which were a constant danger to the population. In many cases, the officers and soldiers of the various contingents made voluntary contributions to help villages in their sectors. Further, Governments of troop-contributing countries provided assistance in the form of new schools or medical centres in their battalions' sectors.

Soon after the invasion, the Israeli forces' presence in the UNIFIL area of deployment was reduced to approximately battalion strength. However, in mid–1983 the activities of a Shi'ite resistance movement against the Israeli occupation, which became increasingly active in the northern part of the occupied territory, began to spill over into the UNIFIL area. Although the area remained relatively quiet until February 1985, there were occasional attacks against the Israeli forces by resistance groups, particularly in the form of roadside bombs, and counter-measures by the Israeli forces, mainly in the form of cordon-and-search operations in the Shi'ite villages. UNIFIL could not prevent counter-measures by the Israeli forces, but endeavoured, by pressure and persuasion, to mitigate violence, and protect the civilian population as much as possible. It also provided medical care and humanitarian assistance to the affected population.

In April 1984, three months after the death of Major Haddad, Major-General Antoine Lahad, also a former officer of the Lebanese National Army, took over the command of the *de facto* forces, which were now calling themselves the "South Lebanon Army" (SLA). According to available information, the strength of the SLA had been increased to approximately 2,100 as of October 1984. Although Israel gave the SLA an expanded role in the northern part of the occupied territory, it did not make any determined attempt to increase its activities in the UNIFIL area.

More serious problems were encountered by UNIFIL when new local militias, armed and uniformed by Israel, began to appear in its area towards the end of June 1982.* Like the SLA, these militias were not recognized by the Lebanese Government or by the established local authorities. Acting with the assistance of the IDF and under its control, they attempted to set up check-points and conduct patrols in the villages. They were generally ill-disciplined and their actions were deeply resented by the local inhabitants and often led to friction with them. UNIFIL was under standing instructions to disarm the local militias and to contain their activities whenever they were not accompanied and directly protected by the Israeli forces. A number of incidents occurred at UNIFIL check-points when militiamen refused to submit to having their vehicles searched or to surrender their weapons.

Until February 1985, the incidents outlined above were exceptions rather than the rule, and the situation in the UNIFIL area was generally quiet—much quieter than in other parts of Lebanon during those years of turmoil. This was widely recognized by the Lebanese Government and the local population. Each time the mandate

* S/15357.

of UNIFIL neared its expiration, many *mukhtars* (village mayors) would write to the Secretary-General to beseech him not to withdraw the Force, and the Lebanese Government would request its extension in insistent terms.

The Secretary-General repeatedly recommended the extension of UNIFIL's mandate in accordance with the requests of the Lebanese Government. In support of his recommendation, he pointed out that despite the difficulties confronted by it, UNIFIL remained an important element of stability in southern Lebanon. Its presence represented the commitment of the United Nations to support the independence, sovereignty and territorial integrity of Lebanon and to help bring about the withdrawal of the Israeli forces from Lebanese territory, in accordance with Security Council resolutions 425(1978) and 509(1982). A withdrawal of the Force before the Lebanese Government was in a position to assume effective control of the area with its national army and its internal security forces would unquestionably be a serious blow to the prospect of restoring the authority of that Government in southern Lebanon, as well as to the security and welfare of the local population.*

I. **Withdrawal of Israeli forces**

In the mean time, efforts had continued to achieve the withdrawal of the Israeli forces from Lebanon. In the autumn of 1982, the United States had undertaken a diplomatic initiative which led to the signing, on 17 May 1983, of an agreement between Israel and Lebanon. In essence, it provided for the withdrawal of the Israeli and other non-Lebanese forces from Lebanon and for joint security arrangements in southern Lebanon. However, the agreement never came into effect and was eventually abrogated by the Government of Lebanon.

In early September 1983, the Israeli forces, which had been frequently attacked by Lebanese Moslem guerrilla groups, redeployed from the Shuf mountains to south of the Awali River.

In his report of 9 October 1984 to the Security Council,† the Secretary-General noted that there was general agreement that an expanded mandate for UNIFIL and a widening of its area of operation would be key elements in future arrangements for bringing about the withdrawal of Israeli forces from southern Lebanon and ensuring peace and security in the region and the restoration of Lebanese authority and sovereignty. In extending the mandate of UNIFIL on 12

* S/16036.   † S/16776.

October, the Security Council requested the Secretary-General to continue consultations with the Government of Lebanon and other parties directly concerned.

Naqoura talks (November 1984–January 1985)

Following the adoption of the Security Council's resolution, the Secretary-General approached the Governments of Israel and Lebanon and suggested that they begin negotiations as soon as possible on the withdrawal of Israeli forces from Lebanese territory and related security arrangements in southern Lebanon. After consultations with those Governments, he convoked a conference of military representatives of the two countries at UNIFIL headquarters in Naqoura to discuss those topics. The conference began on 8 November 1984 and met intermittently until 24 January 1985.*

From the outset of the conference, the Lebanese representative insisted on the full withdrawal of Israeli forces from Lebanese territory and the subsequent deployment of the Lebanese army together with UNIFIL down to the international boundary, in accordance with Security Council resolution 425(1978). The Israeli representative took the position that UNIFIL should be deployed in the entire area to be evacuated by the Israeli forces, with its main strength being deployed between the Zahrani and the Awali rivers and eastward to the border between Lebanon and Syria. While Israel would accept a limited UNIFIL presence further south, the Israeli representative maintained that local forces should be responsible for security arrangements in the southernmost part of Lebanon. There was little change in these basic positions as the conference progressed.

On 14 January 1985, the Israeli Government announced a plan for the unilateral redeployment of the Israeli forces in three phases, which was formally presented to the Naqoura conference on 22 January. In the first phase, relating to the western sector, the Israel Defence Forces would evacuate the Sidon area and deploy in the Litani–Nabatiyah region. In the second phase, relating to the eastern sector, the IDF would deploy in the Hasbayya area. In the third phase, it would deploy along the Israel-Lebanon international border, while maintaining a security zone in southern Lebanon where local forces (the so-called "South Lebanon Army") would function with IDF backing.

The first phase would be carried out within five weeks. Notification of the timing would be given to the Lebanese Government and the United Nations Secretariat in order to allow them to make ar-

---

* S/17093.

rangements and deploy forces in the areas to be evacuated by the IDF. The timing of each subsequent phase would be decided by the Government. Israeli officials indicated subsequently that the second and third phases of the redeployment were tentatively scheduled to be completed in the spring and summer of 1985.

On 24 January 1985, the Lebanese representative announced at the conference that the Israeli redeployment plan did not satisfy his Government's demand for a detailed plan and timetable for the complete withdrawal of Israeli forces from Lebanese territory. While reiterating his Government's willingness to co-operate with the United Nations with a view to expediting the withdrawal of those forces, he maintained that the role of the United Nations could not be discussed before the presentation of such a detailed plan and timetable by Israel.

At the end of the fourteenth meeting, on that date, the Naqoura conference was adjourned *sine die.*

Withdrawal of Israeli forces from the Sidon area

On 16 February, the Israeli forces proceeded with the first phase of the redeployment plan and withdrew from the Sidon area. Early that morning, the Commander of UNIFIL was informed of the withdrawal and immediately communicated it to the Lebanese army authorities. Those authorities advised General Callaghan the next day that the Lebanese army had taken over the evacuated area without incident.

From early February onwards, and particularly after the withdrawal from Sidon, there was an intensification of guerrilla attacks against the Israeli forces by Shi'ite resistance groups and of Israeli cordon-and-search operations against Shi'ite villages. An increasing number of these operations occurred in the UNIFIL area. In a statement made on 27 February,* the Secretary-General outlined the dilemma faced by UNIFIL. He stated that for obvious reasons the Force had no right to impede Lebanese acts of resistance against the occupying forces, nor did it have the mandate and the means to prevent Israeli countermeasures. In the circumstances, UNIFIL personnel had done their utmost to mitigate violence, protect the civilian population and reduce acts of reprisal to the minimum.

At the request of Lebanon, the Security Council held four meetings from 28 February to 12 March to consider the situation. On 12 March, the Security Council voted on a draft resolution submitted

* *Ibid.*

by Lebanon, but did not adopt it. owing to the negative vote of the United States.

Further withdrawals of the Israeli forces

The Israeli forces carried out the second phase of their redeployment in the course of March and April 1985.* At the end of the second phase, they were redeployed in a strip of land north of the international border extending from the Mediterranean Sea to the Hasbayya area, with a depth varying between about two kilometres at its narrowest point and about 20 kilometres at its widest.

Following the extension of the UNIFIL mandate by the Security Council in April 1985, the Secretary-General initiated a new effort to work out, in consultation with the Lebanese and Israeli authorities, arrangements which would lead to the full withdrawal of the Israeli forces, the deployment of UNIFIL to the international border and the establishment of international peace and security in the area. These efforts were not successful, and the Israeli forces proceeded with the third phase of the unilateral redeployment plan, without change, handing over their positions to the SLA. On 10 June, the Israeli Government announced that the third phase had been completed. It indicated that, while all combat units had been withdrawn from Lebanese territory, some Israeli troops would continue to operate in the "security zone" for an unspecified period of time and act as advisers to the SLA.

Since then, Israel has continued to control a substantial part of southern Lebanon. The boundaries of the area under its control have not been clearly defined but are determined *de facto* by the forward positions of IDF/SLA. It includes the land adjacent to the international border, part of the area where UNIFIL is deployed, and sizeable areas to the north of the UNIFIL area. As of January 1990, IDF/SLA maintained no less than 70 positions in the UNIFIL area of operation.

J. **Situation since 1985**

Since 1985, the situation in the UNIFIL area of operation has remained essentially unchanged. Israel has maintained its presence in Lebanon, on the grounds that this is necessary to ensure Israel's security so long as the Lebanese Government is not able to exercise effective authority and prevent its territory from being used to launch attacks against northern Israel. The Israeli authorities

* S/17557.

have held that UNIFIL, as a peace-keeping force, is not capable of assuming this responsibility. Accordingly, the IDF has improved its fortifications along the border, many of them on Lebanese territory, and strengthened the SLA. It has also gradually established a civilian administration in the area it controls. That administration has assumed responsibilities for police, intelligence, the collection of taxes and other levies and various other functions. It also issues permits required for residents of the Israeli-controlled area to travel to other parts of Lebanon.

The Secretary-General has made every effort, at all levels, to convince the Israeli authorities to complete the withdrawal of their forces from Lebanon. However, with the exception of the withdrawal of the SLA from two positions near Yatar in October 1987, Israel has insisted on maintaining, and indeed strengthening, its control in southern Lebanon.

As a consequence, and indeed as forecast by the Secretary-General in his reports to the Security Council, the IDF/SLA positions in Lebanon have remained targets for attacks by Lebanese groups opposed to the Israeli occupation. Such attacks have generally been on a small scale but occasionally they have involved sizeable and co-ordinated military operations leading sometimes to pitched battles. The main targets have been the positions at the forward edge of the Israeli-controlled area, including those located inside UNIFIL battalion sectors. As a result, UNIFIL has often found itself between two fires: on the one hand, the Lebanese groups attacking the Israeli forces and their Lebanese auxiliary, the SLA; on the other hand, those very forces reacting, often with heavy weapons and with air support from Israel, to the attacks directed against them.

In carrying out its tasks in these difficult circumstances, UNIFIL has sustained numerous casualties, including fatal ones. These have generally been the result of UNIFIL personnel being caught in crossfire or injured by explosive devices intended for others but, at times, members of the Force have themselves become the target.

A serious crisis erupted following an incident late on 11 August 1986, during which two men, one of them a local leader of the Amal movement, were shot and killed by a French sentry in a confrontation at a check-point near the village of Abbasiyah. Shortly afterwards, members of Amal and other armed elements attacked 10 positions manned by French troops. This intense round of attacks ended in the early afternoon of the next day, but sporadic attacks by unidentified persons continued until 28 September 1986, resulting in 3 French soldiers being killed and 24 wounded.

In response to these events, UNIFIL took urgent measures to improve the security of its troops. A crash programme was launched to provide for additional shelters and to improve the physical defences at positions, certain vulnerable positions were closed, patrolling procedures were revised and additional security precautions were instituted. In December 1986/January 1987, a major redeployment took place following the withdrawal of the French infantry battalion. It resulted in a consolidation of the Force's deployment in fewer but more effective and better protected positions. In addition, the Force reserve, which had previously been drawn from the battalions as the need arose, was established as a permanent composite unit, the Force Mobile Reserve.

K. Financial aspects

Throughout its existence, UNIFIL has had to cope with serious financial problems. When the Force was set up in March 1978, the Council decided, upon a proposal of the Secretary-General, that the costs of the new Force should be considered as expenses of the Organization to be borne by the Members as apportioned by the General Assembly.

However, a number of Member States have refused, for political reasons, to pay their assessed contributions, and as a result there has been a deficit in the UNIFIL Special Account which has steadily increased with the passing of time. In this situation, the United Nations has been forced to fall further and further behind in reimbursing Governments for the costs they have incurred in contributing troops, equipment and supplies to UNIFIL.

In December 1979, on a proposal of the Secretary-General, the General Assembly established a Suspense Account for UNIFIL—supplementing the Special Account—to be financed by voluntary contributions from Governments, international organizations and private sources. The funds in the Suspense Account were to be used solely for reimbursing Governments which contributed troops to UNIFIL.

The Secretary-General has repeatedly appealed to all Member States to pay their assessments without delay. Since 1979, he has also appealed to the Governments of the developed countries to consider making available, as a practical measure, voluntary contributions to UNIFIL's Suspense Account. However, the deficit in the UNIFIL budget has remained serious.

In his report to the Security Council on UNIFIL dated 25 January 1990,* the Secretary-General stated that, as of the beginning of that month, unpaid assessed contributions to the UNIFIL Special Account amounted to $318 million, which was equivalent to the budget of the Force for over two years at the current rate of expenditure. As a result, the Organization was falling far behind in reimbursement of the troop-contributing countries, thus placing an increasingly heavy burden on them, particularly on the less wealthy ones. The Secretary-General expressed on many occasions his extreme concern about the shortfall accumulated over the years in the UNIFIL Special Account, not only for the reasons just mentioned but also because it could jeopardize the functioning of the Force.

L. Conclusion

As is clear from this chapter, UNIFIL has been prevented from implementing the mandate given to it by the Security Council. In these circumstances, the Force has used its best efforts to keep the area where it is deployed free from hostilities and to shield its inhabitants from the worst effects of the violence that nevertheless occurs. It has also provided humanitarian assistance. Despite the continuing impasse, the Security Council has repeatedly extended the mandate of the Force at the request of the Government of Lebanon and on the recommendation of the Secretary-General.

In recommending the extensions, the Secretary-General has emphasized the role played by UNIFIL in controlling the level of violence in its area of operation and thus reducing the risk of a wider conflagration in the region; he has stressed its importance as a symbol of the international community's commitment to the sovereignty, independence and territorial integrity of Lebanon; and he has reiterated the conviction that the solution to the problems of southern Lebanon lies in the full implementation of Security Council resolution 425(1978), which contains the original mandate of UNIFIL.

* S/21102.

Part III **India and Pakistan**

Chapter VII United Nations Military Observer Group in India and Pakistan and United Nations India-Pakistan Observation Mission

A. Background

The United Nations Military Observer Group in India and Pakistan (UNMOGIP) had its origin in the conflict between India and Pakistan over the status of the State of Jammu and Kashmir (referred to here as Kashmir). The United Nations India-Pakistan Observation Mission (UNIPOM) was an administrative adjunct, created when conflict occurred in 1965 along the borders of the two countries outside the UNMOGIP area.

In August 1947, India and Pakistan became independent dominions, in accordance with a scheme of partition provided by the Indian Independence Act of 1947. Under that scheme, the State of Jammu and Kashmir was free to accede to India or Pakistan. The accession became a matter of dispute between the two countries and fighting broke out later that year.

The question first came before the Security Council in January 1948,* when India complained that tribesmen and others were invading Kashmir and that extensive fighting was taking place. India charged that Pakistan was assisting and participating in the invasion. Pakistan denied India's charges and declared that Kashmir's accession to India following India's independence in 1947 was illegal.

B. United Nations Commission for India and Pakistan

Security Council action

On 20 January, the Council adopted resolution 39(1948) establishing a three-member United Nations Commission for India

* S/628.

and Pakistan (UNCIP) "to investigate the facts pursuant to Article 34 of the Charter of the United Nations" and "to exercise. . .any mediatory influence likely to smooth away difficulties. . .".

Although India and Pakistan were consulted on the above resolution, serious disagreement arose between the two Governments regarding its implementation, and the proposed Commission could not be constituted.

On 21 April 1948, the Security Council met again and adopted resolution 47(1948), by which it decided to enlarge the membership of the Commission from three to five (Argentina, Belgium, Colombia, Czechoslovakia and the United States), and instructed it to proceed at once to the subcontinent. There it was to place its good offices at the disposal of the two Governments to facilitate the taking of the necessary measures with respect to both the restoration of peace and the holding of a plebiscite in the State of Jammu and Kashmir. The Commission was also to establish in Jammu and Kashmir such observers as it might require.

Commission action

The United Nations Commission for India and Pakistan arrived in the subcontinent on 7 July 1948 and immediately engaged in consultations with the Indian and Pakistan authorities. On 20 July, the Commission asked the Secretary-General to appoint and send, if possible at once, a high-ranking officer to act as military adviser to the Commission, and further to appoint officers and necessary personnel who would be ready to travel to the Indian subcontinent at a moment's notice in order to supervise the cease-fire if and when it was reached.*

UNCIP mission

After undertaking a survey of the situation in the area, UNCIP unanimously adopted a resolution on 13 August,† proposing to India and Pakistan that their respective high commands order a cease-fire and refrain from reinforcing the troops under their control in Kashmir. The resolution provided for the appointment by the Commission of military observers who, under the Commission's authority and with the co-operation of both commands, would supervise the observance of the cease-fire order. It also proposed to the Governments that they accept certain principles as a basis for the formulation of a truce agreement, and stated that UNCIP would have observers stationed where it deemed necessary.

* S/1100, annex 25.   † S/995, section 1.

c. **Supervision of the cease-fire, 1948–1965**

Military adviser

On 19 November 1948, the Commission received an urgent communication from the Minister for Foreign Affairs of Pakistan concerning alleged reinforcements of the Indian troops in Kashmir and attacks by those troops against positions held by forces of the Azad (Free) Kashmir movement.* There was immediate need for an independent source of information on the military situation in the State, and UNCIP recommended urgently that a military adviser be appointed and proceed forthwith to the subcontinent. It further requested the Secretary-General to provide an adequate number of military observers to assist the adviser. On 11 December 1948,† UNCIP submitted to India and Pakistan some new proposals for the holding of a plebiscite in Kashmir upon the signing of a truce agreement, which were accepted by the two Governments.‡ On 1 January 1949, both Governments announced their agreement to order a cease-fire effective one minute before midnight, local time, on that day.§

Arrival of observers

The Secretary-General appointed Lieutenant-General Maurice Delvoie of Belgium as Military Adviser to the Commission. General Delvoie arrived in the mission area on 2 January 1949. On 15 January, the Indian and Pakistan high commands conferred in New Delhi and formalized the cease-fire in Kashmir. The UNCIP Military Adviser, who was invited to join the conference, presented to them a plan for the organization and deployment of the military observers in the area.‖ This plan was put into effect on the Pakistan side on 3 February, and on the Indian side on 10 February 1949. A first group of seven United Nations military observers had arrived on 24 January. Their number was increased to 20 in early February. These observers, under the command of the Military Adviser, formed the nucleus of UNMOGIP.

Observers' tasks

In accordance with the Military Adviser's plan, the observers were divided into two groups, one attached to each army.

* S/1196, annex 1.   † S/1196, annex 3.   ‡ S/1196, annexes 4 and 5.
§ S/1196, annex 6.   ‖ S/1430, annex 47.

The senior officer of each group established a "control headquarters" under the direct command of the Military Adviser and in close liaison with the commander of the operations theatre on his side. Each group was divided into teams of two observers, attached to the tactical formations in the field and directly responsible to the control headquarters. The control headquarters on the Pakistan side was located at Rawalpindi. The one on the Indian side was first established at Jammu; later, at the end of March, it was transferred to Srinagar.

The tasks of the observers, as defined by the Military Adviser, were to accompany the local authorities in their investigations, gather as much information as possible, and report as completely, accurately and impartially as possible to the observer in charge of the group.

Any direct intervention by the observers between the opposing parties or any interference in the armies' orders were to be avoided. The local commanders might bring alleged violations of the cease-fire by the other side to the attention of the observers for their action. These arrangements remained in effect until the conclusion of the Karachi Agreement *(see below)*.

The administrative arrangements laid down for the UNMOGIP observers and the general principles under which they function are the same as those for the United Nations Truce Supervision Organization in Palestine *(see Part Two, chapter II)*.

Plebiscite Administrator

With the entering into force of the cease-fire, the situation became quieter. After a brief visit to New York, UNCIP returned to the subcontinent on 4 February 1949 and resumed negotiations with the parties towards the full implementation of Security Council resolution 47 (1948). Earlier in the year, Fleet Admiral Chester W. Nimitz, of the United States, had been appointed by the Secretary-General, in consultation with the two parties and with UNCIP, as United Nations Plebiscite Administrator.

Supervision of the Karachi Agreement

On 18 July 1949, military representatives of the two Governments met at Karachi under the auspices of UNCIP, and on 27 July they signed an Agreement establishing a cease-fire line.* The Agreement specifies that UNCIP would station observers where it deemed necessary, and that the cease-fire line would be verified mutually on the ground by local commanders on each side with the

* S/1430, annex 26.

assistance of the United Nations military observers. Disagreements were to be referred to the Commission's Military Adviser, whose decision would be final. After verification, the Adviser would issue to each high command a map on which would be marked the definitive cease-fire line. The Agreement further sets forth certain activities which are prohibited on either side of the cease-fire line, such as the strengthening of defences or the increase of forces in certain areas, as well as the introduction of additional military potential into Kashmir.

Listing of cease-fire breaches

Interpretations of the Agreement were agreed upon during the demarcation of the cease-fire line on the ground and during the resulting adjustment of forward positions by both armies. An agreed list of acts to be considered as breaches of the cease-fire was established by the Military Adviser on 16 September 1949.

This list was later revised with the agreement of the parties and, in its final form,* encompassed six categories of activity, namely: (1) crossing of the cease-fire line, (2) firing and use of explosives within five miles of the line, (3) new wiring and mining of any positions, (4) reinforcing existing forward defended localities with men or warlike stores, (5) forward movement from outside Kashmir of any warlike stores, equipment and personnel, except for relief and maintenance, and (6) flying of aircraft over the other side's territory.

While the Karachi Agreement established a cease-fire line in Kashmir, it did not include the border between Pakistan and that State, which runs in a general easterly direction from the southern extremity of the cease-fire line at Manawar. In this connection, the Chief Military Observer agreed on 11 February 1950, at the request of both parties, that the UNMOGIP observers would investigate all incidents on the border between Pakistan and Kashmir reported to them by both armies, solely for the purpose of determining whether or not military forces from either side were involved.

UNCIP report to the Security Council

In September 1949, UNCIP decided to return to New York to report to the Security Council. In a press statement issued on 22 September on this subject,† the Commission recalled that Security Council resolution 47(1948) of 21 April 1948 envisaged three related but distinct steps: a cease-fire, a truce period during which

---

* S/6888.   † S/1430, annex 41.

the withdrawal of forces would take place and, finally, consultations to establish the conditions by means of which the free will of the people of Kashmir would be expressed. The first objective had been achieved but, despite the Commission's efforts, no agreement could be secured on the other two.

Concluding that the possibilities of its mediation had been exhausted, UNCIP decided to return to New York. However, it reaffirmed its belief that a peaceful solution of the problem of Kashmir could be reached, and expressed the hope that its report to the Council would further this purpose.

Termination of UNCIP

Before leaving the subcontinent, the Chairman of the Commission, on 19 September, addressed letters to the two Governments informing them of the above decision. In so doing, he stressed that the Military Adviser and the military observers would remain and pursue their normal activities.*

On 17 December 1949, following the Commission's return to New York, the Security Council decided to request the Council President, General A.G.L. McNaughton of Canada, to meet informally with the representatives of India and Pakistan and examine with them the possibility of finding a mutually satisfactory basis for dealing with the Kashmir problem. On 14 March 1950, after examining the reports of UNCIP and of General McNaughton, the Council adopted resolution 80(1950), by which it decided to terminate the United Nations Commission for India and Pakistan.

Appointment of a United Nations representative

At the same time, the Security Council decided to appoint a United Nations representative who was to exercise all of the powers and responsibilities devolving upon UNCIP. Sir Owen Dixon, of Australia, was appointed by the Council as United Nations Representative for India and Pakistan. A Chief Military Observer (Brigadier H. H. Angle, of Canada) was appointed by the Secretary-General as head of UNMOGIP.

Continuance of UNMOGIP

By resolution 91(1951) of 30 March 1951, the Security Council decided that UNMOGIP should continue to supervise the

* S/1430, annex 40.

cease-fire in Kashmir, and requested the two Governments to ensure that their agreement regarding the cease-fire would continue to be faithfully observed. The United Nations Representative (at the time, Frank P. Graham, of the United States, who had succeeded Sir Owen Dixon) subsequently pointed out, in his report of 15 October 1951,* that the debate in the Security Council leading to the adoption of resolution 91(1951) had indicated that it was the Council's intention that the Representative should deal only with the question of the demilitarization of Kashmir. The Representative was therefore not concerned with the existing arrangements for the supervision of the cease-fire, the responsibility for which the Council had placed with UNMOGIP.

Since that time, UNMOGIP has functioned as an autonomous operation, directed by the Chief Military Observer under the authority of the Secretary-General. Its headquarters alternates between Srinagar in summer (mid-May to mid-November) and Rawalpindi in winter. An operational staff office is maintained in one of those two cities when it is not hosting the headquarters. The supervision of the cease-fire in the field is carried out by a number of field observation teams stationed on both sides of the cease-fire line and also along the border between Pakistan and Kashmir.

Between 1949 and 1964, the number of military observers fluctuated between 35 and 67, according to need. Just before the outbreak of the hostilities of 1965, there were 45 observers, provided by 10 countries: Australia, Belgium, Canada, Chile, Denmark, Finland, Italy, New Zealand, Sweden and Uruguay.

Brigadier Angle served as Chief Military Observer until his death in an air crash in July 1950, and he was later replaced by Lieutenant-General Robert H. Nimmo, of Australia. Like the UNCIP Military Adviser, the Chief Military Observer of UNMOGIP, during the initial years, had the status of an observer, and continued to receive his military salary from his Government. In 1959, General Nimmo was given an appointment as an official of the United Nations Secretariat with the rank of Assistant Secretary-General. This administrative arrangement, which had been also applied to the Chief of Staff of UNTSO, was to become the general rule for all heads of United Nations peace-keeping operations.

Role and activities of UNMOGIP

With the conclusion of the Karachi Agreement in 1949, the situation along the cease-fire line became more stable. Incidents

* S/2375.

took place from time to time, but they were generally minor and were dealt with in accordance with the provisions of the Agreement. This situation continued until 1965.

The role and activities of UNMOGIP were described by the Secretary-General in a report dated 3 September 1965* in this manner:

> The United Nations maintains UNMOGIP with its 45 observers along the CFL (cease-fire line) of almost 500 miles, about half of which is in high mountains and is very difficult of access. UNMOGIP exercises the quite limited function of observing and reporting, investigating complaints from either party of violations of the CFL and the cease-fire and submitting the resultant findings on those investigations to each party and to the Secretary-General, and keeping the Secretary-General informed in general on the way in which the cease-fire agreement is being kept. Because the role of UNMOGIP appears frequently to be misunderstood, it bears emphasis that the operation has no authority or function entitling it to enforce or prevent anything, or to try to ensure that the cease-fire is respected. Its very presence in the area, of course, has acted to some extent as a deterrent, but this is not the case at present. The Secretary-General exercises responsibility for the supervision and administrative control of the UNMOGIP operation.

D. The hostilities of 1965 and the establishment of UNIPOM

Background

In early 1965, relations between India and Pakistan were strained again because of their conflicting claims over the Rann of Kutch at the southern end of the international border.

The situation steadily deteriorated during the summer of 1965, and, in August, military hostilities between India and Pakistan erupted on a large scale along the cease-fire line in Kashmir. In his report of 3 September 1965,† the Secretary-General stressed that the cease-fire agreement of 27 July 1949 had collapsed and that a return to mutual observance of it by India and Pakistan would afford the most favourable climate in which to seek a resolution of political differences.

Security Council action for a cease-fire

On 4 September 1965, the Security Council, by resolution 209(1965), called for a cease-fire and asked the two Governments to co-operate fully with UNMOGIP in its task of supervising the ob-

* S/6651.   † *Ibid.*

servance of the cease-fire. Two days later, the Council adopted resolution 210(1965), by which it requested the Secretary-General "to exert every possible effort to give effect to the present resolution and to resolution 209(1965), to take all measures possible to strengthen the United Nations Military Observer Group in India and Pakistan, and to keep the Council promptly and currently informed on the implementation of the resolutions and on the situation in the area".

From 7 to 16 September, the Secretary-General visited the subcontinent in pursuit of the mandate given to him by the Security Council. In his report of 16 September to the Council,* he noted that both sides had expressed their desire for a cessation of hostilities, but that each side had posed conditions which made the acceptance of a cease-fire very difficult for the other. In those circumstances, the Secretary-General suggested that the Security Council might take a number of steps: first, it might order the two Governments, pursuant to Article 40 of the United Nations Charter,† to desist from further military action; second, it might consider what assistance it could provide in ensuring the observance of the cease-fire and the withdrawal of all military personnel by both sides; and, third, it could request the two Heads of Government to meet in a country friendly to both in order to discuss the situation and the problems underlying it, as a first step in resolving the outstanding differences between their two countries.

On 20 September, after the hostilities had spread to the international border between India and West Pakistan, the Council adopted resolution 211(1965), by which it demanded that a cease-fire take effect at 0700 hours GMT on 22 September 1965 and called for a subsequent withdrawal of all armed personnel to the positions held before 5 August. The Council also requested the Secretary-General to provide the necessary assistance to ensure supervision of the cease-fire and the withdrawal of all armed personnel.

Establishment of UNIPOM

In Kashmir, the supervision called for by the Security Council was exercised by the established machinery of UNMOGIP. For this purpose, its observer strength was increased to a total of 102 from the same contributing countries as before.

† In order to prevent an aggravation of a situation, the Security Council, under Article 40 of the Charter, before making recommendations or deciding on measures to be taken, may call upon the parties concerned to comply with provisional measures it deems necessary or desirable, without prejudice to the rights, claims or position of those parties.

* S/6686.

Since the hostilities extended beyond the Kashmir cease-fire line, the Secretary-General decided to set up an administrative adjunct of UNMOGIP, the United Nations India-Pakistan Observation Mission (UNIPOM), as a temporary measure for the sole purpose of supervising the cease-fire along the India-Pakistan border outside the State of Jammu and Kashmir.*

The function of UNIPOM was primarily to observe and report on breaches of the cease-fire called for by the Security Council. In case of breaches, the observers were to do all they could to persuade the local commanders to restore the cease-fire, but they had no authority or power to order a cessation of firing. Ninety observers from 10 countries (Brazil, Burma (now Myanmar), Canada, Ceylon (now Sri Lanka), Ethiopia, Ireland, Nepal, the Netherlands, Nigeria and Venezuela) were assigned to UNIPOM.

The Mission was closely co-ordinated both administratively and operationally with UNMOGIP. The Chief Military Observer of UNMOGIP, General Nimmo, was initially also placed in charge of UNIPOM. After the arrival of the newly appointed Chief Officer of UNIPOM, Major-General B. F. Macdonald, of Canada, in October 1965, General Nimmo was asked by the Secretary-General to exercise oversight functions with regard to both operations.

Further Security Council action

On 27 September 1965, after learning that the cease-fire was not holding, the Security Council adopted resolution 214(1965), by which it demanded that the parties urgently honour their commitments to the Council to observe the cease-fire, and called upon them to withdraw all armed personnel as necessary steps in the full implementation of resolution 211(1965).

As cease-fire violations continued to occur and there were no prospects of the withdrawal of troops, the Security Council met again in November and adopted resolution 215(1965) of 5 November. By this decision, the Council called upon the Governments of India and Pakistan to instruct their armed personnel to co-operate with the United Nations and cease all military activity.

The Security Council further demanded the prompt and unconditional execution of the proposal already agreed to in principle by India and Pakistan that their representatives meet with a representative of the Secretary-General to formulate an agreed plan and schedule of withdrawals. In this connection, the Secretary-General,

* S/6699/Add.3.

after consultation with the parties, appointed Brigadier-General Tulio Marambio, of Chile, as his representative on withdrawals.

On 15 December, the Secretary-General reported* that the two parties directly involved, India and Pakistan, had informed him of their desire that the United Nations should continue its observer function after 22 December 1965, which was the end of the first three months of the cease-fire demanded by the Security Council in its resolution 211(1965) of 20 September 1965.

In the circumstances, the Secretary-General indicated his intention to continue the United Nations activities relating to the cease-fire and withdrawal provisions of the resolution by continuing UNIPOM for a second period of three months and maintaining the added strength of the Military Observer Group.

Tashkent agreement

On 10 January 1966, the Prime Minister of India and the President of Pakistan, who had met in Tashkent, USSR, at the invitation of the Chairman of the Council of Ministers of the USSR, announced their agreement that the withdrawal of all armed personnel of both sides to the positions they had held prior to 5 August 1965 should be completed by 25 February 1966 and that both sides should observe the cease-fire terms on the cease-fire line.†

Withdrawal plan

The principles of a plan and schedule of withdrawals were subsequently agreed upon by military representatives of India and Pakistan, who had held meetings for that purpose since 3 January 1966 at Lahore and Amritsar under the auspices of General Marambio, the Secretary-General's representative on withdrawals. The plan for disengagement and withdrawal was agreed upon by the military commanders of the Indian and Pakistan armies in New Delhi on 22 January.‡

At a joint meeting on 25 January, under the auspices of the Secretary-General's representative, the parties agreed upon the ground rules for the implementation of the disengagement and withdrawal plan.§ The plan was to be implemented in two stages and the good offices of UNMOGIP and UNIPOM were to be requested to ensure that the action agreed upon was fully implemented. In the event of disagreement between the parties, the decision of General Marambio would be final and binding on both sides. The good of-

---

* S/6699/Add.11.   † S/7221.   ‡ S/6719/Add.5, annex.   § *Ibid.*

fices of UNMOGIP and UNIPOM were similarly requested for the implementation of the second stage of the agreement, as were the good offices of the Secretary-General's representative on withdrawals.

Termination of UNIPOM

On 26 February 1966*, the Secretary-General reported that the withdrawal of the troops by India and Pakistan had been completed on schedule on 25 February, and that the withdrawal provisions of the Security Council's resolutions had thus been fulfilled by the two parties. The responsibilities of the Secretary-General's representative on withdrawals came to an end on 28 February and his mission ceased on that date. As planned, UNIPOM was terminated on 22 March 1966 and the 59 additional observers appointed in September 1965 to the Military Observer Group were gradually withdrawn. By the end of March 1966, the observer strength of UNMOGIP was reduced to 45, drawn from the same 10 contributing countries. From that date until December 1971, UNMOGIP functioned on the basis of the Karachi Agreement in much the same way as it had done before September 1965.

E. **Hostilities of 1971 and their aftermath**

Background

At the end of 1971, hostilities broke out again between the Indian and Pakistan forces. They started along the borders of East Pakistan and were related to the movement for independence which had developed in that region and which ultimately led to the creation of Bangladesh.

Secretary-General's actions

When tension was mounting in the summer of 1971, Secretary-General U Thant, invoking his responsibilities under the broad terms of Article 99† of the United Nations Charter, submitted a memorandum to the Security Council on 20 July‡ in which he drew

† Article 99 of the Charter states: "The Secretary-General may bring to the attention of the Security Council any matter which in his opinion may threaten the maintenance of international peace and security."

* S/6179/Add.6.   ‡ S/10410.

attention to the deteriorating situation in the subcontinent and informed the Council of the action he had taken in the humanitarian field.

On 20 October,* the Secretary-General sent identical messages to the heads of the Governments of India and Pakistan expressing increasing anxiety over the situation and offering his good offices with a view to avoiding any development that might lead to disaster. In these messages, he recalled the efforts of the Chief Military Observer of UNMOGIP to ease tension and prevent military escalation along the cease-fire line in Kashmir.

In early December, after the outbreak of hostilities, the Secretary-General submitted a series of reports† to the Security Council on the situation along the cease-fire line in Kashmir, based on information received from the Chief Military Observer. The reports showed that from 20 October onwards, both India and Pakistan greatly reinforced their forces along the cease-fire line. Both sides admitted that violations of the Karachi Agreement were being committed by them, but they continued to use the machinery of UNMOGIP to prevent escalation. However, on 3 December, hostilities broke out along the cease-fire line, with exchanges of artillery and small-arms fire and air attacks by both sides. The Secretary-General pointed out that he could not report on military developments in other parts of the subcontinent since the United Nations had no observation machinery outside Kashmir.

General Assembly resolution

On 4 December, the Security Council met to consider the situation in the subcontinent, but it could not reach agreement and decided two days later to refer the matter to the General Assembly. On 7 December, the Assembly considered the question referred to it and adopted resolution 2793(XXVI), calling upon India and Pakistan to take forthwith all measures for an immediate cease-fire and withdrawal of their armed forces to their own side of the borders.

Between 7 and 18 December, the Secretary-General submitted another series of reports‡ on the situation along the cease-fire line in Kashmir. Fighting continued, with varying intensity, until 17 December, 1930 hours local time, when a cease-fire announced by the two Governments went into effect. By that time, a number of positions on both sides of the 1949 cease-fire line had changed hands.

---

* *Ibid.*   † S/10412 and Add.1,2.   ‡ S/10432 and Add.1-11.

Security Council action

The Security Council met again on 12 December, and, on 21 December, adopted resolution 307(1971), by which it demanded that a durable cease-fire in all areas of conflict remain in effect until all armed forces had withdrawn to their respective territories and to positions which fully respected the cease-fire line in Kashmir supervised by UNMOGIP.

Following the adoption of this resolution, the representative of India stated that Kashmir was an integral part of India. In order to avoid bloodshed, he added, his Government had respected the cease-fire line supervised by UNMOGIP, but there was a need to make some adjustments in that line and India intended to discuss and settle this matter directly with Pakistan. The representative of Pakistan insisted that Kashmir was disputed territory whose status should be settled by agreement under the aegis of the Security Council.

Reports on the cease-fire

Subsequent reports of the Secretary-General* indicated that following a period of relative quiet, complaints of violations of the cease-fire were received by the Chief Military Observer of UNMOGIP in late January from the military commands of both sides. The Secretary-General observed that, pending the withdrawals of the armed forces, the cease-fire under Security Council resolution 307(1971) must be regarded, for the time being and for practical purposes, as a simple cease-fire requiring the parties to refrain from any firing or forward movement along the lines where the respective armies were in actual control at the time the cease-fire had come into effect on 17 December.

In order to report to the Secretary-General on the observance of the cease-fire, the observers must have the co-operation of the parties and enjoy freedom of movement and access along the lines of control, but these conditions were not met. In this connection, the Secretary-General remarked, discussions aimed at securing the co-operation of the parties had been satisfactorily completed with Pakistan but were still continuing with the Indian military authorities.

* S/10467 and Add.1-3.

Functioning of UNMOGIP

On 12 May 1972, the Secretary-General reported to the Security Council* that, while the Pakistan military authorities continued to submit to UNMOGIP complaints of cease-fire violations by the other side, the Indian military authorities had stopped doing so. The situation concerning the functioning of UNMOGIP remained unchanged and, as a result, the Secretary-General could not keep the Council fully informed of developments relating to the observance of the cease-fire. The Secretary-General expressed the hope that, in keeping with the demand of the Security Council, the cease-fire would be strictly observed and that both sides would take effective measures to ensure that there was no recurrence of fighting. He noted in this connection that the UNMOGIP machinery continued to be available to the parties, if desired.

On the same day,† India informed the Secretary-General that its efforts to open direct negotiations with Pakistan had made some progress; it hoped the talks between the two countries would take place at the highest level as early as possible in a positive and constructive spirit, with a view to achieving durable peace in the subcontinent. India also indicated that many incidents had been satisfactorily settled at flag meetings between local commanders. India had refrained from sending to the Secretary-General lists of cease-fire violations by Pakistan in the firm belief that if Pakistan was indeed ready and willing to settle differences and disputes between the two countries in a truly friendly and co-operative spirit, direct negotiations provided the best means.

During May and June, Pakistan brought to the Secretary-General's attention long lists of alleged cease-fire violations by India in Kashmir and other sectors. In a letter dated 5 June, ‡ Pakistan stated that there were no flag meetings between Pakistan and Indian military commanders with regard to incidents along the cease-fire line in Kashmir, although such meetings had been held for incidents along the international border. It was clear that incidents along the cease-fire line should be investigated by UNMOGIP observers, and flag meetings held under the auspices of UNMOGIP, since both the 1949 Karachi Agreement and Security Council resolution 307(1971) prescribed UNMOGIP's responsibilities in this regard. It was therefore the view of the Pakistan Government that the activation of the machinery of UNMOGIP on the Indian side of the cease-fire line in Kashmir would serve to prevent incidents.

---

* S/10467/Add.4. † S/10648. ‡ S/10681.

India took a different position. As a result of the war, the Karachi Agreement of 1949 had, in India's view, ceased to be operative and the mandate of UNMOGIP had lapsed, since it had related specifically to the supervision of the cease-fire line under that Agreement and did not extend to the actual line of control that had come into existence in December 1971. India noted that there was no formal agreement on the location of that line or on the machinery for the maintenance of a durable cease-fire on all fronts.

In July 1972, the Prime Minister of India and the President of Pakistan agreed at Simla in India to define a Line of Control in Kashmir. The Line of Control was agreed by both parties in December 1972 and delineated on the ground by the representatives of the two armies. It followed, with minor deviations, the same course as the cease-fire line established in the Karachi Agreement of 1949. However, the positions of India and Pakistan on the functioning of UNMOGIP remained unchanged.

Financial aspects

Like the United Nations Truce Supervision Organization (UNTSO), UNMOGIP is financed from the regular budget of the United Nations. From the inception of its operation until December 1989 UNMOGIP's total expenditures were approximately $67.7 million. For the biennium 1990–1991 the total resources approved by the General Assembly for UNMOGIP's budget were $8.6 million.

Present situation

Given the disagreement between the two parties about UNMOGIP's mandate and functions, the Secretary-General's position has been that UNMOGIP can be terminated only by a decision of the Security Council. In the absence of such a decision, UNMOGIP has been maintained with the same administrative arrangements. Its task is to observe, to the extent possible, developments pertaining to the strict observance of the cease-fire of 17 December 1971 and to report thereon to the Secretary-General. The military authorities of Pakistan have continued to lodge with UNMOGIP complaints about cease-fire violations. The military authorities of India have lodged no complaints since January 1972 and have restricted the activities of the United Nations' observers on the Indian side of the Line of Control. They have, however, continued to provide accommodation, transport and other facilities to UNMOGIP.

The Observer Group's Headquarters has continued to alternate between Rawalpindi and Srinagar.

The number of observers, which stood at 44 at the end of 1971, had been reduced to 36 by June 1990 as a result of a decision by certain contributing countries to withdraw their observers. As of the latter date, the observers were provided by eight contributing countries: Belgium, Chile, Denmark, Finland, Italy, Norway, Sweden and Uruguay.

Chapter VIII

United Nations Observation Group in Lebanon

Background

In May 1958, armed rebellion broke out in Lebanon when President Camille Chamoun (a Maronite Christian) made known his intention to seek an amendment to the Constitution which would enable him to be re-elected for a second term. The disturbances, which started in the predominantly Moslem city of Tripoli, soon spread to Beirut and the northern and north-eastern areas near the Syrian border, and assumed the proportions of a civil war.

On 22 May,* the Lebanese Government requested a meeting of the Security Council to consider its complaint "in respect of a situation arising from the intervention of the United Arab Republic in the internal affairs of Lebanon, the continuance of which is likely to endanger the maintenance of international peace and security". It charged that the United Arab Republic† was encouraging and supporting the rebellion by the supply of large quantities of arms to subversive elements in Lebanon, by the infiltration of armed personnel from Syria into Lebanon, and by conducting a violent press and radio campaign against the Lebanese Government.

On 27 May, the Security Council decided to include the Lebanese complaint on its agenda but, at the request of Iraq, agreed to postpone the debate to permit the League of Arab States to try to find a settlement of the dispute. After the League had met for six days without reaching agreement, the Council took up the case and, on 11 June, adopted resolution 128(1958), by which it decided to dispatch urgently to Lebanon an observation group "so as to ensure that there is no illegal infiltration of personnel or supply of arms or other *matériel* across the Lebanese borders". The Secretary-General was authorized to take the necessary steps to dispatch the observation group, which was asked to keep the Council informed through him.

This resolution, supported by both Lebanon and the United Arab Republic, formed the basis for the establishment of the United Nations Observation Group in Lebanon (UNOGIL).

† From February 1958 until October 1961, Egypt and Syria joined together to form the United Arab Republic.

* S/4007.

Creation of UNOGIL

Following adoption of the Security Council's 11 June resolution, Secretary-General Dag Hammarskjöld told the Council that the necessary preparatory steps had already been taken. The Observation Group proper would be made up of highly qualified and experienced men from various regions of the world. They would be assisted by military observers, some of whom would be drawn from UNTSO and could be in Beirut on the very next day. Hammarskjöld stressed that the Group would not be a police force like the United Nations Emergency Force (UNEF) deployed in Sinai and the Gaza Strip.

Following the adoption of the resolution, the Secretary-General appointed Galo Plaza Lasso of Ecuador, Rajeshwar Dayal of India and Major-General Odd Bull of Norway as members of UNOGIL. Plaza acted as Chairman.

In order to start the operation without delay, 10 observers were immediately detached from UNTSO for assignment with UNOGIL. Five of them arrived in Beirut on 12 June and began active reconnaissance the following morning. The plan was to cover as many areas as possible and to probe further each day in the direction of the Syrian border so as to observe any illegal infiltration of personnel and supply of arms across the border. The number of observers was rapidly increased with new arrivals and reached 100 by 16 June. They were drawn from 21 countries: Afghanistan, Argentina, Burma (now Myanmar), Canada, Ceylon (now Sri Lanka), Chile, Denmark, Ecuador, Finland, India, Indonesia, Ireland, Italy, Nepal, the Netherlands, New Zealand, Norway, Peru, Portugal, Sweden and Thailand.

The contributing countries were selected by the Secretary-General in accordance with the same criteria as those he had developed for UNEF in 1956, namely the agreement of the host Government and exclusion of nationals of the permanent members of the Security Council and of "special interest" countries. Two helicopters with Norwegian pilots were placed at the disposal of the Group on 23 June and they were supplemented shortly thereafter by four light observation aircraft.

Method of operation

The three members of UNOGIL assembled in Beirut on 19 June under the personal chairmanship of Dag Hammarskjöld, who had arrived in the area the day before. As outlined by the

Secretary-General, the role of UNOGIL was strictly limited to observation, to ascertain whether illegal infiltration of personnel or supply of arms or other *matériel* across the Lebanese borders was occurring. It was not UNOGIL's task to mediate, arbitrate or forcefully to prohibit illegal infiltration, although it was hoped that its very presence on the borders would deter any such traffic. The borders meant those between Lebanon and Syria, since the Armistice Demarcation Line between Israel and Lebanon was covered by UNTSO and not involved in the present case.

It was decided that the Group should discharge its duties by the following methods:*

(a) The UNOGIL military observers would conduct regular and frequent patrols of all accessible roads from dawn to dusk, primarily in border districts and the areas adjacent to the zones held by the opposition forces. Following the practice already established by UNTSO, the patrolling was to be carried out in white jeeps with United Nations markings, equipped with two-way radio sets.

(b) A system of permanent observation posts was to be established and manned by military observers. These posts were in continuous radio contact with UNOGIL headquarters in Beirut, with each other, and with the patrolling United Nations jeeps. There were initially 10 such stations sited with a view to being as close as possible to the dividing-line between the opposing forces, as near to the frontier as possible or at points commanding supposed infiltration routes or distribution centres. The observers at these stations attempted to check all reported infiltration in their areas and to observe any suspicious development.

(c) An emergency reserve of military observers was to be stationed at headquarters and main observation posts for the purpose of making inquiries at short notice or investigating alleged instances of smuggling.

(d) An evaluation team was to be set up at headquarters to analyse, evaluate and co-ordinate all information received from observers and other sources.

(e) Aerial reconnaissance was to be conducted by light aeroplanes and helicopters, the former being equipped for aerial photography. The aircraft were in radio communication with headquarters and military observers in the field.

(f) The Lebanese Government would provide the Observation Group with all available information about suspected infiltration. Based on this information, instructions would be given to observers for maintenance of special vigilance within the areas in question. The

* S/4040.

Group would also request the military observers to make specific inquiries into alleged activities as occasion required.

First UNOGIL report to the Security Council

On 1 July 1958, UNOGIL submitted its first report to the Security Council.* The report, which dealt with the problems of observation arising from the political, military and geographical circumstances prevailing in Lebanon, indicated that the observers were facing difficulties in gaining access to much of the frontier area held by the opposition forces and could provide no substantiated or conclusive evidence of major infiltration.

The Lebanese Government criticized what it called the report's "inconclusive, misleading or unwarranted" conclusions.† It took strong exception to the report and insisted that the United Arab Republic was continuing "massive, illegal and unprovoked intervention in the affairs of Lebanon".

Initially, the military observers encountered serious difficulties in approaching the eastern and northern frontiers, where large areas were in opposition hands. In the early stage, these areas could only be patrolled by aircraft, including photographic and night reconnaissance. But the situation greatly improved by mid-July, when UNOGIL finally obtained full freedom of access to all sections of the Lebanese frontier and received assurances of complete freedom to conduct ground patrols throughout the area north of Tripoli and to establish permanent observation posts anywhere in that area. Arrangements were also made for inspection by military observers of all vehicles and cargoes entering Lebanon across the northern frontier.‡

Dispatch of United States forces

In the mean time, however, new complications arose outside Lebanon's borders. On 14 July 1958, the Hashemite Kingdom of Iraq was overthrown in a *coup d'état* and replaced with a republican régime. This event had serious repercussions both on Lebanon and Jordan. On the same day, President Chamoun requested United States intervention to protect Lebanon's political independence and territorial integrity.

On 15 July, the Security Council was convened at the request of the representative of the United States, who informed it of his Government's decision to respond positively to the Lebanese request.

* S/4040 and Add.1.   † S/4043.   ‡ S/4051.

He stated that United States forces were not in Lebanon to engage in hostilities of any kind but to help the Lebanese Government in its efforts to stabilize the situation, brought on by threats from outside, until such time as the United Nations could take the necessary steps to protect the integrity and independence of Lebanon. He added that his Government was the first to admit that the dispatch of United States forces to Lebanon was not an ideal way to solve the current problems and that these forces would be withdrawn as soon as the United Nations could take over.

Secretary-General's position

During the same meeting, the Secretary-General made a statement reviewing the actions he had taken under the mandate given to him in the Security Council's resolution of 11 June. He stated that he had acted solely with the purpose stated by the Council, "to ensure that there is no illegal infiltration of personnel or supply of arms or other *matériel* across the Lebanese borders". His actions had had no relation to developments that must be considered as the internal affairs of Lebanon, nor had he concerned himself with the wider international aspects of the problem other than those referred to in the resolution. As a matter of course, he had striven to give the observation operation the highest possible efficiency. Hammarskjöld also mentioned his own diplomatic efforts in support of the operation, which now had full freedom of movement in the northern area as well as in the rest of Lebanon.

On 16 July, UNOGIL submitted an interim report* stating that on the previous day it had completed the task of obtaining full freedom of access to all sections of the frontier of Lebanon. The next day, in a second interim report,† the Group expressed its intention to suggest to the Secretary-General that a force of unarmed non-commissioned personnel and other ranks should be assigned to it. It also indicated that the number of observers would have to be raised to 200, with additional aircraft and crews. With the envisaged increase in the observer force, and the addition of enlisted personnel and supporting equipment, it would be possible to undertake direct and constant patrolling of the actual frontier. In transmitting this report, the Secretary-General stated that he fully endorsed the plan contained in it.

* *Ibid.*   † S/4052.

Events in Jordan

On 17 July,* the representative of Jordan requested the Security Council to give urgent consideration to a complaint by his Government of interference in its domestic affairs by the United Arab Republic. The Council decided on the same day to consider this complaint concurrently with the Lebanese complaint.

During the ensuing discussions, the representative of the United Kingdom stated that his Government had no doubt that a fresh attempt was being prepared to overthrow the régime in Jordan. In response to an appeal by the Jordanian Government, British forces were being dispatched to Jordan to help its King and Government to preserve the country's political independence and territorial integrity. This action would be brought to an end if arrangements could be made by the Council to protect the lawful Government of Jordan from external threats and so maintain international peace and security.

At the beginning of the Council's debate, the Soviet Union submitted a draft resolution, later revised,† by which the Council would call upon the United Kingdom and the United States "to cease armed intervention in the domestic affairs of the Arab States and to remove their troops from the territories of Lebanon and Jordan immediately". The United States proposed a draft resolution‡ which would request the Secretary-General "immediately to consult the Government of Lebanon and other Member States as appropriate with a view to making arrangements for additional measures, including the contribution and use of contingents, as may be necessary to protect the territorial integrity and independence of Lebanon and to ensure that there is no illegal infiltration of personnel or supply of arms or other *matériel* across the Lebanese borders". A third draft resolution§ was later submitted by Sweden to have the Council request the Secretary-General to suspend the activities of the observers in Lebanon until further notice.

The Soviet and Swedish draft resolutions were rejected by majorities, while the United States proposal was vetoed by the Soviet Union.

Following those votes, Japan proposed a draft resolution‖ under which the Secretary-General would be requested to make arrangements for such measures, in addition to those envisaged by the Council's resolution of 11 June 1958, as he might consider necessary in the light of the present circumstances, "with a view to enabling the United Nations to fulfil the general purposes established in that resolution, and which will, in accordance with the Charter, serve to

---

* S/4053.   † S/4047/Rev.1.   ‡ S/4050/Rev.1.   § S/4054.
‖ S/4055/Rev.1.

ensure the territorial integrity and political independence of Lebanon, so as to make possible the withdrawal of the United States forces from Lebanon". This draft resolution was also rejected, owing to a Soviet negative vote.

Secretary-General's plan

Following the rejection of the Japanese proposal, the Secretary-General stated that, although the Security Council had failed to take additional action in the grave emergency facing it, the United Nations responsibility to make all efforts to live up to the purposes and principles of the Charter remained. He was sure that he would be acting in accordance with the Council's wishes if he used all opportunities offered to him, within the limits set by the Charter, towards developing those efforts, so as to help prevent a further deterioration of the situation in the Middle East and to assist in finding a road away from the dangerous point now reached. The continued operation of UNOGIL being acceptable to all Council members would imply concurrence in the further development of the Group, so as to give it all the significance it could have, consistent with its basic character as determined by the Council in its resolution of 11 June 1958 and the purposes and principles of the Charter. He indicated that, should the members of the Council disapprove of the way these intentions were to be translated by him into practical steps, he would, of course, accept the consequences of its judgement.

The Secretary-General's plan was to increase the strength of UNOGIL as soon as possible to enable it to carry out fully its mission and thus expedite the withdrawal of the United States troops. The number of personnel, which stood at 200 on 17 July 1958, was increased to 287 by 20 September and to 591 in mid-November, including 32 non-commissioned officers in support of ground operations and 90 such officers in the air section. In November, UNOGIL had 18 aircraft, six helicopters and 290 vehicles, and 49 permanently manned posts of all types had been established.

Further UNOGIL report

On 30 July, UNOGIL submitted a periodic report on its activities and observations.* It stated that the military observers were operating with skill and devotion, often in conditions of considerable danger and difficulty. Intensive air patrolling had been carried out by day and by night, and air observations had been checked

* S/4069.

against the results of ground patrolling and observation. The Group reached the conclusion that the infiltration which might be taking place could not be anything more than of limited scale and was largely confined to small arms and ammunition.

With regard to illegal infiltration of personnel, UNOGIL stated that the nature of the frontier, the existence of traditional tribal and other bands on both sides of it and the free movement of produce in both directions were among the factors which must be taken into account in making an evaluation. In no case, however, had the observers, who had been vigilantly patrolling the opposition-held areas and had frequently observed armed bands there, been able to detect the presence of persons who had undoubtedly entered from across the border for the purpose of fighting. From the observations made of the arms and organization in the opposition-held areas, the fighting strength of opposition elements was not such as to be able successfully to cope with hostilities against a well-armed regular military force.

The United States troops, which had landed in Beirut on 15 July, were confined at all times to the beach area and there were no contacts between them and the United Nations military observers. However, UNOGIL indicated in its report that the impact of the landing of those forces in the Beirut area on the inhabitants of opposition-held areas had occasioned difficulties and caused setbacks in carrying out the tasks of the observers.

General Assembly emergency session

During the discussions in the Security Council in July, both the USSR and the United States proposed the convening of an emergency special session of the General Assembly, but the matter was not taken up until 7 August. In the intervening period, the leaders of France, India, the USSR, the United Kingdom and the United States held consultations through exchanges of letters in an effort to find a way out of the impasse. The idea of a "summit" meeting on the Middle East was advanced, but no agreement could be reached. On 7 August, the Security Council met again and decided to call an emergency special session of the Assembly.

That session took place from 8 to 21 August 1958. By the time the Assembly convened, two events which had an important bearing on the developments in the Middle East had occurred. First, General Fuad Chehab, who was acceptable to the Moslem leaders, had been elected President of Lebanon, and this effectively removed from the scene the controversial question of a second term for Chamoun. Second, the new Iraqi revolutionary Government had accepted the obligations of States under the United Nations Charter and had been recognized by the United Kingdom and the United States.

In a report of 14 August,* UNOGIL indicated that just before the election of President Chehab there had been a noticeable reduction of tension throughout the country and a comparable absence of armed clashes between Government and opposition forces. Since 31 July, there had been a virtual nation-wide truce with only occasional reports of sporadic firing in some areas. The report also indicated that by dint of their perseverance and tact in dealing with difficult and often dangerous situations, the observers had won back the ground lost after 15 July. Most of the permanent stations in opposition-held areas envisaged by the Group had been established, and other stations were expected to be set up shortly.

At the end of the emergency special session, the General Assembly unanimously adopted, on 21 August, a proposal submitted by 10 Arab States. This became resolution 1237(ES-III), by which the Assembly requested the Secretary-General to make forthwith, in consultation with the Governments concerned and in accordance with the Charter, such practical arrangements as would adequately help to uphold Charter purposes and principles in relation to Lebanon and Jordan in the present circumstances, and thereby facilitate the early withdrawal of the foreign troops from the two countries.

Secretary-General's Special Representative

In a report dated 29 September to the General Assembly,† the Secretary-General commented on the practical arrangements mentioned in the Assembly's August resolution.

He noted that, in the case of Lebanon, the United Nations had already made extensive plans for observing the possible infiltration or smuggling of arms across the border. The work of the Observation Group had had to be re-evaluated within the new practical arrangements to be made. As to Jordan, its Government had indicated that it did not accept the stationing of a United Nations force in Jordan nor the organization of a broader observation group like UNOGIL. But it would accept a special representative of the Secretary-General to assist in the implementation of the resolution. Consequently, the Secretary-General asked Pier P. Spinelli, the Under-Secretary in charge of the United Nations Office at Geneva, to proceed to Amman and to serve as his Special Representative, on a preliminary basis.

* S/4085.   † A/3934/Rev.1.

With regard to the withdrawal issues, the Secretary-General had been informed that Lebanon and the United States were discussing a schedule for the completion of the withdrawal of the United States forces, and that they hoped this might take place by the end of October. Jordan and the United Kingdom were also discussing the fixing of dates for the withdrawal of the British troops from Jordan, which would begin during October.

In its fourth report to the Security Council, which was circulated on 29 September 1958,* UNOGIL stated that, during the period being reviewed, its military observers had not only been able to re-establish confidence in the independent nature of their activities, but had won for themselves the trust and understanding of all sections of the population. Despite the presence of a considerable number of men under arms, there had been no significant clashes between the Lebanese army and organized opposition forces. No cases of infiltration had been detected and, if any infiltration was still taking place, its extent must be regarded as insignificant.

Withdrawal of United Kingdom and United States forces

In a letter dated 1 October,† the United Kingdom informed the Secretary-General that it had agreed with the Jordanian Government that the withdrawal of British troops should begin on 20 October. On 8 October,‡ the United States announced that, by agreement with the Lebanese Government, it had been decided to complete the withdrawal of United States forces by the end of October. The withdrawal of United States troops was completed by 25 October, and of the British troops by 2 November. Some of the UNOGIL observers played a role in assisting in the evacuation of the British forces from Jordan.

Termination of UNOGIL

In a letter dated 16 November 1958,§ the Minister for Foreign Affairs of Lebanon stated that cordial and close relations between Lebanon and the United Arab Republic had resumed their normal course. In order to dispel any misunderstanding which might hamper such relations, the Lebanese Government requested the Security Council to delete the Lebanese complaint from its agenda.

In its final report, dated 17 November 1958,‖ UNOGIL recommended that the operation should be withdrawn since its task might be regarded as completed. On 21 November,¶ the Secretary-

* S/4100.   † A/3937.   ‡ A/3942.   § S/4113.   ‖ S/4114.   ¶ S/4116.

General submitted to the Security Council a plan for the withdrawal of the operation, formulated by the Observation Group, which was acceptable to Lebanon.

In accordance with that plan, the closing down of stations and substations preparatory to the withdrawal of UNOGIL began on 26 November and was completed by the end of the month. The observers were withdrawn in three phases, with the key staff, the personnel required for air service and the logistic components leaving last. The withdrawal was completed by 9 December.

Chapter IX United Nations Yemen Observation Mission

Background

A civil war which broke out in Yemen in September 1962 contained the seeds of a wider conflict with international dimensions because of the involvement of Saudi Arabia and the United Arab Republic. Saudi Arabia shared an extended border with Yemen, much of it still undefined. The United Arab Republic (Egypt) had had a special relationship with Yemen in the past. In March 1958, Yemen joined it to form the United Arab States, but this association was dissolved in December 1961, shortly after Syria seceded from the United Arab Republic.

A further factor in the situation was that Yemen had long claimed that the Aden Protectorate was legally part of its territory. The British-controlled Government of the South Arabian Federation, which included the Aden Protectorate, therefore also closely followed developments in Yemen.

On 19 September 1962, Imam Ahmed bin Yahya died and was succeeded by his son, Imam Mohammed Al-Badr. A week later, a rebellion led by the army overthrew the new Imam and proclaimed the Yemen Arab Republic. The new Government was recognized by the United Arab Republic on 29 September and by the USSR the next day, but other major Powers with interests in the area, including the United Kingdom and the United States, withheld action on the question of recognition.

Following his overthrow, Imam Al-Badr managed to escape from San'a, the capital, and, with other members of the royal family, rallied the tribes in the northern part of the country. With financial and material support from external sources, the royalists fought a fierce guerrilla campaign against the republican forces. The revolutionary Government accused Saudi Arabia of harbouring and encouraging Yemeni royalists, and threatened to carry the war into Saudi Arabian territory. The Imam, on the other hand, claimed that the army rebellion was fostered and aided by Egypt, which denied the charge. At the beginning of October, large numbers of United Arab Republic forces were dispatched to Yemen at the request of the revolutionary Government to assist the republican forces in their fight against the royalists.

187

On 27 November, the Permanent Mission of Yemen to the United Nations, which was still staffed by the royalists, addressed a letter to the Secretary-General urging the United Nations to establish an inquiry to ascertain whether or not the rebellion was fostered from Cairo. This letter was informally circulated to the United Nations missions. A delegation of Yemeni republicans which had arrived in New York by that time let it be known that they would not object to a United Nations on-the-spot investigation.

The General Assembly, which began its seventeenth session in New York in September 1962, had before it credentials from both the royalist and republican régimes in Yemen. It took up the question of the representation of Yemen on 20 December, the very last day of its session. On that day, the Credentials Committee decided, by a vote of 6 to none, with 3 abstentions, to recommend that the Assembly accept the credentials submitted by the President of the Yemen Arab Republic. Later on the same day, the Assembly approved, by 73 votes to 4, with 23 abstentions, the Committee's report.

King Hussein of Jordan earlier that month had suggested that the presence of United Nations observers might be useful in finding a solution.

Secretary-General's initiative

Secretary-General U Thant undertook a peace initiative, which eventually led to the establishment of the United Nations Yemen Observation Mission (UNYOM).

In a report dated 29 April 1963,* the Secretary-General stated that, since the autumn of 1962, he had been consulting regularly with the representatives of the Governments of the Arab Republic of Yemen, Saudi Arabia and the United Arab Republic about "certain aspects of the situation in Yemen of external origin, with a view to making my office available to the parties for such assistance as might be desired towards ensuring against any developments in that situation which might threaten peace of the area". He had requested Ralph J. Bunche, Under-Secretary for Special Political Affairs, to undertake a fact-finding mission in the United Arab Republic and Yemen. As a result of the activities carried out by Bunche on his behalf, and by Ellsworth Bunker, who had been sent by the United States Government on a somewhat similar but unconnected mission, he had received from each of the three Governments concerned formal confirmation of their acceptance of identical terms of disengagement in Yemen.

* S/5298.

Under those terms, Saudi Arabia would terminate all support and aid to the royalists of Yemen and would prohibit the use of Saudi Arabian territory by royalist leaders for carrying on the struggle in Yemen. Simultaneously with that suspension of aid, Egypt would undertake to begin withdrawal from Yemen of the troops that had been sent at the request of the new Government, the withdrawal to be phased and to take place as soon as possible. A demilitarized zone would be established to a distance of 20 kilometres on each side of the demarcated Saudi Arabia–Yemen border, and impartial observers would be stationed there to check on the observance of the terms of disengagement. They would also certify the suspension of activities in support of the royalists from Saudi Arabian territory and the outward movement of the Egyptian forces and equipment from the airports and seaports of Yemen.

The Secretary-General asked Lieutenant-General Carl C. von Horn of Sweden, Chief of Staff of UNTSO, to visit the three countries concerned to consult on the terms relating to the functioning of United Nations observers in implementation of the terms of disengagement.

In a second report, dated 27 May,* the Secretary-General told the Council that on the basis of information provided by General von Horn, he concluded that United Nations observers in the area were necessary and should be dispatched with the least possible delay. The personnel required would not exceed 200, and it was estimated that the observation function would not be required for more than four months. The military personnel in the Yemen operation would be employed under conditions similar to those applying to other United Nations operations of this nature. The total cost was estimated to be less than $1 million, and he hoped that the two parties principally involved, Saudi Arabia and Egypt, would undertake to bear this cost. He submitted more detailed estimates of the costs of the proposed Mission in a supplemental report on 3 June.†

In a further report, ‡ submitted on 7 June, the Secretary-General informed the Security Council that Saudi Arabia had agreed to accept a "proportionate share" of the costs of the operation, while Egypt agreed in principle to provide $200,000 in assistance for a period of two months, which would be roughly half the costs of the operation for that period. Thus, there would be no financial implications for the United Nations in getting the Observation Mission established and for its maintenance for an initial two-month period. The Secretary-General announced his intention to proceed with the organization and dispatch of the Mission without delay.

---

* S/5321.   † S/5323.   ‡ S/5325.

Security Council action establishing UNYOM

The next day, the USSR* requested the convening of the Council to consider the Secretary-General's reports on developments relating to Yemen, since the reports contained proposals concerning possible measures by the United Nations to maintain international peace and security, which, under the Charter, should be decided by the Council.

After considering the reports, the Council adopted, on 11 June 1963, resolution 179(1963), requesting the Secretary-General to establish the observation operation as he had defined it, and urging the parties concerned to observe fully the terms of disengagement set out in his 29 April report and to refrain from any action that would increase tension in the area. The Council noted with satisfaction that Saudi Arabia and Egypt had agreed to defray, over a period of two months, the expenses of the observation function called for in the terms of disengagement.

This resolution constituted the basis for the establishment of UNYOM. It did not set a specific time-limit for the Mission, although two months was mentioned in the preamble in connection with its financing. The Secretary-General took the position that he could extend UNYOM without a decision of the Security Council if he considered that its task had not been completed, provided that he could obtain the necessary financial support.

Reports on UNYOM operations

In his first report on the operation, which was submitted to the Security Council on 4 September 1963,† the Secretary-General pointed out that the Mission's task would not be completed on the expiration of the two-month period, and for that reason he had sought and received assurances from both parties that they would defray the expenses of the operation for a further two months.

In his second report, dated 28 October, ‡ the Secretary-General reported that there had been no decisive change in the situation in Yemen and, because of the limiting and restrictive character of the UNYOM mandate, the Mission would have to be withdrawn by 4 November 1963, since there would be no financial support for it after that date. However, three days later, he informed the Council§ that Saudi Arabia and Egypt had agreed to participate in the financing of UNYOM for a further two-month period and, accordingly, preparations for the withdrawal of the Mission had been cancelled. He in-

* S/5326.   † S/5412.   ‡ S/5447.   § S/5447/Add.1.

dicated that, although no Security Council meeting was required for the extension of UNYOM, he had consulted Council members to ascertain that there would be no objection to the proposed extension.

On 2 January 1964,* before the expiration of the third two-month period, the Secretary-General reported that he considered that the continuing functioning of UNYOM was highly desirable, that the two Governments concerned had agreed to continue their financial support for another two months, and that he had engaged in informal consultations with the members of the Council before announcing his intention to extend the Mission. This process was repeated at the beginning of March, May and July 1964, and UNYOM was extended for successive periods of two months until 4 September 1964.

In late August 1964, Saudi Arabia informed the Secretary-General that it found itself unable to continue the payment of expenses resulting from the disengagement agreement, and Egypt indicated that it had no objection to the termination of UNYOM on 4 September. The Secretary-General therefore advised the Council of his intention to terminate the activities of the Mission on that date.†

Organization of UNYOM

Following the adoption of resolution 179(1963), the Secretary-General appointed General von Horn as Commander of UNYOM and took steps to provide the Mission with the required personnel and equipment. The resolution had requested the Secretary-General to establish UNYOM as he had defined it in his report of 29 April 1963, and he selected the various components of the Mission accordingly. In selecting those components and the contributing countries, he informally consulted the parties concerned. Practical considerations were also taken into account, including the proximity of the existing United Nations peace-keeping operations, namely UNTSO and UNEF.

In the initial stage, UNYOM was composed mainly of six military observers, a Yugoslav reconnaissance unit of 114 personnel and a Canadian air unit of 50 officers and men. In addition, 28 international staff members and a small military staff were assigned to UNYOM headquarters. The military observers were detailed from UNTSO and the reconnaissance unit personnel were drawn from the Yugoslav contingent of UNEF, which had experience in United Nations peace-keeping operations in similar terrain. The UNEF air base at El Arish provided support for the Canadian air unit, including six aircraft and a similar number of helicopters.

* S/5501.   † S/5927.

The strength and composition of UNYOM remained unchanged until November 1963, when a reappraisal of its requirements in terms of personnel and equipment was undertaken. It was felt that in view of the co-operation shown by the parties and the peaceful and friendly attitude of the people in the area covered by the Mission, it was no longer necessary to maintain a military unit in the demilitarized zone; therefore, it was decided to withdraw progressively the Yugoslav reconnaissance unit and to deploy instead up to 25 military observers, while the aircraft of the Mission were reduced to two. The new observers were provided by Denmark, Ghana, India, Italy, the Netherlands, Norway, Pakistan, Sweden and Yugoslavia.

With the arrival of General von Horn and the first group of military personnel, UNYOM began operations on 4 July 1963. In August, General von Horn resigned, and his deputy, Colonel Branko Pavlović of Yugoslavia, took over as acting Commander until September 1963 when Lieutenant-General P. S. Gyani of India, then Commander of UNEF, was temporarily detailed from that Force and appointed Commander of UNYOM.

Secretary-General's Special Representative

At the end of October 1963,* when the Secretary-General thought UNYOM had to be withdrawn for lack of financial support, he announced his intention to maintain a civilian presence in Yemen after the withdrawal of the Observation Mission, and he had in mind the appointment of Pier P. Spinelli, head of the United Nations Office at Geneva, as his Special Representative for this purpose. After the withdrawal plan was cancelled, as mentioned earlier, the idea of appointing Spinelli was retained, particularly since General Gyani had to return to his command in UNEF.

In November 1963, upon the departure of General Gyani, Spinelli was appointed Special Representative of the Secretary-General, as well as head of UNYOM. Spinelli assumed this dual responsibility until the end of the Mission.

Functioning of UNYOM

The mandate of UNYOM stemmed from the disengagement agreement entered into by the three Governments concerned, namely, Saudi Arabia, the United Arab Republic and the Arab Republic of Yemen, set out in the report of the Secretary-General of 29 April 1963.† The function and authority of UNYOM as

* S/5447.   † S/5298.

defined in the agreement were considerably more limited than in the case of other United Nations observation missions. For example, its establishment was not based on any cease-fire agreement and there was no cease-fire to supervise. The tasks of UNYOM were limited strictly to observing, certifying and reporting in connection with the intention of Saudi Arabia to end activities in support of the royalists in Yemen and the intention of Egypt to withdraw its troops from that country.

To carry out these tasks in the initial stage, detachments of the Yugoslav reconnaissance unit were stationed in Jizan, Najran and Sa'dah in the demilitarized zone and the surrounding areas. They manned check-posts and conducted ground patrolling. In addition, air patrolling was carried out by the Canadian air unit, which had bases at San'a as well as Jizan and Najran, particularly in the mountainous central part of the demilitarized zone where there were few passable roads. The six military observers detailed from UNTSO, who were stationed at San'a, and the two positions at Al Hudaydah were primarily responsible for observing and certifying the withdrawal of Egyptian troops.

In order to check on the reduction or cessation of assistance from Saudi Arabia to the royalists, a pattern of check-points and air/ground patrolling was established to cover all main roads and tracks leading into Yemen and the demilitarized zone. Air and ground patrols were carried out daily with varied timings and routes, the patrol plan being prepared and co-ordinated every evening.

Experience quickly showed that air and ground patrolling had two main limitations, namely, that traffic could be observed only by day while, for climatic reasons, travel during hours of darkness was customary in the area, and that cargoes could not be checked. These problems were met by periodically positioning United Nations military observers at various communication centres for 40 hours or more, so that traffic could be observed by day or night and cargoes checked as necessary. Arrangements were also made to have Saudi Arabian liaison officers assigned to United Nations check-points and check cargoes when requested by United Nations observers.

Various complaints were received by UNYOM from one or the other of the parties concerned. They fell mainly into two categories: on the one hand, allegations of offensive actions by Egyptian forces against the royalists in Yemen and in Saudi Arabian territory, and, on the other, alleged activities in support of the royalists emanating from Saudi Arabia. UNYOM authorities would transmit these complaints to the parties involved and, whenever possible and appropriate, investigate them.

In accordance with the disengagement agreement, the responsibilities of UNYOM concerned mainly, in addition to the cities of San'a and Al Hudaydah, the demilitarized zone on each side of the demarcated portion of the Saudi Arabia–Yemen border. It did not extend to the undefined portion of that border nor to the border between Yemen and the British-controlled South Arabian Federation.

From the very start, the Secretary-General pointed out that UNYOM, because of its limited size and function, could observe and report only certain indications of the implementation of the disengagement agreement. However, despite its shortcomings, the Mission did have a restraining influence on hostile activities in the area. The Secretary-General repeatedly expressed the view that the responsibility for implementing the agreement lay with Saudi Arabia and Egypt and progress could be best achieved through negotiations between them.

With this in view, he informed the Security Council that UNYOM could, within limits, serve as an intermediary and as an endorser of good faith on behalf of the parties concerned, and that it was his intention to have the Mission perform these roles to the maximum of its capability. When Spinelli was appointed Special Representative of the Secretary-General and head of UNYOM in November 1963, he devoted a great deal of his time and attention to good-offices efforts and held extensive discussions with officials of the three Governments concerned. These discussions were of an exploratory character to try to ascertain whether there were areas of agreement between the parties which might, through bilateral discussions or otherwise, lead to further progress towards disengagement and the achievement of a peaceful situation in Yemen.

Secretary-General's assessment

The assessment of the Secretary-General on the functioning of UNYOM and the implementation of the disengagement agreement, as set out in his successive periodic reports to the Security Council, are outlined below.

In his first report on this subject, which was dated 4 September 1963,* the Secretary-General found no encouraging progress towards effective implementation of the agreement, although both parties had expressed a willingness to co-operate in good faith with UNYOM. He

---

* S/5412.

noted reluctance by each side to fulfil its undertakings regarding the agreement before the other side did so.

His second report, which was submitted on 28 October 1963* indicated limited progress. He stated that although the developments observed by UNYOM were far short of the disengagement and regularization of the situation which had been hoped for, they were in a limited way encouraging in that the scale of fighting had been reduced and conditions of temporary truce applied in many areas.

On 2 January 1964,† he reported that UNYOM observations tended to confirm that, during the period under review, no military aid of significance had been provided to the royalists from Saudi Arabia, and that there had been a substantial net withdrawal of Egyptian troops from Yemen. Ground operations had further decreased in intensity. The Secretary-General reiterated his belief that the solution of the problem lay beyond the potential of UNYOM under its original mandate, and he referred to the extensive discussions his Special Representative had had with members of the three Governments concerned with a view to furthering progress towards disengagement and the achievement of a peaceful situation in Yemen.

A later report, submitted on 3 March 1964, ‡ raised a new problem: Yemeni and Egyptian sources asserted that large quantities of supplies were being sent to the royalists from the Bayhan area across the frontier with the South Arabian Federation. The Secretary-General pointed out in this connection that since that frontier was not included in the disengagement agreement, United Nations observers did not operate in that area. However, he mentioned that the nature and extent of the military operations carried out by the royalists during January and February would seem to indicate that arms and ammunition in appreciable amounts had been reaching them from that source.

The Secretary-General also reported that the royalists appeared to be well provided with money and to have engaged foreign experts to train and direct their forces, and that they had recently launched attacks against Egyptian troops. From the developments observed by UNYOM, he felt that progress towards the implementation of the disengagement agreement had been very disappointing during the period under review; a state of political and military stalemate existed inside the country, which was unlikely to be changed as long as external intervention in various forms continued from either side. On the other hand, he noted certain encouraging factors, particularly the increasing unity of feeling and purpose within the Arab world arising from a Conference of Arab Heads of State held in Cairo in

* S/5447.   † S/5501.   ‡ S/5572.

mid-January 1964 and the resulting improvement in relations between Saudi Arabia and Egypt. The Secretary-General expressed the hope that the meeting to be held between the two parties in Saudi Arabia would result in some progress towards the implementation of the agreement and towards an understanding between the two Governments to co-operate in promoting political progress and stability in Yemen.

In his report dated 3 May 1964,* the Secretary-General stated that there was no progress in troop reduction towards the implementation of the disengagement agreement and that no actual end of the fighting appeared to be in sight. He noted, however, that the two parties had reported noticeable progress in discussions of a number of problems at issue between them, and that a meeting between President Nasser of Egypt and Crown Prince Feisal of Saudi Arabia would be held in Cairo in the near future.

On 2 July,† the Secretary-General reported that the military situation in Yemen had remained fairly quiet over the past two months, that no military aid by Saudi Arabia to the Yemeni royalists had been observed and that some slight progress in Egyptian troop reduction appeared to have occurred. Once again he appealed to the parties concerned to meet at the highest level with a view to achieving full and rapid implementation of the disengagement agreement.

Termination of UNYOM

In his final report, dated 2 September 1964,‡ the Secretary-General again acknowledged the failure of the parties to implement the disengagement agreement and the difficulties UNYOM faced in observing and reporting on these matters. There had been a substantial reduction in the strength of the Egyptian forces in Yemen but it seemed that the withdrawal was a reflection of the improvement in the situation of the Yemeni republican forces rather than the beginning of a phased withdrawal in the sense of the agreement. There were also indications that the Yemeni royalists had continued to receive military supplies from external sources. Noting that UNYOM had been able to observe only limited progress towards the implementation of the agreement, he reiterated his view that UNYOM's terms of reference were restricted to observation and reporting only, and that the responsibility for implementation lay with the two parties to the agreement. He stated that UNYOM had actually accomplished much more than could have been expected of it in the circumstances, and that during the 14 months of its presence in

* S/5681.   † S/5794.   ‡ S/5927.

Yemen, the Mission had exercised an important restraining influence on hostile activities in the area.

On 4 September 1964, the activities of UNYOM ended and its personnel and equipment were withdrawn.

Shortly after the withdrawal of UNYOM, relations between the parties steadily improved and issues were resolved between them. There has been no consideration of the matter in United Nations organs since the termination of that Mission.

Chapter X

Representative of the Secretary-General in the Dominican Republic

Background

Towards the end of April 1965, a political crisis developed in the Dominican Republic, resulting in civil strife that had considerable international repercussions. On 24 April, the three-man junta headed by Donald Reid Cabral was overthrown by a group of young officers and civilians who sought the return to office of former President Juan Bosch, who had been deposed by a military *coup* in September 1963, and the restoration of the 1963 Constitution.

Bosch's supporters were opposed by a group of high-ranking officers of the Dominican armed forces, with the result that two rival governments emerged in the Dominican Republic during the first weeks of the civil war. The pro-Bosch forces organized themselves into what was called the "Constitutional Government", headed by Colonel Francisco Caamaño Deñó. The opposing forces established a civilian-military junta which called itself the "Government of National Reconstruction", headed by General Antonio Imbert Barrera.

The military phase of the Dominican crisis took place mainly in Santo Domingo, capital of the country, where heavy fighting broke out between the two contending factions on 25 April 1965.

On 28 April, the United States announced that its troops had been ordered to land in the Dominican Republic. On the following day, the United States representative informed the Security Council of his Government's action and of its call for a meeting of the Council of the Organization of American States (OAS). His letter* asserted that the President of the United States had ordered troops ashore in the Dominican Republic in order to protect United States citizens there and escort them to safety. The President had acted, the letter stated, after being informed by the military authorities in the Dominican Republic that lives of United States citizens were in danger, that their safety could no longer be guaranteed, and that the assistance of United States military personnel was required.

---

* S/6310.

On 29 April,* the Secretary-General of the OAS informed the United Nations Secretary-General that the OAS Council had appealed for the suspension of armed hostilities in the Dominican Republic. On 1 May,† the Assistant Secretary-General of the OAS informed the Security Council that the Tenth Meeting of Consultation of Ministers for Foreign Affairs of the American Republics had decided on that day to establish a committee, composed of representatives of Argentina, Brazil, Colombia, Guatemala and Panama, and had instructed it to proceed immediately to Santo Domingo to bring about the restoration of peace and normality and to offer its good offices to the contending factions there with a view to achieving a cease-fire and the orderly evacuation of persons.

On 1 May, the USSR requested an urgent meeting of the Security Council to consider the question of the armed intervention by the United States in the internal affairs of the Dominican Republic.‡

The Security Council considered this question at 29 meetings held between 3 May and 26 July 1965.

Security Council action, May 1965

On 6 May,§ the Assistant Secretary-General of the OAS transmitted to the Security Council the text of a resolution by which the Tenth Meeting of Consultation had requested OAS members to make available land, air and naval contingents or police forces for the establishment of an inter-American force, to operate under its authority. The purpose of the force would be to help restore normal conditions in the Dominican Republic, maintain the security of its inhabitants and the inviolability of human rights, and create an atmosphere of peace and conciliation that would allow the functioning of democratic institutions.

On 14 May, Jordan, urging action by the Security Council, submitted, together with Malaysia and the Ivory Coast, a draft resolution whereby the Council would call for a strict cease-fire, invite the Secretary-General to send, as an urgent measure, a representative to the Dominican Republic to report on the situation, and call upon all concerned in the Dominican Republic to co-operate with that representative in carrying out his task.

The three-Power text was unanimously adopted by the Council the same day, as resolution 203(1965).

---

* S/6313.   † S/6364, annex.   ‡ S/6316.   § S/6333/Rev.1.

Representative's activities

In a report dated 15 May,* the Secretary-General informed the Council that he had appointed José Antonio Mayobre, Executive Secretary of the Economic Commission for Latin America, as his Representative in the Dominican Republic. An advance party, led by Major-General I. J. Rikhye as Military Adviser, had arrived in Santo Domingo earlier that day. The Military Adviser was assisted by two military observers at any one time from three made available from Brazil, Canada and Ecuador.

On 18 May,† the Secretary-General informed the Council that his Representative had left for Santo Domingo on 17 May. He had asked Mayobre to notify formally all the parties concerned of the Council's call for a strict cease-fire and to convey to all those involved in the conflict his most earnest appeal to heed that call so that a propitious climate for finding a solution might be brought about.

On 19 May, ‡ the Secretary-General reported that, shortly after his arrival, Mayobre had met with Colonel Caamaño, President of the "Constitutional Government", and with General Imbert, President of the "Government of National Reconstruction".

Late in the evening of 18 May, Mayobre had informed the Secretary-General by telephone of heavy fighting in the northern section of the capital and of the numerous casualties caused by it. It had not been possible to persuade General Imbert to agree to a cease-fire, although he had expressed willingness to agree to a suspension of hostilities some time on 19 May to facilitate the work of the Red Cross in searching for the dead and wounded.

Appeal by the Security Council President

At the Council's meeting on 19 May, the Council President made a statement, which was supported by all Council members, requesting the Secretary-General to convey to his Representative the Council's desire that his urgent efforts be devoted to securing an immediate suspension of hostilities so that the Red Cross's work in searching for the dead and wounded might be facilitated.

Communications from the OAS

Also on 19 May,§ the OAS transmitted the text of a second report submitted by the Special Committee of the Tenth

* S/6358.   † S/6365.   ‡ S/6369.   § S/6370.

Meeting of Consultation. The Committee said that efforts to arrange for a meeting between Colonel Caamaño and General Imbert to iron out their differences had proved unsuccessful, and that the Committee had issued an appeal to the parties for strict compliance with the cease-fire agreed upon in the Act of Santo Domingo, signed on 5 May, formalizing a cease-fire achieved earlier through the efforts of the Papal Nuncio in Santo Domingo. The report added that the presence of the United Nations in the Dominican Republic had created a factor which had compromised and interfered with the task of the Committee. It recommended that the Meeting of Consultation agree upon the measures necessary to re-establish peace and normality in the Republic, and that the Security Council be requested to suspend all action until regional procedures had been exhausted.

The OAS also transmitted to the Council* the text of a resolution adopted by the Meeting of Consultation on 20 May, entrusting the OAS Secretary-General with negotiating a strict cease-fire and with providing his good offices for establishing a climate of peace and reconciliation that would permit democratic institutions to function. The resolution asked him to co-ordinate his action, in so far as relevant, with that of the Representative of the United Nations Secretary-General.

Further reports by the Secretary-General

The Secretary-General informed the Security Council† that his Representative, on the morning of 19 May, had met with representatives of the Dominican Red Cross, the International Red Cross and the Pan American Sanitary Bureau, and had suggested that they meet with the leaders of the two factions engaged in the fighting and request a 12-hour suspension of hostilities to remove the dead and wounded from the battle area. On 21 May,‡ the Secretary-General reported on further information from his Representative that, following negotiations with the leaders of the two factions, agreement had been reached for the suspension of hostilities for 24 hours beginning on 21 May, at 1200 hours local time.

Further Security Council action

During a Council meeting of 21 May, the Secretary-General said that his Representative had reported that the cease-fire of 21 May was effective. The Red Cross, which had gone into the battle area early that morning, had been fully engaged in its

* S/6372/Rev.1.   † S/6371.   ‡ S/6371/Add.1.

humanitarian task. In view of the need to evacuate the sick and wounded to less congested hospitals, the Representative was trying to obtain an extension of the truce.

On 22 May, France submitted a draft resolution by which the Council would request that the suspension of hostilities in Santo Domingo be transformed into a permanent cease-fire, and would invite the Secretary-General to report to it on the implementation of the resolution. This was adopted as resolution 205(1965).

On 25 May, the Council President noted that it appeared that a *de facto* cessation of hostilities continued to prevail in Santo Domingo and that the Secretary-General had informed him that it was being observed. He therefore suggested that the Council adjourn, on the understanding that it could reconvene if the situation required it.

Further OAS communications

On 2 June,* the OAS advised the Security Council that the Tenth Meeting of Consultation had appointed an *ad hoc* committee—composed of representatives of Brazil, El Salvador and the United States—to assist all parties in the Dominican Republic to achieve a climate of peace and to enable democratic institutions to function. It also informed the Council of the arrival in Santo Domingo of the Chairman of the Inter-American Commission on Human Rights in response to requests made by both of the contending Dominican groups.†

Security Council consideration, 3-11 June 1965

The question of the Dominican Republic was again considered by the Council at four meetings held between 3 and 11 June. The Council was convened at the request of the USSR to take up two communications from the "Constitutional Government", asking for the dispatch of the United Nations Commission on Human Rights to the Dominican Republic to investigate atrocities allegedly carried out by General Imbert's forces against the civilian population in Santo Domingo.

The question of the scope of the mandate of the Secretary-General's Representative arose during these meetings from suggestions made by France, Jordan and Uruguay to enlarge Mayobre's staff to enable him to supervise the cease-fire and to investigate complaints of human rights violations. They considered that his mandate was suf-

* S/6401. † S/6404.

ficiently wide to cover both tasks. The suggestions were supported by the USSR.

Bolivia, the Ivory Coast, Malaysia, the United Kingdom and the United States, on the other hand, expressed doubt as to the advisability of extending Mayobre's mandate at that stage. The United States observed, in this connection, that the Inter-American Human Rights Commission, which had been sent to Santo Domingo, was actively investigating human rights violations.

Secretary-General's position

The Secretary-General stated that his Representative's current mandate involved observing and reporting, functions which did not include the actual investigation of complaints and charges about specific incidents, other than those connected with cease-fire violations. Investigative functions would require a directive from the Security Council, a substantially larger staff and increased facilities. Moreover, he could give no assurance that such added responsibility would receive from the contending parties the co-operation necessary to secure effective implementation by his Representative.

The Secretary-General remarked that his Representative was keeping a watchful eye on all aspects of the situation and was reporting what he observed. The size of his staff was under constant review, and he would be provided with the necessary assistance as the circumstances demanded.

Security Council consideration, 16-21 June 1965

On 16 June,* the Secretary-General reported that an exchange of fire had taken place on the morning of 15 June between Colonel Caamaño's forces and troops of the Inter-American Peace Force (IAPF). There was no evidence, however, as to which side had started the firing. By nightfall his Representative had arranged for a cessation of hostilities.

In a later report,† the Secretary-General informed the Council that, on 16 June, fighting between the Caamaño forces and the IAPF had been renewed along the newly established IAPF positions manned by United States troops. Although the firing had stopped on the evening of 16 June, the situation remained very tense.

This situation was discussed by the Security Council from 16 to 21 June. During these meetings, the Council received from the OAS the text of proposals for a political settlement submitted on 18 June‡

* S/6447.   † S/6459.   ‡ S/6457, annex I.

by the OAS *ad hoc* committee to the "National Reconstruction Government" and the "Constitutional Government". The principal points in the OAS proposals were: general elections within six to nine months, under OAS supervision; a general amnesty for all who had participated in the civil strife; surrender of all arms in the hands of civilians to the OAS; establishment of a provisional government which would exercise its authority under an institutional act and would call elections; and the convening of a constitutional assembly within six months following assumption of office by the elected government.

On 21 June, the Secretary-General informed the Security Council that he had just received a report from his Representative which stated that the cease-fire had been effective since 16 June.

Secretary-General's report, 16 July 1965

On 16 July, the Secretary-General submitted a report on the situation in the Dominican Republic covering the period from 19 June to 15 July 1965.*

Despite a number of isolated incidents, the cease-fire in Santo Domingo had been maintained. The Secretary-General indicated that, as of 26 June, the IAPF was composed of 1,700 troops from six Latin American countries and 12,400 from the United States, of which 1,400 would be withdrawn shortly. He went on to report that the situation outside Santo Domingo—which had been potentially explosive since May, owing mainly to deteriorating economic conditions, to the ineffectiveness of civilian authority and to military and police repression—had become more acute following an abortive uprising by armed civilians at San Francisco de Macorís on 25 June and an attack against a police post at Ramón Santana on 2 July.

The Secretary-General drew attention to repeated complaints of violations of human rights in Santo Domingo as well as in the provinces, involving alleged executions, arbitrary arrests, and cases of missing persons following arrest. He also drew attention to the worsening economic situation. In his Representative's view, an early political solution accompanied by an emergency programme of external financial and technical assistance was essential.

Security Council meetings, July 1965

The Security Council resumed consideration of the question at four meetings held between 20 and 26 July.

* S/6530.

The Council President ultimately summed up the agreed views of the members of the Council:

- Information received by the Council as well as the Secretary-General's reports showed that, in spite of the Council's resolutions of 14 and 22 May 1965, the cease-fire had been repeatedly violated. Acts of repression against the civilian population and other violations of human rights, as well as data on the deterioration of the economic situation in the Dominican Republic, had been brought to the Council's attention.
- Members of the Council had condemned gross violations of human rights in the Republic, expressed the desire that such violations should cease, and indicated again the need for the strict observance of the cease-fire in accordance with the Council's resolutions.
- The Council members considered it necessary that the Council continue to watch the situation closely and that the Secretary-General continue to report on it.

Secretary-General's reports, 22 July 1965–5 January 1966

In a report covering the period between 22 July and 17 August 1965,* the Secretary-General informed the Security Council that, except for a few minor incidents, the cease-fire had been maintained. While his Representative continued to receive complaints of alleged cases of arbitrary arrest by forces of the "Government of National Reconstruction", the situation in general had improved. The report referred to negotiations for a political settlement being carried out by the OAS *ad hoc* committee on the basis of new proposals the committee had submitted to the two contending parties on 9 August 1965.†

A proposed Act of Dominican Reconciliation‡ provided that the parties would accept a provisional government presided over by Héctor García Godoy as the sole and sovereign government of the Dominican Republic, and that they would accept a proposed Institutional Act§ as the constitutional instrument under which the provisional government would exercise its authority. The latter Act also provided for: a proclamation of a general amnesty by the provisional government; the disarmament and incorporation of the "Constitutionalist" zone into the security zone; a procedure for the recovery of arms in the hands of civilians; the reintegration of "Constitutionalist" military personnel who had participated in the conflict; and, finally, a procedure to be followed for the withdrawal of the IAPF.

---

* S/6615.   † S/6608.   ‡ S/6608, annex I.   § S/6608, annex III.

In a report covering the period of 17 August to 2 September 1965,* the Secretary-General reported the resignation on 30 August of the members of the "Government of National Reconstruction" headed by General Imbert, and the signing, on 31 August, of an amended text of the Act of Reconciliation by the leaders of the "Constitutional Government". On the same day, the chiefs of the armed forces and the national police had signed a declaration in which they had pledged acceptance of the Act of Reconciliation and the Institutional Act, and support of Dr. García Godoy as provisional President.

On 3 September, García Godoy was installed as President of the Provisional Government.

On 23 October,† the Secretary-General reported to the Security Council that since the inauguration of the Provisional Government much progress had been made in efforts to restore normal conditions in the Dominican Republic. Little progress had been made, however, towards the reintegration of "Constitutionalist" military personnel into the regular armed forces, owing mainly to continuing tension between the high command of the Republic's armed forces and "Constitutionalist" officers. The situation had been aggravated by acts of terrorism and violence, and armed clashes between civilians and elements of the police and regular Dominican troops.

In subsequent reports, the Secretary-General informed the Council that the Government had announced that troops of the Dominican armed forces had been ordered to return to their barracks and that law and order in Santo Domingo would be maintained by the national police with the assistance of the IAPF. By 25 November,‡ he reported, the situation had improved and the country was returning to normalcy. The bulk of the IAPF had been withdrawn from the capital and the national police were gradually assuming responsibility for the maintenance of law and order. There had also been some improvement in the relations between the civilian authorities and the armed forces.

In a report issued on 3 December,§ the Secretary-General informed the Council that the Provisional Government had promulgated a law calling for national elections to be held on 1 June 1966.

Later in December, the Secretary-General reported on new disturbances. The main disturbance took place on 19 December‖ at Santiago, where former "Constitutionalist" forces and Dominican air force units engaged in heavy fighting that resulted in many casualties, including 25 dead. The Santiago incident was followed by a wave of terrorist activities in Santo Domingo which caused the deaths of eight persons and considerable material damage. The

* S/6649. † S/6822. ‡ S/6975. § S/6991. ‖ S/7032.

reports indicated that mixed patrols of the IAPF, Dominican troops and national police faced a difficult task in maintaining order, as they were continually stoned and shot at by roving civilian groups.

Tension had again subsided by 25 December. On the evening of 3 January 1966, President García Godoy announced that within a few hours an important group of military personnel would leave the country on missions abroad. The Secretary-General concluded his report by stating that, while Santo Domingo had remained calm since 1 January, the situation there was reported to be tense and unstable.*

Secretary-General's observations

The Secretary-General, in the introduction to his annual report on the work of the Organization covering the period from 16 June 1964 to 15 June 1965,† discussed the problems and character of the United Nations role in the Dominican Republic situation. He described the task of his Representative there as a "new United Nations mission in the peace-keeping category".

The situation, the Secretary-General wrote, was of unusual complexity and had considerable international repercussions, particularly with regard to the unilateral military involvement of the United States in the initial stage and to the later role of the Inter-American Peace Force. While his Representative's mandate had been a limited one, the effect of his role had been significant, since he had played a major part in bringing about a cessation of hostilities on 21 May 1965, and had supplied information as to the situation both in Santo Domingo and in the interior of the country.

His presence had undoubtedly been a moderating factor in a difficult and dangerous situation, the Secretary-General said, adding that this had been the first time a United Nations peace mission had operated in the same area and dealt with the same matters as an operation of a regional organization, in this instance the OAS.

Further, the Secretary-General maintained the view that the developments in the Caribbean should stimulate thought by everyone concerning the character of the regional organizations and the nature of their functions and obligations in relation to the responsibilities of the United Nations under the Charter.

* S/7032/Add.4. † A/6001/Add.1.

Secretary-General's reports, January-February 1966

In one of eight reports covering developments in the Dominican Republic during January 1966,* the Secretary-General informed the Council that, on 6 January 1966, President García Godoy had issued decrees appointing a new Minister of the Armed Forces and new armed services chiefs, and providing for the transfer abroad of several high-ranking military officers, including Commodore Francisco Rivera Caminero, former Minister of the Armed Forces, and Colonel Caamaño Deñó, former "Constitutionalist" leader. The implementation of these decrees had met with some resistance from the Dominican armed forces, which at one point occupied radio and telecommunications buildings in Santo Domingo. However, by the end of January, 11 high-ranking former "Constitutionalist" officers had left the Dominican Republic to take up diplomatic posts abroad.

In six reports issued during February,† the Secretary-General reported to the Security Council several serious incidents and acts of terrorism which occurred in and outside Santo Domingo, beginning 7 February. As a result, economic activity in the city and nearby commercial areas had come to an almost complete standstill. Tension remained high from 12 to 15 February as hostile acts directed against IAPF military police and troops took place in Santo Domingo. A general strike was called off one day after a speech by President García Godoy, broadcast on 16 February, in which he announced orders to put into effect decrees concerning changes and transfers in the Dominican armed forces and ordered all public employees to return to work. The new Minister of the Armed Forces was sworn in on the same day and new chiefs of staff of the army, navy and air force were appointed on 26 February. Also, a new chief of the national police had been appointed by the Provisional Government.

Secretary-General's reports, March-May 1966

In 17 reports issued from March to May 1966, ‡ the Secretary-General informed the Security Council that, though fewer in number, acts of terrorism and other disturbances continued to occur in Santo Domingo and in the interior of the country. He stated that the electoral campaign had officially opened on 1 March.

In connection with national elections on 1 June 1966, the Central Electoral Board issued on 15 March a proclamation providing for the election of a President and Vice-President of the Republic, 27 Senators and 74 Deputies for a period of four years beginning

---

* S/7232/Add.4-11.   † S/7032/Add.12-17.   ‡ S/7032/Add.18-34.

1 July 1966, and for the election, for a period of two years, of 70 mayors and 350 aldermen and their alternates. On 11 May, President García Godoy, in a televised speech, expressed concern over certain signs of pressure exerted by minority groups intent upon disturbing the electoral process. He appealed to all sectors of the population to maintain a peaceful and orderly atmosphere for the elections, and indicated that the problem of the presence of the IAPF in the country should be solved before 1 July. On 13 May,* the OAS *ad hoc* committee announced that IAPF personnel would be confined to barracks on election day. This was followed by an announcement on 18 May by President García Godoy of his decision to confine all armed forces to barracks from 19 May until election day. On 29 May,† the OAS *ad hoc* committee indicated, in a press statement, that 41 observers invited by the OAS would observe elections in 21 provinces of the Republic and in the National District. The observers would submit a report to the Provisional Government.

At midnight on 30 May, the electoral campaign officially ended. On that day, the Provisional President sent a communication to the Tenth Meeting of Consultation of OAS Foreign Ministers informing it that he had instructed the Dominican representative to the OAS to request a meeting of the Tenth Meeting of Consultation to ask for withdrawal of the IAPF from Dominican territory.

Election of 1 June 1966

During June and July 1966, the Secretary-General submitted four reports‡ to the Council dealing mainly with the elections on 1 June and related events. According to those reports, the elections had proceeded on schedule in a calm and orderly manner. On 21 June, the final results of elections were announced by the Central Electoral Board. They showed 769,265 votes for Joaquín Balaguer, 525,230 for Juan Bosch and 39,535 for Rafael F. Bonnelly.

Installation of the Government, July 1966

In a report dated 2 July,§ the Secretary-General informed the Security Council that on 1 July, Joaquín Balaguer and Francisco Augusto Lora had been sworn in as President and Vice-President, respectively, of the Dominican Republic by the President of the National Assembly. In his inaugural address, President Balaguer stated that the country was returning to a system of law and that no one would be permitted to live outside legal norms. He set

* S/7032/Add.32.   † S/7032/Add.34.   ‡ S/7338/Add.1-3.
§ S/7338/Add.5.

forth a policy of austerity to place the Republic's economic, administrative and financial structure on a sounder footing. His Government would support the OAS and would work within it to ensure that national sovereignty would never again be infringed by foreign troops. While his Government intended to act drastically if extremists sought to disturb the peace, it would protect opponents against persecution and would ensure that the symbols of past oppression would disappear for ever from Dominican life.

Phased withdrawal of the IAPF

Early in July, a plan for the withdrawal of the IAPF in four phases was approved by the OAS *ad hoc* committee in agreement with the Dominican Government.

On 24 June,* the OAS Secretary-General had transmitted to the Security Council the text of a resolution adopted by the Tenth Meeting of Consultation that day. By this resolution, the Meeting of Consultation—noting that the purposes of the Tenth Meeting had been fully achieved inasmuch as popular elections had been held in the Dominican Republic, the results of which had given that nation a constitutional and democratic Government—directed that the withdrawal of the IAPF should begin before 1 July 1966 and should be completed within 90 days. It further asked the OAS *ad hoc* committee, in agreement with the Dominican Government, to give the IAPF the necessary instructions concerning the dates for and the manner of effecting the withdrawal.

From 3 August to 21 September 1966, the Secretary-General, on the basis of information received from the office of his Representative in Santo Domingo, submitted a series of reports to the Security Council† giving a detailed account of the withdrawal of the United States and the Latin American contingents (Brazil, Costa Rica, El Salvador, Honduras, Nicaragua and Paraguay) of the IAPF and of its military equipment. This withdrawal was completed on 21 September 1966.

Withdrawal of the United Nations Mission

In a letter of 13 October addressed to the Secretary-General, ‡ the Dominican Republic's Minister for Foreign Affairs expressed the appreciation of his country to the United Nations for its efforts to bring about the restoration of peace and harmony in the Republic, and stated that, in the view of his Government, the objec-

---

* S/7379.   † S/7338/Add.6-15.   ‡ S/7551.

tives of the Security Council's resolution of 14 May 1965 having been achieved, it would be advisable to withdraw the United Nations Mission from the Dominican Republic.

In a report issued on 14 October,* the Secretary-General informed the Security Council that in the light of the developments which had recently taken place in the Dominican Republic, including the installation on 1 July 1966 of the newly elected Government and the withdrawal of the IAPF, he had initiated arrangements for the withdrawal of the Mission in the Dominican Republic, which was expected to be completed shortly.

The withdrawal of the United Nations Mission was completed on 22 October 1966.

* S/7552.

Part V # The Congo

Chapter XI **United Nations Operation in the Congo**

A. Introduction

Background

The United Nations Operation in the Congo (Opération des Nations Unies au Congo, or ONUC), which took place in the Republic of the Congo (now Zaire) from July 1960 until June 1964, is by far the largest peace-keeping operation ever established by the United Nations in terms of the responsibilities it had to assume, the size of its area of operation and the manpower involved. It included, in addition to a peace-keeping force which comprised at its peak strength nearly 20,000 officers and men, an important Civilian Operations component. Originally mandated to provide the Congolese Government with the military and technical assistance it required following the collapse of many essential services and the military intervention by Belgian troops, ONUC became embroiled by the force of circumstances in a chaotic internal situation of extreme complexity and had to assume certain responsibilities which went beyond normal peace-keeping duties. The policy followed by Secretary-General Dag Hammarskjöld in the Congo brought him into direct conflict with the Soviet Union and serious disagreement with some other Powers. The Operation cost the life of Hammarskjöld and led to a grave political and financial crisis within the United Nations itself.

With an area of some 2,345,000 square kilometres (about 1 million square miles), approximately the size of Western Europe, the Congo/Zaire is the third largest country in Africa, after the Sudan and Algeria. Encompassing the greatest part of the Congo basin in the very heart of Africa, the country has an important strategic position. The Congo is also exceptionally rich in minerals, much of them in the province of Katanga.

At the time of independence, the Congo had a population of about 14 million. The wind of change that had swept across Africa after the Second World War left the Territory largely untouched. The Belgian colonial administration practised a policy of paternalism which gave the indigenous population one of the highest living standards on the continent, but little political and educational advancement. Few Congolese studied beyond the secondary level and, at the time of independence, there were among them only 17 university graduates and no doctors, lawyers or engineers.

Little political activity was allowed the Congolese population until 1959. Early that year, the Belgian Government, confronted with increasing disturbances, announced its intention to prepare the Congo for independence, and soon embarked upon a radical decolonization plan. A charter granting freedom of speech, of the press and of association was put into effect in August 1959, and elections to municipal and territorial councils were held in December. In January 1960, at a round-table conference of Congolese leaders convened in Brussels, Belgium agreed to grant independence to the Congo as of 30 June that same year.

From then on it was a race against time to get the Congo ready for independence. Provisional executive councils with the participation of Congolese leaders were established at the central and provincial levels in March 1960. The *"Loi fondamentale"*, which was to serve as the constitution for the Congo, was adopted by the Belgian Parliament and promulgated by King Baudouin of Belgium on 19 March. General and provincial elections leading to the establishment of the Congolese Parliament and the provincial assemblies were held during the same month.

The Parliament convened in the early part of June and, by 23 June, after lengthy debate, the newly elected representatives worked out a compromise whereby the two rival dominant Congolese leaders were elected to the two key positions in the new political structure: Joseph Kasa-Vubu as President of the Republic and Patrice Lumumba as Prime Minister. Thus, the apparatus for the independent State was completed barely six days before independence.

On 29 June 1960, a treaty of friendship, assistance and co-operation between Belgium and the Congo was signed by the representatives of the two Governments (but never ratified). Under that treaty, most of the administrative and technical personnel of the colonial administration would remain in the Congo on secondment to the Congolese Government. The treaty also provided that the two military bases at Kamina and Kitona would be ceded to Belgium and that the Belgian Government could, at the request of the Congolese Government, call out the Belgian troops from the bases to assist the latter Government in maintaining law and order. Belgium hoped that with this massive assistance and the guarantees accompanying it, it would be possible to ensure a smooth transition from colonial status to independence. Its main hope lay in the *Force publique,* the 25,000-man security force which had maintained law and order in the country in a forceful and effective way during the colonial times and which would continue to be commanded by Belgium's Lieutenant-General Emile Janssens, with an all-Belgian officer corps. It was what the Belgians called at the time the *"Pari congolais",* the Congolese gamble.

Dag Hammarskjöld, who had visited the Belgian Congo in January 1960, was keenly conscious of the serious problems that would confront the Congolese Government after independence. He felt that the Congo would need, in addition to massive assistance from Belgium, extensive United Nations technical aid that had no political strings attached. With this in mind, he asked his Under-Secretary for Special Political Affairs, Ralph J. Bunche, to attend the independence ceremony in Leopoldville (now Kinshasa) as his personal representative and to take the opportunity to discuss with the Congolese authorities the technical assistance which the United Nations could provide. Bunche arrived in Leopoldville on 26 June and stayed on after the independence ceremony to work out an extensive United Nations technical assistance programme for the country.

Shortly after independence, Congolese soldiers of the *Force publique* became restive and petitioned for more promotion opportunity. Their petition was dismissed by General Janssens. He made it clear that so far as the *Force publique* was concerned, independence had changed nothing. On 5 July, a mutiny broke out in the Leopoldville garrison and spread to several other cities during the following days. As some mutineers attacked Belgians and other Europeans, and in some cases committed rape and other atrocities, most Belgian administrators and technicians fled the country, and this led to the collapse of a number of essential services throughout the country.

The Belgian Ambassador to the Congo repeatedly urged Prime Minister Lumumba to request the assistance of Belgian troops, under the friendship treaty, to maintain law and order, but Lumumba adamantly refused. Instead, he attempted to regain control of the *Force publique* by agreeing to the Congolese soldiers' demand for reform. He renamed the *Force publique* the *Armée nationale congolaise* (ANC), dismissed General Janssens and appointed Victor Lundula, a Congolese, as Commander of the Army with the rank of Major-General, and Joseph Mobutu, also a Congolese, as its Chief of Staff with the rank of Colonel. All Congolese soldiers and non-commissioned officers were promoted by one grade pending further measures to Africanize the entire officer corps.

As disorder spread and intensified, Ralph Bunche, who was in Leopoldville at the time, strongly advised the Belgian Ambassador not to call in Belgian troops without the prior agreement of the Congolese Government. At the same time, he was in close touch with the Congolese authorities and the Secretary-General in New York to work out a plan to help the Government control and strengthen the Congolese army through United Nations assistance. Hammarskjöld envisaged sending a large number of United Nations military advisers, experts and technicians for this purpose. He felt that if the Congolese Government were to request such military personnel as technical assistance of a military nature, rather than as military assistance, he could take immediate action on his own authority without referring the matter to the Security Council.

The Congolese Government agreed to this course of action and, on 10 July, submitted a formal request to the Secretary-General for technical assistance of a military nature, including military advisers, experts and technicians, to assist it in developing and strengthening the national army for the twin purposes of national defence and the maintenance of law and order.

Belgian intervention and Security Council action

However, a new situation developed on the next day when the Belgian Government ordered its troops into the Congo without the agreement of the Congolese Government, for the declared purpose of restoring law and order and protecting Belgian nationals. Belgian troops landed at Leopoldville, Matadi, Luluabourg (now Kananga) and Elisabethville (now Lubumbashi), in Katanga. Their intervention, which was followed in some cases by heavy fighting with Congolese soldiers, further increased tension and disorder throughout the country. On 11 July, shortly after the arrival of Belgian troops in Elisabethville, Moïse Tshombé, the provincial president, proclaimed the independence of Katanga, the richest province of the Congo, which provided the country with more than half of its revenues.

On 12 July, President Kasa-Vubu and Prime Minister Lumumba sent a joint telegram* to the Secretary-General requesting United Nations military assistance. They said that the essential purpose of the requested military aid was "to protect the national territory of the Congo against the present external aggression which is a threat

* S/4382.

to international peace". The next day, they cabled a further message*
to the Secretary-General to make it clear that they were not asking
for aid to restore the internal situation but to respond to Belgian aggression.

On 13 July, Hammarskjöld, invoking Article 99 of the United Nations Charter—which empowers the Secretary-General to bring to the
attention of the Security Council any matter which in his opinion may
threaten international peace and security—requested an urgent
meeting of the Council to consider the situation in the Congo.† The
Council met on the same evening. In an opening statement, Hammarskjöld outlined his ideas about the actions that the Council might take
in response to the request of the Congolese Government. In essence,
he recommended the establishment of a United Nations peace-
keeping force to assist that Government in maintaining law and order
until, with technical assistance from the United Nations, the Congolese
national security forces were able fully to meet their tasks. He
assumed that, were the United Nations to act as proposed, the Belgian
Government would withdraw its forces from Congolese territory.

At the same meeting, during the night of 13/14 July, the Security
Council adopted resolution 143(1960), by which it called upon the
Government of Belgium to withdraw its troops from the territory of
the Congo and decided "to authorize the Secretary-General to take
the necessary steps, in consultation with the Government of the
Republic of the Congo, to provide the Government with such military
assistance as might be necessary until, through that Government's
efforts with United Nations technical assistance, the national security
forces might be able, in the opinion of the Government, to meet fully
their tasks". It requested the Secretary-General to report to the
Security Council as appropriate.

The Council resolution was adopted by 8 votes in favour (including the USSR and the United States) to none against, with 3 abstentions.

Secretary-General's principles governing
the United Nations Force

In his first report on the implementation of the
resolution‡ the Secretary-General outlined the principles which
would govern the organization and activities of the United Nations
Force in the Congo, its composition and the action he had taken or
envisaged taking to establish it.

The proposals the Secretary-General set out for the Force were
as follows:

* *Ibid.*   † S/4381.   ‡ S/4389.

(a)   The Force was to be regarded as a temporary security force to be deployed in the Congo with the consent of the Congolese Government until the national security forces were able, in the opinion of that Government, to meet fully their tasks.

(b)   Although dispatched at the request of the Congolese Government and remaining there with its consent, and although it might be considered as serving as an arm of the Congolese Government for the maintenance of law and order and protection of life, the Force was necessarily under the exclusive command of the United Nations, vested in the Secretary-General under the control of the Security Council. The Force was thus not under the orders of the Congolese Government and could not be permitted to become a party to any internal conflict.

(c)   The host Government, when exercising its sovereign rights with regard to the presence of the United Nations Force in its territory, should be guided by good faith in the interpretation of the Force's purpose. Similarly, the United Nations should be so guided when it considered the question of the maintenance of the Force in the host country.

(d)   The United Nations should have free access to the area of operation and full freedom of movement within that area as well as all the communications and other facilities required to carry out its tasks. A further elaboration of this rule obviously required an agreement with the Government specifying what was to be considered the area of operation.

(e)   The authority granted to the United Nations Force could not be exercised within the Congo either in competition with the representatives of its Government or in co-operation with them in any joint operation. This principle applied also a fortiori to representatives and military units of Governments other than the host Government. Thus, the United Nations Operation must be separate and distinct from activities by any national authorities.

(f)   The units of the Force must not become parties to internal conflicts. They could not be used to enforce any specific political solution of pending problems or to influence the political balance decisive for such a solution.

(g)   The basic rules of the United Nations for international service were applicable to all United Nations personnel employed in the Congo Operation, particularly as regards loyalty to the aims of the Organization.

(h)   The United Nations military units were not authorized to use force except in self-defence. They were never to take the initiative in the use of force, but were entitled to respond with force to an attack with arms, including attacks intended to make them withdraw from positions they occupied under orders from the Commander, acting under the authority of the Security Council. The basic element of influence in this principle was clearly the prohibition of any initiative in the use of armed force.

With regard to the composition of the Force, the Secretary-General reiterated the principle that, while the United Nations must preserve its authority to decide on this matter, it should take full account of the views of the host Government. He recalled that in order to limit the scope of possible differences of opinion with host Governments, the United Nations had in recent operations followed two principles: not to include units from any of the permanent members of the Security Council nor units from any country which, because of its geographical position or for other reasons, might be considered as having a special interest in the situation that had called for the operation. He indicated his intention to seek, in the first place, the assistance of African States for the United Nations Force in the Congo. The Force would be built around a core of military units from African States and should also include suitable units from other regions to give it a truly international character. In selecting the contingents, the Secretary-General would necessarily be guided by considerations of availability of troops, language and geographical distribution within the region.

In order to set up the Force speedily, the Secretary-General said, he had accepted offers of troops by Ethiopia, Ghana, Guinea, Morocco and Tunisia. These five countries would provide seven battalions, with a total strength of 4,000 men. Arrangements were being made to air-lift the battalions to the Congo as soon as possible. An offer of troops from Mali had also been received and would be activated at a later stage.

With the deployment of the seven battalions, the first phase of the buildup of the Force would be completed. For the second phase, the Secretary-General had requested troops from three European countries and one Asian and one Latin American country. In one of those cases—Sweden—he had asked and secured permission to transfer to the Congo on a temporary basis the Swedish battalion of the United Nations Emergency Force (UNEF) in Gaza, thus bringing the total strength of the Force to eight battalions.

Requests for aircraft, signal and other logistic support, as well as for air transport facilities, had been addressed to a number of non-African nations.

As soon as Security Council resolution 143(1960) was adopted, the Secretary-General appointed Ralph J. Bunche as his Special Representative in the Congo to head the new Operation. He also appointed Lieutenant-General Carl C. von Horn, of Sweden, as Supreme Commander of the United Nations Force in the Congo. General von Horn, who until then had occupied the post of Chief of Staff of the United Nations Truce Supervision Organization (UNTSO), would be assisted in the initial stage by a small personal staff of officers drawn from UNTSO.

On the evening of 15 July 1960, less than 48 hours after the adoption of the Council's resolution, an advance party of the Tunisian contingent, consisting of about 90 officers and men, landed at Leopoldville. They were followed on succeeding days by the remainder of the Tunisian battalion and personnel of the Ethiopian, Ghanaian, Guinean and Moroccan battalions. Bunche, who was appointed temporary Commander of the Force pending the arrival of General von Horn, immediately deployed these units in sensitive localities in Leopoldville, Stanleyville (now Kisangani), Matadi, Thysville and Coquilhatville (now Mbandaka). On 18 July, General von Horn and his staff officers arrived in Leopoldville and immediately set up Force headquarters at the airport.

As the responsibilities of the United Nations in the Congo expanded, the Secretary-General requested and obtained more battalions and support personnel. The Force reached a total of 19,828 at its peak strength by July 1961. From then on, as some of its responsibilities were fulfilled, the strength of the Force was progressively reduced. In addition to the military units, ONUC had a Civilian Operations component which employed some 2,000 experts and technicians to provide the Congolese Government with extensive assistance in the administrative, technical and humanitarian fields.

While its original mandate as outlined in Council resolution 143(1960) remained valid, ONUC was given new responsibilities and new tasks during the four years of its operation. The history of ONUC may be divided into four periods, as follows: restoration of law and order and withdrawal of Belgian forces (July–August 1960); constitutional crisis (September 1960–September 1961); termination of the secession of Katanga (September 1961–February 1963); and consolidation of the Congolese Government (February 1963–June 1964). Each of these periods is dealt with separately below.

B. Restoration of law and order and withdrawal of Belgian forces (July–August 1960)

ONUC objectives

The two main objectives of ONUC during the initial phase were to help the Congolese Government restore law and order and bring about the speedy withdrawal of the Belgian forces. These objectives were closely related.

In a statement made in the Security Council just before the adoption of resolution 143(1960), the representative of Belgium stated that his Government had no political designs in the Congo and that when the United Nations Force had moved into position and was able to ensure the effective maintenance of order and the security of persons in the Congo, his Government would withdraw its forces.

Immediately after the adoption of the resolution, Bunche initiated negotiations with the Belgian Ambassador in Leopoldville in order to work out agreement for the speedy and orderly withdrawal of the Belgian forces in accordance with the resolution and in the light of the undertaking given by the Belgian Government. The United Nations plan was to bring its forces into the Congo as rapidly as possible and deploy them in various parts of the country, first of all in those positions occupied by Belgian troops. Once deployed, United Nations troops would restore law and order and ensure the protection of civilians in co-operation with the Congolese Government and speed up the withdrawal of the Belgian forces from the area.

Withdrawal of Belgian troops outside Katanga

The first troops of the United Nations Force arrived at Leopoldville on the evening of 15 July and were deployed the next morning at the radio station and the power station and along the main thoroughfare of the capital. Their presence had an immediate calming effect in an extremely tense situation. On 16 July, the Belgian Ambassador informed Bunche that, consequent upon the arrival of the United Nations troops, the first contingents of the Belgian armed forces had left Leopoldville and returned to their bases on that same day. On 19 July, Bunche reported to the Secretary-General that the United Nations was now in a position to guarantee that contingents of the United Nations Force drawn from both African and European countries would arrive during the week in sufficient numbers to ensure order and protect the entire population of Leopoldville, African and European. In the light of this assurance, it was decided that the Belgian forces would begin to withdraw completely from the Leopoldville area and return to their bases on 20 July. This withdrawal operation was to be completed by the afternoon of 23 July.

As more United Nations troops were flown into the Congo, they were deployed in other areas such as Thysville, Matadi, Luluabourg, Coquilhatville and Stanleyville. In each of these places, ONUC immediately began its task of maintaining law and order and protecting the local population, and initiated discussions with the Belgian representative to bring about the withdrawal of Belgian troops at an early date.

Although this speed could be achieved only through strenuous efforts, the Congolese Government did not consider it fast enough. On 17 July 1960, Lumumba and Kasa-Vubu addressed an ultimatum to the Secretary-General, warning that if the Belgian forces were not completely withdrawn within 48 hours, they would request troops from the Soviet Union. The Secretary-General brought the matter before the Security Council, which—by resolution 145(1960) of 22 July 1960, adopted unanimously—commended the action taken by the Secretary-General and called upon Belgium to speed up the withdrawal of its troops.

The original plan was therefore continued without change. As soon as new United Nations contingents arrived, they were deployed in the positions occupied by Belgian troops. They brought about the complete withdrawal of the Belgian troops from Leopoldville and the surrounding area on 23 July 1960, and from the whole of the Congo, except Katanga and the two bases, by the beginning of August 1960.

Withdrawal from Katanga

The next step was the entry of United Nations troops into the province of Katanga. On this question, the Secretary-General ran into a grave conflict with Prime Minister Lumumba, who wanted ONUC to help his Government put down the secession of Katanga by force. The Secretary-General refused to do this, taking the position that under its mandate ONUC could not use force except in self-defence, and could not be a party to, or in any way intervene in or be used to influence the outcome of, any internal conflict in the Congo. He also encountered serious difficulties with the Katangese secessionist authorities and the Belgian Government. The Katangese authorities strongly opposed the entry of United Nations troops and, citing this opposition, the Belgian Government was reluctant to withdraw its forces from Katanga.

On 4 August 1960, the Secretary-General, who had arrived in Leopoldville a few days earlier, sent Bunche to Elisabethville to make arrangements with the Belgian representative there for the entry of United Nations troops into Katanga, which, if no difficulties arose, would take place on 6 August. But in the face of unqualified and unyielding opposition by the Katangese secessionist authorities, Bunche concluded that the entry of United Nations troops could not be achieved without bloodshed. The Secretary-General therefore decided to postpone the original plan and brought the matter before the Security Council.

By resolution 146(1960) of 9 August 1960, the Security Council confirmed the authority conferred upon the Secretary-General by its previous resolutions and called upon Belgium immediately to withdraw its troops from Katanga, under speedy modalities determined by the Secretary-General. At the same time, while declaring that the entry of the United Nations Force into Katanga was necessary, the Council reaffirmed that the Force should not in any way intervene in any internal conflict in the Congo or be used to influence the outcome of any such conflict, constitutional or otherwise. The resolution was adopted by 9 votes to none, with 2 abstentions (France and Italy).

After the adoption of the resolution, the Secretary-General returned to the Congo and, on 12 August, personally led the first United Nations unit into Katanga. But Prime Minister Lumumba strongly criticized the manner in which the Secretary-General had implemented the Council's resolutions and refused henceforth to cooperate with him. In view of the Prime Minister's reaction, the Secretary-General once again referred the matter to the Security Council.

The Council met on 21 August 1960, but did not vote on any resolution. During the discussion, the Secretary-General indicated that, in the absence of any new directive, he would consider his interpretation of the ONUC mandate as upheld. He also made known his intention to appoint an Advisory Committee, composed of Member States which had contributed troops to the United Nations Force, to advise him on future policy on the Congo.

The entry of United Nations troops into Katanga on 12 August 1960 set off a process of withdrawal of Belgian troops from the province, which was completed by the beginning of September. At that time, Belgian troops were also withdrawn from the military bases of Kamina and Kitona, which were taken over by ONUC.

Thus, despite difficult circumstances, ONUC brought about the withdrawal of Belgian troops from the whole of the Congo within six weeks. However, the secession of Katanga remained unresolved.

Maintenance of law and order

The maintenance of law and order was the heaviest of all the tasks falling upon ONUC. In order to carry out that task, the Secretary-General set up a United Nations Force which at its peak strength numbered nearly 20,000. But even at its peak strength, the Force was hardly sufficient and was severely strained, inasmuch as its responsibilities had to encompass such a vast land as the Congo.

On their arrival in the Congo, United Nations soldiers were officially instructed that they were members of a peace force, not a fighting force, that they had been asked to come in response to an appeal from the Congolese Government, that their task was to help in restoring order and calm in a troubled country and that they should give protection against acts of violence to all the people, Africans and Europeans alike. They were also told that although they carried arms, they were to use them only in self-defence; they were in the Congo to help everyone and to harm no one.

What ONUC sought to do was to assist the Congolese authorities to perform their normal duties, for instance by undertaking joint patrols with the local police for the maintenance of law and order in a given area. When, however, this was not possible on account of the breakdown of the security forces, the United Nations Force had to perform the normal security duties in the place of Congolese authorities. But in so doing it sought the consent and co-operation of the Congolese Government. Such was the case in Leopoldville during the Operation's first stage, when United Nations soldiers performed police duties along the city's main arteries to ensure the protection of its essential services.

Following these procedures, the Force restored law and order, protected life and property, and ensured the continued operation of essential services wherever it was deployed. In many areas it brought under control unruly ANC elements, many of whom laid down their arms voluntarily or at the request of their Government.

Thus the Force carried out its task of maintaining law and order with success in the initial phase of the Operation.

However, the internal situation in August began to worsen rapidly. Tribal rivalries, which had plagued the country before independence, flared up that month with added intensity in Kasai between Baluba and Lulua tribesmen. The Baluba of the Luluabourg area fled *en masse* to their tribal lands in the Bakwanga region, where their leader, Albert Kalonji, proclaimed the secession of South Kasai.

In Equateur and Leopoldville provinces, there was increasing opposition to the Government. To put down opposition and secessionist movements, Prime Minister Lumumba arrested some opposition leaders, and anti-Government newspapers were suspended. At the end of August, ANC troops were sent to South Kasai, and many civilians were killed, including women and children. Other ANC troops were being massed near the northern border of Katanga in preparation for an invasion of the province. During those days, elements of the ANC, which the Government was using to achieve its political objectives but which it was not always able to control, were a constant danger to the civilian population.

Without the co-operation of the Congolese Government which it had come to assist, ONUC faced a frustrating situation. Its activities were further hampered when the Government itself resorted to actions which tended to endanger law and order, or restrict human rights. Whenever this happened, ONUC endeavoured to induce and persuade Congolese authorities to change their course of action, and, to the extent possible, took measures to ensure the protection of the threatened persons. But it refused to use force to subdue Congolese authorities, or the ANC under their orders. Even when its own personnel were attacked, ONUC intervened only to prevent further excesses and to urge the Congolese Government to take disciplinary action against the culprits.

c. Constitutional crisis (September 1960– September 1961)

Introduction

On 5 September 1960, a constitutional crisis developed, when President Kasa-Vubu, invoking the authority conferred upon him by the *Loi fondamentale,* decided to dismiss Prime Minister Lumumba.* The crisis lasted 11 months, during which time there was no legal government and the country was divided into four opposing camps, each with its own armed forces. ONUC therefore could only deal with *de facto* authority and do whatever it could to avert civil war and protect the civilian population. It attempted to prevent the leaders who wielded power from subduing opponents by force and at the same time encouraged those leaders to seek a solution through negotiation and conciliation.

Dismissal of Lumumba

In the days following Kasa-Vubu's dismissal of Lumumba, utter confusion prevailed in Leopoldville. Lumumba refused to recognize Kasa-Vubu's decision and, in turn, dismissed Kasa-Vubu as Chief of State. Parliament supported Lumumba, although it refused to endorse his decision to dismiss the Chief of State, but Parliament itself was soon suspended by Kasa-Vubu. Each contending party sought the support of the army and, whenever it could, ordered the arrest of its opponents. On 14 September 1960,† Colonel Joseph Mobutu imposed by a *coup* an army-backed régime run by a Council of Commissioners (*Collège des Commissaires*) and supporting Kasa-Vubu. But the *coup* was not fully effective in that Lumumba and his supporters resisted the Commissioners' authority.

Emergency measures

At the outset of the crisis, ONUC took emergency measures to avoid violence and bloodshed.‡ It decided on the night of 5/6 September 1960 to close the Leopoldville airport to prevent the arrival of rival troops. The following day, in view of the likely dangerous effect of inflammatory speeches on an already disturbed populace and after a number of violent demonstrations had taken place in the city, it temporarily closed down the Leopoldville radio station. These measures were lifted by 13 September 1960, as soon as the tension had subsided to below the explosive level.

In response to appeals from political and other leaders of all sides in Leopoldville, ONUC agreed to protect the threatened leaders, and in so doing it endeavoured to show absolute impartiality. ONUC guards were stationed around the residences of both Kasa-Vubu and Lumumba. Protection was also given to the other leaders, though not to the same extent.

* S/4531.   † S/4557.   ‡ S/4531.

Containment of hostilities

In the following months, ONUC endeavoured to prevent or control hostilities between the various Congolese factions.

In South Kasai, ONUC helped in arranging a cease-fire between ANC troops and Kalonji's secessionist army and in establishing a neutral zone under ONUC control. It also persuaded the ANC command to withdraw its troops from the northern border of Katanga.

In northern Katanga, where violent fighting broke out between pro-Tshombé gendarmes and the anti-Tshombé Baluba population, ONUC put an end to the fighting by setting up, in agreement with both parties, neutral zones under its protection.

Protected areas were set up at various times and places, to which threatened persons, Africans and Europeans alike, could repair for safety. Neutral zones were established to stop tribal warfare. During this period of unrest, Europeans, many of whom were settlers in scattered, remote areas, were often threatened by hostile local authorities or populations. Whenever possible, ONUC took measures to rescue and protect them and, if they so desired, to evacuate them to safer areas.

The contending parties turned to ONUC for recognition and support. ONUC continued its policy of avoiding intervening or taking sides in the internal conflicts. While it recognized the unimpaired status of Kasa-Vubu as Chief of State, it refused to help him achieve political aims by force and, in particular, to recognize the Council of Commissioners supported by him.

Security Council and General Assembly consideration

The crisis was examined by the Security Council from 14 to 17 September 1960 and, when the Council failed to take a decision, by an emergency special session of the General Assembly from 17 to 20 September.

By resolution 1474(ES-IV) of 20 September 1960, the Assembly requested the Secretary-General to continue to take vigorous action in line with the Security Council's resolutions. In an effort to resolve the constitutional crisis, it appealed to all Congolese to seek a speedy solution, by peaceful means, of all their internal conflicts, and requested the Advisory Committee on the Congo to appoint a conciliation commission to assist them in that endeavour.

The Conciliation Commission was composed of Ethiopia, the Federation of Malaya, Ghana, Guinea, India, Indonesia, Liberia, Mali,

Morocco, Nigeria, Pakistan, Senegal, the Sudan, Tunisia and the United Arab Republic. Subsequently Guinea, Indonesia, Mali and the United Arab Republic withdrew from the Commission.

During the meeting of the Security Council, two Congolese delegations, one appointed by Kasa-Vubu and the other by Lumumba, were sent to New York, but neither could win recognition. Two months later, during the fifteenth regular session of the General Assembly in December, Kasa-Vubu himself came to New York as the head of his delegation, which was seated by the Assembly after a long and heated debate. The Assembly's decision considerably enhanced Kasa-Vubu's personal prestige, but did not bring an immediate solution to the crisis.

Four rival groups

In the mean time, the internal situation rapidly worsened in the Congo. While the Council of Commissioners consolidated its position in Leopoldville, Antoine Gizenga, acting on behalf of Lumumba, succeeded in establishing a "government" in Stanleyville which was formally recognized as the legitimate government of the Republic by a number of Member States. With the support of the local ANC troops, led by General Victor Lundula, Gizenga extended his authority beyond Orientale province to Kivu and the northern part of Katanga.

At the same time, the secessionist authorities headed by Moïse Tshombé and Albert Kalonji consolidated their hold, respectively, over southern Katanga and South Kasai, with the active assistance of certain foreign Powers. Thus the Congo came to be divided into four rival camps, each relying more on armed force than on popular support.

ONUC casualties

In carrying out its mission of peace, the United Nations Force suffered many casualties. On 8 November 1960, a patrol of 11 Irish soldiers was ambushed by tribesmen in northern Katanga and eight of them were killed. Another incident occurred on 24 November when ANC troops attacked the Ghanaian Embassy in Leopoldville. The Tunisian unit which guarded the Embassy incurred several casualties, including one fatality.

Here again, when the authorities in power indulged in actions which endangered peace and order, or violated human rights, ONUC could not always prevent those actions, but sought to redress the situation by the use of persuasion or good offices. Thus ONUC could not prevent a number of political arrests made by the various local régimes. At the time, those régimes endeavoured to strengthen their armed forces by importing arms and military equipment from abroad. While ONUC did its best to stop such imports, its forces were insufficient to control all points of entry, and therefore it could not prevent quantities of arms and equipment from being smuggled into different parts of the country.

Lumumba's death

From the beginning of the constitutional crisis, ONUC troops vigilantly guarded Lumumba's residence and, so long as he remained there, he was safe. However, it was not possible to protect him when he voluntarily left his residence, as he did on the night of 27/28 November 1960, in an apparent attempt to get to Stanleyville, his political stronghold.* Before he could get there, he was arrested by ANC soldiers controlled by Mobutu near Port-Francqui (now Ilebo) and brought back to Leopoldville. Once Lumumba was arrested by the de facto authorities of Leopoldville, ONUC was not in a position to take forcible action to liberate him from his captors, but it exerted all possible pressure to secure lawful, humane treatment for him. Upon learning of the arrest, the Secretary-General sent a succession of messages to President Kasa-Vubu,† expressing his concern over the event and stressing the importance of giving the prisoner all the guarantees provided by law. Similarly repeated representations were later made to the President by Rajeshwar Dayal of India, at the time Special Representative of the Secretary-General in the Congo. ONUC could not do more without exceeding the mandate given it by the Security Council and without using force.

Lumumba remained detained in Thysville until 17 January, when he and two other political prisoners, Joseph Okito and Maurice Mpolo, were transferred to Elisabethville in Katanga. This move brought strong protests from both the Secretary-General and the United Nations Conciliation Commission for the Congo, which was then in the territory. In particular, the Secretary-General took immediate action to urge the authorities concerned to return Lumumba to Leopoldville province and to apply the normal legal rules. But no remedial action was taken, and, four weeks later, the news came from Katanga that the three prisoners had been murdered. The circumstances of their death were later investigated by a United Nations commission,

* S/4571.   † S/4571, annexes I and II.

which accepted as substantially true evidence indicating that the prisoners had been killed on 17 January 1961 and probably in the presence of high officials of the Katanga provincial government.*

Following Lumumba's death, there was a series of reprisals and counter-reprisals by pro-Lumumba and anti-Lumumba factions, including summary executions of political leaders. The civil war, already under way in northern Katanga, threatened to spread to other regions.

Several troop-contributing countries withdrew their national contingents from ONUC,† reducing its strength from 20,000 to less than 15,000. At United Nations Headquarters, the Soviet Union called for Hammarskjöld's dismissal and announced that it would not, henceforth, recognize him as Secretary-General.

Authorization to use force

The Security Council met again on 15 February 1961, and after long debate adopted, on 21 February, resolution 161(1961), by which it authorized ONUC to use force, as a last resort, to prevent civil war in the Congo. It urged that the various Congolese armed units be reorganized and brought under discipline and control, and urged the immediate evacuation of all Belgian and other foreign military and paramilitary personnel and political advisers not under United Nations command, as well as mercenaries. It also urged the convening of Parliament and the taking of the necessary protective measures in that connection.

Provisional government

After January 1961, a number of steps were taken by various Congolese leaders attempting to resolve the crisis. On 25 January, a preliminary round-table was sponsored by Kasa-Vubu in Leopoldville. It was boycotted by pro-Lumumba and pro-Tshombé leaders, which considerably limited its usefulness. However, at the end of the conference, Kasa-Vubu decided to replace the Council of Commissioners by a provisional government headed by Joseph Iléo, a decision which was considered by the United Nations Conciliation Commission as a step in the right direction.

---

* S/4976.   † S/4640.

Situation in the Congo: February-April 1961

The period immediately following the adoption of the Security Council's resolution of 21 February 1961 was a critical one for the United Nations Operation in the Congo. Thinly deployed throughout the country, the United Nations Force had great difficulty in coping with its overwhelming tasks, and this difficulty increased with its reduction in strength.

The difficulties were compounded by the hostile attitude of the *de facto* authorities of Leopoldville and Elisabethville. These authorities interpreted the Council's new resolution as an attempt to subdue them by force and, in retaliation, ordered a number of harassing measures against ONUC and its personnel. The most serious of these was an attack by ANC troops on the United Nations garrison in Matadi on 4 March 1961, which forced the garrison to withdraw from the port city.*

In order to cope with these difficulties and to implement the resolution, the Secretary-General took urgent action to increase the strength of the United Nations Force. New contributions of personnel were obtained from several Governments, bringing the total of the United Nations troops to more than 18,000 in April 1961.

In April, the situation began to improve, first because of the increased strength of the Force, and secondly, because after patient negotiations, ONUC reached an agreement with President Kasa-Vubu on 17 April 1961† for the implementation of the Security Council's February resolution.

The limited use of force, as authorized by the Council, was resorted to by ONUC at the beginning of April 1961 to stop the civil war, which was spreading dangerously in northern Katanga. Since mid-March 1961, Katangese gendarmerie led by foreign mercenaries had launched an offensive against the anti-Tshombé forces in northern Katanga in a determined effort to crush all opposition there. On 27 March, ‡ the United Nations Force Commander warned Tshombé to stop the offensive, but the warning was unheeded and his gendarmes entered Manono three days later and prepared to attack Kabalo. It was at this point that United Nations troops intervened, stopped the gendarmes and established control of the area between Kabalo and Albertville (now Kalemie).

* S/4761.   † S/4807, annex I.   ‡ S/4791.

Further casualties

At the end of April, a tragic incident occurred when a Ghanaian detachment of ONUC in Port-Francqui was suddenly attacked and overpowered by ANC troops, and 44 of its members ruthlessly massacred. It was generally agreed that this brutal assault was mainly an act by undisciplined and unpredictable armed troops. Thereafter, the ONUC command made it a rule not to station small units in isolated areas.

Another series of incidents was related to the ANC campaign, late in 1961, to occupy northern Katanga. In connection with this military campaign, which is described in the section below on the problem of Katanga, a number of grave incidents were caused by undisciplined ANC elements. At the beginning of November 1961, ANC soldiers of the Leopoldville group assaulted several Belgian women in Luluabourg. On 11 November, ANC soldiers of the Stanleyville group massacred 13 ONUC aircrew members of Italian nationality in Kindu. Two days later, ANC soldiers of the same group, who had just entered Albertville, began looting houses and threatening civilians there. On 1 January 1961, 22 European missionaries and an undetermined number of Africans were killed in Kongolo by ANC soldiers, also from Stanleyville, in an incident reminiscent of the Kindu massacre.

Conciliation efforts

During the first days of the constitutional crisis, ONUC endeavoured to prevent the leaders holding the reins of power from using force to subdue their opponents within or outside the zones they controlled and, at the same time, it encouraged all leaders to seek a solution of their differences through negotiation and conciliation.

Conciliation efforts were also made by the United Nations Conciliation Commission, established under the Assembly's resolution of 20 September 1960 *(see above)*. This Commission, which was composed of representatives of African and Asian countries which contributed troops to the United Nations Force, visited the Congo at the beginning of 1961. After spending seven weeks in that country, the Commission concluded that, while there was among most leaders a general feeling of weariness and a sincere desire to achieve a peaceful solution to the crisis, a small number of other leaders, among the very persons holding the reins of power, appeared to prefer a military rather than a political and constitutional solution. Because of those leaders' unco-operative and intransigent attitude, the Commission's attempts to reconcile the opposing groups had not led to positive results. The Commission also came to the conclusion that the crisis could be solved only if Parliament was reconvened and a national unity government was approved by it, and that one of the main obstacles to a speedy solution was foreign intervention in the internal affairs of the Congo.

Tananarive Conference

In the mean time, at the beginning of March 1961, a conference was held in Tananarive (now Antananarivo), Madagascar, on the proposal of Moïse Tshombé. It was attended by a number of top Congolese leaders, but Antoine Gizenga, who had at first agreed to come, did not show up. The Tananarive Conference proposed that the Congo be turned into a confederation of sovereign States. Under the proposed arrangement, the central Government would be abolished, and legislative and executive powers would be vested in the individual States. The Conference proposals also provided for the establishment of new States, but did not determine the criteria to be followed in that connection. This decision led some Congolese leaders, through personal ambition and tribal animosities, to lay claim for the creation of a score of new States. But the influence of the Tananarive Conference was short-lived. Soon afterwards, Kasa-Vubu and other leaders revised their positions and made it clear that the decisions of Tananarive were mere statements of intention and, unless approved by Parliament, had no force of law.

Coquilhatville meeting

The following month, on 24 April 1961, a more important conference was convened in Coquilhatville, on the proposal of Kasa-Vubu. Gizenga again refused to attend. Tshombé came and sought to have the Conference endorse the Tananarive proposals. When his attempt was opposed by the overwhelming majority of the representatives, he decided to boycott the Conference. As he prepared to fly back to Elisabethville, he was arrested by the Leopoldville authorities, although he was released about a month later. The Conference continued nevertheless, and, at the conclusion of its work, it recommended a reorganization of the governmental structure of the Congo on a federal basis. From the outset, it had been made clear that Conference decisions would have to be endorsed by Parliament, and during the Conference, on 12 May, President Kasa-Vubu announced that Parliament would be reopened in the near future and requested United Nations assistance and protection for this purpose.

While carefully avoiding interference in the discussions between the Congolese leaders, ONUC assisted them whenever it was requested to do so. Thus it placed a guard at the site of the preliminary round-table conference in Leopoldville. It agreed to facilitate Gizenga's trip to Tananarive when he first accepted to go there. Before the Coquilhatville Conference, a Congolese leader, Cléophas Kamitatu, went to Stanleyville on an ONUC aeroplane in an effort to bring about a *rapprochement* between Gizenga and Kasa-Vubu. ONUC also made representations for Tshombé's release.

Reopening of Parliament

After Kasa-Vubu announced his intention to reconvene Parliament, ONUC spared no effort to help achieve this purpose. An essential condition for reconvening Parliament was a *rapprochement* between leaders of the Leopoldville and Stanleyville groups. To these two groups belonged the great majority of parliamentarians, and if one of them refused to attend meetings of Parliament, there would be no quorum. But the memory of Patrice Lumumba's death and its aftermath was still vivid, and leaders of the two groups were divided by deep suspicion and distrust. Through good offices and persuasion, ONUC officials did everything possible to dissipate their mutual suspicion and lay the groundwork for negotiations between them.

After Kasa-Vubu called the parliamentary session in Leopoldville, Gizenga condemned his action as illegal and ordered Parliament to meet in Kamina. Thanks to ONUC's good offices, Gizenga softened his stand and agreed not to insist on Kamina, provided that full protection was given to parliamentarians by ONUC. Later, a meeting between Leopoldville and Stanleyville representatives was arranged at Leopoldville, under ONUC auspices, to consider the modalities of the reopening of Parliament.* The Stanleyville representatives were brought to Leopoldville in an ONUC aircraft and the meeting took place at ONUC headquarters. After long discussions, an agreement was reached by the representatives of the two groups. At their joint request, ONUC accepted the responsibility for making arrangements for the session of Parliament and ensuring full protection to the parliamentarians.

* S/4841.

In accordance with a request made by both delegations, ONUC also sought to persuade Congolese leaders of South Kasai and southern Katanga to subscribe to the agreement on the reconvening of Parliament. Both Kalonji and Tshombé, who was released from confinement by the Leopoldville authorities on 22 June 1961, promised to co-operate. Tshombé signed a protocol calling for the reconvening of Parliament,* but he changed his position after he returned to Elisabethville.

Parliament reopened on 22 July with more than 200—out of a total of 221—members attending. Most of them were brought to Leopoldville with the assistance of ONUC.

Government of national unity

On 2 August 1961, Prime Minister Cyrille Adoula, at the request of President Kasa-Vubu, constituted a Government of national unity, which was unanimously approved by both Chambers.†

With the act of approval of the national unity Government, the constitutional crisis was ended. In response to a letter from Prime Minister Adoula, the Secretary-General confirmed‡ that the United Nations would deal with his Government as the Central Government of the Republic and would render to it whatever aid and support the United Nations was in a position to give to the Congo.

Adoula endeavoured to secure Gizenga's co-operation, with the active assistance of other Stanleyville leaders and ONUC. His efforts seemed successful at first. On 7 August 1961, Gizenga recognized the Adoula Government as the sole legal Government of the Republic. Four weeks later, he came back to Leopoldville to assume the post of Deputy Prime Minister and accompanied Adoula in that capacity to a conference of non-aligned nations in Belgrade, Yugoslavia. However, Gizenga left again for Stanleyville at the beginning of October, ostensibly to collect some personal effects, and refused to return to Leopoldville despite the many appeals from Adoula. While he was in Stanleyville, he attempted to form a new party, the *Parti national lumumbiste* (PANALU), and made several statements strongly hostile to the Government.

On 8 January 1962, the Chamber of Representatives adopted a resolution§ ordering Gizenga to return to Leopoldville without delay to answer charges of secessionism. Gizenga refused, and his defiant attitude led to fighting, on 13 January 1962, between gendarmes supporting him and ANC troops loyal to the Government, which was easily won by the latter. Thereafter, Gizenga was dismissed from the

---

* S/4841/Add.2.   † S/4913.   ‡ S/4923.   § S/5053/Add.1, annex I.

post of Deputy Prime Minister following a motion of censure by the Chamber of Representatives.*

D. Termination of the secession of Katanga (September 1961– February 1963)

United Nations resolutions

Along with the breakdown of law and order and foreign armed intervention, the secession of Katanga was one of the main problems which confronted the Congo when it appealed to the United Nations for help. However, the Security Council's resolution of 14 July 1960 contained no mention of this point. In a second resolution, of 22 July, the Council requested all States to refrain from any action which might undermine the territorial integrity and political independence of the Congo. In August, the Council called for the immediate withdrawal of Belgian troops from Katanga; however, it emphasized that the United Nations was not to take sides in Congolese internal conflicts, constitutional or otherwise, nor was the Organization to be used to influence the outcome of any such conflict.

Secretary-General's position

The Secretary-General's position was that, while ONUC originated from a request by the Congolese Government, the purpose of United Nations intervention as determined by the Security Council was not to achieve the domestic aims of the Government but to preserve international peace and security. The United Nations Force therefore could not, under the Council's decision, be used on behalf of the Central Government to subdue or to force the provincial government into a specific line of action in regard to an internal political controversy. At the same time, the problem of Katanga clearly had an international dimension.

What the United Nations sought to do was to encourage efforts at reconciliation and to eliminate foreign interference, which had been instrumental in bringing about the secession of Katanga and which had helped it to endure. The withdrawal of Belgian troops from Katanga, which occurred in August 1960, did not end the secession

---

* S/5053/Add.1, annex VI.

of the province, and Tshombé's secessionist régime was able to consolidate its hold over southern Katanga, with active foreign assistance. While Belgian officers, supplemented by an increasing number of foreign mercenaries, continued to strengthen the gendarmerie, Tshombé imported large quantities of arms and war *matériel,* including aircraft, from abroad. With his improved armed forces, he launched a merciless extermination campaign against the Baluba and other political and tribal enemies. Helping to maintain law and order in Katanga and protecting large parts of the Katangese population against the brutal lawlessness of the gendarmerie accordingly became one of the principal aspects of the ONUC effort, along with the removal of the foreign political advisers, military and paramilitary personnel and mercenaries.

Union Minière du Haut-Katanga

In carrying out its functions in Katanga, ONUC continually found itself opposed by certain foreign financial interests which, in effect, controlled the economy of the province. These interests centred about the vast industrial and mining complex of the Union Minière du Haut-Katanga—with headquarters in Brussels, Belgium—which had apparently committed itself to Tshombé's secessionist policies.

The Union Minière supported Tshombé in four principal ways. Firstly, it paid nearly all of its taxes not to the Central Government, to which they were due, but to the Katangese provincial authorities. Secondly, it shipped its production not by way of the traditional "national" route, but by way of Portuguese Angola; this enabled it to credit hard-currency export duties to the account of the provincial government. Thirdly, the Congo's part of Union Minière stock was withheld from the Central Government and kept in Brussels. Fourthly, the firm allowed its industrial facilities at Elisabethville and other places to be used by the mercenary-led gendarmerie for military purposes, including the making of some implements of war.

Non-recognition of Katanga

Despite Tshombé's efforts and the powerful financial and political support he enjoyed, his separatist movement never gained official international recognition, either in Belgium or elsewhere. Moreover, neither Belgium nor any other Government publicly espoused the cause of Katangese secession. In fact, after the establishment of the coalition Government in Brussels in the spring of 1961, its Minister for Foreign Affairs, Paul-Henri Spaak, announced publicly his Government's opposition to the secession of Katanga.

Mercenaries

The problem of foreign elements who sought to influence the Congo's destiny in their own interests came to light soon after the country's accession to independence.

In the beginning, the bulk of these persons were Belgian professional military and civilian officials placed at the disposal of the Central Government of the Congo under the treaty of friendship with Belgium, which was signed in June 1960 but never ratified. After the severance of diplomatic relations between the Congo and Belgium, many of these men gathered in Katanga, where they gained prominent positions in the provincial administration and the gendarmerie. From these vantage points they vigorously promoted secession. In effect, they waged war on the Congolese Government at whose disposal they had been placed by their Government. Later these Belgians were joined by other nationalities.

On 21 February 1961, the Security Council urged "the immediate withdrawal and evacuation from the Congo of all Belgian and other foreign military and paramilitary personnel and political advisers not under the United Nations Command, and mercenaries". Implicit in this language was the finding that while the Congo was admittedly and direly in need of assistance from outside, and especially of personnel to carry out technical and professional tasks which the Congolese had not hitherto been trained to perform, there were other types of foreign personnel whose actions were incompatible with genuine Congolese independence and unity. In certain parts of the Congo, and especially in Katanga, such personnel had come to play an increasingly questionable role, obstructing the application of United Nations resolutions and, in effect, working in their own interest and in the interest of certain financial concerns, to break up the country into a balkanized congeries of politically and economically unviable states.

Secretary-General's efforts, 1961

Immediately after the adoption of the resolution of 21 February, the Secretary-General undertook intensive diplomatic efforts to bring about the withdrawal of the foreign military and political personnel.

The Belgian Government took the position that there must be no discrimination against Belgians in engaging non-Congolese technical personnel; as for military personnel and mercenaries, the Belgian Government divided them into several categories. Of these, it undertook to recall those whom it considered it had the legal right to request to return. But it would take no such action in respect of mercenaries or of Belgian personnel directly engaged by the Congolese Government, arguing that it was up to the Secretary-General to agree with the Congolese authorities on how to deal with them. The Secretary-General expressed the view that the measures indicated by the Belgian Government fell far short of full compliance with the Security Council's resolution.

The exchanges with Belgium continued, fairly inconclusively, until the change of government in the first half of 1961, when some progress was made. A new Belgian Government notified 23 of its nationals serving in Katanga as political advisers to return to Belgium. It also acted to prevent the recruitment of mercenaries proper. But the effectiveness of these efforts soon became open to doubt. On 30 October 1961, the Government at Brussels acknowledged that this was the case and took more vigorous steps—including the withdrawal of passports from recalcitrant Belgians.

Tshombé, however, would not co-operate with ONUC. He continued to recruit foreign personnel, whose influence in the councils of the provincial government in fact tended to rise sharply. The complexion of the group also changed noticeably as mercenaries replaced Belgian professional officials. Thus the traditional colonial administrative and military elements were being supplemented through an influx of non-Belgian adventurers and soldiers of fortune, including outlawed elements previously involved in extremist, repressive and separatist policies. They drew political sustenance from the substantial non-Congolese community to which Katanga's extractive and processing industries had given rise.

Repatriation and expulsion of some foreign elements, 1961

Only after the United Nations had strengthened its position in April 1961 did the Katanga secessionist authorities, acting while Tshombé was under detention in the west, officially accept resolution 161(1961) of 21 February.

Those authorities drew up lists of persons whom they considered as falling within the terms of the resolution. By the end of June 1961, 44 Belgian nationals were thus selected for repatriation and the cases of 22 others were under consideration. It was noted, however, that persons clearly not coming under the resolution had been included for political reasons, while others notorious for their activities had been omitted. ONUC representatives continued to press for revision of the lists, and brought home to the provincial authorities their determination to take drastic action, if need be, to comply with the United Nations mandate.

In April 1961,* 30 members of a mercenary unit known as the *"Compagnie internationale"* were apprehended by ONUC personnel and evacuated from the Congo. By mid-June an estimated 60 more mercenaries had withdrawn from Katanga, and on 24 June the *Compagnie* was formally dissolved by the provincial government.

On 7 June 1961, following discussions with the Katangese authorities, the United Nations Force Commander dispatched a military mission to Katanga to help the authorities there to remove non-Congolese elements falling under the resolution. The mission reported that there were 510 foreign and non-commissioned officers active in the Katangese gendarmerie, as against 142 Congolese "cadres". Of the non-Congolese, 208 were the remaining Belgian professional military men; 302 were mercenaries.

But despite the unrelenting efforts of ONUC, the provincial authorities refused to take effective action to remove the foreign elements, without whom the secessionist movement might have collapsed. For its part, the Belgian Government said it was prepared to help in the removal of its professional and non-commissioned officers who had been serving the Congo and were currently in command of the gendarmerie, but it professed itself unable to do anything about "volunteers" and mercenaries. Persuasion by the Secretary-General, who discussed the matter with Foreign Minister Spaak at Geneva on 12 July 1961, was unavailing in this regard.

Gradually, the United Nations was compelled to shift to more vigorous and direct measures to achieve compliance with the Security Council's resolution. Tshombé's chief military adviser was compelled to leave in June 1961, and a prominent political adviser was apprehended, taken to Leopoldville, and evacuated in July. ONUC warned the Katangese authorities that it was prepared to compel the evacuation of other advisers and officers. Five French officers in politically sensitive gendarmerie posts were dismissed and repatriated, and a joint commission was established to list foreign

* S/4790.

political advisers, both those in official posts and others acting unofficially, who were to be repatriated.

Formation of the Adoula Government

The formation of the Adoula Government, enjoying unquestionable and internationally recognized authority, was of crucial importance in enabling the United Nations to proceed with the elimination of foreign elements.

Before the formation of a legal government, United Nations efforts had been restricted by the requirement of avoiding political interference or support of one Congolese faction against another. Now the United Nations was able to do more effectively what the 11-month constitutional crisis had impeded—that is, help the Government remove the foreign elements that had provided the teeth of the attempt to sever, in their own interests, the Congo's richest province from the rest of the country.

Government ordinance on expulsions

Soon after the reopening of Parliament, Tshombé somewhat softened his stand and allowed the parliamentarians of his party in Katanga to participate in the work of Parliament. However, he himself remained in Elisabethville and showed no intention of relinquishing the powers he held in Katanga. For weeks, ONUC representatives urged Tshombé to co-operate in removing the remaining foreign elements, but to little avail.

When all attempts at negotiations failed, in order to remove what it believed to be the main obstacle to a peaceful solution to the Katanga question, Prime Minister Adoula's Government formally requested the expulsion of the mercenaries serving in Katanga and requested ONUC to assist it in carrying out the decision. An ordinance was issued on 24 August calling for expulsion of all foreign officers and mercenaries standing behind the secessionist policy.*

Round-up of mercenaries

On 28 August 1961, ONUC proceeded to round up the mercenaries for deportation. In the face of inflammatory rumours about an invasion by the ANC which had been disseminated by Godefroid Munongo, the provincial Minister of the Interior, certain security precautions were taken by ONUC in Elisabethville, including

---

* S/4940, annex I.

surveillance over Radio Katanga, gendarmerie headquarters and some other key points. Inflammatory broadcasts were thus prevented, and appeals for calm were put on the air.

Tshombé, who had been fully informed of the objectives of ONUC's action, expressed his readiness to co-operate. He broadcast a statement to the effect that the Katangese authorities accepted the decisions of the United Nations, and that the services of foreign military personnel were being terminated by his government.*

At that point, ONUC representatives met with the Elisabethville consular corps, which offered to assume the responsibility, together with two senior Belgian officers formerly in the gendarmerie, for the orderly repatriation of the foreign personnel, most of whom were Belgians. In the interest of avoiding violence, ONUC accepted this arrangement, and suspended its own rounding-up operation.

However, the foreign military men being selected for repatriation were in the main personnel whose withdrawal had earlier been agreed to by the Belgian Government. By 9 September 1961, 273 had been evacuated and 65 were awaiting repatriation. But, while some of the volunteers and mercenaries had left, many others—about 104 of whom were known to be in Katanga—were "missing". They were reinfiltrating into the gendarmerie, distributing arms to groups of soldiers over whom they could assert control, and getting ready for violent resistance.

At the same time, the political police *(Sûreté)*, under Munongo and largely directed by foreign officers, launched a campaign of assaults and persecution against anti-Tshombé Baluba tribesmen in Elisabethville. An effort was made to convince the world that ONUC's actions were causing disorder. The terrorized Baluba streamed out of the city and sought safety by camping in primitive conditions near ONUC troop quarters. ONUC arranged protection for the encampment, into which 35,000 Baluba had crowded by 9 September, creating a serious food and health problem, as well as a continuing danger of tribal violence.

Attack on ONUC

When ONUC realized that the Katangese authorities had no intention of fulfilling their promises, it pressed its demand for the evacuation of foreign personnel of the Katangese security police and of the remaining mercenaries. The Katangese, however, led by Tshombé, had manifestly fallen back under the domination of the foreign elements, and had let themselves be persuaded to launch

* S/4940.

violent action against ONUC. ONUC's plans for a solution of the difficulties in Elisabethville were rejected, and when, on 13 September 1961, it applied security precautions similar to those of 28 August, the United Nations troops were violently attacked by gendarmes led by non-Congolese personnel.

In the morning of 13 September, Tshombé requested a cease-fire, but the attacks on United Nations troops continued.* From the building housing the Belgian Consulate in Elisabethville, where a number of Belgian officers were known to be staying, sustained firing was directed at United Nations troops. The United Nations base at Kamina was attacked, as were the United Nations garrison and installations at Albertville. Reluctantly, United Nations troops had to return the fire. All over Elisabethville, and elsewhere in Katanga, the foreign officers who had gone into hiding reappeared to lead operations against ONUC personnel.

Efforts to reinforce the troops were frustrated by the depredations of a Katangese jet fighter, piloted by a mercenary, which quickly managed to immobilize ONUC's unarmed air transport craft. The jet also played havoc with the ground movements of ONUC, which had deliberately refrained from securing offensive weapons such as fighter-planes or tanks as incompatible with its mission as a peace force.

Dag Hammarskjöld's death

In the mean time, the Secretary-General had arrived in Leopoldville at Prime Minister Adoula's invitation to discuss future prospects of the United Nations Operation in what was hoped would be a new setting created by the completion of the principal tasks assigned by the Security Council and General Assembly. He intended also to bring about a reconciliation between Leopoldville and Elisabethville. Confronted instead with a situation of confused fighting in Elisabethville, Hammarskjöld devoted himself to the task of securing a cessation of hostilities and achieving reconciliation among Congolese factions. In quest of a cease-fire, he flew to Ndola, in what was then Northern Rhodesia, to meet Tshombé. On this flight, on the night of 17 September 1961, his aeroplane crashed and he was killed, together with seven other United Nations staff members and the Swedish crew.†

---

* S/4940/Add.2.   † S/4940/Add.5,9.

Cease-fire, September 1961

The Secretary-General's mission was immediately taken up by the authorities of ONUC in Leopoldville. Mahmoud Khiari, the Chief of ONUC Civilian Operations, flew to Ndola and, on behalf of the United Nations forces, signed a military cease-fire agreement on 20 September.* It was understood as an express condition that the agreement would not affect the application of the Security Council and General Assembly resolutions. A protocol for carrying out the provisions of the cease-fire was signed on 13 October 1961 at Elisabethville.† While the protocol allowed firing back in case of attack, it prohibited Katangese and ONUC troop movements. In approving this protocol, the United Nations stressed its military nature, reemphasized its support of the unity, integrity and independence of the Congo, and insisted on continued enforcement of the Security Council resolution which called for the removal of mercenaries.

Katangese violations of the cease-fire

Although prisoners were exchanged and certain positions held by ONUC in Elisabethville during the fighting were duly released, in accordance with the protocol, Tshombé's régime was soon flouting the provisions of the cease-fire agreement. In Leopoldville, his emissaries made it clear that nothing less than independence along the lines of the Tananarive decisions would be acceptable to the Elisabethville authorities. Meanwhile, the remaining Katangese mercenaries were leading the gendarmerie in a long series of violations of the cease-fire agreement, going so far as to launch offensive air action along the Kasai-Katanga frontier. This was strongly protested by the United Nations. While strictly abiding by the cease-fire in Katanga, ONUC took steps to prevent the recurrence of the September situation when it had found itself powerless to stop the attacks of Katanga's jet fighters. Three Member States—Ethiopia, India and Sweden—provided jet fighter squadrons to the United Nations Force to strengthen its defensive capacity.

At the same time, however, the Force's ground strength was being whittled away. The Tunisian contingent had been withdrawn in August 1961 because of events in Tunisia; the Ghanaian contingent subsequently withdrew, and certain other ONUC units were reduced. Not unaware of these developments, Tshombé and the foreign elements supporting him were determined to turn secession into an accomplished fact. ONUC-sponsored talks between the Central

* S/4940/Add.7   † S/4940/Add.11, annex I.

Government and Katanga were subjected to stalling tactics. At least 237 persons, chiefly mercenaries falling under the provisions of the Security Council's resolution, remained in Katanga, many of whom donned civilian clothing.

ANC offensives

Despairing of a peaceful solution, the Central Government attempted to deal with Katanga's secession independently, by the use of force, in late October 1961. The strength of the national army was built up on the border of northern Katanga in preparation for entry into that region. At the beginning of November, a detachment of the ANC entered northern Katanga in the Kamina area, but was immediately repelled by Katangese gendarmes. Later, ANC units from Stanleyville succeeded in reaching Albertville, Nyunzu, Kongolo and other towns of northern Katanga. To facilitate this move, the Government had requested ONUC assistance for the transport of its troops. The request was turned down because, as had been the case from the outset, it remained against ONUC principles to become a party to an internal conflict.

Security Council authorizes ONUC to remove mercenaries

In the latter part of November 1961, the Security Council was convened once again to examine the situation in the Congo. By resolution 169(1961) of 24 November 1961, the Council strongly deprecated the secessionist activities in Katanga and authorized the Secretary-General to use force to complete the removal of mercenaries.

After the adoption of the resolution, Tshombé launched an inflammatory propaganda campaign against ONUC which soon degenerated into incitement to violence. The results were not long in coming. On 28 November 1961, two senior United Nations officials in Elisabethville were abducted and badly beaten; later an Indian soldier was murdered and an Indian major abducted. Several members of the United Nations Force were detained, and others were killed or wounded. Road-blocks were established by the gendarmerie, impeding ONUC's freedom of movement and endangering its lifelines. It subsequently became known that this was part of a deliberate plan to cut off the United Nations troops in Elisabethville, and either force them to surrender or otherwise destroy them. For one week, United Nations officials sought to settle the crisis by peaceful negotiations. But when it became evident that, in the face of the bad faith displayed by Katangese authorities, no commitments could be relied upon, and that, while pretending to negotiate, those authorities were preparing for more assaults, ONUC finally decided to take action to regain and assure its freedom of movement.

Fighting of December 1961

ONUC had few troops in Elisabethville when fighting broke out on 5 December 1961. Until 14 December, ONUC forces endeavoured to hold their positions and to maintain communications between units while reinforcements were hurriedly flown in from other parts of the Congo. On 15 December, having received enough reinforcements, ONUC troops moved to seize control of those positions in Elisabethville necessary to ensure their freedom of movement. In so doing, they worked their way around the perimeter of the city, in order to keep destruction and civilian casualties to the strict minimum. This objective was achieved within three days.*

From the outset of the hostilities, United Nations military and civilian officers did their best, in co-operation with the International Committee of the Red Cross, to relieve the distress caused to innocent civilians. Persons caught in areas where firing had been initiated by the gendarmerie were escorted to safety, at the risk of ONUC personnel's lives; food supplies were provided where needed; special arrangements for the evacuation of women and children were made by ONUC. Notwithstanding the shortage of troops, ONUC employed a whole battalion to guard the Baluba refugee camp, where more than 40,000 anti-Tshombé Baluba lived under United Nations protection.† ONUC troops, on the one hand, prevented them from raiding Elisabethville and, on the other, protected them from the gendarmes who launched several attacks on the camp.

Kitona Declaration

On 19 December 1961, having ensured the positions necessary for its security, ONUC ordered its troops to hold fire unless fired upon.‡ The same day, Tshombé left Elisabethville to confer with Prime Minister Adoula at Kitona, the United Nations military base in Leopoldville province. After that, major fighting between ONUC and Katangese forces ceased. ONUC immediately turned its efforts to the re-establishment of normal conditions in Elisabethville. It co-operated

---

* S/4940/Add.18.   † *Ibid.*   ‡ S/4940/Add.19.

closely with the local police to stop looting, to rid private houses of squatters and, in general, to restore and maintain law and order.

The Kitona meeting was arranged with the assistance of ONUC and the United States Ambassador in the Congo following a request by Tshombé on 14 December 1961, when the fighting in Elisabethville was in full swing. After meeting Prime Minister Adoula all day long on 20 December, Tshombé signed early in the morning of 21 December an eight-point Declaration.* In this Declaration, he accepted the application of the *Loi fondamentale,* recognized the authority of the Central Government in Leopoldville over all parts of the Congo and agreed to a number of steps aimed at ending the secession of Katanga. He also pledged himself to ensure respect for the resolutions of the Security Council and the General Assembly and to facilitate their implementation.

In accordance with the provisions of the Kitona Declaration, Tshombé sent 14 parliamentarians from Katanga to Leopoldville to participate in the session of Parliament. Three Katangese officials were also dispatched to the capital to participate in discussions for the modification of the constitutional structure of the Congo. In both cases, ONUC ensured the safety of the representatives during their journey to and from Leopoldville and their stay there.

While making the concessions contained in the Declaration, Tshombé stated that he had no authority to decide on the future of Katanga, and he summoned the provincial Assembly to meet in Elisabethville to discuss the Declaration. On 15 February, that Assembly decided to accept the "draft declaration" of Kitona only as a basis for discussions with the Central Government.

Following this action, Prime Minister Adoula invited Tshombé to meet with him in Leopoldville to discuss the procedure for carrying out the provisions of the Declaration,† but attempts at peaceful resolution through the talks failed; the agreement was not implemented owing to the procrastination and intransigence of the Katangese leader. The talks were suspended in June 1962 without agreement.‡

Secretary-General's Plan of National Reconciliation

Given the failure of the negotiations, after consultation with various Member States, Secretary-General U Thant, in August 1962, proposed a "Plan of National Reconciliation",§ which was ultimately accepted by both Adoula and Tshombé. It provided for: a federal system of government; division of revenues and foreign-

---

* S/5038.   † S/5053/Add.8.   ‡ S/5053/Add.10, annex 46.

§ S/5053/Add.13, annex I.

exchange earnings between the Central and provincial governments; unification of currency; integration and unification of all military, paramilitary and gendarme units into the structure of a national army; general amnesty; reconstitution of the Central Government giving representation to all political and provincial groups; withdrawal of representatives abroad not serving the Central Government; and freedom of movement for United Nations personnel throughout the Congo.

End of the secession of Katanga

After acceptance of the Plan of National Reconciliation, a draft federal constitution was prepared by United Nations experts,* and amnesty was proclaimed by the Central Government in late November 1962. On the Katanga side, however, no substantial steps were taken to implement the Plan. In this situation, U Thant requested Member States, on 11 December,† to bring economic pressure on the Katangese authorities, particularly by stopping Katanga's export of copper and cobalt. But before that action became effective, the Katangese fired, without provocation, on United Nations positions. Although the firing continued for six days, ONUC did not fire back but tried to resolve the situation by negotiation.

Immediately after the breakdown of the negotiations, ONUC began action to restore the security of its troops and their freedom of movement, the first phase being the clearing of the road-blocks from which Katangese troops had been directing fire at ONUC personnel. Ethiopian, Indian and Irish troops took part in the operations.

Wherever ONUC troops appeared, the gendarmerie offered little or no resistance. By 30 December 1962, all the Katangese road-blocks around Elisabethville had been cleared and ONUC forces were in effective control of an area extending approximately 20 kilometres around the city. Meanwhile, around Kamina, Ghanaian and Swedish troops, advancing in a two-pronged attack, had succeeded in occupying that town on the morning of 30 December. Thus, the first phase of the operations was completed.‡

The second phase started on 31 December,§ when Indian troops of the United Nations Force began to move towards Jadotville (now Likasi). The next day, ONUC advance elements reached the Lufira River, which they crossed by nightfall, although both bridges had been destroyed. On 2 January 1963, having met some gendarmerie resistance on the other side of that river, ONUC troops resumed their advance and reached Jadotville on 3 January, where they were

---

* S/5053/Add.13, annex XI.   † S/5053/Add.14, annexes XIII-XV.
‡ S/5053/Add.14.   § *Ibid.*

greeted by the cheers of the population. At the same time, ONUC troops also reached the town of Kipushi, south of Elisabethville.

By 4 January, ONUC troops had secured themselves in the Elisabethville, Kipushi, Kamina and Jadotville areas. In all these areas, measures were taken to restore essential services and protect the local population.

In the mean time, Tshombé, who had left Elisabethville on 28 December 1962, had proceeded through Northern Rhodesia to Kolwezi, his last stronghold. To avoid useless bloodshed and destruction of industrial installations, the United Nations ordered its troops to slow their advance towards Kolwezi while the Secretary-General continued his efforts to persuade Tshombé to cease all resistance.

On 14 January 1963, the Secretary-General received, through Belgian Government channels, a message from Tshombé and his ministers meeting at Kolwezi.* They announced their readiness to end the secession of Katanga, to grant ONUC troops complete freedom of movement and to arrange for the implementation of the Plan of National Reconciliation. They asked that the Central Government immediately put into effect the amnesty called for in the Plan in order to guarantee the freedom and safety of the Katangese government and of all who worked under its authority.

The Secretary-General welcomed Tshombé's message and informed him on 15 January† that the United Nations would do its utmost to assist in the fulfilment of the promise implicit in Tshombé's statement. On 15 January,‡ President Kasa-Vubu and Prime Minister Adoula separately confirmed that the amnesty proclamation of November 1962 remained valid. It was also announced, on 16 January, that Joseph Iléo had been appointed Minister of State Resident at Elisabethville, for the purpose of facilitating the process of reintegration.

On 16 January, Tshombé informed the Secretary-General that he was prepared to discuss at Elisabethville arrangements for ONUC's entry into Kolwezi. The next day, after four hours of discussions at ONUC headquarters, the Acting Representative of the United Nations at Elisabethville, the general officer commanding ONUC troops in the Katanga area and Tshombé signed a document in which Tshombé undertook to facilitate the peaceful entry of ONUC into Kolwezi, to be completed by 21 January.§ It was understood that pending arrangements for the integration of the gendarmerie, the security of its members would be fully ensured by ONUC. They would not be treated as prisoners of war and would be able to continue to wear their uniforms in Kolwezi.

---

* S/5053/Add.15, annex V.   † S/5053/Add.15, annex VI.
‡ S/5053/Add.15, annexes VII and VIII.   § S/5053/Add.15, annex IX.

As agreed, Indian troops of ONUC entered Kolwezi in the afternoon of 21 January. Meanwhile, the situation became increasingly volatile in northern Katanga because of sizeable groups of disorganized but heavily armed gendarmes. Consequently, in the morning of 20 January, Indonesian troops disembarked at Baudouinville (now Moba) and shortly thereafter secured the town and its airport. On the same day, a Nigerian unit starting from Kongolo and a Malayan unit coming from Bukavu cleared the Kongolo pocket where there had remained a considerable gendarme force.

By 21 January, the United Nations Force had under its control all important centres hitherto held by the Katangese, and quickly restored law and order there. The Katangese gendarmerie ceased to exist as an organized fighting force. Thanks to the skill and restraint displayed by ONUC troops, the casualties incurred during the fighting were relatively light. In the 24 days of activity, ONUC casualties were 10 killed and 77 wounded. Katangese casualties also appeared to have been low.

At the beginning of January 1963, 22 officials and officers representing the Central Government arrived at Elisabethville to make up an administrative commission to prepare the way for the integration of the provincial administration into the Central Government. Iléo and his party arrived on 23 January to assume their duties. Shortly before that, Prime Minister Adoula had requested ONUC to give Iléo all the assistance and co-operation he might require. It had been agreed between the Central Government and ONUC that all the military forces in Katanga would be placed under the single command of ONUC. At ONUC's suggestion, Adoula declared that gendarmes who rejoined the Congolese National Army by a certain date would retain their ranks.

Progress was also achieved with regard to the economic reintegration of Katanga. On 15 January, an agreement on foreign exchange was signed at Leopoldville by the representatives of the Central Government and a representative of the Union Minière, who had come from Belgium, in the presence of the Director of the Bank of Katanga. In brief, that agreement provided that the Union Minière would remit all its export proceeds to the Congolese Monetary Council, which would in turn allocate to the Union Minière the foreign exchange it needed to carry out its operations. The allocation of foreign exchange by the Central Government to the provincial authorities was to be discussed separately by that Government and the provincial authorities of southern Katanga.

Under a decree of 9 January 1963, the Monetary Council assumed control of the "National Bank of Katanga" and ensured the resumption of the Bank's operations, with ONUC's assistance.

Thus, the secession of Katanga had been brought to an end, and with this an important phase of ONUC's operations had been completed.

E. Consolidation of the Congolese Government (February 1963– June 1964)

Introduction

While the period from the end of the Katangese secession until ONUC's withdrawal in June 1964 is the main subject of this section, with the Congolese Central Government authority now extended to the whole country, it is convenient first to consider ONUC's early efforts to assist that Government in regard to civilian operations and the retraining of the Congolese army and security forces.

Civilian Operations

A main objective of ONUC was to provide the Congolese Government with technical assistance for the smooth operation of all essential services and the continued development of the national economy. The situation faced by ONUC at the beginning immediately assumed unprecedented proportions. In the absence of functioning governmental and economic machinery which could receive and use expert advice and training services, the Secretary-General at once mobilized the resources of the United Nations family of organizations under the authority of a Chief of Civilian Operations. A consultative group of experts was set up, consisting of senior officials of the United Nations and the specialized agencies concerned.

The first task was to restore or maintain minimum essential public services. Engineers, air traffic controllers, meteorologists, radio operators, postal experts, physicians, teachers and other specialists were rushed into the country. An emergency project was carried out to halt the silting of the port of Matadi and to restore navigation. In response to the Central Government's appeal, the United Nations agreed, in August 1960, to provide $5 million to finance essential governmental services as well as essential imports.

In the economic and financial fields, ONUC helped in setting up and managing monetary, foreign exchange and foreign trade controls, without which the country's slender resources might have been drained away and all semblance of a monetary system might have collapsed.

In all these fields, as well as in agriculture, labour and public administration, ONUC's efforts were designed chiefly to improve the ability of the Congolese authorities to discharge their responsibilities towards the population despite the precipitate departure of non-Congolese technicians and administrators. As it soon became obvious that the needs would continue for some time, the Secretary-General proposed and the General Assembly, by resolution 1474(ES-IV) of 20 September 1960, approved the establishment of a United Nations Fund for the Congo, financed by voluntary contributions. Its purpose was to restore the economic life of the country and to carry on its public services as well as possible.

The Assembly's action coincided with the outbreak of the constitutional crisis of September 1960. As a result of that crisis, ONUC could not deal with any authorities, except for President Joseph Kasa-Vubu, on the nation-wide plane, and could not furnish advice at the ministerial level. As the emergency conditions continued, however, the ONUC effort did not flag, and was carried on in co-operation with those Congolese authorities exercising *de facto* control in the provinces or localities where United Nations Civilian Operations were being undertaken.

Famine conditions in some areas, and widespread unemployment, led the Secretary-General to institute refugee relief and relief-work programmes. The worst conditions developed in South Kasai in the second half of 1960, where it was reported that some 200 persons were dying daily from starvation as a result of disruptions caused by tribal warfare. For six months, the United Nations shipped and distributed food and medical supplies in the area. While several thousand persons died before the United Nations effort began, the number of lives saved approximated a quarter of a million.

In the mean time, foreign exchange reserves were running low, owing to the political and economic situation. Accordingly, in June 1961, an agreement was arrived at between President Kasa-Vubu and the Secretary-General, by which the United Nations put funds at the disposal of the Republic for financing a programme of essential imports. It was agreed that such assistance must benefit the population of the country as a whole.

Despite the constitutional crisis, United Nations training services continued as a long-range operation. They were regarded as an investment in the development of human resources so as to fill the huge void caused by the shortage of indigenous operational and executive personnel. Training courses were organized for air traffic controllers, agricultural assistants, farm mechanics, foresters, medical assistants, labour officials, police commissioners, etc. To train Congolese operators and instructors, a telecommunications training centre was set up; to train primary and secondary school teachers and inspectors, a national pedagogical institute was established. Undergraduate medical studies were fostered. A national school of law and administration was opened to produce competent civil servants; a technical college was set up to train junior engineers, public works foremen and the like. Fellowships for study abroad were awarded to school directors, medical students, police officers, social workers and others in need of training, for whom adequate facilities were not available in the Congo. Furthermore, a programme was prepared for the reorganization and retraining of the Congolese National Army *(see section below)*.

In 1960 and 1961, ONUC Civilian Operations were able to provide about 600 experts and technicians to do the jobs of departing Belgian personnel. These experts and technicians, drawn from some 48 nationalities, were made available to the Congo by the United Nations and its specialized agencies for work in a variety of fields, such as finance and economics, health, transport, public administration, agriculture, civil aviation, public works, mining and natural resources, postal services, meteorology, telecommunications, judicature, labour, education, social welfare, youth training and community development. In addition, a large number of secondary school teachers were recruited with the assistance of the United Nations Educational, Scientific and Cultural Organization. These assistance programmes continued at about the same level until 1964, despite financial and other difficulties.

The end of the Katangese secession in January 1963 brought with it new responsibilities for the United Nations Civilian Operations programme, since experts became urgently needed to help the Central Government in the reintegration of services previously under Katangese rule, such as postal services, customs and excise, immigration, civil aviation, telecommunications and banking. An expert mission was required to survey the 40 rail and road bridges destroyed or damaged.

As a result of the various training programmes set up by ONUC, it became possible in 1963 to replace some international personnel by qualified Congolese, particularly in the postal, meteorological, telecommunications and civil aviation services. In 1963, 55 of the 130 medical assistants sent abroad for training in 1960-1961 under World Health Organization auspices returned to the Congo and were assigned to various parts of the country.

Reorganization of the Congolese armed forces, 1960-1963

Nearly all the grave incidents mentioned in earlier sections were caused by military elements of Congolese armed forces, whether they were part of the Congolese National Army, the Katangese gendarmerie or the Kalonji forces in South Kasai. From the outset, it was considered an essential task of ONUC to assist the Congolese Government in establishing discipline in the armed forces. These forces were to be brought under a unified command, the rebellious elements eliminated and the remaining ones reorganized and retrained. ONUC offered the Congolese Government full support and co-operation to achieve these objectives.

The United Nations Operation in the Congo took its first step towards the reorganization of the Congolese National Army when the Deputy Commander of the United Nations Force was appointed adviser to the ANC at the end of July 1960, at the request of Prime Minister Lumumba. Shortly thereafter, the ANC began to re-form in new units and to engage in the training of its officers and men. This programme was interrupted at the end of August because of the Government's plan to invade Kasai and Katanga, and later ONUC was compelled to abandon it altogether because of the political struggle which began in September 1960.

After the Adoula Government was set up, in August 1961, ONUC's efforts were resumed and the new Deputy Force Commander prepared a reorganization programme to be carried out in full co-operation with the Government.

Nevertheless, difficulties were later encountered in regard to ONUC assistance in this area. After December 1962, it became clear that Prime Minister Adoula wanted the Secretary-General to request six countries—Belgium, Canada, Israel, Italy, Norway and the United States—to provide personnel and *matériel* for reorganizing and training the various armed services.*

* S/5240/Add.2.

The Secretary-General had doubts—which were shared by the Advisory Committee composed of ONUC troop-contributors—about the advisability of the United Nations assuming sponsorship of what was, essentially, bilateral military assistance by a particular group of States. He therefore concluded that it was not feasible to grant Adoula's specific request, although he continued to hope that a way would be found to make it possible for the ANC to receive the necessary training assistance through ONUC. That hope was not realized, however, and eventually the programme for the training of the ANC was carried out outside the United Nations.

F. Winding up of ONUC

Situation in February 1963

On 4 February 1963,* the Secretary-General reported to the Security Council on the extent to which the mandates given to ONUC by the Council's resolutions had been fulfilled and on the tasks still to be completed.

Regarding the maintenance of the territorial integrity and political independence of the Congo, the secession of Katanga was ended and there was no direct threat to Congo's independence from external sources. That part of the mandate was largely fulfilled.

The mandate to prevent civil war, given in February 1961, was also substantially fulfilled as was, for all practical purposes, the removal of foreign military and paramilitary personnel and mercenaries.

Assistance in maintaining law and order was continuing and, with the vast improvements in that regard, a substantial reduction of ONUC forces was being made.

In view of these accomplishments, the phase of active involvement of United Nations troops was concluded, and a new phase was beginning, which would give greater emphasis to civilian operations and technical assistance.

General Assembly resolution of 18 October 1963

No specific termination date for the United Nations Force in the Congo had been set by any Security Council resolution. However, the General Assembly had, on 27 June 1963 at its fourth special session, adopted resolution 1876(S-IV) appropriating funds

* S/5240.

for the Force, which, in the absence of any subsequent action, would in effect have established 31 December 1963 as the terminal date for ONUC's military phase.

In a report to the Security Council dated 17 September 1963,* the Secretary-General stated that, in the light of the Assembly's resolution, he was proceeding with a phasing-out schedule for the complete withdrawal of the Force by the end of 1963. He drew attention, however, to a letter dated 22 August 1963 from Prime Minister Adoula who, while agreeing with the substantial reduction of the Force that had already been carried out, saw a need for the continued presence of a small United Nations force of about 3,000 officers and men through the first half of 1964.

In this connection, the Secretary-General expressed the opinion that cogent reasons existed in support of prolonging the stay of the Force. There could be no doubt that the presence of a United Nations Force in the Congo would continue to be helpful through the first half of 1964, or longer. But the time must come soon when the Government of the Congo would have to assume full responsibility for security and for law and order in the country.

Acting upon the Congolese Government's request for reduced military assistance up to 30 June 1964, the General Assembly decided, on 18 October 1963, by resolution 1885(XVIII), to continue the *ad hoc* account for the United Nations Operation in the Congo until 30 June 1964, and authorized an expenditure of up to $18.2 million to that effect.

In accordance with the Assembly's resolution, the United Nations Force in the Congo was maintained beyond 1963, but its strength was gradually brought down from 6,535 in December 1963 to 3,297 in June 1964.

Secretary-General's report, 29 June 1964

The Secretary-General, in a report of 29 June 1964,† affirmed his earlier conclusions that most of ONUC's objectives had been fulfilled. He indicated his intention to continue technical assistance, within available financial resources, after ONUC's withdrawal.

As to maintenance of law and order, he noted considerable deterioration in a number of localities, especially in Kwilu, Kivu and northern Katanga. He observed, however, that maintenance of law and order, which was one of the main attributes of sovereignty, was principally the responsibility of the Congolese Government, and that

* S/5428.   † S/5784.

ONUC's role had been limited to assisting the Government, to the extent of its means, when it was requested to do so.

The Secretary-General recalled the difficulties ONUC had encountered in attempting to assist the Government in training and reorganizing the Congolese security forces. He said the ANC was now an integrated body of 29,000 soldiers with a unified command, but was still insufficiently trained and officered to cope with a major crisis.

In view of the uncertainties affecting the Congo, the Secretary-General observed, the question was often asked why the stay of ONUC had not been extended beyond the end of June 1964. First, he said, the Congolese Government had not requested an extension. Secondly, a special session of the General Assembly would be required to extend any mandate.

In any case, the Secretary-General concluded, a further extension would provide no solution to the Congo's severe difficulties. The time had come when the Congolese Government would have to assume full responsibility for its own security, law and order, and territorial integrity. He believed this was the position of the Congolese Government, since it had not requested a further extension of ONUC.

Withdrawal of the Force

On 30 June 1964, the United Nations Force in the Congo withdrew from that country according to plan. With the completion of the military phase of ONUC, the Civilian Operations programme was formally discontinued. However, the overall programme of technical assistance which had been supplied by the United Nations family of organizations continued under the responsibility of the Office of the Resident Representative of the United Nations Development Programme.

Part VI # West New Guinea (West Irian)

Chapter XII

United Nations Temporary Executive Authority and United Nations Security Force

Background

The territory of West New Guinea (West Irian) had been in the possession of the Netherlands since 1828. When the Netherlands formally recognized the sovereign independence of Indonesia in 1949, the status of West Irian remained unresolved. It was agreed in the Charter of Transfer of Sovereignty—concluded between the Netherlands and Indonesia at The Hague, Netherlands, in November 1949—that the issue would be postponed for a year, and that "the *status quo* of the presidency of New Guinea" would be "maintained under the Government of the Netherlands" in the mean time. The ambiguity of the language, however, led the Netherlands to consider itself the sovereign Power in West New Guinea, since this would be a continuation of the *"status quo"*. Indonesia, on the other hand, interpreted the Dutch role there to be strictly administrative, with the implication that West Irian would be incorporated into Indonesia after a year.

The status of the territory was still being disputed when Indonesia brought the matter before the United Nations in 1954.* Indonesia claimed that the territory rightfully belonged to it and should be freed from Dutch colonial rule. The Netherlands maintained that the Papuans of West New Guinea were not Indonesians and therefore should be allowed to decide their own future when they were ready to do so.

The future of the territory was discussed at the General Assembly's regular sessions from 1954 to 1957 and at the 1961 session, but no resolutions on it were adopted.

In December 1961, when increasing rancour between the Indonesian and Dutch Governments made the prospect of a negotiated settlement even more elusive, U Thant, who had been appointed Acting Secretary-General following the death of Dag Hammarskjöld, undertook to resolve the dispute through his good offices. Consulting

* A/2694.

with the Indonesian and Dutch Permanent Representatives to the United Nations, U Thant suggested that informal talks take place between the parties in the presence of former United States Ambassador Ellsworth Bunker, who would act as U Thant's representative. The parties agreed, and talks were begun in early 1962.

A sharpening of tension between the two Governments occurred shortly thereafter, however, when Indonesia landed paratroops in West New Guinea. The Netherlands charged that the landings constituted an act of aggression, but Indonesia refuted this on the grounds that "Indonesians who have entered and who in future will continue to enter West Irian are Indonesian nationals who move into Indonesia's own territory now dominated by the Dutch by force".* U Thant urged restraint by both parties but declined a Dutch request to send United Nations observers to the scene, noting that such action could only be considered if both Governments made the request.†

Further incidents were reported by the Netherlands during the first months of 1962, and there were intermittent lulls in the progress of Ambassador Bunker's talks. A number of communications from the Netherlands and from Indonesia were circulated as documents of the Security Council in connection with this question.

In one such letter, ‡ dated 16 May, the Prime Minister of the Netherlands, stating that Indonesia had landed more parachutists on West New Guinea and had continued its aggressive acts, requested that the Acting Secretary-General make an appeal to Indonesia to remind it of its primary obligations under the United Nations Charter and to refrain from all aggressive acts against the territory and people of West New Guinea. He added that the Netherlands' presence in New Guinea was of a temporary nature and that his Government was prepared to give its fullest co-operation to the Secretary-General's efforts to find an honest and just solution for the territory on the basis of Article 73 of the Charter—concerning responsibilities of administering Powers towards non-self-governing territories—and General Assembly resolutions on the question of colonialism.

In a reply dated 22 May, § U Thant stated that, while he was concerned about developments in the area and had appealed already to the parties to exercise the utmost restraint, he could not accept the suggestion to approach Indonesia with an appeal which would imply that he was taking sides in the controversy. He did, however, keep a close eye on the situation, frequently consulting with the representatives of both countries and appealing to them to resume formal negotiations on the basis of Ambassador Bunker's proposals.

---

* S/5128.   † S/5124.   ‡ S/5123.   § S/5124.

The Acting Secretary-General was at last able to announce, on 31 July 1962, that a preliminary agreement had been reached, and that official negotiations were to take place under his auspices. The final negotiations were held at United Nations Headquarters under the chairmanship of U Thant, with Ambassador Bunker continuing to act as mediator. An agreement was signed at New York by Indonesia and the Netherlands on 15 August 1962. Ratification instruments* were exchanged between the two countries on 20 September 1962 and, the next day, the General Assembly took note of the agreement in resolution 1752(XVII) of the same date, authorizing the Secretary-General to carry out the tasks entrusted to him therein.

The agreement provided for the administration of West New Guinea (West Irian) to be transferred by the Netherlands to a United Nations Temporary Executive Authority (UNTEA), to be headed by a United Nations Administrator who would be acceptable to both parties and who would be appointed by the Secretary-General. Under the Secretary-General's jurisdiction, UNTEA would have full authority after 1 October 1962 to administer the territory, to maintain law and order, to protect the rights of the inhabitants and to ensure uninterrupted, normal services until 1 May 1963, when the administration of the territory was to be transferred to Indonesia.

The agreement also stipulated that the Secretary-General would provide a United Nations Security Force (UNSF) to assist UNTEA with as many troops as the United Nations Administrator deemed necessary. In "related understandings" to the main agreement, it was established that United Nations personnel would observe the implementation of the cease-fire that was to become effective before UNTEA assumed authority. The United Nations was therefore entrusted with a dual peace-keeping role in addition to its administrative responsibilities as the executive authority.

Arranging a cease-fire

To pave the way for the arrival in West Irian of UNTEA and UNSF, a cease-fire between Indonesian and Netherlands forces had to be enforced. The memorandum of understanding concerning the cease-fire—presented on 15 August 1962 in a note to the Acting Secretary-General from the representatives of Indonesia and the Netherlands†—requested that U Thant undertake immediately some of the functions outlined in the main agreement, so as to effect a cessation of hostilities as soon as possible. Such action would constitute

* A/5170, annex C.   † A/5170, annex B.

an "extraordinary measure", because the General Assembly would not be voting on the establishment of UNTEA and UNSF until it convened in late September.

U Thant responded promptly, stating that he was prepared to undertake the responsibilities mentioned in the note. The memorandum on the cessation of hostilities specified that the Secretary-General would assign United Nations personnel to perform certain tasks, including: observing the cease-fire; protecting the security of Dutch and Indonesian forces; restoring the situation in the event of breaches of the cease-fire; assisting in informing Indonesian troops in the jungle of the existence of the cease-fire; and providing a non-military supply line to Indonesian troops.

Although there was no explicit reference to military observers in the memorandum, U Thant selected them to perform these tasks. Furthermore, he agreed to dispatch them without the prior authorization of the General Assembly or the Security Council, a step never before taken by a Secretary-General. Reference was made in the memorandum to UNSF and its law-and-order maintenance role, with the implication that the Secretary-General should address this responsibility with all possible speed.

U Thant appointed Brigadier-General (later Major-General) Indar Jit Rikhye, his Military Adviser, to head the military observer team that was to supervise all arrangements for the cease-fire. Six Member States (Brazil, Ceylon (now Sri Lanka), India, Ireland, Nigeria and Sweden) agreed to provide 21 observers for this purpose. They were drawn from troops of these nations then serving either in the United Nations Emergency Force or the United Nations Operation in the Congo.

The observer force was assembled in West Irian within days of the signing of the agreement at United Nations Headquarters. The observers were informed at that time that the Netherlands military command had proclaimed a cease-fire as of 0001 GMT on 18 August 1962, and had ordered its ground forces to concentrate in the main garrison towns, although air and naval forces continued to patrol the territory. After a visit to Djakarta by General Rikhye, contacts were established with the Indonesian troops in the jungle. In this connection, frequent radio broadcasts on both the Netherlands-owned and Indonesian stations told the troops that hostilities had ceased. Printed pamphlets carrying the cease-fire message were dropped from aeroplanes over the jungle.

Besides supervising the cease-fire, the United Nations observers helped resupply the Indonesian troops with food and medicines and helped them regroup in selected places. The effort was successful owing to the full co-operation of the Indonesian and Netherlands authorities. Aerial support was given by the Thirteenth United States Task Force for the Far East and the Royal Canadian Air Force. Most of the emergency supplies were provided by the Netherlands military command, which also treated any Indonesian troops who were seriously ill. United Nations aircraft landed supplies in four staging areas: Sorong, Fakfak, Kaimana and Merauke.

By 21 September 1962, General Rikhye was able to report that all Indonesian forces in West Irian had been located and concentrated, that resupply had been assured and that over 500 Indonesian political detainees had been repatriated in accordance with the memorandum. The observers' mandate had thus been fulfilled and all actions concerning the cessation of hostilities had been completed without incident.

Establishment of UNSF and UNTEA

With the cessation of hostilities, the next step was to ensure the maintenance of law and order in the territory. In addition to supervising the observer team, General Rikhye had been charged with making preliminary arrangements for the arrival of UNSF.

Article VIII of the Indonesian-Netherlands agreement stipulated the role and purpose of such a force:

> The Secretary-General will provide the UNTEA with such security forces as the United Nations Administrator deems necessary; such forces will primarily supplement existing Papuan (West Irianese) police in the task of maintaining law and order. The Papuan Volunteer Corps, which on the arrival of the United Nations Administrator will cease being part of the Netherlands armed forces, and the Indonesian armed forces in the territory, will be under the authority of, and at the disposal of, the Secretary-General for the same purpose. The United Nations Administrator will, to the extent feasible, use the Papuan (West Irianese) police as a United Nations security force to maintain law and order and, at his discretion, use Indonesian armed forces. The Netherlands armed forces will be repatriated as rapidly as possible and while still in the territory will be under the authority of the UNTEA.*

UNSF was thus essentially an internal law and security force—the "police arm" of UNTEA—whose responsibilities would range from ensuring the smooth implementation of UNTEA's administrative mandate to supervising the buildup of a viable, local police force.

In the memorandum of understanding on the cessation of hostilities, it was provided that UNSF would commence its duties as soon as possible after the General Assembly adopted an enabling

* A/5170, annex A.

resolution, but no later than 1 October 1962. In fact, the UNSF Commander arrived in West Irian weeks before the Assembly resolution was passed.

Major-General Said Uddin Khan, of Pakistan, appointed by U Thant as Commander of UNSF, arrived in Hollandia on 4 September for preliminary discussions with Netherlands authorities and for a survey of future requirements. Similar efforts had already been exerted to some extent by General Rikhye, who had been charged earlier with making preliminary arrangements for the arrival of UNSF. The two men co-operated closely before and after the establishment of UNSF in West Irian.

UNSF activities prior to UNTEA

UNSF comprised 1,500 Pakistan troops, made available at the request of the Secretary-General, as were the support units of Canadian and United States aircraft and crews.

By 3 October, an advance party of 340 men of UNSF had arrived in the territory. On 5 October, the balance of the Pakistan contingent took up its positions. Also included in UNSF were some 16 officers and men of the Royal Canadian Air Force, with two aircraft, and a detachment of approximately 60 United States Air Force personnel with an average of three aircraft. These provided troop transport and communications. The Administrator also had under his authority the Papuan Volunteer Corps, the civil police, the Netherlands forces until their repatriation, and Indonesian troops, totalling approximately 1,500.

Establishment of UNTEA

UNSF was created to uphold the authority of UNTEA. Whereas groundwork for the arrival of UNSF troops had been laid in West Irian prior to the General Assembly's recognition of the agreement, it was not until Assembly resolution 1752(XVII) was adopted that personnel associated with UNTEA were dispatched. This resolution, which would make the United Nations directly responsible for the administration of the western half of New Guinea, was approved by a vote of 89 to none, with 14 abstentions.

In the resolution, the Assembly took note of the agreement between Indonesia and the Netherlands concerning West New Guinea (West Irian), acknowledged the role conferred by it upon the

Secretary-General, and authorized him to carry out the tasks entrusted to him in the agreement.

Upon adoption of the resolution, U Thant noted that for the first
time in its history the United Nations would have temporary executive
authority established by and under the jurisdiction of the Secretary-
General over a vast territory. He dispatched his Deputy Chef de
Cabinet, José Rolz-Bennett, as his Representative in West New Guinea
(West Irian), where he would make preliminary arrangements for the
transfer of administration to UNTEA. Rolz-Bennett arrived in the territory on 21 September 1962, the date the enabling resolution was
passed.

Transfer of administration to UNTEA

Under the agreement, neither Dutch nor Indonesian
officials were to hold any of the top administrative positions during
the seven-month transition period. In addition, three quarters of the
Dutch civil servants of lesser rank had decided to leave the territory
before 1 October, thereby creating a vacuum that would have to be
filled to prevent a disruption of essential functions and services. In
some instances, this was accomplished by promoting Papuan officials
to the vacant posts. There was, however, a great shortage of adequately trained Papuans.

Rolz-Bennett immediately set about assembling an emergency
task force to be deployed in key areas of the administration, recruiting
international as well as Dutch and Indonesian personnel. The
Netherlands Governor of the territory and his senior officials assisted
in this effort; measures were also taken by the Netherlands Government to encourage Dutch officials to remain and serve the Temporary
Executive Authority. In addition, the Indonesian Government was requested to provide urgently a group of civil servants to fill certain
high-priority posts. This request was made with a view to the gradual
phasing-in of Indonesian officials, whose presence thus facilitated
the subsequent transfer of administrative responsibilities to Indonesia.
In all, 32 nationalities were represented in UNTEA, among them both
Dutch and Indonesian personnel.

The transfer of the administration from the Netherlands to
UNTEA took place on 1 October 1962 and, in conformity with article
VI of the agreement and its related aide-mémoire, the United Na-
tions flag was raised and flown side by side with the Netherlands flag.

Before his departure from the territory on 28 September, the
Netherlands Governor, Peter Johannis Plateel, appealed to the

population to give its support to the United Nations administration. In messages from the Secretary-General and from Rolz-Bennett (who was designated as Temporary Administrator for approximately six weeks), the population was informed that UNTEA would endeavour to ensure the welfare of the inhabitants. The Temporary Administrator signed an order effective 15 October granting amnesty to all political prisoners sentenced prior to 1 October 1962.

On 1 October, Indonesia and the Netherlands established liaison missions to UNTEA in Hollandia/Kotabaru. An Australian liaison mission replaced one which had formerly served in Hollandia/Kotabaru as an administrative liaison between the authorities of the territory of Papua/New Guinea and West New Guinea, and now provided effective liaison with UNTEA on matters of mutual interest.

The United Nations Administrator, Djalal Abdoh, of Iran, was appointed by the Secretary-General on 22 October 1962, under article IV of the agreement. On 15 November, he arrived in the territory to take up his assignment and Rolz-Bennett returned to Headquarters the following day.

Activities after the creation of UNTEA

The agreement between the Netherlands and Indonesia entrusted to UNTEA a number of broad powers: to "administer the territory" (article V); to appoint government officials and members of representative councils (articles IX and XXIII); to legislate for the territory, subject to certain qualifications (article XI); and to guarantee civil liberties and property rights (article XXII).

Once the international team that comprised UNTEA was assembled in the capital of the territory, they immediately began to address the vast economic and social problems facing them.

The very nature of the country presented major difficulties. Roads were practically non-existent, with a total length estimated at 900 kilometres. There was no other means of land transportation, which made air transport of all supplies from ports to the hinterland essential. Coupled with the difficulties of physical movement were problems of communication. Telephone systems existed only inside the major towns. UNSF was, however, able to tackle adequately the problems which faced it.

The transfer of authority implied a need to adapt existing institutions from the Dutch pattern to an Indonesian pattern. The first problem was to rebuild the officer and inspection cadres which had almost completely disappeared with the exodus of Dutch officers, and to reinstate a sense of loyalty and discipline in the rank and file, at the same time keeping the police service serving the public. The second problem was to reorient the entire service, substituting the Indonesian language and procedures for those of the Dutch so that there would be no upheaval when UNTEA handed over the reins of government to the Republic of Indonesia.

In accordance with the terms of article VII of the Indonesia-Netherlands agreement, the Papuan Volunteer Corps ceased to be part of the Netherlands armed forces upon the transfer of administration to UNTEA. The Corps, consisting of some 350 officers and men, was concentrated at Manokwari and was not assigned any duties in connection with the maintenance of law and order. As Dutch officers and non-commissioned officers left the area, they were replaced by Indonesian officers. This process was completed on 21 January 1963, when the command of the Corps was formally transferred to an Indonesian officer and the last Dutch officers left the territory.

During the period of UNTEA administration, the Papuan police were generally responsible for the maintenance of law and order in the territory. Before the transfer of administration to UNTEA, all the officers of the police corps were Dutch, there being no qualified Papuans. By the time UNTEA had assumed responsibility for the territory, almost all officers of Dutch nationality had left, having been temporarily replaced by officers from the Philippines who, in turn, were later replaced by Indonesians. By the end of March 1963, the entire corps was officered by Indonesians. However, in accordance with the provisions of article IX of the agreement, the chief of police continued to be an international recruit.

On 1 October 1962, when authority was transferred to UNTEA, the Indonesian troops in the territory consisted of those who had been brought in by parachute during the Dutch-Indonesian conflict and those who had infiltrated the territory. Agreement was reached with the Indonesian authorities to replace a large number of these troops with fresh territorial troops from Indonesia. It was also agreed that the number of Indonesian troops in the territory would not exceed the strength of the Pakistan contingent of UNSF, except with the prior consent of the UNTEA administration.

The withdrawal of the Netherlands naval and land forces from the territory was effected in stages in accordance with a timetable agreed upon by the Temporary Administrator, the Commander of UNSF and the Commander-in-Chief of the Netherlands forces in the territory. By 15 November 1962, this process had been completed without incident.

The situation was generally calm throughout the period of UNTEA. On 15 December 1962, however, two incidents involving the police and a small group of Indonesian troops occurred in Sorong and Doom. One police constable was killed and four wounded. Order was immediately restored by UNSF units while the civil administration continued to perform its normal functions. The area remained quiet for the rest of the temporary administration. In general, the inhabitants of the territory were law-abiding and the task of maintaining peace and security presented no problems. The United Nations Administrator had no occasion to call on the Indonesian armed forces in that connection but only for the purpose of occasional joint patrols with elements of the Pakistan contingent.

With regard to UNTEA's responsibility to uphold the rights of the territory's inhabitants (as outlined in article XXII of the agreement), the Administration ensured the free exercise of those rights by the population, and UNTEA courts acted as their guarantor. One of UNTEA's first concerns was, in fact, the reactivation of the entire judiciary since, with the departure of Netherlands personnel from various judiciary organs, the administration of justice practically came to a standstill. Once UNTEA was established, all the vacant positions in the judicial offices were filled through recruitment of qualified judicial officers from Indonesia.

UNTEA was also responsible for opening and closing the New Guinea Council and for appointing new representatives to the Council, in consultation with the Council's members. On 4 December 1962, the Council members met in the presence of the Administrator and took their new oath of office. The Council's Chairman and all members pledged to support loyally the provisions of the agreement and swore allegiance to UNTEA. As it seemed desirable that members should return to their constituencies in order to explain personally to their constituents the new political situation of the territory, the session was closed on 5 December, after consultation with the Chairman.

During the period of UNTEA's administration, a number of vacancies in the membership of the New Guinea Council occurred because of resignation, departure or absence of members. At the request of the Council's Chairman to fill some of these vacancies, the United Nations Administrator, in conformity with article XXIII, signed appropriate decrees appointing two new members. However, no consultation could take place with representative councils since none existed in the districts from which the two members were appointed.

In addition to the New Guinea Council, there were 11 representative councils, known as regional councils, in the various districts. On 14 February 1963, the Administrator opened the new regional council at Ransiki, Manokwari, elections to which had been held in December 1962.

The United Nations Administrator also toured the territory extensively in conjunction with article X of the agreement, which required that UNTEA widely publicize and explain the terms of the agreement. He took part in all public functions in order to explain personally those parts of the agreement which related to the United Nations presence in the territory and the changes that would take place on 1 May 1963. These efforts supplemented a United Nations information campaign which, with the help of special features, texts, posters and discussion groups, helped prepare the population for the transfer of administration to Indonesia, and informed them regarding the provisions of the agreement on the question of self-determination.

Articles XVII through XXI addressed the issue of self-determination. The relevant clauses of the agreement required that Indonesia make arrangements, with the assistance and participation of the United Nations Representative and his staff, to give the people of the territory the opportunity to exercise freedom of choice. The inhabitants were to make the decision to "remain with Indonesia" or to "sever their ties with Indonesia", under the auspices of a plebiscite to be held no later than 1969.

Day-to-day problems of the territory were addressed and handled smoothly by the civilian administration under UNTEA. In the sphere of public health, UNTEA had to deal with an epidemic of cholera which had begun to spread on the south-west coast of the island shortly after its administration was established. In this, it received valuable assistance from the World Health Organization, which provided a health team and the necessary medical supplies. The administration was able not only to contain the epidemic within a short period but also to declare the whole territory free of cholera. The administration also vigorously pursued plans for establishing hospitals and clinics in various parts of the territory.

In the economic sphere, the administration was mainly concerned with maintaining stability and dealing with a serious unemployment problem. Only 32 of a total of 317 Netherlands officials engaged in public works had been willing to stay on after UNTEA's takeover. Contractors stopped work, and gradually maintenance and repair services came to a halt. Over 3,500 men were idle. In a land where only 300,000 people (a third of the population) were in regular contact with the administration and where skilled labour was at a premium, this was a significant figure. With the co-operation of the Indonesian liaison mission, UNTEA was able to reactivate work on existing projects and draw up plans for similar projects which would be useful for the development of the territory. Forty-five projects were completed by the end of UNTEA, and 32 others were under construction. UNTEA was also able to keep in check the general price level of commodities, most of which had to be imported, and ensure adequate supplies for the population.

All costs incurred by UNTEA during its administration were borne equally by the Netherlands and Indonesia in compliance with article XXIV of the agreement. Consultations between the Secretariat and the representatives of the two Governments regarding the preparation of the UNTEA budget had taken place shortly after the agreement was signed. Later, at Hollandia/Kotabaru, a committee composed of the representatives of the two sides met under the chairmanship of the Deputy Controller of the United Nations and agreed on an UNTEA budget for the period 1 October 1962 to 30 April 1963, which was subsequently approved by the Secretary-General. As the budget committee doubted that UNTEA would be able to collect any revenue, no estimates of income were prepared. The Department of Finance was, however, able to collect a total of 15 million New Guinea florins by the end of the UNTEA period through taxes and customs duties. This was credited to the final budget figure.

On 31 December 1962, the Netherlands flag was replaced by the Indonesian flag, which was raised side by side with the United Nations flag, as contemplated in an aide-mémoire attached to the agreement.

In the last months of 1962 and the beginning of 1963, a number of communications from Papuan leaders and various groups in the territory were addressed to the Secretary-General and the United Nations Administrator requesting that the period of UNTEA administration in West Irian be shortened. On 21 November 1962, a joint declaration by the representatives of the New Guinea Council was transmitted to the Secretary-General asking for the early transfer of the administration to Indonesia. A demonstration to the same effect took place on 15 January 1963, when a petition was presented to the Administrator by 18 political leaders from the area of Hollandia/Kotabaru.

These requests were brought to the attention of the Secretary-General in January 1963 by Sudjarwo Tjondronegoro, head of the Indonesian Liaison Mission to UNTEA. After consultation with the representative of the Netherlands, the Secretary-General decided that any shortening of UNTEA would not be feasible. However, he sent his Chef de Cabinet, C. V. Narasimhan, in February 1963, to consult with the United Nations Administrator and the Government of Indonesia, with a view to facilitating the entry of Indonesian officials into the administration of West Irian in order to ensure the continuity and expansion of all essential services. Following these consultations, the Chef de Cabinet announced in Djakarta that the transfer of administration would take place as scheduled on 1 May 1963, and that the replacement of Netherlands officials by Indonesian officials would be accelerated. By the end of March 1963, Indonesian nationals occupied the second highest post in every administrative department in all six divisions in the territory.

The gathering momentum of the phasing-in operation was accompanied by an encouraging development in a different sphere. The resumption of diplomatic relations between Indonesia and the Netherlands was announced on 13 March 1963. Thus began a new era in the relationship between the two countries, one which notably helped UNTEA's work as the time approached for the transfer of authority.

In April, the Indonesian Government announced that a Papuan member of the New Guinea Council, E. J. Bonay, would be installed on 1 May as the first Governor of Irian Barat (the Indonesian name for West Irian). He would be assisted by an Indonesian deputy, and the territory would be administered as a province of the Republic of Indonesia.

The number of Indonesian officials in the Administration towards the end of April reached 1,564, while Papuans and other indigenous people of West Irian occupied 7,625 civil service posts. Only 11 Netherlands officials remained; they were to leave upon the transfer of authority to Indonesia. Stores of goods were procured to ensure adequate supplies for a period after the transfer. Direct negotiations between the Netherlands and Indonesia for the purchase of a number of Dutch interests proceeded smoothly. The economy had been largely stabilized, health and education services were in good order, and all the provisions of the agreement leading up to the transfer of administration fully implemented.

During the last days of April, some 30 Indonesian warships arrived in Biak and Hollandia for the ceremony, as had service squadrons of aircraft of the Indonesian air force. The Pakistan units of UNSF began their withdrawal to Biak, ready for embarkation; the various UNSF garrisons were replaced by incoming Indonesian troops.

Transfer of administration to Indonesia

In accordance with article XII of the agreement, the UNTEA Administrator transferred full administrative control to the representative of the Indonesian Government, Tjondronegoro, on 1 May 1963. The ceremony was performed in the presence of the Chef de Cabinet as the Secretary-General's personal representative for the occasion, and the Indonesian Foreign Minister. At that time, the United Nations flag was taken down.

Secretary-General's observations

On the completion of UNTEA, the Secretary-General declared* that it had been a unique experience, which had once again proved the capacity of the United Nations to undertake a variety of functions, provided that it received adequate support from its Member States. He also announced that, in consultation with Indonesia, he had decided in principle to designate a few United Nations experts, serving at Headquarters and elsewhere, to perform the functions envisaged in article XVII of the agreement, in so far as the article required that the Secretary-General advise, assist and participate in arrangements which were the responsibility of Indonesia for the act of free choice. Those experts would visit West Irian as often as necessary and spend as much time as would enable them to report fully to him, until he appointed a United Nations representative to preside over them as a staff.

Looking to the future, the Secretary-General stated that he was confident that Indonesia would scrupulously observe the terms of the 1962 agreement, and would ensure the exercise by the territory's population of their right to express their wishes as to their future.

In accordance with the Indonesia-Netherlands agreement, the Secretary-General on 1 April 1968 appointed a representative, Fernando Ortiz-Sanz, to advise, assist and participate in arrangements which were the responsibility of Indonesia for the act of free choice, on retaining or severing ties with Indonesia.

In a report† submitted to the Secretary-General, the Government of Indonesia stated that between 14 July and 2 August 1969, the enlarged representative councils (consultative assemblies) of West New Guinea (West Irian), which included 1,026 members, were asked

---

* A/5501, chapter II.15.   † A/7723, annex II.

to pronounce themselves, on behalf of the people of the territory, as to whether they wished to remain with Indonesia or sever their ties with it. All those councils chose the first alternative without dissent.

The representative of the Secretary-General reported* that within "the limitations imposed by the geographical characteristics of the territory and the general political situation in the area, an act of free choice has taken place in West Irian in accordance with Indonesian practice, in which the representatives of the population have expressed their wish to remain with Indonesia".

Those reports were transmitted by the Secretary-General to the General Assembly, which, by resolution 2504(XXIV) of 19 November 1969, acknowledged with appreciation the fulfilment by the Secretary-General and his representatives of the task entrusted to them under the 1962 agreement.

---

* A/7723, annex I.

Part VII # Cyprus

Chapter XIII

United Nations Peace-keeping Force in Cyprus

A. Background

The Constitution

The Republic of Cyprus became an independent State on 16 August 1960, and a Member of the United Nations one month later. The Constitution of the Republic, which came into effect on the day of independence, had its roots in agreements reached between the heads of Government of Greece and Turkey at Zurich on 11 February 1959. These were incorporated in agreements reached between those Governments and the United Kingdom in London on 19 February. On the same day, the representatives of the Greek Cypriot and Turkish Cypriot communities accepted the documents concerned, and accompanying declarations by the three Governments, as "the agreed foundation for the final settlement of the problem of Cyprus". The agreements were embodied in treaties—the Treaty of Establishment and the Treaty of Guarantee, signed by Cyprus, Greece, Turkey and the United Kingdom, and the Treaty of Alliance, signed by Cyprus, Greece and Turkey—and in the Constitution, signed in Nicosia on 16 August 1960.

The settlement of 1959 envisaged Cyprus becoming a republic with a régime specially adapted both to the ethnic composition of its population (approximately 80 per cent Greek Cypriot and 18 per cent Turkish Cypriot) and to what were recognized as special relationships between the Republic and the three other States concerned in the agreements. Thus, the agreements recognized a distinction between the two communities and sought to maintain a certain balance between their respective rights and interests. Greece, Turkey and the United Kingdom provided a multilateral guarantee of the basic articles of the Constitution. In the event of a breach of the Treaty of Guarantee, the three Powers undertook to consult on concerted action, and, if this proved impossible, each of them reserved the right to take action "with the sole aim of re-establishing the state of affairs" set out in the Treaty. Both the union of Cyprus with any other State and the partitioning of the island were expressly forbidden. The settlement also permitted the United Kingdom to retain sovereignty over two areas to be maintained as military bases, these areas being in fact excluded from the territory of the Republic of Cyprus.

The Constitution assured the participation of each community in the exercise of the functions of the Government, while seeking in a number of matters to avoid supremacy on the part of the larger community and assuring also partial administrative autonomy to each community. Under the Constitution, the President, a Greek Cypriot, and the Vice-President, a Turkish Cypriot, were elected by their respective communities, and they designated separately the members of the Council of Ministers, comprising seven Greek Cypriots and three Turkish Cypriots. The agreement of the President and Vice-President was required for certain decisions and appointments, and they had veto rights, separately or jointly, in respect of certain types of legislation, including foreign affairs. Human rights and fundamental freedoms, as well as the supremacy of the Constitution, were guaranteed.

The application of the provisions of the Constitution encountered difficulties almost from the birth of the Republic and led to a succession of constitutional crises and to accumulating tension between the leaders of the two communities.

On 30 November 1963, the President of the Republic, Archbishop Makarios, publicly set forth 13 points on which he considered that the Constitution should be amended. He did so on the stated grounds that the existing Constitution created many difficulties in the smooth functioning of the State and the development and progress of the country, that its many *sui generis* provisions conflicted with internationally accepted democratic principles and created sources of friction between Greek and Turkish Cypriots, and that its effects were causing the two communities to draw further apart rather than closer together.

The President's proposals would have, among other things, abolished the veto power of the President and the Vice-President, while having the latter deputize for the President in his absence. The Greek Cypriot President of the House of Representatives and the Turkish Cypriot Vice-President would have been elected by the House as a whole and not, as under the Constitution, separately by its Greek and Turkish members. The constitutional provisions regarding separate majorities for enactment of certain laws by the House of Representatives would have been abolished, unified municipalities established, and the administration of justice and the security forces unified. The proportion of Turkish Cypriots in the public service and the military forces would have been reduced, and the Greek Cypriot Communal Chamber abolished, though the Turkish community would have been able to retain its Chamber.

No immediate response was forthcoming from the Vice-President to this proposed programme, but the Turkish Government, to which the President's proposals had been communicated "for information purposes", rejected them promptly and categorically. Subsequently, the Turkish Cypriot Communal Chamber described the President's claim that the Constitution had proved an obstacle to the smooth functioning of the Republic as "false propaganda" and contended that the Greek Cypriots had never attempted to implement the Constitution in good faith. The Turkish Cypriots maintained that the structure of the Republic rested on the existence of two communities and not of a majority and a minority. They refused to consider the amendments proposed by the other side, which were in their opinion designed to weaken those parts which recognized the existence of the Turkish Cypriot community as such.

Whatever possibility might have existed at the time for calm and rational discussion of the President's proposals between the two communities disappeared indefinitely with the outbreak of violent disturbances between them a few days later, on 21 December 1963.

In the afternoon of 24 December 1963, the Turkish national contingent, stationed in Cyprus under the Treaty of Alliance and numbering 650 officers and other ranks, left its camp and took up positions at the northern outskirts of Nicosia in the area where disturbances were taking place. On 25 December, the Cyprus Government charged that Turkish war-planes had flown at tree-level over Cyprus, and during the next several days there were persistent reports of military concentrations along the southern coast of Turkey and of Turkish naval movements off that coast.

Mission of the personal representative

In the face of the outbreak of intercommunal strife, the Governments of the United Kingdom, Greece and Turkey, on 24 December 1963, offered their joint good offices to the Government of Cyprus, and on 25 December they informed that Government, "including both the Greek and Turkish elements", of their readiness to assist, if invited to do so, in restoring peace and order by means of a joint peace-making force under British command, composed of forces of the three Governments already stationed in Cyprus under the Treaties of Alliance and Establishment. This offer having been accepted by the Cyprus Government, the joint force was established on 26 December, a cease-fire was arranged on 29 December, and on 30 December it was agreed to create a neutral zone along the cease-fire line ("green line") between the areas occupied by the two communities in Nicosia. That zone was to be patrolled by the joint peace-making force, but in practice the task was carried out almost exclusively by its British contingent. It was further agreed that a conference of representatives of the Governments of the United Kingdom, Greece and Turkey and of the two communities of Cyprus would be convened in London in January 1964. These arrangements were reported to the Security Council in a letter dated 8 January from the Permanent Representative of the United Kingdom to the United Nations.*

Meanwhile, on 26 December 1963,† the Permanent Representative of Cyprus requested an urgent meeting of the Security Council to consider his Government's complaint against Turkey. The meeting was held on 27 December. The Secretary-General met with the Permanent Representative of Cyprus to explore the best way in which the United Nations could assist in restoring quiet in the country. The representative of Cyprus, as well as the representatives of Greece, Turkey and the United Kingdom, requested the Secretary-General to appoint a personal representative to observe the peace-making operation in Cyprus.

After consultations, during which agreement was reached with all concerned regarding the functions of the representative, the Secretary-General, on 17 January 1964, appointed Lieutenant-General P. S. Gyani, of India, as his personal representative and observer, to go to Cyprus initially until the end of February. The Secretary-General stated that his function would be to observe the progress of the peace-making operation. General Gyani was to report to the Secretary-General on how the United Nations observer could function and be most effective in fulfilling the task as outlined in the request made by the Government of Cyprus and agreed to by the Governments of Greece, Turkey and the United Kingdom. Gyani's mandate was later extended until the end of March.

The London Conference, which met on 15 January 1964, failed to reach agreement, and proposals to strengthen the international peace-making force were rejected by the Government of Cyprus, which insisted that any such force be placed under the control of the United Nations. From Nicosia, General Gyani reported a rapid and grave deterioration of the situation, involving scattered intercommunal fighting with heavy casualties, kidnappings and the taking of hostages (many of whom were killed), unbridled activities by

* S/5508.   † S/5488.

irregular forces, separation of the members of the two communities, and disintegration of the machinery of government, as well as fears of military intervention by Turkey or Greece. The British peace-making force was encountering increasing difficulties. While Gyani's presence had been helpful in a number of instances, attention was turning increasingly to the possibility of establishing a United Nations peace-keeping operation.

B. Establishment of the United Nations operation

Creation of the Force

On 15 February, the representatives of the United Kingdom and of Cyprus requested urgent action by the Security Council.* On the same day, the Secretary-General appealed to all concerned for restraint.† He was already engaged in intensive consultations with all the parties about the functions and organization of a United Nations force, and, on 4 March, the Security Council unanimously adopted resolution 186(1964), by which it noted that the situation in Cyprus was likely to threaten international peace and security, and recommended the creation of a United Nations Peace-keeping Force in Cyprus (UNFICYP), with the consent of the Government of Cyprus.

The Council also called on all Member States to refrain from any action or threat of action likely to worsen the situation in the sovereign Republic of Cyprus or to endanger international peace, asked the Government of Cyprus, which had the responsibility for the maintenance and restoration of law and order, to take all additional measures necessary to stop violence and bloodshed in Cyprus, and called upon the communities in Cyprus and their leaders to act with the utmost restraint.

As for the Force, the Council said its composition and size were to be established by the Secretary-General, in consultation with the Governments of Cyprus, Greece, Turkey and the United Kingdom. The Commander of the Force was to be appointed by the Secretary-General and report to him. The Secretary-General, who was to keep the Governments providing the Force fully informed, was to report periodically to the Security Council on its operation. The Force's function should be, in the interest of preserving international peace and security, to use its best efforts to prevent a recurrence of fighting and,

* S/5543, S/5545.   † S/5554.

as necessary, to contribute to the maintenance and restoration of law and order and a return to normal conditions. The Council recommended that the stationing of the Force should be for a period of three months, all costs pertaining to it being met, in a manner to be agreed upon by them, by the Governments providing the contingents and by the Government of Cyprus. The Secretary-General was also authorized to accept voluntary contributions for that purpose. By the resolution, the Council also recommended the designation of a Mediator to promote a peaceful solution and an agreed settlement of the Cyprus problem.

The Minister for Foreign Affairs of Cyprus promptly informed the Secretary-General that his Government consented to the establishment of the Force.*

Operational establishment of UNFICYP

On 6 March,† the Secretary-General reported the appointment of General Gyani as Commander of UNFICYP, and referred to his approaches to several Governments about the provision of contingents. Negotiations with prospective troop-contributing Governments encountered certain delays, relating to political as well as financial aspects of the operation.

Meanwhile, as the situation in Cyprus deteriorated further, the Secretary-General on 9 March addressed messages to the President of Cyprus and to the Foreign Ministers of Greece and Turkey, appealing for restraint and a cessation of violence. The Government of Turkey sent messages to President Makarios on 12 March, and to the Secretary-General on 13 March, stating that unless assaults on the Turkish Cypriots ceased, Turkey would act unilaterally under the Treaty of Guarantee to send a Turkish force to Cyprus until the United Nations Force, which should include Turkish units, effectively performed its functions. ‡ The Secretary-General replied immediately that measures to establish the United Nations Force were under way and making progress, and he appealed to Turkey to refrain from action that would worsen the situation. §

At the request of the representative of Cyprus,‖ the Security Council held an emergency meeting on 13 March and adopted resolution 187(1964). The resolution noted the Secretary-General's assurances that the Force was about to be established, called on Member States to refrain from action or threats likely to worsen the situation in Cyprus or endanger international peace, and requested

---

* S/5578.   † S/5579.   ‡ S/5596.   § S/5600.   ‖ S/5598.

the Secretary-General to press on with his efforts to implement resolution 186(1964).

Upon the arrival of troops of the Canadian contingent on 13 March, the Secretary-General reported that the Force was in being.* However, it did not become established operationally until 27 March, when sufficient troops were available to it in Cyprus to enable it to discharge its functions. The three-month duration of the mandate, as defined in resolution 186(1964), began as of that date. This development marked a new phase in the Cyprus situation. The Secretary-General noted† that UNFICYP was a United Nations Force, operating exclusively under the mandate given to it by the Security Council and, within that mandate, under instructions given by the Secretary-General. It was an impartial, objective body which had no responsibility for political solutions and would not try to influence them one way or another.

The Force now consisted of the Canadian and British contingents (the latter's incorporation in UNFICYP having been negotiated with the British Government), and advance parties of Swedish, Irish and Finnish contingents. The main bodies of the last-mentioned three contingents arrived in April. A Danish contingent of approximately 1,000 as well as an Austrian field hospital arrived in May, along with additional Swedish troops transferred from the United Nations Operation in the Congo. By 8 June 1964, the Force had reached a strength of 6,411. As units of the new contingents arrived, certain units of the British contingent, which had formed part of the old peace-making force and had been taken into UNFICYP, were repatriated.

UNFICYP was thus established in 1964, with military contingents from Austria, Canada, Denmark, Finland, Ireland, Sweden and the United Kingdom, and civilian police units from Australia, Austria, Denmark, New Zealand and Sweden. This national composition has remained largely unchanged except for the reduction of the Irish, Finnish and Swedish contingents to token units in 1973, 1977 and 1987 respectively, and the withdrawal of the New Zealand, Danish and Austrian police units in 1967, 1975 and 1977 respectively.

Under the terms of the 1960 Treaty of Alliance, Greece was given the right to maintain an army contingent of 950 officers and men in the island, and Turkey a contingent of 650. As already noted, the Turkish contingent left its camp when the intercommunal strife broke out and was deployed in tactical positions astride the Kyrenia road north of Nicosia, where it remained until 1974. The Government of Cyprus, contending that the Turkish move was a breach of the Treaty,

---

* S/5593/Add.2.   † S/5593/Add.3.

unilaterally abrogated it on 4 April 1964. However, both contingents remained on the island.

During the early stages of the functioning of UNFICYP, the Secretary-General proposed that the Turkish Government should either order its contingent to retire to its barracks or accept his offer to put both the Greek and Turkish national contingents under United Nations command, though not as contingents of UNFICYP. Greece accepted the latter suggestion. Turkey put forward the condition that the Force Commander, before issuing orders to the Turkish contingent for any task or movement requiring a change in its present position, must have the prior consent of the Turkish Government. As the Secretary-General considered this condition unacceptable, the two national contingents were not placed under United Nations command.

Force Commanders

Following the retirement of General Gyani in June 1964, General K. S. Thimayya, of India, was appointed Force Commander and remained in that post until his death in December 1965. Brigadier A. J. Wilson, of the United Kingdom, served as Acting Commander until May 1966 when Lieutenant-General I. A. E. Martola, of Finland, was appointed Commander. He was succeeded by Lieutenant-General Dewan Prem Chand, of India, in December 1969, Major-General J. J. Quinn, of Ireland, in December 1976, Major-General Günther G. Greindl, of Austria, in March 1981, and Major-General Clive Milner, of Canada, in April 1988.

Special Representatives

In his report of 29 April 1964,* the Secretary-General referred to the necessity of appointing a high-level political officer, and on 11 May he announced the appointment of Galo Plaza Lasso as his Special Representative in Cyprus. Plaza served until his appointment as Mediator in September (*see below*). The following have subsequently served as Special Representatives of the Secretary-General: Carlos A. Bernardes (1964–1967), P. P. Spinelli (Acting) (1967), Bibiano F. Osorio-Tafall (1967–1974), Luis Weckmann-Muñoz (1974–1975), Javier Pérez de Cuéllar (1975–1977), Rémy Gorgé (Acting) (1977–1978), Reynaldo Galindo-Pohl (1978–1980), Hugo J. Gobbi (1980–1984), James Holger (Acting) (1984–1988) and Oscar Camilión since 1988.

* S/5671.

Mediation

On 25 March 1964, in accordance with the Security Council's recommendation in resolution 186(1964) that the Secretary-General designate a mediator for the purpose of promoting a peaceful solution and agreed settlement of the Cyprus problem, the Secretary-General appointed Sakari S. Tuomioja, a Finnish diplomat, as Mediator. Tuomioja died on 9 September. One week later, the Secretary-General appointed Galo Plaza Lasso, of Ecuador, to succeed him. After several rounds of consultations with all concerned, the Mediator in March 1965 submitted a report to the Secretary-General* in which he analysed the situation in the island, the positions of the parties and the considerations that would have to be taken into account in devising a settlement. On that basis, the Mediator offered observations under three headings: independence, self-determination and international peace; the structure of the State; and the protection of individual and minority rights. The Mediator recommended that the parties concerned, and in the first instance the representatives of the two communities, should meet together for discussions on the basis of his observations.

The report was commented upon favourably by the Governments of Cyprus and Greece. Turkey, however, rejected the report in its entirety and considered that Plaza's functions as a Mediator had come to an end upon its publication. Plaza resigned in December 1965, and the Secretary-General's efforts to bring about a resumption of the mediation function did not meet with success.

In these circumstances, the Secretary-General, on 4 March 1966, instructed his Special Representative in Cyprus, Carlos A. Bernardes, to employ his good offices with the parties in and outside Cyprus with a view to discussions, at any level, of problems of a local or a broader nature. Thereafter, the Special Representatives of the Secretary-General were engaged in a mission of good offices on his behalf, with a view to promoting an agreed settlement. In 1975, the Security Council, by resolution 367(1975), requested the Secretary-General to undertake a new mission of good offices, a mission the Council has reaffirmed periodically in connection with the extension of the mandate of UNFICYP.

* S/6253.

C. **UNFICYP operations until 1974**

Deployment and organization

When UNFICYP was established in 1964, the contingents were deployed throughout the island and an effort was made as far as possible to match their areas of responsibility (zones or districts) with the island's administrative district boundaries. This was meant to facilitate a close working relationship with Cyprus Government District Officers, and with the local Turkish Cypriot leaders.

All districts were covered according to the intensity of the armed confrontation. The capital, Nicosia, initially was manned by two UNFICYP contingents (Canadian and Finnish), organized in a single Nicosia zone under Canadian command. The districts of Kyrenia and Lefka were manned by one contingent each. The remaining two contingents covered the districts of Larnaca, Limassol and Paphos.

Over the years, there have been numerous redeployments of UNFICYP contingents to secure better use of available troops in relation to the requirements of the mandate and to cover any new areas of tension.

In Nicosia, UNFICYP troops were positioned for an observation role along the length of the "green line". In two other districts, Kyrenia and Lefka, United Nations posts were deployed between the two defence lines; observation and patrolling took place from those posts. On the rest of the island, UNFICYP troops were generally deployed in areas where confrontation was likely to arise, and they were so positioned as to enable them to interpose themselves between the opposing sides in areas of tension and wherever incidents might cause a recurrence of fighting. Observation squads, backed by mobile patrols, were regularly deployed into areas that were likely to be potential areas of trouble.

Guiding principles for UNFICYP

On the basis of the experience gained during the first six months of operation of the Force, guiding principles, which remain in effect to this day, were summarized by the Secretary-General in his report of 10 September 1964,* as follows:

> The Force is under the exclusive control and command of the United Nations at all times. The Commander of the Force is appointed by and responsible exclusively to the Secretary-General. The contingents com-

---

* S/5950.

prising the Force are integral parts of it and take their orders exclusively from the Force Commander.

The Force undertakes no functions which are not consistent with the provisions of the Security Council's resolution of 4 March 1964. The troops of the Force carry arms which, however, are to be employed only for self-defence, should this become necessary in the discharge of its function, in the interest of preserving international peace and security, of seeking to prevent a recurrence of fighting, and contributing to the maintenance and restoration of law and order and a return to normal conditions. The personnel of the Force must act with restraint and with complete impartiality towards the members of the Greek and Turkish Cypriot communities.

As regards the principle of self-defence, it is explained that the expression "self-defence" includes the defence of United Nations posts, premises and vehicles under armed attack, as well as the support of other personnel of UNFICYP under armed attack. When acting in self-defence, the principle of minimum force shall always be applied and armed force will be used only when all peaceful means of persuasion have failed. The decision as to when force may be used in these circumstances rests with the Commander on the spot. Examples in which troops may be authorized to use force include attempts by force to compel them to withdraw from a position which they occupy under orders from their commanders, attempts by force to disarm them, and attempts by force to prevent them from carrying out their responsibilities as ordered by their commanders.

With further reference to the question of the use of force, the Secretary-General had reported to the Security Council on 29 April 1964* that the Force Commander was seeking to achieve the objectives of UNFICYP by peaceful means and without resorting to armed force, the arms of the Force being carried only for self-defence. Despite these efforts and the Secretary-General's appeals, fighting continued. The Secretary-General emphasized that "the United Nations Force was dispatched to Cyprus to try to save lives by preventing a recurrence of fighting. It would be incongruous, even a little insane, for that Force to set about killing Cypriots, whether Greek or Turkish, to prevent them from killing each other". Yet this was the dilemma facing UNFICYP, which could not stand idly by and see an undeclared war deliberately pursued or innocent civilians struck down.

When the UNFICYP Civilian Police (UNCIVPOL) became operational on 14 April 1964, the Secretary-General outlined the following duties for it:† establishing liaison with the Cypriot police; accompanying Cypriot police patrols which were to check vehicles on the roads for various traffic and other offences; manning United Nations police posts in certain sensitive areas, namely, areas where tension existed and might be alleviated by the presence of UNFICYP police elements; observing searches of vehicles by local police at road-

* S/5671. † S/5679.

blocks; and investigating incidents where Greek or Turkish Cypriots were involved with the opposite community, including searches for persons reported as missing.

Liaison arrangements

In view of the comprehensive functions of UNFICYP as laid down by the Security Council in resolution 186(1964), the United Nations operation in Cyprus became involved, from its inception, in carrying out a vast array of activities that affected almost every aspect of life in Cyprus, often in difficult conditions. All of UNFICYP's functions were of necessity carried out in contact and consultation with the Government of Cyprus and the Turkish Cypriot authorities, and also, on many occasions, with the Governments of Greece and Turkey, and depended for their success on the co-operation of all concerned.

The legal framework of relations with the host Government was provided on 31 March 1964, when the Secretary-General and the Foreign Minister of Cyprus concluded an exchange of letters constituting an agreement on the status of UNFICYP.*

From the outset, UNFICYP made arrangements for close and continuous liaison with the Government of Cyprus and with the Turkish Cypriot leadership. Liaison was likewise maintained at various levels of the administrative and military establishments of both sides, including field military units in the areas of confrontation.

In situations of military confrontation, UNFICYP, not being empowered to impose its views on either party, of necessity negotiated with both, since the consent of both was and is required if peaceful solutions are to be found and violence averted. Time and again, communications, messages and appeals were sent to civilian leaders and military commanders of both sides in Cyprus, calling upon them to exercise restraint, refrain from provocative actions, observe the cease-fire, co-operate with the Force and contribute to a return to normal conditions. This was done either with regard to specific problems or, as in October and November 1964, in an effort to generate an across-the-board programme of action in pursuance of the mandate.

At the same time, the efforts of UNFICYP to carry out its mandate were impeded by the parties' conflicting interpretations of the duties of the Force under that mandate. To the Cyprus Government, UNFICYP's task was to assist it in ending the rebellion of the Turkish Cypriots and extending its authority over the entire territory of the

* S/5634, annexes I and II.

Republic. To the Turkish Cypriots, a "return to normal conditions" meant having UNFICYP restore, by force if necessary, the status of the Turkish Cypriot community under the 1960 Constitution, while the Cyprus Government and its acts should not be taken as legal. The Secretary-General in his reports rejected both these interpretations, which, if followed, would have caused UNFICYP to affect basically the final settlement of the Cyprus problem. This he considered to be in the province of the Mediator, not of UNFICYP.

Freedom of movement of UNFICYP

The agreement on the status of UNFICYP mentioned above provides for the freedom of movement of the Force throughout Cyprus, subject to a minor qualification relating to large troop movements, and entitles UNFICYP to use roads, bridges, airfields, etc. Freedom of movement has been regarded from the outset as an essential condition for the proper functioning of the Force; indeed, the function of preventing a recurrence of fighting depends for its implementation entirely on the freedom of movement of the military and police elements of UNFICYP. The Force encountered many difficulties in this regard.

On 10 November 1964, the Force Commander reached an agreement with the Commander of the Cyprus National Guard, declaring the whole island open to UNFICYP except for certain stipulated areas (covering about 1.65 per cent of the country) that were accessible only to the Force Commander or to senior officers of UNFICYP. Arrangements were also negotiated for UNFICYP access to the Limassol docks, which were used by the Cyprus Government for the importation of military stores. Also in November 1964, it was agreed that the Cyprus security forces would henceforth refrain from searching UNFICYP personnel and vehicles.

During 1965, the Force Commander carried out a thorough review of UNFICYP's reconnaissance procedures, with a view to reducing friction to a minimum. Nevertheless, incidents of obstruction and harassment of UNFICYP continued. In certain cases, these even involved firing at UNFICYP soldiers, manhandling of UNFICYP officers and other unacceptable practices. Both the National Guard and Turkish Cypriot fighters were involved in incidents of this kind, especially during periods of tension.

Supervision of the cease-fire

UNFICYP's operating procedures to prevent a recurrence of fighting and to supervise the cease-fire were worked out pragmatically in the light of the impasse that persisted between the two sides. The Force instituted a system of fixed posts and frequent patrols, intervention on the spot and interposition to prevent incidents from escalating into serious fighting, demarcation of cease-fire lines where appropriate, and the submission of proposals or plans for remedying situations of military tension or conflict. Thus, UNFICYP endeavoured to secure the withdrawal or elimination of fortifications erected by the two sides, and submitted numerous proposals to that end, designed to reduce the armed confrontation in the island without prejudice to the security requirements of both sides. Wherever violent incidents broke out, UNFICYP made every effort, by persuasion, negotiation and interposition, to stop the fighting; it assisted civilians, evacuated the wounded and endeavoured to resolve the underlying security and other problems.

Despite the efforts of UNFICYP, sporadic violence continued in the island after the Force became operational, punctuated by outbreaks of severe fighting in which United Nations troops would find themselves at times fired upon by both sides, and forced to return the fire. Serious incidents occurred in the Tylliria area on 4 April 1964, at Ayios Theodhoros on 22 April, and in the area north of Nicosia from 25 to 29 April. A number of UNFICYP soldiers were killed as they sought to carry out their duties during continued scattered fighting in May. A major outbreak of fighting occurred from 5 to 8 August in the Tylliria area, reducing the Turkish Cypriot bridgehead there to the village of Kokkina. This was followed by aerial attacks on Government forces by Turkish fighter aircraft, and led on 8 and 9 August to meetings of the Security Council, which adopted resolution 193(1964), which, *inter alia,* called for an immediate cease-fire. The Governments of Cyprus and Turkey accepted the cease-fire without conditions.*

In August and September 1964, the Secretary-General engaged in intensive negotiations with the parties on the explosive issue of the periodic partial rotation of the Turkish national contingent stationed in Cyprus under the Treaty of Alliance (which the Cyprus Government had abrogated, but which Turkey considered to remain valid). This was linked to the question of the reopening of the Nicosia–Kyrenia road, which the Turkish Cypriots had closed to Greek Cypriot traffic. On 25 September, U Thant announced in the Security

* S/5879.

Council that agreement had been reached for the reopening of the road under the exclusive control of UNFICYP, and for the unimpeded rotation of the Turkish national contingent.

The road was reopened on 26 October 1964, and UNFICYP continued until 1974 to supervise the movement of Greek Cypriot civilians on it and to ensure that no armed personnel except those of UNFICYP were allowed to use it. The first rotation of the Turkish national contingent under this agreement was carried out on the same day, with UNFICYP assistance and under UNFICYP observation. UNFICYP also performed observation functions in connection with checking the incoming Turkish troops and their stores by Cyprus Government officials at Famagusta harbour. These functions, too, continued to be carried out, twice a year, until 1974. It should be noted that the UNFICYP functions relating to the Turkish national contingent concerned relations between the Governments of Cyprus and Turkey and therefore did not fall strictly within the terms of UNFICYP's mandate; they were assumed at the request of all concerned, in the interest of maintaining the peace, reducing tension in the island, and creating favourable conditions for carrying out other aspects of UNFICYP's mandate.

As a result of this arrangement, the situation in the island improved somewhat, and in his report of December 1964,* the Secretary-General reported that fighting had virtually ceased. However, the underlying tensions continued, and UNFICYP had little or no success in inducing the parties to scale down their military confrontation or dismantle their fortifications, which were the cause of recurrent incidents.

Return to normal conditions

UNFICYP normalization efforts evolved on an *ad hoc* basis and employed persuasion and negotiation exclusively. The principal objective was to restore conditions that would enable the people of the island, Greek Cypriot and Turkish Cypriot alike, to go about their daily business without fear for their lives and without being victimized, and in this connection to restore governmental services and economic activities disrupted by the intercommunal strife. A significant aspect of UNFICYP's procedures under this heading concerned humanitarian and relief assistance. All of UNFICYP's efforts were so framed as to avoid prejudicing the positions and claims of the parties in respect of a final political settlement. However, its task was

* S/6102.

made difficult by the reluctance of the two communities to modify their positions in the absence of such a settlement.

From the beginning of the United Nations operation, UNFICYP undertook *ad hoc* measures designed to save lives, minimize suffering and, to the extent possible, restore essential civilian activities. These measures included:

(a) Escorts for essential civilian movements, including persons, food and essential merchandise, on the roads of Cyprus, especially for members of the Turkish Cypriot community who feared abduction.

(b) Harvest arrangements, including escorts and patrols, to enable farmers to till their lands in the vicinity of positions held by members of the other community; agricultural arrangements, including grain deliveries by the Turkish Cypriots to the Cyprus Grain Commission; maintenance of abandoned citrus orchards, etc.

(c) Arrangements for government property in Turkish Cypriot–controlled areas; water and electricity supplies to the Turkish Cypriot sectors; postal services; payment of social insurance benefits; efforts to normalize the public services, including arrangements to re-employ Turkish Cypriot civil servants, etc.

(d) Co-operation with the Red Cross and the Cyprus Joint Relief Commission in providing relief assistance for refugees (mainly Turkish Cypriots). UNFICYP also made intensive efforts to alleviate hardships resulting from the economic restrictions that had been imposed on the Turkish Cypriot community.

In October and November 1964, UNFICYP initiated a major effort to persuade the Government and the Turkish Cypriot leadership to drop most economic and security restrictions directed at members of the other community, to restore free movement and contacts for all, and to consider the return of displaced persons, with UNFICYP assistance. This comprehensive approach resulted in some improvement of the situation, but the basic political problem continued to limit the effectiveness of UNFICYP's normalization efforts.

On 21 April 1965, President Makarios informed the Special Representative of the Secretary-General and the Force Commander that the Government planned a normalization programme in three districts—Larnaca, Limassol and Ktima. This move came in response to UNFICYP's suggestions for a withdrawal of troops from fortified posts, elimination of road-blocks and the lifting of economic restrictions. However, the Turkish Cypriots, noting the limited geographical scope of the programme and the continuation of economic restrictions, declined to remove their defences.

The crisis of 1967

In January 1967, General George Grivas, the Greek Commander of the Cyprus National Guard, deployed a battalion of troops in the Kophinou area. These remained in place despite an understanding reached by UNFICYP with the local Turkish Cypriot commander to avoid incidents. As the National Guard unit was reinforced on 28 February, Turkish Cypriot fighters moved forward at nearby Ayios Theodhoros, where they also manhandled senior UNFICYP officers. There was severe friction between UNFICYP and Turkish Cypriot fighters in Kophinou, and the situation also deteriorated in the Paphos and Lefka districts.

In September 1967,* the Government announced a normalization programme that included the unmanning of armed posts and fortifications and complete freedom of movement, initially in the Paphos and Limassol districts. The Turkish Cypriot side assured UNFICYP that it would not seek to occupy the vacated positions.

In November 1967,† the Cyprus police sought to resume the practice of patrolling Ayios Theodhoros, passing through the Turkish Cypriot quarter, and informed UNFICYP that the National Guard would, if necessary, escort the policemen. On 15 November, heavy fighting broke out, and the National Guard overran most of Ayios Theodhoros and part of Kophinou. The Turkish Government protested to the Secretary-General, who requested the Cyprus and Greek Governments to bring about a withdrawal of the National Guard from the areas it had occupied. The withdrawal was carried out on 16 November. On 18 and 19 November, there were several Turkish overflights of Cyprus, and armed clashes spread to the Kokkina and Kyrenia areas.

These events set off a severe political crisis. The Secretary-General appealed to the President of Cyprus and to the Prime Ministers of Greece and Turkey, on 22 and 24 November 1967, ‡ to avoid an outbreak of hostilities, and he sent a personal representative to the three capitals. In the second appeal, the Secretary-General urged the three parties to agree upon a staged reduction and ultimate withdrawal of non-Cypriot armed forces, other than those of the United Nations, and he offered the assistance of UNFICYP in working out a programme of phased withdrawals and helping to maintain quiet.

The Security Council met on 24 November and, after consultations with the representatives of the parties, unanimously approved a consensus statement noting with satisfaction the efforts of the

* S/8141.   † S/8248.   ‡ S/8248/Add.3,5.

Secretary-General and calling upon all the parties to assist and co-operate in keeping the peace.

On 3 December 1967,* the Secretary-General addressed a third appeal to the President of Cyprus and to the Prime Ministers of Greece and Turkey, in which he called for Greece and Turkey to carry out an expeditious withdrawal of their forces in excess of their contingents in Cyprus. He added:

> "With regard to any further role that it might be considered desirable for UNFICYP to undertake, I gather that this could involve, subject to the necessary action by the Security Council, enlarging the mandate of the Force so as to give it broader functions in regard to the realization of quiet and peace in Cyprus, including supervision of disarmament and the devising of practical arrangements to safeguard internal security, embracing the safety of all the people of Cyprus. My good offices in connection with such matters would, of course, be available to the parties on request."

All three Governments welcomed the Secretary-General's appeal,† and Turkey supported the enlargement of the UNFICYP mandate to include supervision of the disarmament in Cyprus of forces constituted after 1963. The Security Council, at a meeting on 22 December 1967, adopted resolution 244(1967), by which, among other things, it noted the Secretary-General's three appeals and the replies of the three Governments.

In response to the Secretary-General's appeals, Greece and Turkey reached an agreement under which Greek national troops were withdrawn from Cyprus between 8 December 1967 and 16 January 1968. However, as no agreement was reached by Greece and Turkey on the issue of reciprocity, UNFICYP did not take on the task of checking that no Greek or Turkish forces in excess of their respective contingents remained in Cyprus.

At the same time, a formula was devised for informal meetings between Glafcos Clerides and Rauf R. Denktash, representing the Greek Cypriot and Turkish Cypriot communities, respectively. After an initial meeting in Beirut, Lebanon, on 2 June, they held meetings in Nicosia.

The intercommunal security situation in Cyprus improved during 1968, and in January 1969, President Makarios confirmed that he intended to extend normalization measures, including freedom of movement for the Turkish Cypriots, throughout the island. The Secretary-General suggested that the Turkish Cypriot leadership should respond by allowing the free movement of Greek Cypriots through Turkish Cypriot areas, but this was not accepted.

---

* S/8248/Add.6.   † S/8248/Add.7,8.

Arms imports

From the beginning of the Cyprus operation, the Secretary-General reported that the influx of arms and military equipment was a cause of concern for UNFICYP with regard to the discharge of its mandate. UNFICYP kept a careful watch on all imports of such arms and equipment, but the question whether it could take any additional action in this regard under resolution 186(1964) remained a controversial one. An agreement was concluded on 10 September 1964 to have UNFICYP present at the unloading of military equipment at Famagusta and Limassol, but additional material was being imported at Boghaz, unobserved by UNFICYP.

The issue came to a head when it became known in December 1966 that the Cyprus Government had imported a quantity of arms for distribution to the Cyprus police. On 12 January 1967, the Cyprus Government indicated to the Secretary-General that the imported arms would not be distributed for the time being, that the Secretary-General would be advised in due time if their distribution should become necessary, and that, in the mean time, the Force Commander could make periodic inspections.

In March 1970, increasing tension within the Greek Cypriot community culminated in an attempt on the life of President Makarios and the subsequent killing of a former Minister of the Interior, Polycarpos Georghadjis.

Clandestine activity by pro-enosis (union with Greece) elements continued in 1971, and in view of that, the Government of Cyprus in January 1972 imported a large quantity of arms and ammunition. To minimize the resultant increase in tension, UNFICYP negotiated a provisional agreement on 10 March, whereby the Cyprus Government undertook to keep the imported arms in safe-keeping and open to inspection by the Force Commander. On 21 April,* the Secretary-General reported that an improved arrangement had been agreed upon, under which the weapons and munitions, except for the high explosives, would be stored in a fenced area within the perimeter of an UNFICYP camp. The fenced area would be in the charge of unarmed Cyprus police personnel, but control of the camp perimeter and access to it would be the responsibility of UNFICYP. The high-explosive munitions were stored at Cyprus police headquarters, but the fuses were removed and stored at the UNFICYP camp. A system of double locks and keys was devised for both storage areas.

UNFICYP continued to carry out its functions under both these agreements until 1974. The weapons and arms are still stored in the

* S/10564/Add.1.

UNFICYP camp, but the responsibility for their security now rests with UNFICYP alone. The Cyprus police have no involvement with them other than periodic verification carried out jointly with UNFICYP.

UNFICYP reductions

The consolidation of the security situation that was achieved by the beginning of 1965, however limited and tenuous, made possible a gradual reduction of the strength of UNFICYP. From a total (military personnel and police) of 6,275 in December 1964, the Force was reduced one year later to 5,764, and to 4,610 by the end of 1966. The strength of the Force in December 1967 was 4,737.

The general lessening of tension throughout the island in 1968, in addition to creating a favourable atmosphere for the Clerides/Denktash intercommunal talks, also led to a further significant reduction in the strength of the Force. Steps were taken, in co-operation with the Government of Cyprus and the Turkish Cypriot leadership, to ensure that the effectiveness of the Force would not be adversely affected. Between April and December 1968, its strength was brought down to 3,708.

Further reductions took place gradually over the next two years; thereafter, the strength of UNFICYP from 1970 to 1972 remained stable at approximately 3,150. The strength of the Irish battalion was reduced from 420 to 150 during this period. In this connection, Austria, at the request of the Secretary-General, agreed in 1972 to augment its contingent, which had consisted of the UNFICYP field hospital and an UNCIVPOL unit, by providing also a battalion of 276 ground troops.

In October and November 1973, personnel of the Austrian, Finnish, Irish and Swedish contingents of UNFICYP were transferred to the Middle East to form the advance elements of the United Nations Emergency Force. Replacements for the Austrian, Finnish and Swedish personnel were promptly sent to Cyprus by the Governments concerned; however, at the request of the Secretary-General, Ireland agreed to dispatch additional troops only to the Middle East, and the Irish contingent in Cyprus was reduced to a token detachment at UNFICYP headquarters.

A further reduction of 381 troops was made in the spring of 1974. However, this was soon overtaken by the events of July 1974 which made it necessary to increase the strength of the Force once again.

D. *Coup d'état* and Turkish intervention of 1974

Events from the *coup d'état* of 15 July to 30 July

On 15 July 1974, the National Guard, under the direction of Greek officers, staged a *coup d'état* against the Cyprus Government headed by President Makarios. In view of the seriousness of the matter in relation to international peace and security and in view of the United Nations involvement in Cyprus, the Secretary-General requested the President of the Security Council on 16 July to convene a meeting of the Council.* The Permanent Representative of Cyprus also requested a meeting.† The Council met on 16 and 19 July.

On 20 July, the Turkish Government, invoking the Treaty of Guarantee of 1960, launched an extensive military operation on the north coast of Cyprus which resulted eventually in the occupation of the main Turkish Cypriot enclave north of Nicosia and areas to the north, east and west of the enclave, including Kyrenia. The Council met on the same day and adopted resolution 353(1974), by which it called upon all parties to cease firing and demanded an immediate end to foreign military intervention, requested the withdrawal of foreign military personnel present otherwise than under the authority of international agreements, and called on Greece, Turkey and the United Kingdom to enter into negotiations without delay for the restoration of peace in the area and constitutional government in Cyprus. The Council also called on all parties to co-operate fully with UNFICYP to enable it to carry out its mandate—thus indicating that UNFICYP was expected to continue to function despite the radically changed circumstances. The cease-fire called for by the Council was announced for 1600 hours, local time, on 22 July.

The fighting resumed on 23 July, especially in the vicinity of Nicosia International Airport, which, with the agreement of the local military commanders of both sides, was declared a United Nations–protected area and was occupied by UNFICYP troops. The Secretary-General reported to the Council on the breakdown of the cease-fire, and sent messages‡ to the Prime Ministers of Greece and Turkey and to the Acting President of Cyprus, expressing his great anxiety and requesting measures to ensure observance of the cease-fire. The Council on 23 July adopted resolution 354(1974), reaffirming the pro-

* S/11334.   † S/11335.   ‡ S/11368.

visions of resolution 353(1974) and demanding that the parties comply immediately with paragraph 2 of that resolution, which called on them to stop firing and refrain from action which might aggravate the situation.

UNFICYP activities

As a consequence of these events, UNFICYP was faced with a situation that had not been foreseen in its mandate. As laid down by the Security Council in resolution 186(1964), the functions of UNFICYP were conceived in relation to the intercommunal conflict in Cyprus, not to large-scale hostilities arising from action by the armed forces of one of the guarantor Powers.

On 15 July, as soon as the *coup d'état* was reported, UNFICYP was brought to a high state of readiness. Additional liaison officers were deployed at all levels, and increased observation was maintained throughout the island in all areas of likely intercommunal confrontation. Special measures were taken to ensure the security of the Turkish Cypriot community. A few cases of firing into the Turkish enclave north of Nicosia were reported; the firing was stopped through liaison with the National Guard.

On 20 July, the day of the Turkish landings, UNFICYP was placed on full alert. An increased level of observation was maintained throughout the entire island, and additional precautions were taken to safeguard isolated Turkish Cypriot villages. The National Guard reacted to the Turkish operations by strong simultaneous attacks in other parts of the island against most of the Turkish Cypriot quarters and villages. The best UNFICYP could achieve under the circumstances was to arrange local cease-fires to prevent further loss of life and damage to property, as the Turkish Cypriot fighters, who were mainly deployed to protect isolated villages and town sectors, were heavily outnumbered. When the war situation made it necessary on 21 July to evacuate foreign missions to the British Sovereign Base Area at Dhekelia, UNFICYP played a major part in the organization and execution of that humanitarian operation. In all areas, including the Kyrenia sector, intensified United Nations patrolling was carried out, a close watch was maintained over the battle zone and all possible efforts were made to promote the safety of civilians.

The Secretary-General reported to the Security Council his understanding that UNFICYP should, and indeed must, use its best efforts to ensure, as far as its capabilities permitted, that the cease-fire called for by the Council was maintained. Obviously, a United Nations peace-keeping force, in a deeply serious situation such as the one prevailing in Cyprus, could not be expected to stand by and not make the maximum effort to ensure that a resolution of the Security Council was put into effect. For this reason, the Special Representative, the Force Commander and all the personnel of UNFICYP made every effort to restore the cease-fire, to ensure that it was observed and to prevent any incidents from escalating into a full recurrence of fighting. In this connection, UNFICYP assisted in delineating the positions of the parties as at 1600 hours on 22 July. Additional United Nations observation posts were established in the confrontation areas, and extensive patrolling was carried out in order to maintain a United Nations presence throughout the island.

In addition, the Secretary-General requested reinforcements from the contributing countries; they arrived between 24 July and 14 August, increasing the total strength of the Force by 2,078 all ranks to a total of 4,444. UNFICYP was redeployed to meet the new situation, two new operational districts were established on both sides of the Turkish bridgehead, and the general level of surveillance throughout the island was increased accordingly. Because of the suffering caused by the hostilities, UNFICYP undertook an increasing number of humanitarian tasks to assist the afflicted population of both communities.

Tripartite Conference and the Geneva Declaration

As called for in Security Council resolution 353(1974), the Foreign Ministers of Turkey, Greece and the United Kingdom began discussions in Geneva on 25 July, and on 30 July they agreed on the text of a declaration concerning the situation in Cyprus, which was immediately transmitted to the Secretary-General.* By the Geneva Declaration, the Foreign Ministers agreed on certain measures that involved action by UNFICYP. Thus:

(a) A security zone of a size to be determined by representatives of Greece, Turkey and the United Kingdom, in consultation with UNFICYP, was to be established at the limit of the areas occupied by the Turkish armed forces. This zone was to be entered by no forces other than those of UNFICYP, which was to supervise the prohibition of entry. Pending the determination of the size and character of the security zone, the existing area between the two forces was not to be entered by any forces.

* S/11398.

(*b*) All the Turkish enclaves occupied by Greek or Greek Cypriot forces were to be immediately evacuated and would continue to be protected by UNFICYP. Other Turkish enclaves outside the area controlled by the Turkish armed forces would continue to be protected by an UNFICYP security zone and could, as before, maintain their own police and security forces.

(*c*) In mixed villages, the functions of security and police were to be carried out by UNFICYP.

(*d*) Military personnel and civilians detained as a result of the recent hostilities were to be either exchanged or released under the supervision of the International Committee of the Red Cross (ICRC) within the shortest time possible.

At the meeting of the Security Council held on 31 July, the Secretary-General made a statement referring to the above functions envisaged for UNFICYP. The Council, on 1 August, adopted resolution 355(1974), taking note of the Secretary-General's statement and requesting him "to take appropriate action in the light of his statement and to present a full report to the Council, taking into account that the cease-fire will be the first step in the full implementation of Security Council resolution 353(1974)".

Immediately after the adoption of resolution 355(1974), the Secretary-General instructed his Special Representative in Cyprus and the Commander of UNFICYP to proceed, in co-operation with the parties, with the full implementation of the role of UNFICYP as provided for in that resolution. UNFICYP promptly informed the parties that it stood ready to carry out all the functions devolving upon it under the resolution and it repeatedly appealed for observance of the cease-fire.

The Secretary-General's interim report of 10 August 1974* pursuant to resolution 355(1974) gave an account of the action taken to carry out the various provisions of the Geneva Declaration. The military representatives of Greece, Turkey and the United Kingdom had been meeting since 2 August together with a representative of UNFICYP, but they had not as yet determined the size of the security zone. Accordingly, UNFICYP action regarding that zone had been limited to participation in the deliberations.

Concerning the Turkish enclaves occupied by Greek or Greek Cypriot forces, UNFICYP stood ready to assume its protective functions as soon as they had been evacuated by those forces. In the mean time, UNFICYP's protective functions in respect of Turkish enclaves had continued, including regular patrols, assistance to the population, escorts and convoys for relief supplies (food, medicaments, etc.),

* S/11433.

and visits to detainees, together with the ICRC, to ensure that their treatment was satisfactory. These protective functions were also being carried out in the Turkish enclaves outside the area controlled by the Turkish forces mentioned in the Declaration, as well as in mixed villages.

On 12 August,* the Secretary-General reported that the National Guard had evacuated a number of Turkish Cypriot villages, and UNFICYP had assumed the responsibility for the protection of those areas.

The second round of fighting

Following the breakdown of the Geneva Conference on 14 August, fighting resumed in Cyprus. In the circumstances, UNFICYP resorted to *ad hoc* emergency operating procedures. Armoured reconnaissance units of UNFICYP maintained observation over the battle zone wherever possible. During the night of 14/15 August, and again on 15/16 August, UNFICYP achieved a partial cease-fire in Nicosia to allow all the non-combatants to be evacuated. It made major efforts throughout the country to put an end to the fighting, but was unable to do so in certain combat areas, where UNFICYP posts had to be withdrawn. In a few such areas, killing of civilians took place.

The resumption of heavy fighting on 14 August had placed UNFICYP units in an extremely difficult and dangerous position, resulting in severe casualties. The Security Council noted that development with concern in its resolution 359(1974) of 15 August; it recalled that UNFICYP was stationed in Cyprus with the full consent of the Governments of Cyprus, Turkey and Greece; it demanded that all parties concerned fully respect the international status of the United Nations Force and refrain from any action which might endanger the lives and safety of its members; it further demanded that all parties co-operate with the Force in carrying out its tasks, including humanitarian functions, in all areas of Cyprus and in regard to all sections of the population. After negotiations, the Turkish forces declared a cease-fire at 1800 hours, local time, on 16 August.

On the same day, the Council adopted resolution 360(1974), by which it recorded its "formal disapproval of the unilateral military actions undertaken against the Republic of Cyprus" and urged the parties to comply with its previous resolutions and to resume without delay the negotiations called for in resolution 353(1974).

* S/11353/Add.20.

Humanitarian functions

During the events of July and August 1974, UNFICYP assumed important humanitarian functions, and the Security Council, in its resolution 359(1974), took notice of these tasks. On 22 July, a special humanitarian and economics branch had been set up at UNFICYP headquarters. Every effort was made to protect the civilian population caught up in the hostilities—including both Cypriots and foreigners. In co-operation with the ICRC, a wide range of relief assistance was organized for Greek and Turkish Cypriots. However, it soon became evident that a more systematic and larger scale of operation was needed, since approximately one third of the population of the island had become homeless or was otherwise in need. Accordingly, on 20 August, the Secretary-General designated the United Nations High Commissioner for Refugees as Co-ordinator of United Nations Humanitarian Assistance for Cyprus.* In resolution 361(1974) of 30 August, the Security Council, noting that a large number of people in Cyprus were in dire need, and "mindful of the fact that it is one of the foremost purposes of the United Nations to lend humanitarian assistance in situations such as the one currently prevailing in Cyprus", requested the Secretary-General to continue to provide emergency humanitarian assistance to all parts of the island's population in need of such assistance. UNFICYP assisted the Co-ordinator in carrying out his functions.

E. **UNFICYP since 1974**

Since its establishment in 1964, the main objective of the United Nations operation in Cyprus, as of all other United Nations peace-keeping operations, has been to foster peaceful conditions in which the search for an agreed, just and lasting settlement of the problem could best be pursued. The main instrument for maintaining calm and preventing strife in the island has been and remains the United Nations Peace-keeping Force, which continues effectively to carry out its task of conflict control. Accordingly, the Secretary-General has reported to the Security Council, at the end of every six-month mandate period, that in the light of the situation on the ground and of political developments, the continued presence of UNFICYP remains indispensable, both in helping to maintain calm in the island and in creating the best conditions for his good offices

* S/11488.

efforts. For its part, the Security Council has regularly extended the mandate of the Force for six-month periods.

Until June 1983, the parties concerned consistently informed the Secretary-General of their concurrence in the proposed extension of the stationing of the Force in the island. Following the Turkish Cypriot proclamation on 15 November 1983 of the "Turkish Republic of Northern Cyprus", which was deplored and considered legally invalid by the Security Concil, the Government of Cyprus as well as the Governments of Greece and the United Kingdom have continued to indicate their concurrence, but Turkey and the Turkish Cypriot community have indicated that they were not in a position to accept the resolutions extending the mandate. Despite their divergent positions, all the parties have continued to co-operate with UNFICYP, both on the military and the civilian levels.

The function of the United Nations Peace-keeping Force in Cyprus was originally defined by the Security Council in its resolution 186(1964) of 4 March 1964 in the following terms ". . . in the interest of preserving international peace and security, to use its best efforts to prevent a recurrence of fighting and, as necessary, to contribute to the maintenance and restoration of law and order and a return to normal conditions".

That mandate, which was conceived in the context of the confrontation between the Greek Cypriot and Turkish Cypriot communities in 1964, has been periodically extended by the Security Council. In connection with the hostilities in July and August 1974, the Security Council adopted a number of resolutions which have affected the functioning of UNFICYP and have required the Force to perform certain additional functions relating, in particular, to the maintenance of the cease-fire.

That cease-fire came into effect at 1800 hours on 16 August 1974. Immediately afterwards, UNFICYP inspected the areas of confrontation and recorded the deployment of the military forces on both sides. Lines drawn between the forward defended localities became respectively the National Guard and Turkish forces cease-fire lines. In the absence of a formal cease-fire agreement, the military *status quo*, as recorded by UNFICYP at the time, became the standard by which it was judged whether any changes constituted violations of the cease-fire. The military *status quo* was subsequently clarified further and adjusted in numerous local agreements between the units of UNFICYP and of the sides concerned. Most of those agreements were eventually consolidated in a simple set of rules which UNFICYP communicated to the military forces on both sides in early 1989.

It is an essential feature of the cease-fire that neither side can exercise authority or jurisdiction or make any military moves beyond its own forward military lines. In the area between the lines, which is known as the United Nations buffer zone, UNFICYP maintains the *status quo* (including innocent civilian activity and the exercise of property rights) without prejudice to an eventual political settlement concerning the disposition of the area. UNFICYP discharges its responsibilities in that area, with a view to safeguarding the legitimate security requirements of both sides, while giving due regard to humanitarian considerations.*

The cease-fire lines extend approximately 180 kilometres from Kato Pyrgos on the north-west coast to the east coast at Dherinia. The United Nations buffer zone between the lines varies in width from less than 20 metres in Nicosia to some 7 kilometres near Athienou. It covers about 3 per cent of the island, including some of the most valuable agricultural land.

UNFICYP keeps the cease-fire lines and the buffer zone under constant surveillance through a system of observation posts and patrols. High-powered binoculars and night observation devices are used in this work. The Force maintains a patrol track, which runs the length of the buffer zone and is used for surveillance, monitoring of agricultural activities, the resupply of observation posts and rapid reaction to any incidents.

In Nicosia, the cease-fire lines of the two sides are in close proximity and, consequently, the most serious incidents have tended to occur in that city. In May 1989, UNFICYP reached an agreement with both sides whereby they unmanned their positions and ceased their patrols in certain sensitive locations. The opposing troops were thus moved further apart, although the cease-fire lines were left unchanged. As a result, the number of incidents in Nicosia has been reduced.

Both sides in the island have frequently expressed concern about the strength and development of the military forces on the other side. This subject is of concern to UNFICYP as well, and it has proposed to both sides that it conduct inspections to verify such developments. In the absence of any agreement on this proposal, UNFICYP monitors the opposing forces by overt means to the best of its ability.

In accordance with its mandate, UNFICYP encourages the fullest possible resumption of normal civilian activity in the buffer zone. To this end, four villages and certain other areas in the buffer zone have been designated as civilian use areas, which means that they are

* S/12253.

freely accessible and are policed by local civilian police. Elsewhere in the buffer zone, no civilian movement or activity is permitted unless specifically authorized by UNFICYP. In Nicosia, in view of the security implications, such authorization is given only with the concurrence of both sides. The main civilian activity in the buffer zone is farming.

UNFICYP provides its good offices, as necessary, in regard to the supply of electricity and water across the lines, facilitates normal contacts between Greek and Turkish Cypriots by making available meeting facilities, provides emergency medical services, including medical evacuations, and delivers mail and Red Cross messages across the lines.

UNFICYP discharges certain humanitarian functions for the Greek Cypriots living in the northern part of the island, mostly in the Karpas peninsula. The Force delivers to them supplies provided by the Cyprus Government and the Cyprus Red Cross Society as well as pensions and welfare payments. Further, UNFICYP personnel verify that any permanent transfers to the southern part of the island are voluntary. UNFICYP also delivers supplies to the Maronites living in three villages in the northern part of the island and generally assists them in humanitarian matters.

UNFICYP periodically visits Turkish Cypriots living in the southern part of the island and helps them maintain contact with their relatives in the north.

The United Nations civilian police maintains close co-operation and liaison with the Cyprus police and the Turkish Cypriot police on matters having intercommunal aspects. Together with the line units they contribute to law and order in the buffer zone and assist in investigations and in the Force's humanitarian activities.

UNFICYP co-operates with the United Nations High Commissioner for Refugees, as co-ordinator of United Nations humanitarian assistance to needy displaced persons in Cyprus, and with the United Nations Development Programme, in particular to facilitate projects involving both communities.

F. Financial aspects

The arrangements for the financing of UNFICYP were laid down by the Security Council in paragraph 6 of resolution 186(1964), by which the Council:

"Recommends that the stationing of the Force shall be for a period of three months, all costs pertaining to it being met, in a manner to be agreed upon by them, by the Governments providing the contingents and by the Government of Cyprus; the Secretary-General may also accept voluntary contributions for that purpose".

In accordance with Council resolutions, the Secretary-General has issued regular and special appeals to all Member States or members of specialized agencies to make voluntary contributions to defray the costs of the Force. As of 30 June 1990, pledges of such contributions from 76 Member States and one non-member State, in addition to miscellaneous receipts, totalled $444.7 million. The costs to be borne by the United Nations for the operation of UNFICYP since 1964 through December 1990 were estimated at $635.7 million. Accordingly, the UNFICYP deficit stood at $191.0 million.

In order to provide contingents for UNFICYP, the troop-contributing Governments divert from national duty troops and other resources at an ongoing cost to them currently estimated by them at $32.8 million for each six-month period. This figure includes (a) the troops' regular pay and allowances and normal *matériel* expenses for which, under existing arrangements, the United Nations is not required by the troop contributors to reimburse them; these therefore constitute costs of maintaining the Force which are being financed directly by the troop-contributing Governments, and (b) certain extra and extraordinary costs that troop contributors incur in respect of UNFICYP for which, under existing arrangements, they would be entitled to claim reimbursement from the United Nations, but which they have agreed to finance at their own expense as a further contribution to the United Nations operation in Cyprus.

In view of the nature of the financial arrangements, payments to troop-contributing Governments for costs for which they seek United Nations reimbursement can only be made as and when voluntary contributions or other income are received, and after the operational costs incurred directly by the United Nations have been met.

As a result of this situation, the United Nations has fallen further and further behind in meeting its obligations in respect of the reimbursement claims of the troop contributors. The last disbursement under this heading, made in February 1990, enabled the Organization to meet those Governments' claims through December 1980. This means that the troop-contributing countries not only absorb at their own expense considerable costs incurred in maintaining their contingents but are, in effect, financing the deficit. Since the troop-contributing countries are also, in many cases, substantial voluntary contributors to the UNFICYP Special Account, it will be realized that those Governments carry a disproportionate burden in keeping UNFICYP in operation.

The Secretary-General has repeatedly voiced his profound concern about the worsening financial situation confronting UNFICYP. He has urged the Security Council to decide that the United Nations' share of the costs of UNFICYP should be financed from assessed (i.e. obligatory) contributions and not from voluntary contributions. The troop-contributing countries have likewise expressed their growing concern. However, despite the Secretary-General's repeated appeals, the deficit of the UNFICYP account continues to worsen.

Part VIII # Operations established in 1988 and 1989

UN Good Offices Mission in Afghanistan and Pakistan

UN Iran–Iraq Military Observer Group

UN Angola Verification Mission

UN Transition Assistance Group in Namibia

UN Observer Group in Central America

Chapter XIV

United Nations Good Offices Mission in Afghanistan and Pakistan

A. Introduction

In April 1988, the efforts of the United Nations to end the war in Afghanistan were enhanced when, under its auspices, the Geneva Accords on the Settlement of the Situation Relating to Afghanistan were concluded and a group of military observers was deployed to monitor their implementation. While the mission was considered to be an extension of the exercise of the Secretary-General's good offices which had mediated the negotiations that led to the Geneva Accords, its use of military personnel brought it within the definition of a peace-keeping operation and it functioned in a manner similar to other such operations.

B. Background

On 27 December 1979, Soviet forces entered Afghanistan, in response to a reported request from the Afghan Government for assistance against insurgent movements. More than 100,000 Soviet troops were eventually deployed; they soon became embroiled in a protracted conflict with the factions of the Afghan resistance, or *mujahideen*.

Security Council debate of the issue in January 1980 failed to produce a resolution. In order to circumvent the deadlock, the matter was referred, under the "Uniting for Peace" procedure (as provided for in General Assembly resolution 377(V) of 3 November 1950), to an emergency session of the General Assembly, which, by resolution ES-6/2 of 14 January 1980, strongly deplored the armed intervention and called for the "immediate, unconditional and total withdrawal of the foreign troops from Afghanistan".

On 11 February 1981, Secretary-General Kurt Waldheim appointed Javier Pérez de Cuéllar, then Under-Secretary-General for Special Political Affairs, as his Personal Representative on the Situation Relating to Afghanistan. In visits to the region in April and August 1981, the Under-Secretary-General held extensive discussions with the Governments of Afghanistan and Pakistan to determine the substantive issues to be negotiated in resolving the conflict. The acceptance by the parties of his suggested four-point agenda started the negotiating process which ultimately produced the Geneva Accords.

Geneva negotiations

Upon his assumption of the post of Secretary-General in January 1982, Javier Pérez de Cuéllar designated Diego Cordovez, who had succeeded him as Under-Secretary-General for Special Political Affairs, as his Personal Representative. Beginning in June 1982 and over the next six years, Cordovez acted as intermediary in a series of indirect negotiations between the Governments of Afghanistan and Pakistan at the Palais des Nations in Geneva and in the area.

The conclusion of the Geneva Accords was finally expedited by a growing desire on the part of the Soviet Government to withdraw its forces from Afghanistan. In February 1988, Moscow announced that it would start repatriating its troops in May. The last round of talks ended on 8 April 1988 when Under-Secretary-General Cordovez announced that all the instruments comprising the settlement had been finalized and were open for signature.

The Geneva Accords

The Accords, known formally as the Agreements on the Settlement of the Situation Relating to Afghanistan, consisted of four instruments: a bilateral agreement between the Republic of Afghanistan and the Islamic Republic of Pakistan on the principles of mutual relations, in particular on non-interference and non-intervention; a declaration on international guarantees, signed by the Union of Soviet Socialist Republics and the United States of America; a bilateral agreement between Afghanistan and Pakistan on the voluntary return of refugees; and an agreement on the interrelationships for the settlement of the situation relating to Afghanistan, signed by Afghanistan and Pakistan and witnessed by the USSR and the United States.

This last instrument contained provisions for the timetable and modalities of the withdrawal of Soviet troops from Afghanistan. It also provided for arrangements to assist the parties to ensure the smooth and faithful implementation of the provisions of the instruments of the Accords and to consider alleged violations. Representatives of the Governments of Afghanistan and Pakistan were to meet for this purpose whenever required. The Secretary-General was asked to appoint a Representative to lend his good offices to the parties. The Representative would be assisted in his tasks by a support staff, organized as the United Nations Good Offices Mission in Afghanistan and Pakistan (UNGOMAP), which would investigate and report on any possible violations of the instruments. The mandate of UNGOMAP was derived from the instruments and, accordingly, comprised the monitoring of (1) non-interference and non-intervention by the parties in each other's affairs, (2) the withdrawal of Soviet troops from Afghanistan, and (3) the voluntary return of refugees. The *modus operandi* and logistic support of UNGOMAP were set out in a "Memorandum of Understanding" annexed to the fourth instrument.

UNGOMAP's operations in the field would be directed by a senior military officer designated as Deputy to the Representative. UNGOMAP would be organized into two small headquarters units, one in Kabul and the other in Islamabad, which would each consist of five military officers and a small civilian component. The Deputy Representative would act on behalf of the Representative and would maintain contact with liaison officers designated by each party.

The Memorandum made provision for the deployment of up to 40 additional military officers "whenever considered necessary by the Representative of the Secretary-General or his Deputy". These military officers would be organized into inspection teams to ascertain on the ground any violations of the instruments comprising the settlement. They would all be temporarily redeployed from existing United Nations peace-keeping operations; the nationalities of the observers were subject to approval by the parties.*

C. Establishment of UNGOMAP

The Accords were signed by the four countries in Geneva on 14 April 1988. On the same day, the Secretary-General informed the Security Council of the role requested of him in their implementation. He stated his intention to dispatch 50 military observers to the area, subject to the concurrence of the Council.†

* S/19835.   † S/19834.

On 22 April, he submitted a second letter with the texts of the Accords, including the Memorandum. On 25 April, the President of the Council informed the Secretary-General by letter of the Council's provisional agreement to the proposed arrangements. Formal consideration and decision were deferred until later. On 31 October 1988, in resolution 622, the Security Council confirmed its agreement to the measures envisaged in the letters.*

The Secretary-General immediately initiated the creation of UNGOMAP. He retained Diego Cordovez as his Representative and appointed Major-General Rauli Helminen, of Finland, as Deputy to the Representative (Major-General Helminen was succeeded by Colonel Heikki Happonen, also of Finland, in May 1989). Fifty military officers were temporarily seconded from the United Nations Truce Supervision Organization, the United Nations Disengagement Observer Force and the United Nations Interim Force in Lebanon. Ten countries contributed to the mission: Austria, Canada, Denmark, Fiji, Finland, Ghana, Ireland, Nepal, Poland and Sweden.

The first elements of an advance party arrived in the Mission area on 25 April 1988. The two headquarters units in Kabul and Islamabad, with the combined total complement of 50 military officers, were operational well in advance of 15 May, when the instruments entered into force.

D. Operations

Monitoring of withdrawal

The strength of the Soviet forces stationed in Afghanistan on 14 May 1988 was declared to be 100,300, all ranks, about two thirds of whom were combat troops. They had already handed over some positions to the armed forces of Afghanistan, but still controlled 18 main garrisons. Soviet forces were present in 17 of the 30 provinces of Afghanistan. At the outset of its operations, UNGOMAP received from military representatives of the USSR in Afghanistan detailed information on the plan and schedule for the withdrawal of the Soviet troops.

This included a map indicating the location of the main garrisons, the routes to be used by the troops as they left Afghanistan, and the crossing-points on the Afghan-Soviet border which they would use, namely the towns of Hayratan and Torghundi. Starting on 14 May, UNGOMAP met regularly with the Afghan and Soviet military

* S/19835, S/19836.

representatives. At these meetings, the Mission received information on the ongoing withdrawal as well as on any changes made to the original schedule.

UNGOMAP established three permanent outposts on the Afghanistan side: at the border points of Hayratan and Torghundi, and at the Shindand air base which was used for withdrawal by air. Each was normally manned by two officers whose task was to monitor the withdrawal of the Soviet troops.

UNGOMAP's operations also entailed visiting garrisons during or immediately after the departure of Soviet forces. In areas where uncertain security conditions prevented the presence of United Nations observers at the garrisons, the numbers of troops departing were recorded either at the airports of Kabul, Kunduz and Shindand or at the border-crossing points.

First phase

On 15 August 1988, the Soviet military representatives informed UNGOMAP that 10 main garrisons had been evacuated and handed over to the Afghan armed forces; 8 main garrisons remained under Soviet control. The latter were located in Kabul, to the north of Kabul and in north-west Afghanistan.

In accordance with the stipulations of the fourth instrument of the Geneva Accords, slightly over 50 per cent of the Soviet troops had been withdrawn three months after the entry into force of the Accords. A total of 50,183 Soviet troops had been repatriated by land and air. Numbers of fixed-wing aircraft, helicopters and vehicles had also been withdrawn.

Second phase

UNGOMAP had been informed, on 14 May 1988, that the completion of the first phase of the withdrawal in August would be followed by a three-month pause. This would facilitate preparations for the second phase of the withdrawal, which was to be completed by 15 February 1989. Shortly before the withdrawal was due to resume, however, the Soviet representatives announced that it was being postponed in the light of prevailing conditions. They reaffirmed that it would be completed in accordance with the Geneva Accords. Between 15 August 1988 and 1 January 1989, UNGOMAP did not observe any significant withdrawal of Soviet troops.

On 25 January 1989, the Soviet military representatives informed UNGOMAP of the manner in which the final withdrawal of troops would be completed. Over a short period of days in the first half of February, troops would be repatriated both by air and by road in grouped convoys. This duly took place. On 14 February, an UNGOMAP team visited the remaining main garrison in Tashqurghan and confirmed that it had been evacuated on 12 February.

Despite some delays in prior notification of the withdrawal and the need occasionally to limit UNGOMAP's movement for security reasons, the mission concluded that the withdrawal of Soviet troops had been completed in compliance with the fourth instrument of the Geneva Accords. After the completion of the withdrawal, UNGOMAP closed its three outposts at Hayratan and Torghundi and at the Shindand air base.

Monitoring of non-interference and non-intervention

Numerous complaints of alleged violations of the first instrument, on non-interference and non-intervention, were submitted to UNGOMAP from the outset of its mission by both parties. Complaints submitted by Afghanistan included allegations of political activities and propaganda hostile to the Government of Afghanistan taking place in Pakistan, border crossings of men and *matériel* from Pakistan to Afghanistan, cross-border firings, acts of sabotage, rocket attacks on major urban centres, violations of Afghan airspace by Pakistan aircraft, the continued presence in Pakistan of training camps and arms depots for Afghan opposition groups, and direct involvement by Pakistan military personnel inside Afghanistan, as well as restrictions placed on refugees who wished to return to Afghanistan. Complaints lodged by Pakistan included allegations of political activities and propaganda hostile to the Government of Pakistan, bombings and violations of its airspace by Afghan aircraft, acts of sabotage and cross-border firings, including the use of SCUD missiles against Pakistan territory.

Despite the constraints often encountered in the course of its operations, UNGOMAP made every effort to investigate complaints lodged by the two parties and it submitted regular reports to them. However, a number of difficulties unavoidably hampered the effectiveness of the work of UNGOMAP's inspection teams. These included the rough nature of the terrain, the time which lapsed before many of the alleged incidents were reported, and the security conditions prevailing in the area of operation.

Two outposts were established on the Pakistan side in November 1988—one in Peshawar and one in Quetta—to enhance UNGOMAP's capacity to carry out its investigations promptly. In April 1989, it further strengthened its presence on the Pakistan side of the border by setting up permanent presences at Torkham, Teri Mangal and Chaman.

The fourth instrument of the Geneva Accords had provided that the two parties would hold joint meetings to consider the reports submitted by UNGOMAP. After initial difficulties, the first in a series of joint meetings was held in March 1989. The venue for these meetings alternated between the two UNGOMAP headquarters units in Islamabad and Kabul. The parties were thus able to review their obligations under the Geneva Accords, and UNGOMAP was able to improve its monitoring and investigating procedures.

Implementation of the third instrument: voluntary return of refugees

UNGOMAP maintained close co-operation with the United Nations High Commissioner for Refugees (UNHCR), and it stood ready to discharge its task under the third instrument, the Agreement on the Voluntary Return of Refugees. In particular, it was ready to monitor the situation inside Afghanistan and inform UNHCR of the safety conditions necessary for the return and resettlement of refugees. Up to 5 million refugees were estimated to be living in Pakistan and Iran. However, fighting continued, conditions remained unstable, and only a limited number of refugees returned to Afghanistan.

E. Financial aspects

UNGOMAP was financed from the regular budget of the United Nations. On 29 April 1988, the General Assembly's Advisory Committee on Administrative and Budgetary Questions (ACABQ) agreed to the request of the Secretary-General to enter into financial commitments to cover temporarily the cost of UNGOMAP's operation as an unforeseen and extraordinary expense of the Organization. On 21 December 1988, in resolution 43/218, the General Assembly agreed to a non-recurrent appropriation to allow the Secretary-General to carry out his role under the Geneva Agreements on the Settlement of the Situation Relating to Afghanistan. In 1990, the

ACABQ granted further authorization to cover the costs of UNGOMAP's operation. UNGOMAP's total expenditures from its inception until its termination in March 1990 amounted to approximately $14 million.

F. Termination of UNGOMAP

The Memorandum of Understanding provided that UNGOMAP's operation would cease two months after the completion of all the time-frames envisaged for the implementation of the instruments. The longest explicit time-frame contained in the instruments was the 18 months provided in the third instrument for the arrangements to assist the voluntary return of refugees. The implementation of this instrument did not begin—as Pakistan noted in November 1989—and the first instrument had an implicit time-frame, so the duration of UNGOMAP's mandate envisaged in the Accords, i.e., 20 months from May 1988, became a matter of interpretation. Accordingly, on 9 January 1990, 20 months after May 1988, the Secretary-General, having consulted the parties and having obtained the concurrence of the countries contributing UNGOMAP's military personnel, sought the consent of the Security Council to an extension of UNGOMAP's mandate, indicating that more needed to be done for the implementation of the Geneva Accords. Two days later, the Council adopted resolution 647 extending the existing arrangements for two months.*

In March 1990, the Secretary-General again held consultations with the signatories of the Geneva Accords but was unable to obtain the consensus necessary for a further extension of UNGOMAP's mandate. Consequently, and in view of the mandate he had been given under General Assembly resolution 44/15 of 1 November 1989 to encourage and facilitate the early realization of a comprehensive political settlement in Afghanistan, he informed the Security Council that he intended to redeploy 10 military officers as military advisers to his Personal Representative in Afghanistan and Pakistan (a post established in May 1989 and held since then by Mr. Benon Sevan) to assist in the further implementation of his responsibilities under the Assembly's resolution. For this purpose one officer was retained from each of the 10 countries which had contributed military observers to UNGOMAP. UNGOMAP's mandate thus ended on 15 March 1990.

* S/21071.

Chapter XV

United Nations Iran-Iraq Military Observer Group

A. Introduction

In August 1988, after almost eight years of war, and following a period of intensive negotiations between the Secretary-General and the two Foreign Ministers, the Islamic Republic of Iran and the Republic of Iraq agreed to a suggestion of the Secretary-General, which combined the coming into force of a cease-fire and the beginning of direct talks between the two Foreign Ministers under the auspices of the Secretary-General. The United Nations Iran-Iraq Military Observer Group (UNIIMOG) was established to verify, confirm and supervise the cessation of hostilities and the withdrawal of all forces to the internationally recognized boundaries without delay. It was deployed in the region several days before the formal commencement of the cease-fire on 20 August 1988.

B. Background

United Nations involvement during the conflict

Attempts by the United Nations to seek an end to the war dated back to 1980, when an outbreak of armed conflict between Iran and Iraq prompted Secretary-General Kurt Waldheim to offer his good offices to work for a peaceful settlement of the conflict. On 23 September 1980, in accordance with Article 99 of the United Nations Charter, he brought to the attention of the Security Council the threat to the maintenance of international peace and security. In resolution 479 of 28 September 1980, the Council, *inter alia,* called upon Iran and Iraq to refrain immediately from any further use of force and to settle their dispute by peaceful means.

On 11 November, Olof Palme, former Prime Minister of Sweden, was appointed as the Secretary-General's Special Representative to Iran and Iraq and shortly thereafter undertook a mission to the region. Some progress was made over the freeing of merchant shipping caught by the hostilities in the Shatt al-Arab waterway and, in 1981 and 1982, over the exchange of limited numbers of prisoners of war. Yet a settlement remained elusive.

While these efforts stalled over the issues of responsibility for the war and control of the Shatt al-Arab, the United Nations was able to play a role in the issue of the bombing of purely civilian population centres of both countries. Furthermore, missions dispatched by the Secretary-General confirmed the use of chemical weapons and investigated the situation of prisoners of war in both countries.

Military inspection teams

The year 1984 saw the establishment of the first resident United Nations presence in the area. On June 9, Secretary-General Javier Pérez de Cuéllar appealed to both sides to refrain from deliberate military attacks on purely civilian centres of population.* When both Iran and Iraq agreed to this, the Secretary-General informed the Security Council of his decision to deploy inspection teams in the region. Their task would be to investigate alleged attacks on civilian areas. This became known as the truce in the "war of the cities" and lasted for some nine months.

By the end of June, two teams, each composed of three officers seconded from the military personnel of the United Nations Truce Supervision Organization (UNTSO) and one senior official of the United Nations Secretariat, were installed in Baghdad and Tehran. Their presence in the capitals four years later helped to expedite the establishment of UNIIMOG.

In 1986 and 1987, escalation of the war had increasing international repercussions. Attacks on merchant shipping in the Persian Gulf, including repeated strikes against commercial oil tankers, became more frequent. In response, several countries unilaterally dispatched mine-sweeping and escort craft in an attempt to facilitate safe commercial passage through international waters.

In January 1987, the Secretary-General undertook a new diplomatic initiative to reach a settlement. Enlisting the co-operation of all the members of the Council at a meeting in his office on 23 January 1987, he suggested a number of elements for their consideration. On 20 July, after extensive consultations, the Council adopted resolution 598(1987), which included those elements and the cease-fire which came into effect one year later. The Secretary-General's endeavours benefited from a growing readiness by the five perma-

* S/16611.

nent members to work together to seek an end to this long-standing conflict.

Resolution 598(1987)

In the preamble to resolution 598(1987), the Council reaffirmed its resolution 582(1986) (which, *inter alia*, had called for an immediate cease-fire, the withdrawal of all forces to the internationally recognized boundaries without delay and a comprehensive exchange of prisoners of war); expressed its deep concern that the conflict between Iran and Iraq continued unabated with further heavy loss of human life and material destruction; deplored the initiation and continuation of the conflict, the bombing of purely civilian population centres, attacks on neutral shipping or civilian aircraft, the violation of international humanitarian law and other laws of armed conflict, and, in particular, the use of chemical weapons contrary to obligations under the 1925 Geneva Protocol. It expressed its deep concern that further escalation and widening of the conflict might take place, its determination to bring to an end all military actions between Iran and Iraq, and its conviction that a comprehensive, just, honourable and durable settlement should be achieved between Iran and Iraq. The Council recalled the provisions of the Charter of the United Nations, and in particular the obligation of all Member States to settle their international disputes by peaceful means in such a manner that international peace and security and justice are not endangered. Finally, it determined that there existed a breach of the peace as regards the conflict between Iran and Iraq, and recorded that it was acting under Articles 39 and 40 of the Charter of the United Nations.

In the operative paragraphs, it demanded, *inter alia,* that, as a first step towards a negotiated settlement, Iran and Iraq observe an immediate cease-fire, discontinue all military actions on land, at sea and in the air, and withdraw all forces to the internationally recognized boundaries without delay; it requested the Secretary-General to dispatch a team of United Nations observers to verify, confirm and supervise the cease-fire and withdrawal and further requested the Secretary-General to make the necessary arrangements in consultation with the parties and to submit a report thereon to the Security Council; it urged that prisoners of war be released and repatriated without delay after the cessation of active hostilities in accordance with the Third Geneva Convention of 12 August 1949; called upon Iran and Iraq to co-operate with the Secretary-General in implementing the resolution and in mediation efforts to achieve a comprehensive, just and honourable settlement, acceptable to both sides, of all outstanding issues, in accordance with the principles contained in the Charter of the United Nations, and upon all other States to refrain from any act which might lead to further escalation and widening of the conflict.

The Council requested the Secretary-General to explore, in consultation with Iran and Iraq, the question of entrusting an impartial body with inquiring into responsibility for the conflict and to report to the Council as soon as possible; to assign a team of experts to study the question of reconstruction; and, in consultation with Iran and Iraq and with other States of the region, to examine measures to enhance the stability of the region. He was asked to keep the Security Council informed on the implementation of the resolution.

Iraq welcomed the resolution and informed the Secretary-General of its readiness to co-operate with him and the Security Council in its implementation. Iran, while not rejecting the resolution, criticized "fundamental defects and incongruities" in it.*

In September 1987, the Secretary-General travelled to Tehran and Baghdad, and a period of intense diplomatic activity ensued, with negotiations in the region and at United Nations Headquarters in New York. In October, the Secretary-General tabled the implementation plan of the resolution which he had originally presented to the Council in September. In the spring of 1988, the Secretary-General met repeatedly with representatives of both countries in an attempt to reach accord on the implementation of resolution 598. In March 1988, the Secretary-General invited both sides to send special emissaries to New York for consultations which took place in April 1988.

Meanwhile, the war continued, with the ever present risk of a widening of the hostilities. Naval vessels sent by a number of countries to escort merchant shipping in the Persian Gulf were involved in incidents with one or other of the combatants. On 3 July 1988, the *USS Vincennes,* a United States cruiser, mistakenly shot down an Iranian commercial airliner, killing all 290 passengers and crew on board.

Acceptance of resolution 598(1987)

On 17 July 1988, Iran notified the Secretary-General of its formal acceptance of resolution 598, expressing the need to save life and to establish justice and regional and international peace and security. The following day, Iraq also reaffirmed its agreement with the principles embodied in the resolution.†

* S/19045, S/18993.   † S/20020, S/20023.

Between 26 July and 7 August, the Secretary-General met with the Foreign Minister of Iran nine times and with the Representatives of Iraq six times in talks aimed at bringing about implementation of the resolution. After these intensive efforts, and with the assistance of regional diplomacy, on 6 August the President of Iraq declared his readiness for a cease-fire to be followed by direct talks. In letters dated 8 August 1988, the Secretary-General informed the Permanent Representatives of Iran and Iraq that both Governments had agreed that direct talks between their Foreign Ministers should be held under his auspices, immediately after the establishment of the cease-fire, in order to reach a common understanding of the other provisions of Security Council resolution 598 and the procedures and timing for their implementation.

Resolution 598 addressed the need both for verification and supervision of a cease-fire and for mediation to resolve all outstanding issues between the two countries. In pursuance of the latter, on 1 September 1988 the Secretary-General appointed Ambassador Jan Eliasson, of Sweden, as his Personal Representative on Issues Pertaining to the Implementation of Security Council Resolution 598(1987).

Technical mission

With formal agreement to a cease-fire in sight, the Secretary-General sent a technical mission to Iran and Iraq from 25 July to 2 August to work out the modalities for the dispatch of the United Nations observer group. Lieutenant-General Martin Vadset, of Norway, Chief of Staff of UNTSO, led the mission, which included a senior political adviser, a civilian logistics expert and four military observers from UNTSO. It was assisted by the small teams which had been stationed in Baghdad and Tehran since 1984. In the course of three working days in Tehran and three in Baghdad, the mission held detailed discussions with the political and military authorities in both capitals about the method of operation of the military observer group called for in resolution 598, its deployment in each of the two countries, and the co-operation and facilities it would require from both parties.

c. Establishment of UNIIMOG

The information furnished by the technical mission was used in defining the terms of reference and concept of operations of UNIIMOG. On 7 August, the Secretary-General presented to the Security Council a report* containing his proposals for the composition and precise mandate of UNIIMOG once a date for the cease-fire had been agreed. This was achieved on 8 August, when he announced the agreement of both Iran and Iraq to a cease-fire with effect from 0300 GMT on 20 August; direct talks between the two countries would begin under his auspices on 25 August in Geneva.†

UNIIMOG's mandate, in accordance with resolution 598, is "to verify, confirm and supervise the cease-fire and withdrawal". Its terms of reference were set out in the Secretary-General's report of 7 August in the following terms:

(a) to establish with the parties agreed cease-fire lines on the basis of the forward defended localities occupied by the two sides on D-Day but adjusting these, as may be agreed, when the positions of the two sides are judged to be dangerously close to each other;

(b) to monitor compliance with the cease-fire;

(c) to investigate any alleged violations of the cease-fire and restore the situation if a violation has taken place;

(d) to prevent, through negotiation, any other change in the *status quo*, pending withdrawal of all forces to the internationally recognized boundaries;

(e) to supervise, verify and confirm the withdrawal of all forces to the internationally recognized boundaries;

(f) thereafter, to monitor the cease-fire on the internationally recognized boundaries, investigate alleged violations and prevent, through negotiation, any other change in the *status quo*, pending negotiation of a comprehensive settlement;

(g) to obtain the agreement of the parties to other arrangements which, pending negotiation of a comprehensive settlement, could help to reduce tension and build confidence between them, such as the establishment of areas of separation of forces on either side of the international border, limitations on the number and calibre of weapons to be deployed in areas close to the international border, and patrolling by United Nations naval personnel of certain sensitive areas in or near the Shatt al-Arab.‡

In his report of 7 August, the Secretary-General also drew attention to four essential conditions that had to be met for UNIIMOG to be effective. First, it had to have at all times the full confidence and backing of the Security Council. Secondly, it had to enjoy the full co-operation of the two parties. Thirdly, it had to be able to function as an integrated and efficient military unit. Fourthly, adequate financial arrangements had to be made to cover its costs.

* S/20093.   † S/20095.   ‡ S/20093.

The Secretary-General further recommended that the guidelines which had been applied to the peace-keeping forces which had been set up since 1973 should be applied *mutatis mutandis* to UNIIMOG. In particular, the Group would be under the command of the United Nations, vested in the Secretary-General, under the authority of the Security Council, which the Secretary-General would keep fully informed. UNIIMOG would act with complete impartiality. It would proceed on the assumption that the parties would take all the necessary steps to comply with the decisions of the Security Council, including giving it the freedom of movement and communication and other facilities that would be necessary for the performance of its tasks. It would be composed of a number of military contingents to be provided by Member States, at the request of the Secretary-General. The contingents would be selected in consultation with the two parties and with the Security Council, bearing in mind the accepted principle of equitable geographical representation.

In its resolution 619(1988) of 9 August, the Security Council approved the Secretary-General's report and decided to establish UNIIMOG immediately for a period of six months. Major-General Slavko Jović, of Yugoslavia, was appointed to the post of Chief Military Observer, which he still holds.

The total military strength of UNIIMOG is approximately 400 all ranks. Military observers have been contributed by Argentina, Australia, Austria, Bangladesh, Canada, Denmark, Finland, Ghana, Hungary, India, Indonesia, Ireland, Italy, Kenya, Malaysia, New Zealand, Nigeria, Norway, Peru (withdrew in October 1989), Poland, Senegal, Sweden, Turkey, Uruguay, Yugoslavia and Zambia. New Zealand operates an air unit, and the Observer Group also includes military police provided by Ireland and medical orderlies from Austria. At the beginning of the operation, and pending the establishment of a civilian-operated communications system, a signals unit from Canada ensured the vital communications which UNIIMOG needed. Like other peace-keeping operations, UNIIMOG also includes international and locally recruited civilian staff.

Advance parties

On 10 August 1988, one day after the enabling resolution of the Security Council, the first elements of UNIIMOG's two advance parties arrived in Iran and Iraq. Each group consisted of twelve military observers (nine of whom were temporarily drawn from UNTSO) in addition to team leaders and a civilian component. In the days before the arrival of the main body of military observers, the advance parties established liaison with Iranian and Iraqi authorities and conducted reconnaissance of the forward locations where UNIIMOG would be deployed.

Cease-fire

The cease-fire came into effect at 0300 GMT on 20 August 1988. By that time, 307 military observers and the main elements of the Canadian signals unit were present in Iran and Iraq and 51 patrols were deployed on the first day. These patrols had the double task of establishing the forward defended localities occupied by the two sides when the cease-fire came into effect and of defusing confrontations resulting from actual or alleged breaches of the cease-fire. In some areas there still exists disagreement between the two sides over the precise position of the forward defended localities on 20 August 1988, and this remains one of the principal causes of tension at certain points on the line.

Deployment

It was originally envisaged that UNIIMOG Group Headquarters would be divided between Baghdad and Tehran, with its Iran detachment headquarters at Bakhtaran, and the Iraq detachment headquarters alongside Group Headquarters at Baghdad. To increase efficiency, however, and to release more military observers for patrol duty on the cease-fire lines, group and detachment headquarters were merged into a single UNIIMOG headquarters in Baghdad and another in Tehran.

The Chief Military Observer and his senior staff, known as the "Command Group", spend alternate weeks at each headquarters. An Assistant Chief Military Observer is permanently stationed in each capital and directs UNIIMOG's operations in the country concerned, under the overall command of the Chief Military Observer.

In the field, the military observers are deployed in four sectors on the Iranian side, with sector headquarters at Saqqez, Bakhtaran, Dezful and Ahwaz, and three on the Iraqi side, with sector headquarters at Sulaymaniyah, Ba'qubah and Basra. Each sector controls a number of team sites, which are located as far forward as possible in order to minimize the time spent by military observers travelling between team site and cease-fire line. The length of the cease-fire line monitored by a team site varies from 70 kilometres in the south to 250 kilometres in the north.

The air wing of UNIIMOG consists of three fixed-wing aircraft, for communications, observation, and freight and passenger duties. It was envisaged that UNIIMOG would also operate a squadron of United Nations helicopters for observation of no man's land and the cease-fire lines. It has not yet, however, proved possible to obtain the agreement of one of the parties to this arrangement. As a result, UNIIMOG military observers have to use helicopters which are provided by the parties themselves and which can therefore fly only behind the respective cease-fire line. This inhibits UNIIMOG's ability to maintain close observation of the cease-fire.

D. Operations

The cease-fire lines, which extend approximately 1,400 kilometres, cover a wide variety of terrain. UNIIMOG's method of patrolling is adapted accordingly. Teams of two or more military observers conduct mobile patrols by vehicle, by helicopter, by boat in the southern marshes, and by mule-back or on foot in the mountains of the north. In winter some patrols use skis. UNIIMOG deploys a daily average of 64 patrols which operate around the clock.

The patrols' primary task is to check that the side to which they are assigned is complying with the cease-fire. They do this through their own regular observation of the forward defended localities and by verifying complaints received from the other side; they also transmit complaints to their counterparts on the opposite side of the cease-fire line. Wherever possible, they negotiate a return to the *status quo* with the commanders on the spot. Where this is not possible, the matter is referred to the relevant sector headquarters so that it can be taken up with the liaison authorities of the side concerned.

In addition to investigating alleged violations, the military observers have engaged in such humanitarian and confidence-building measures as the exchange of war dead found on the battlefield.

Military observers from both sides of the cease-fire lines maintain radio communications across no man's land and also meet regularly in it. Plans to open three crossing-points to enable passage of United Nations personnel and vehicles across the cease-fire lines have yet to be realized.

Cease-fire violations

From the inception of its mission, UNIIMOG has received frequent complaints of alleged cease-fire violations; in the first nine weeks, 1,072 such complaints were recorded, but the number has since declined steadily as the cease-fire has stabilized. All complaints are investigated; of those which have been confirmed, many have been minor in nature.

However, more significant violations have occurred. On 23-24 August, shortly after the commencement of the cease-fire, several hundred Iranian soldiers were taken prisoner in a serious incident near Eyn-e Khowsh. Efforts since then to secure their release, and that of smaller groups of prisoners taken by both sides since the cease-fire, have not succeeded.

A serious violation began on 13 September 1988 when Iran started flooding an area of no man's land in the Khusk region. This created a water obstacle between the forward positions occupied by the two armies, which in this area lie immediately to the east of the internationally recognized border. The area under flooding has been the scene of several military confrontations. The Secretary-General has stressed that "it remains essential that the *status quo* be restored without further delay".*

Other violations have included the movement of troops, the establishment of new observation posts or other positions forward of the forward defended localities, and the reinforcement of defensive positions by wiring, mining, improving bunkers and general engineering works. In all such cases UNIIMOG endeavours to persuade the side concerned to stop work and restore the *status quo*.

Relations with the parties

Preliminary agreements concerning the status of UNIIMOG were concluded with the Government of Iraq on 5 November 1988 and with the Government of the Islamic Republic of Iran on 28 March 1989. They embody the principles of the Charter of the United Nations and of the Convention on the Privileges and Immunities of the United Nations, as well as the experience of previous United Nations peace-keeping operations. They are intended to ensure UNIIMOG's ability to function independently and, in particular, the freedom of movement and communications and other facilities that are necessary for the performance of its tasks.

* S/21200.

Both Iran and Iraq have established interdepartmental groups to co-ordinate co-operation with UNIIMOG and both have provided liaison officers, as well as the logistic facilities requested of them.

E. Financial aspects

In his report of 7 August 1988, the Secretary-General recommended to the Security Council that the costs of UNIIMOG should be considered as expenses of the Organization to be borne by Members in accordance with Article 17, paragraph 2, of the Charter. He further informed the Council that he intended to recommend to the General Assembly that the assessments to be levied on Member States should be credited to a special account which would be established for this purpose. The General Assembly duly accepted this recommendation in resolution 42/233 adopted on 17 August 1988.

In mid-1990, the cost of the operation to the United Nations was running at approximately $58 million per annum. As of 30 June 1990, $24.4 million, equivalent to about 14 per cent of the sums levied on Member States since the beginning of the mission, were still outstanding.

F. Conclusion

Of the several peace-keeping missions established since 1988, UNIIMOG conforms more closely than most to the traditional concept of peace-keeping. The United Nations military observers are deployed to monitor a cease-fire between two hostile parties, while diplomatic initiatives are pursued to reach a comprehensive settlement. The tension remaining in the area highlights the continuing need for mediation and peace-making. Yet it also testifies to the value of the observers, without whose prompt actions hostilities could have broken out once more. To enable it to perform this valuable role effectively, UNIIMOG is dependent upon the full co-operation of both parties, the continued commitment of the troop-contributing countries, and the financial security essential for all peace-keeping missions.

Chapter XVI

United Nations Angola Verification Mission

Background

The deployment of the United Nations Angola Verification Mission (UNAVEM) in January 1989 resulted from a complex international diplomatic process which initiated both the implementation of Security Council resolution 435(1978), leading to the independence of Namibia, and the withdrawal of Cuban troops from Angola.

Intensive efforts to obtain the agreement of all concerned to the early implementation of Security Council resolution 435(1978) on the independence of Namibia were halted by the failure in January 1981 of the "Pre-Implementation Meeting" in Geneva. Thereafter, the question of independence for Namibia became linked with that of the withdrawal of the Cuban troops which had been stationed in Angola since shortly before that country's independence in 1975. This "linkage" was opposed both by the General Assembly and by the Security Council which, in its resolution 566(1985), rejected "South Africa's insistence on linking the independence of Namibia to irrelevant and extraneous issues as incompatible with resolution 435(1978)". The United States Government nevertheless pursued its efforts, led by Dr. Chester Crocker, Assistant Secretary of State for African Affairs, to mediate between the countries primarily concerned in order to negotiate a complex of agreements relating both to Namibia's independence and to Cuban troop withdrawal from Angola.

Meanwhile, the military situation in southern Angola continued to deteriorate. The Namibian national liberation movement, the South West Africa People's Organization (SWAPO), carried out from bases there its armed struggle against the South African authorities in Namibia. The latter made frequent incursions into Angola, by land, sea and air, and at times occupied large tracts of that country's territory. The Security Council adopted a number of resolutions, including resolution 602 on 25 November 1987, in which it demanded unconditional withdrawal of South African forces from Angolan territory, to be monitored by the Secretary-General.

335

Technical mission

In response to this resolution, the Secretary-General dispatched a mission to Luanda to hold technical discussions with the Angolan Government. The mission, which spent one week in the region in early December 1987, was composed of United Nations civilian officials and three military officers seconded from the United Nations Truce Supervision Organization. It received detailed briefings on the continuing hostilities and travelled to Cunene province to investigate the situation on the ground. Upon its return to New York it reported to the Secretary-General on South African troop concentrations and military activities in Angola.*

The 1988 agreements

During the course of 1988, considerable progress was made in the United States-mediated talks between Angola, Cuba and South Africa. In August of that year, the Governments concerned reached agreement on a series of practical steps that brought about a *de facto* cessation of hostilities in southern Angola and the withdrawal of South African forces from that country.

In November, provisional agreement was reached in Geneva on the redeployment and withdrawal of Cuban troops from Angola. On 13 December 1988, in Brazzaville, Congo, representatives of the three Governments signed a Protocol recommending to the Secretary-General that 1 April 1989 be established as the date for implementation of Security Council resolution 435.† They undertook to meet in New York the following week for the formal signature of two documents, a tripartite agreement between Angola, Cuba and South Africa, and a bilateral agreement between Angola and Cuba.

The two agreements were duly signed by the Foreign Ministers of the three countries at a ceremony at United Nations Headquarters on 22 December 1988. In the tripartite agreement, Angola, Cuba and South Africa agreed to request the Secretary-General to seek authority from the Security Council to commence implementation of resolution 435(1978) on Namibia's independence on 1 April 1989 and to co-operate fully with the Secretary-General in implementing the resolution. In addition, they undertook to ensure that their respective territories would not be used for acts of war, aggression or violence against the territorial integrity, inviolability of borders or the independence of any State of south-western Africa. In the bilateral agreement, Angola and Cuba agreed upon a timetable for the

* S/19359.   † S/20325.

repatriation of the 50,000 Cuban troops which were then in Angola.*

Timetable of withdrawal

This timetable was set out in detail in an appendix to the bilateral agreement. By 1 April 1989, the first day of the implementation of resolution 435, 3,000 Cuban troops would have been withdrawn. In the ensuing 27 months, the remaining troops would redeploy northwards and would be repatriated in phases. By 1 August 1989, all Cuban soldiers would move to positions north of the "adjusted 15th parallel".† By 31 October 1989, they would be redeployed to the north of the "adjusted 13th parallel". ‡

Meanwhile, the original total of 50,000 Cuban troops would be steadily reduced. By 1 November 1989, 25,000 would be withdrawn (50 per cent); by 1 April 1990 this figure would rise to 33,000 (66 per cent), and by 1 October 1990 to 38,000 (76 per cent). The complete withdrawal of all Cuban troops would be achieved by 1 July 1991.

United Nations involvement

It had for some years been envisaged that the United Nations could play a part in verification of any agreement that might be negotiated on the phased withdrawal of Cuban troops from Angola.

When it became clear that agreement was imminent on this matter, the Secretariat conducted consultations in New York with delegations from Angola and Cuba about the manner in which the United Nations would verify the withdrawal of Cuban troops, if so requested by the two parties and subject to the approval of the Security Council. Agreement was quickly reached on a set of modalities which would enable United Nations military observers to keep an exact record of the movements of Cuban troops and military equipment through the ports and airport which the Angolan and Cuban authorities intended to use for the withdrawal. In the light of the continuing hostilities in Angola, these modalities also took account of the

† For the purposes of the operation, the "adjusted 15th parallel" was determined to be a direct line from a point on the coast 30 kilometres south of Namibe to a point on the west bank of the Cunene River, 30 kilometres south of the 15th parallel; thence northwards up the west bank of the Cunene River to the 15th parallel; and thence eastwards along the 15th parallel to the Angolan-Zambian border.

‡ The "adjusted 13th parallel" is a line running 30 kilometres south of the 13th parallel from the coast to the 16th meridian; thence northwards up the 16th meridian to the 13th parallel; and thence eastwards to the Angolan-Zambian border.

* A/43/989, S/20346, S/20345.

Cuban authorities' concerns that the military security of their troops should not be compromised.

Establishment of UNAVEM

On 17 December, prior to, but contingent upon, the signature of the two agreements described above, Cuba and Angola requested the Secretary-General to recommend to the Security Council the establishment of a United Nations military observer group.* Its task would be to verify compliance with the bilateral agreement, in accordance with the arrangements which had already been agreed between the two countries and the Secretariat.

On the same day, the Secretary-General issued a report containing his recommendations on how this task might be carried out. On 20 December, by resolution 626(1988), the Security Council approved the Secretary-General's report and decided to establish UNAVEM for a period of 31 months, i.e., until one month after the completion of Cuban troop withdrawal on 1 July 1991. The necessary arrangements came into effect on 22 December when the tripartite and bilateral agreements between Angola, Cuba and South Africa were signed.

Composition

UNAVEM comprises a number of unarmed military observers, with command in the field being exercised by a Chief Military Observer. The observers have been contributed by Algeria, Argentina, Brazil, the Congo, Czechoslovakia, India, Jordan, Norway, Spain and Yugoslavia. On 23 December 1988, the Security Council accepted the Secretary-General's proposal that Brigadier-General Péricles Ferreira Gomes, of Brazil, be appointed Chief Military Observer; he has retained this position since then.

Deployment

UNAVEM became operational on 3 January 1989 when an advance party of 18 military observers arrived in Luanda to verify the departure of the first 450 Cuban soldiers on 10 January. Thereafter, the strength rose to 70 military observers, assisted by international and local civilian staff.

The observer group's headquarters is located at Luanda, and military teams have been deployed at the ports (Cabinda, Lobito,

* S/20036, S/20037.

Luanda and Namibe) and airport (Luanda) used for the arrival and departure of Cuban troops or military equipment. In addition, two mobile teams have been deployed as necessary to confirm Cuban redeployment northwards in accordance with the agreed plan. The outstation at Namibe was closed in December 1989 and the observer strength was reduced to 60, after the completion of Cuban redeployment north of the "adjusted 13th parallel".

To permit effective verification, the Angolan and Cuban authorities are required to give the Chief Military Observer at least seven days' notification of each departure or arrival of Cuban troops and/or equipment. As normal troop rotation has continued during the withdrawal period, arrivals of troops and equipment are as carefully monitored and computed as departures. The net total of troops withdrawn can be simply calculated at any time by subtracting gross arrivals from gross departures. After each phase of the redeployment of Cuban troops northwards, the Chief Military Observer has dispatched mobile teams to verify that no Cuban troops remain in the areas concerned. He is also authorized to conduct *ad hoc* inspections at any time, either on his own initiative or at the request of a member of the Security Council.

Joint Commission

To ensure liaison between the parties and the United Nations, a Joint Commission was established, consisting of the Chief Military Observer as chairman and one senior officer appointed each by Angola and by Cuba. The Joint Commission's primary responsibilities are to co-ordinate United Nations verification of the bilateral agreement and to resolve any problems which arise. Angola and Cuba also assign liaison officers to accompany the verification teams. In areas already vacated by the Cubans, the officers are Angolan.

Progress of withdrawal

In general, the provisions of the Angolan-Cuban agreement have been scrupulously complied with and, on the whole, the withdrawal has proceeded at a rate slightly ahead of the projected figures. However, the process has not been immune to developments in the ongoing conflict in Angola. On 16 August 1989, President Fidel Castro of Cuba informed the Secretary-General by letter that the Angolan rebel movement, the União Nacional para a Independência Total de Angola (UNITA), had killed six Cuban soldiers in Benguela province and warned that any further incidents of this kind could have an adverse effect on compliance with the timetable for withdrawal of Cuban troops.* After a second attack by UNITA, this time on a Cuban water point near Lobito, in which four Cuban soldiers were killed, the withdrawal was suspended between 24 January and 25 February 1990. As a result there was a shortfall of 619 in the 33,000 troops who were to have been withdrawn by 1 April 1990. By June 1990, however, the rhythm of the agreed withdrawal had been fully restored.

Financial aspects

In resolution 626(1988) of 20 December 1988, the Security Council accepted the Secretary-General's recommendation† that the cost of UNAVEM's operation should be considered as expenses of the Organization to be borne by Member States in accordance with Article 17, paragraph 2, of the United Nations Charter. On 16 February 1989, in resolution 43/231, the General Assembly requested the Secretary-General to establish a special account for this purpose, to which the assessments to be levied on Member States would be credited.

In mid-June 1990, the net cost of the UNAVEM operation to the United Nations amounted to approximately $5.6 million per annum. As of 30 June 1990, contributions outstanding amounted to $3.4 million, equivalent to 23 per cent of the sums levied on Member States since the beginning of the mission.

Conclusion

The efficiency of UNAVEM has been facilitated by Angolan and Cuban co-operation; in fact, the Secretary-General has singled out the mission's success as demonstrating "what can be achieved by a United Nations peace-keeping operation when it receives the full co-operation of the parties concerned".‡

* S/20799.   † S/20338.   ‡ S/20783.

Chapter XVII **United Nations Transition Assistance Group in Namibia**

A. Introduction

The United Nations operation in Namibia marked the culmination of 70 years of pressure by the organized international community—through the League of Nations and then the United Nations—to enable the people of the Territory to live in peace, freedom and independence. Its climax came shortly after midnight on 21 March 1990, when the South African flag was lowered, the Namibian flag was raised, and the Secretary-General of the United Nations, Mr. Javier Pérez de Cuéllar, administered the oath of office to Mr. Sam Nujoma as President of the newly independent State.

Namibia had been the particular concern of the United Nations from its earliest days in 1946. In 1966 the General Assembly terminated the Mandate of South Africa to administer the Territory and placed it under the direct responsibility of the United Nations. From that time onwards, the pace of negotiation quickened, and led, though still at tortuous length and with great complexity, to the Security Council's decision on 16 February 1989 to implement a Settlement Proposal which had first been agreed in 1978.

The agreed settlement was a negotiated compromise and led to a most unusual, indeed *sui generis*, United Nations operation: the *de facto* but illegal occupying Power, South Africa, and the United Nations, in which *de jure* authority reposed but which had not previously been able to establish effective administration in Namibia, were to work together to enable the Namibian people to exercise their right of self-determination. The central objective of the United Nations operation was to create conditions for the holding of free and fair elections for a Constituent Assembly which would draw up a Constitution under which Namibia would proceed to independence as a free and sovereign State. The process, all of which was to take place under United Nations supervision and control, would move step-by-step from a cease-fire in a long and bitter war to the final moment of transition, that of independence. Every step had to be completed, in a democratic manner, to the satisfaction of the Secretary-General's Special Representative, Mr. Martti Ahtisaari.

At its height, nearly 8,000 men and women—civilians, police, military—from more than 120 countries were deployed in Namibia to assist this process. Every step was followed with the closest attention, not only by the people of Namibia themselves but by the members of the Security Council, who had set the process in motion, by the international community at large, by the media and by a multitude of non-governmental organizations.

The complexity of the operation and the intense interest it aroused led the Secretary-General to establish at headquarters in New York a high-level Namibia Task Force, which met daily under his chairmanship, to co-ordinate the Secretariat's role and to provide policy guidance and maximum support to the Special Representative in the field. The Task Force comprised the Secretary-General's Chef de Cabinet, the Under-Secretary-General for Special Political Affairs, the Under-Secretary-General responsible for African questions, the Legal Counsel, the Military Adviser, the Secretary-General's Spokesman and supporting staff.

The United Nations Transition Assistance Group (UNTAG) was an extremely political operation, in which the tasks of each element—civilian, police, military—were bonded together in the field under the Special Representative, with a view to achieving a structural change in society by means of a democratic process, in accordance with an agreed timetable. Though it had elements reminiscent of other United Nations field operations, which have monitored elections and law and order and patrolled borders with peace-keeping forces, it also had numerous novel aspects. It did not fit into the mould of most of the peace-keeping operations described in this book nor did it follow the pattern of the United Nations' previous endeavours in the decolonization process. UNTAG was, in effect, in charge of the process, because each step had to be done to the satisfaction of the Secretary-General's Special Representative. The breadth and depth of the United Nations' political engagement with the process of change, and the integration of high-level Secretariat and UNTAG elements into this process, gave UNTAG its special character, with all tasks being conducted at a brisk pace, in conditions which posed daunting logistics and support problems.

B. **Background**

The context of the Settlement Proposal

Namibia, formerly South West Africa, with an area of 824,269 square kilometres, is a mainly arid country, with a sparse and widely dispersed population, estimated at 1.4 million, which is culturally and linguistically diverse. About half the inhabitants live in the relatively densely populated north-western border area adjacent to Angola.

In 1884, Germany annexed the Territory of South West Africa and retained control of it until the First World War, when an invasion by South Africa resulted in the defeat of German forces in July 1915.

In December 1920, the Permanent Mandates Commission of the League of Nations conferred upon the British Crown for and on behalf of the Government of South Africa (the Mandatory) a class C Mandate over South West Africa (i.e., the Territory could best be administered under the laws of the Mandatory "as an integral portion of the Union of South Africa"). Problems regarding South West Africa arose at almost every session of the Mandates Commission, and the people of the Territory often petitioned the League, complaining of South Africa's administration.

After the Second World War, however, when the Trusteeship Council of the United Nations assumed the responsibilities of the League's Permanent Mandates Commission, the validity of the mandate became a contentious issue. South Africa sought to incorporate South West Africa as a fifth province, and, in 1948, ceased submitting annual reports to the United Nations. That same year, it granted whites living in the Territory direct representation in the South African parliament. In 1950, 1955 and 1956, the International Court of Justice (ICJ), at the request of the General Assembly, gave Advisory Opinions on the South West African question. In the 1950 Advisory Opinion, the Court concluded that South Africa had no legal obligation to conclude a trusteeship agreement with the United Nations, but also held that the Mandate was still in force, and that South Africa had no right to change the Territory's international status. The 1955 and 1956 Advisory Opinions dealt with the voting procedure of the General Assembly in considering reports and petitions on South West Africa and with its right to hear oral petitioners.

In 1962, Ethiopia and Liberia, the only African States which had been members of the League of Nations, brought action against South

Africa at the ICJ, alleging failure on the part of South Africa to fulfil its international obligations in respect of South West Africa. While the case was in progress, a South African Government commission published and began to implement the Odendaal Report, a plan to divide the Territory into 12 regions or "homelands", with over 60 per cent of the land remaining under the control of whites. In 1966 a deeply divided ICJ ruled that Ethiopia and Liberia, even though they had been members of the League of Nations, did not have "any legal right or interest appertaining to them in the subject matter of the present claims, and that accordingly, the Court must decline to give effect to them".

In July 1966, the South West Africa People's Organization (SWAPO)—which, in 1976, was to be recognized by the United Nations General Assembly in resolution 31/146 as "the sole and authentic representative of the Namibian people"—resolved, if necessary, to employ all possible means to achieve national liberation, including armed struggle.

In October 1966, by resolution 2145(XXI), the General Assembly revoked the Mandate and declared the Territory to be the direct responsibility of the United Nations. In May 1967, during its fifth special session, the Assembly, by resolution 2248(S-V), established the United Nations Council for South West Africa, *inter alia*, "to administer South West Africa until independence, with the maximum possible participation of the people of the Territory". In 1968 it adopted the name "Namibia" for the Territory. By its resolutions 264(1969) and 269(1969), the Security Council endorsed the actions of the General Assembly.

In 1970, by resolution 276, the Security Council confirmed the illegality of South Africa's presence in the Territory. The same year, the Council decided to request an Advisory Opinion of the International Court of Justice as to the legal consequences for States of South Africa's continued presence in Namibia notwithstanding resolution 276(1970). In 1971, in its Advisory Opinion, the Court confirmed the Assembly's revocation of the Mandate. It declared that South Africa must withdraw its administration and end its occupation and that Member States were under the obligation to refrain from any support or assistance to South Africa in Namibia.

In 1973, the General Assembly created the post of United Nations Commissioner for Namibia to which Mr. Sean MacBride (Ireland) was appointed. He was succeeded by Mr. Martti Ahtisaari (Finland) (1977-1982), Mr. Brajesh Mishra (India) (1982-1987), and Mr. Bernt Carlsson (Sweden) (1987-1988).

South Africa, however, continued to pursue its own plans for the Territory. In 1975, it convened a constitutional conference in Windhoek of the leaders of the homelands set up under the Odendaal Plan. SWAPO was not invited. The Turnhalle group (named after the building where the conference took place) established an interim government and agreed to aim for independence at the end of 1976.

On 30 January of that year, the Security Council adopted resolution 385, in which it declared that it was imperative to hold free elections under United Nations supervision and control for the whole of Namibia as one political entity. South Africa did not initially accept this plan.

Five Western members of the Security Council—Canada, France, the Federal Republic of Germany, the United Kingdom and the United States—then began to seek a way of implementing resolution 385. This group, which became known as the "Contact Group", worked principally with South Africa, SWAPO and the front-line States (then comprising Angola, Botswana, Mozambique, the United Republic of Tanzania and Zambia) and maintained close contact with the Secretary-General and Martti Ahtisaari, the United Nations Commissioner for Namibia at that time. A round of "proximity talks", held in New York in February 1978, produced the "Proposal for a settlement of the Namibian situation" which, on 10 April 1978, was presented by the Contact Group to the President of the Security Council.*

The Settlement Proposal and
Security Council resolution 435(1978)

The Settlement Proposal contained a negotiated compromise. Described as a "working arrangement" which would "in no way constitute recognition of the legality of the South African presence in and administration of Namibia", it allowed South Africa, through an Administrator-General designated by it, to administer elections, but under United Nations supervision and control exercised through a Special Representative of the Secretary-General, who would be assisted by a "United Nations Transition Assistance Group" (UNTAG). The Contact Group stated that the Proposal addressed all elements of resolution 385, but "the key to an internationally acceptable transition to independence is free elections for the whole of Namibia as one political entity with an appropriate United Nations role". All other elements of the Proposal were intended to facilitate this central objective of a democratic exercise in self-determination.

* S/12636.

The Proposal's detailed provisions were accompanied by a timetable scheduling the actions required from the various parties. Approximately seven months were assigned for a complex series of steps culminating in the holding of elections. Implementation was to begin on "D-Day", as it was called, with a cease-fire in the war between South Africa and SWAPO, accompanied by the confinement to base of all combatants. Within six weeks of D-Day, the level of South Africa Defence Force (SADF) personnel was to be reduced to 12,000 and by 12 weeks after D-Day, to 1,500, confined to two bases in northern Namibia. As regards the local military and paramilitary forces established by South Africa, their command structures were to be dismantled and they were to be demobilized, their arms being placed under guarded supervision. By the beginning of the election campaign, due to start at the thirteenth week, all political prisoners and detainees, wherever they were held, were to be released and all discriminatory or restrictive laws which might abridge or inhibit the objective of free and fair elections were to be repealed. All Namibian refugees were to be allowed to return peacefully so that they could freely participate in the electoral process. Provision was to be made for the peaceful return of former SWAPO forces under United Nations supervision through designated entry points. While primary responsibility for maintaining law and order during the transition period was to remain with the existing police forces, the Administrator-General, to the satisfaction of the Special Representative, was to ensure their good conduct and to take the necessary action to ensure their suitability for continued employment during the transition period. The Special Representative was to make appropriate arrangements for United Nations personnel to accompany the police forces in the discharge of their duties.

As regards the political and electoral process, the Special Representative would have to satisfy himself at each stage as to the fairness and appropriateness of all measures affecting the political process at all levels of administration before such measures took effect. He himself would also be authorized to make proposals in regard to any aspect of the political process. Every adult Namibian was to be eligible, without discrimination or fear of intimidation from any source, to vote, campaign and stand for election to a Constituent Assembly which would draw up and adopt the Constitution for an independent and sovereign Namibia. Voting was to be by secret ballot, provision being made for those who could not read or write. There would be prompt decisions on the dates for the beginning of the electoral campaign and for the elections themselves, as well as on the electoral system, the preparation of voters' rolls and other aspects of electoral procedures. Full freedom of speech, assembly, movement and the press was to be guaranteed. Only when the Special Representative had satisfied himself as to the fairness and appropriateness of the electoral procedures was the official electoral campaign to commence. The implementation of the electoral process, including the proper registration of voters and the proper and timely tabulation and publication of voting results, was to be conducted to the satisfaction of the Special Representative. The Special Representative was also to take steps to guarantee against the possibility of intimidation or interference with the electoral process from any quarter.

One week after the date on which the Special Representative had certified the election, the SADF was to withdraw its remaining personnel, SWAPO bases were to be closed, and the Constituent Assembly was to convene in order to draw up and adopt the Constitution. Whatever additional steps were necessary would be taken prior to the installation of the new Government, and independence. The Contact Group anticipated that this would occur, at the latest, by 31 December 1978.

Walvis Bay could not be included in the Settlement Plan. In 1977, after it had been administered for 55 years as if it were part of the territory of South West Africa, the South African President issued a proclamation by which it was provided that Walvis Bay would be administered as part of the South African Province of the Cape of Good Hope. In November 1977 the General Assembly declared Walvis Bay to be an integral part of Namibia. By resolution 432(1978) the Security Council took a similar position: it "declared that the territorial integrity and unity of Namibia must be assured through the reintegration of Walvis Bay within its territory". In order not to further complicate the difficult negotiations on the conclusion of the Settlement Plan, it was decided to take up the issue of Walvis Bay as soon as the Settlement Plan was executed and Namibian independence achieved.

By Security Council resolution 431(1978), the Secretary-General was requested to appoint a Special Representative for Namibia and to submit a report making recommendations concerning the implementation of the Settlement Proposal. The Secretary-General appointed Martti Ahtisaari as his Special Representative and dispatched a survey mission led by him to the Territory. Upon receiving the report of the mission, the Secretary-General submitted to the Security Council on 29 August 1978* a plan to implement the Proposal and to provide the means that would be required to assist the Special

* S/12827.

Representative in doing so. He pointed out that it would obviously not be possible to complete the process by 31 December 1978 because the plan required approximately seven months for the completion of the stages prior to an election, and it would not be possible to abbreviate this consistently with the objective of holding free and fair elections. The Secretary-General's report stressed the resources that would be required to carry out the plan; with large civilian (including police) and military components and a substantial and complicated logistics structure.

On 29 September 1978,* the Secretary-General made an explanatory statement to the Security Council in reply to various questions which had been raised about his report. On the same day, the Security Council, by resolution 435, approved the Secretary-General's report and his explanatory statement.

From the adoption of resolution 435 to its implementation

Despite the protracted delay which occurred before implementation, and the extensive consultations which took place both within and outside the United Nations framework, resolution 435 established the definitive plan for Namibian independence.

Many rounds of further consultations on matters of detail led to what was planned as a "Pre-Implementation Meeting" of all parties concerned, at Geneva in January 1981. However, because of charges by the Turnhalle group of United Nations partiality in favour of SWAPO, the meeting failed to achieve its objective, namely, the setting of a date for a cease-fire and the start of implementation in the early part of 1981.† The Contact Group resumed its discussions later that year, as did the Secretary-General with all the parties. In July 1982, the Contact Group transmitted to the Secretary-General the text of "Principles concerning the Constituent Assembly and the Constitution for an independent Namibia".‡ These, they noted, had been put forward by their Governments, and all parties to the negotiations had accepted them. The Secretary-General stepped up his own consultations, and an updating of the Secretariat's implementation plans took place. However, other issues began to assume major importance, it being asserted that there could be no implementation of resolution 435 without parallel progress on the withdrawal of Cuban troops from Angola—the so-called "linkage".

In a report to the Security Council on 19 May 1983,§ however, the Secretary-General emphasized the deteriorating situation in the region, and said that the delay in implementing resolution 435 was

---

* S/12869.   † S/14333.   ‡ S/15287.   § S/15776.

having widespread destructive consequences. So far as the United Nations was concerned, the sole outstanding questions related to the choice of an electoral system and the settlement of some final problems relating to UNTAG and its composition. He expressed deep concern "that factors which lie outside the scope of resolution 435" should hamper its implementation. The process of consultation continued thereafter, with the Secretary-General exploring every avenue with the parties to seek to bring about the agreed independence process in full accordance with resolution 435.

"Linkage" remained, however, an apparently insuperable obstacle until a series of meetings took place between Angola, Cuba and South Africa in London, Cairo, New York and Geneva, from May to August 1988, under the mediation of the United States and with the participation of the Soviet Union, with the aim of achieving a regional settlement to the conflict in south-western Africa. The three parties established "Principles for a peaceful settlement in south-western Africa",* and then a sequence of agreed steps necessary to prepare the way for the independence of Namibia in accordance with resolution 435, and to achieve peace in south-western Africa. The various elements of these agreements were embodied in the Geneva Protocol of 8 August 1988, which provided, *inter alia*, for a cessation of hostile acts with effect from 10 August 1988.† SWAPO, although not a party to the Protocol, informed the Secretary-General that it had agreed to comply with the cessation of hostile acts embodied therein.‡

Immediately thereafter, the peace process began to move apace. The Secretary-General, who had remained actively involved in efforts to begin implementation of the resolution 435 process, was invited by the South African State President, P. W. Botha, to visit that country in September 1988 to discuss preparations for the implementation of resolution 435, and the general situation in the region. He told the State President, *inter alia*, that the system of proportional representation had been agreed on for elections in Namibia. From South Africa, the Secretary-General proceeded to Luanda, where he met the President of Angola, José Eduardo dos Santos, to discuss with him progress in regard to the situation in south-western Africa.§

Further meetings between Angola, Cuba and South Africa took place in Brazzaville, Congo, under the continuing mediation of the United States, leading to the signature of the Brazzaville Protocol.‖ By this, the parties agreed to recommend that 1 April 1989 be established as the date for the beginning of implementation of resolution 435. They also agreed to establish a tripartite Joint Commission,

* S/20412, annex. † S/20109, annex. ‡ S/20129. § S/20412.
‖ S/20325.

which the Soviet Union and the United States would attend as observers. The three parties met on 22 December 1988 in New York, at United Nations Headquarters, for signature of a tripartite agreement between them, and for signature by Angola and Cuba of a bilateral agreement relating to the phased withdrawal of Cuban troops from Angola.* In anticipation of the bilateral agreement, the Security Council had decided, in resolution 626(1988) of 20 December 1988, to establish the United Nations Angola Verification Mission (UNAVEM), for a period of 31 months, to verify implementation of the Angolan-Cuban accord (*see chapter XVI*).

On 16 January 1989, the Security Council unanimously adopted resolution 629(1989) in which it decided, *inter alia*, that 1 April 1989 would be the date on which implementation would begin. The Council called on South Africa to reduce the size of its police presence in Namibia, and requested the Secretary-General to prepare an updated report on the implementation of resolution 435, seeking cost-saving measures which would not prejudice the effectiveness of the operation. The Secretary-General's report of 23 January 1989† responded to this request.

The Secretary-General referred to the serious concern which had been expressed to him, particularly by the permanent members of the Security Council, at the size and likely cost of the military component of UNTAG. Under the plan approved by the Council in 1978, this component would have accounted for more than 75 per cent of UNTAG's overall budgeted cost. However, the Movement of Non-Aligned Countries, the Organization of African Unity (OAU), front-line States and SWAPO had told him of their strong opposition to any reduction in its size. In these difficult circumstances, the Secretary-General proposed that the authorized upper limit for the military component of UNTAG should remain at 7,500 but that the Force should initially be deployed with a strength of only 4,650: three infantry battalions, each comprising five line companies, would be deployed, with four battalions in reserve in their home countries, instead of the previously planned deployment of six battalions of three line companies each, with one battalion in reserve. If the Special Representative reported a real need for additional military personnel, the Secretary-General would deploy as many of the reserve battalions as he judged to be necessary, subject to there being no objection from the Security Council.

Meanwhile, the Secretary-General proposed a concept of operations under which the military component would concentrate on certain specific tasks, namely: monitoring the disbandment of the citi-

* S/20346, 20345.   † S/20412.

zen forces, commando units and ethnic forces, including the South West Africa Territorial Force (SWATF); monitoring SADF personnel in Namibia, as well as SWAPO forces in neighbouring countries; and securing installations in the northern border area. Other tasks approved under resolution 435, such as monitoring the cessation of hostile acts by all parties, keeping the borders under surveillance and preventing infiltration, would not, however, be eliminated. Some of them, which were previously to have been carried out by the battalions, would instead be done by military monitors or observers, whose numbers were to be increased from 200 to 300.

In view of the increase in the size of the existing police forces in the Territory, the Secretary-General also proposed an increase in the number of UNTAG police monitors from the 360 stipulated in 1978 to 500.

These changes in the plan resulted in a reduction in the overall budget from an estimated $700 million to $416 million, not including the cost of the repatriation and resettlement operation of the Office of the United Nations High Commissioner for Refugees (UNHCR), which would form the subject of a separate appeal for funding.

The Secretary-General's report also referred to agreements and understandings which had been reached by the parties since the adoption of resolution 435(1978) and which formed part of the United Nations plan for Namibia. These included the 1982 agreement that UNTAG would monitor SWAPO bases in Angola and Zambia;* a number of informal understandings reached in 1982 on the question of impartiality (the "Impartiality Package"); the Constitutional Principles (also finalized in 1982);† and the 1985 agreement on a system of proportional representation for the elections envisaged in resolution 435.‡ The "Impartiality Package" was published on 16 May 1989.§ It included undertakings by the Western Contact Group, the frontline States and Nigeria and SWAPO, with respect to activities within the United Nations system once the Security Council had met to authorize the implementation of resolution 435. It also included corresponding obligations on the part of South Africa in order to ensure free and fair elections in Namibia.

In an explanatory statement on 9 February,‖ the Secretary-General observed that the United Nations was now very close to the absolute minimum lead time required for the effective mobilization of UNTAG and its emplacement in Namibia; he emphasized the urgent need for the Council to adopt, without further delay, the necessary enabling resolution so that the date of 1 April 1989 for the commencement of the implementation of the United Nations plan could be met.

* S/15776. † S/15287. ‡ S/17658. § S/20635. ‖ S/20457.

If the operation began later than 1 April, it would not be possible to complete the electoral process before the onset of the rainy season in mid-November, which would make many tracks in northern Namibia impassable. In his contacts with all concerned, the Secretary-General also stressed that a minimum of six weeks would be needed for the deployment of UNTAG to the Territory. This could not begin until the General Assembly had approved the budget.

On 16 February, in resolution 632(1989) the Council approved the Secretary-General's report and explanatory statement, and decided to implement resolution 435 "in its original and definitive form". Later that day, the Secretary-General presented the proposed UNTAG budget to the General Assembly, again stressing the extreme urgency if the 1 April date were to be maintained. He stated that the lead times for delivery of many essential items of equipment were already past. The Assembly, however, was especially concerned over certain aspects of the procurement of goods and services for UNTAG in southern Africa, and did not adopt the budget until 1 March. Until it had been adopted, the Secretary-General lacked the necessary authority to make official requests to Governments for the resources UNTAG required or to conclude commercial arrangements with other suppliers. Moreover, no reserves existed because of the severe financial crisis to which the Organization had been subjected for several years.

As regards the cease-fire envisaged in resolution 435, the Secretary-General had noted in his report of 23 January that South Africa and SWAPO had already agreed to a de facto cessation of hostilities with effect from 10 August 1988, as provided for in that month's Geneva Protocol. He would send identical letters to South Africa and SWAPO proposing a specific date and hour for the formal cease-fire. These letters were sent on 14 March, proposing that the cease-fire should begin at 0400 hours GMT on 1 April. The Secretary-General requested each of the parties to assure him in writing, no later than 22 March 1989, that it had accepted the terms of the cease-fire and had taken all necessary measures to cease all warlike acts and operations. These included tactical movements, cross-border movements and all acts of violence and intimidation in, or having effect in, Namibia. SWAPO and South Africa formally accepted the proposal on 18 and 21 March 1989 respectively. Each also recalled that it had previously informed the Secretary-General of its acceptance of the cessation of hostilities stipulated in the Geneva Protocol.

While it was inevitable that UNTAG's effective deployment would be retarded by several weeks, because of the delays in the Security Council and General Assembly over the size of the military component and aspects of the budget, resources were already pouring into Namibia and UNTAG's key personnel had begun to assemble there by the end of February. For 70 years, the Territory had been the subject of international debate and violent controversy, first in the League of Nations and then in the United Nations. On the eve of implementation of resolution 435, 31 March 1989, all at last seemed calm and auspicious. The Special Representative of the Secretary-General, Martti Ahtisaari, arrived at Windhoek airport on that day and was welcomed by his South African counterpart, the Administrator-General, Advocate Louis Pienaar.

C. **The structure and deployment of UNTAG**

UNTAG's mandate

UNTAG was essentially a political operation. Its basic mandate was to ensure that free and fair elections could be held in Namibia. Creating the conditions for such elections required UNTAG to carry out a wide variety of tasks, many of which went well beyond those previously undertaken by the more traditional peace-keeping operations described in this volume.

UNTAG had to monitor the cease-fire which was supposed to come formally into effect on the first day of the mandate (but which tragically did not do so, as is described in the next section of this chapter). It had to monitor the rapid reduction and eventual removal of the South African military presence in Namibia, which was an essential condition for free and fair elections and the subsequent transition to independence. It had the difficult task of ensuring that the remaining security forces, the South West Africa Police (SWAPOL), carried out their duties in a manner which was consistent with free and fair elections.

Above all, UNTAG had the political task of ensuring that a major change in political atmosphere took place so that there could be a free and fair campaign in a fully democratic climate. Numerous changes in law, attitude and society had to take place. But Namibia had had no tradition of political democracy and had been subjected to a harsh and discriminatory system of administration for a hundred years. UNTAG's task was to ensure that, despite this, the people of the country could feel sufficiently confident, free from intimidation from any quarter, and adequately informed, to exercise a free choice as regards their political future.

In carrying out these diverse tasks in the limited time available, the Special Representative of the Secretary-General (SRSG) had the assistance of UNTAG, an equally diverse group of international civilian and military personnel. Under the overall leadership of the SRSG and his Deputy, Mr. Legwaila Joseph Legwaila (Botswana), UNTAG consisted of a civilian component, which included a large police element, and a military component, which was commanded by the Force Commander, Lieutenant-General Dewan Prem Chand (India). It was deployed at almost 200 locations throughout the Territory.

At maximum deployment, during the elections from 7 to 11 November 1989, UNTAG's overall strength was almost 8,000, consisting of just under 2,000 civilians (including local employees and more than 1,000 additional international personnel who came specifically for the elections), 1,500 police and approximately 4,500 military personnel.

The civilian component (excluding police)

The civilian component consisted of six elements, of which the largest, the police, is described in the next section. The other five were:

(a)   the Special Representative's Office;

(b)   the Independent Jurist;

(c)   the Office of the United Nations High Commissioner for Refugees (UNHCR);

(d)   the Electoral Division;

(e)   the Division of Administration.

The *Special Representative's Office* had both co-ordinating and line functions. It was responsible for overall co-ordination and liaison with other UNTAG elements, with the Administrator-General's Office and his administration, with the political parties and local interest and community groups, and with the many governmental, and multitudinous non-governmental, observer missions that came to Namibia for the implementation process. Its line functions were mainly in the political and information areas. They involved responsibility for negotiations with the local administration on each of the political processes which had to unfold during implementation of the Settlement Plan and for an extensive information programme which was under the direct supervision of the SRSG.

The SRSG, his Deputy and his Office were located in Windhoek. Initially they operated from a series of makeshift offices, but a headquarters (the Troskie Building) became available at the end of April 1989 and its staffing, including liaison, legal and information personnel, was largely complete by early May 1989. In order to support the SRSG's co-ordination, liaison, information and political activities and to provide him with a steady flow of information about developments throughout the Territory, 42 political offices were established throughout the length and breadth of Namibia. For this purpose, the Territory was divided into 10 regions: Oshakati, Rundu, Tsumeb, Otjiwarongo, Outjo, Swakopmund, Windhoek, Gobabis, Mariental and Keetmanshoop, with a regional director in charge of each one. Within the regions 32 district centres were established, the largest number being in the relatively heavily populated Oshakati region.

Almost all these 42 offices were functioning by mid-May 1989, though one or two additional district centres were opened in the northern part of the Territory in early July 1989. A number of them closed immediately after the elections, but the basic structure of political offices remained, though at a somewhat reduced strength, until the mission closed in March 1990. One of their final tasks was to prepare for the United Nations Development Programme and for the other development agencies and programmes a comprehensive guide to the social, economic and political structures in their areas. This would ensure, during the next phase of international support for Namibia, that the extensive local knowledge acquired by UNTAG would not be lost.

The Settlement Proposal provided for the appointment of an *Independent Jurist* of international standing to advise on any disputes that might arise in connection with the release of political prisoners and detainees. Professor Carl Nörgaard (Denmark) was appointed to that position in 1978. His office was not subject to the direction of the SRSG but had a quasi-autonomous status, though being part of UNTAG and financed from its budget. It was located in central Windhoek, separately from the rest of UNTAG. Professor Nörgaard was himself present during the early months of the mission, when the majority of his work took place. His professional assistant remained in Windhoek until the close of the mission to deal with a residue of cases which continued to come forward until early 1990.

The *Office of the UNHCR* was responsible for the return of Namibian exiles, their reception and their resettlement. All were to be back in Namibia in time to vote, unless they indicated that they did not wish to return. The UNHCR operation was part of the Settlement Plan but was administered by UNHCR and was not financed from the UNTAG budget. However, it came under the overall political structure of UNTAG and UNTAG facilitated its work. The operation was based at UNTAG headquarters in Windhoek, but UNHCR staff were deployed at many locations throughout Namibia, mostly in the northern half of the Territory. The designated entry points for the return of Namibian exiles were Windhoek, Grootfontein and Oshakati, where agreed formalities were completed before the returnees went to reception centres. In addition, a number of secondary reception centres were established for persons who had difficulty for one reason or another in quickly reintegrating into Namibian society.

UNHCR's key personnel arrived in Namibia on or about 1 April. The peak of their activity was during the repatriation operation, from June to September, but they maintained a presence in the Territory beyond independence in March 1990.

The *Electoral Division* was responsible for advising the SRSG on all specialist and technical aspects of the election and for the supervision of the registration and electoral processes. It was also responsible for assisting the SRSG in his and his deputy's negotiations with the South African Administrator-General concerning the electoral legislation and the manner in which the South African authorities would implement it. The Division was based at UNTAG headquarters in Windhoek. Its relatively small core staff was augmented by large numbers of additional staff, from the United Nations system and from Governments, during registration and the election itself.

For the purposes of registration and the elections, the Territory was divided into 23 electoral areas, in each of which an UNTAG official, usually from one of the regional or district political offices, was appointed district supervisor. All the 180 additional staff required for the registration of voters (3 July to 23 September) were provided from within the United Nations system. At the time of the elections themselves, from 7 to 11 November, the need for extra staff was so great that the Secretary-General sought the help of Member States. A total of 885 specialist personnel were made available by the Governments of the following 27 countries: Australia, Canada, China, Congo, Costa Rica, Denmark, Federal Republic of Germany, Finland, France, German Democratic Republic, Ghana, Greece, India, Japan, Kenya, Nigeria, Norway, Pakistan, Poland, Portugal, Singapore,

Soviet Union, Sweden, Switzerland, Thailand, Trinidad and Tobago, United Kingdom.

The *Division of Administration* was responsible for all aspects of the administration of, and logistics support for, all elements of UNTAG, except for some of the military component, the police element and UNHCR, to the extent that they were self-administered or self-supported. UNTAG's policy was to fashion an integrated system of logistics support, with some items provided by the United Nations from its own resources, some by military logistics units and some by civilian contractors. This required the closest possible co-ordination and liaison between the Director of Administration and the Force Commander. Difficulties were encountered in the early weeks of the mission, both because of the pre-implementation delays already referred to and because of the tense situation which existed in the Territory following the events of early April (*see section D*). However, by the time of the elections in November, UNTAG's logistics were in key respects superior to those of the South African authorities who found themselves having to rely on UNTAG's support during the elections, especially in the north.

The Division of Administration was located at UNTAG headquarters in Windhoek. The Director's deputy was based in Grootfontein, close to the concentration of civilian, police and military personnel in the northern part of the Territory. Many members of the Division of Administration were deployed for periods throughout the Territory from time to time. The Director of Administration arrived in Namibia in mid-February 1989, together with key personnel of his staff, and the Division built up rapidly thereafter. The majority departed at the conclusion of the mission after independence in March 1990 but a small "wind-up" team remained for several months thereafter.

Special efforts were devoted to the training of members of the United Nations Secretariat who were selected for political and electoral assignments with UNTAG. Training seminars took place in New York and Geneva in March 1989 for senior officials appointed to the Special Representative's Office and the 42 regional or district offices. These staff subsequently attended conferences in Windhoek at regular intervals during UNTAG's mandate period to discuss with the SRSG the current situation, UNTAG's strategy and the carrying out of their responsibilities at each stage. As for electoral staff, they received training at special seminars in Windhoek and elsewhere in Namibia upon their arrival in the Territory.

The police element

The UNTAG civilian police (CIVPOL) were commanded by a Police Commissioner, who, as Police Adviser, also provided advice to the SRSG and his Deputy on all police-related matters. Commissioner Steven Fanning (Ireland) was appointed to this post on 23 March 1989, having previously advised the SRSG during the long preparations for the UNTAG mission. As Police Commissioner, he was responsible for the organization, deployment and operations of CIVPOL and shared responsibility with the Director of Administration for their administration and support. Their task was to ensure that the South West Africa Police fulfilled their duty of maintaining law and order in an efficient, professional and non-partisan way.

For police purposes, the Territory was divided in two, with a northern and a southern regional co-ordinator (later commander) providing co-ordination at the regional level. The country was further divided into six (later seven) UNTAG police districts. After the first group of 500 police officers had been deployed by May 1989, CIVPOL had 39 police stations; by September, the number had increased to 49.

The first tranche of 500 police monitors was largely deployed in the northern part of the Territory, because of the tense situation which persisted there after the events of early April. Continuing difficulties in the north (*which are described on p. 375*) caused the SRSG to ask for a second tranche of 500 police monitors. After consulting the Security Council, the Secretary-General obtained the agreement of certain Member States to provide the additional officers, who arrived in the Territory between late June and late August. In the latter month, the SRSG requested a third tranche of 500 in order to provide sufficient personnel during the election campaign and the elections themselves. After further consultations with the Security Council and contributing Governments, the Secretary-General began sending this group in mid-September and it was fully deployed by 31 October. The focus of CIVPOL's deployment continued to be in the north and on 1 December 1989, almost two thirds of its strength was in the northernmost quarter of the Territory.

The (finally) 1,500 police officers who served in CIVPOL were contributed, at the request of the Secretary-General, by the following Member States: Austria, Bangladesh, Barbados, Belgium, Canada, Egypt, Fiji, German Democratic Republic, Federal Republic of Germany, Ghana, Guyana, Hungary, India, Indonesia, Ireland, Jamaica, Kenya, Netherlands, New Zealand, Nigeria, Norway,

Pakistan, Singapore, Sweden and Tunisia. Almost all CIVPOL personnel remained in Namibia until independence, after which they were rapidly repatriated, with the exception of officers from Ghana, India, Nigeria and Pakistan who, at the request of the incoming Government, remained for a time in Namibia under bilateral arrangements.

The military component

The military component was responsible for all military aspects of the Settlement Plan. The most important of these were monitoring the cease-fire and the confinement of the parties' armed forces to base; monitoring the dismantling of the South African military presence in Namibia; and maintaining some degree of surveillance over the Territory's borders. The military component was commanded by the Force Commander who was appointed by the Secretary-General after consultation with the Security Council. The Force Commander also advised the SRSG on military matters and reported through him to the Secretary-General. The Force Commander, and frequently also his deputy, participated in the SRSG's daily morning meeting, as did the Deputy Special Representative, the Police Adviser and the Director of the SRSG's Office, together with other senior officials as required.

Lieutenant-General Prem Chand had been appointed as Force Commander–designate in 1980 and had played an active part in the preparations for the UNTAG operation. He arrived in Namibia, with the advance party of the UNTAG military component, on 26 February 1989. The Deputy Force Commander was Brigadier-General Daniel Opande (Kenya). General Prem Chand established his headquarters at the Suiderhof base in Windhoek, on the other side of the city from the Troskie Building, where the Special Representative eventually established UNTAG's overall headquarters. Because of the limited accommodation available in Windhoek, it never proved possible to establish an integrated headquarters for both components of UNTAG. As a result, much travelling was required to ensure the close co-ordination necessitated by the complicated nature of the mission.

The military component, as deployed, consisted of three elements: 300 military monitors and observers; three infantry battalions; and a number of logistics units. The strength approved by the Security Council for initial deployment was 4,650, but the maximum number actually deployed was 4,493, this being due to a reduced requirement of personnel for air support.

The 300 military monitors and observers were contributed by the following Member States: Bangladesh, Czechoslovakia, Finland, India, Ireland, Kenya, Malaysia, Pakistan, Panama, Peru, Poland, Sudan, Togo and Yugoslavia. Of these, 291 had been deployed in Namibia before 1 April, though they were often without transport or communications because of the delays already referred to in the final decision-making for the establishment of UNTAG. The monitors, numbering about 200, were deployed at a variety of locations in Namibia and Angola to monitor the cease-fire, the confinement of the parties' forces to base and the dismantling of the South African military presence. In Namibia they were deployed at all the bases of SADF and SWATF units. In Angola, UNTAG (Angola) was based at Lubango, with outposts for several weeks at Chibemba, where SWAPO forces were concentrated after the events of early April, and with a liaison office in Luanda. They were withdrawn in early January 1990, following the return to Namibia of the great majority of the SWAPO forces, and the Luanda liaison office was closed a month later. UNTAG's military observers were deployed for border surveillance purposes in the Walvis Bay area and along Namibia's southern frontier with South Africa. The military monitors and observers left Namibia between January and April 1990.

The three enlarged infantry battalions approved for initial deployment were provided by Finland, Kenya and Malaysia. Four additional battalions were held in reserve, on seven days' notice to move to Namibia, by Bangladesh, Togo, Venezuela and Yugoslavia. In the event, the reserve battalions were not called to Namibia. The delays already referred to had made it clear that it was not going to be possible to deploy the infantry battalions to Namibia by D-Day, 1 April, as originally envisaged in the Settlement Plan. Under the revised plan they were due to be deployed in late April/early May. The events of early April, however, led to an acceleration of this deployment by approximately two weeks. The Finnish battalion was deployed in the north-eastern part of the Territory by 17 April; the Malaysian battalion in the north-west by 1 May; and the Kenyan battalion in the centre and south, also by 1 May. All three battalions remained in Namibia until after independence, with the Finnish and Malaysian battalions leaving in early April 1990. The incoming Government asked Kenya to retain its battalion in Namibia after independence, under bilateral arrangements, for an initial period of three months, in order to fulfil various tasks, including helping with the training of a Namibian army.

As already noted, the logistics elements in UNTAG's military component worked closely with the civilian logistics elements to provide an integrated logistics support system for the whole operation. The military units consisted of: a signals unit (United Kingdom); an engineer squadron (Australia); an administrative company, including movement control and postal elements (Denmark); supply, transport and maintenance units (Canada and Poland, plus civilian personnel provided by the Federal Republic of Germany); a helicopter squadron (Italy); and a squadron of light transport aircraft (Spain). The military component also included a civilian medical unit contributed by Switzerland. In addition, the Soviet Union and the United States provided air transport for the initial deployment of UNTAG.

For the same reason that applied to the infantry battalions, the deployment of the logistics units was not completed before D-Day. Indeed most of them had little more than advance parties in Namibia at that time and most became fully operational only in late April or early May.

D. **D-Day and its aftermath**

When the SRSG arrived in Windhoek on 31 March 1989 to assume his duties in Namibia, hopes were high. What had seemed an interminable process of negotiation was at last to bear fruit and Namibia's independence seemed in sight. There was concern, of course, that—for the reasons already mentioned, which were beyond the Secretary-General's control—UNTAG would be far from fully deployed on D-Day and would become completely operational only a month or more later. It was recognized that this made it even more essential that all concerned should honour the commitments which they had entered into regarding all aspects of the Settlement Plan. But an informal cease-fire had been in effect, and largely respected, for over seven months and the parties had just reaffirmed in writing their acceptance of a formal cease-fire with effect from 0600 local time on the morning of 1 April.

The previous evening, however, the newly arrived SRSG was told by the South African Administrator-General (AG) that heavily armed SWAPO forces, in combat uniform, had begun moving forward and crossing from Angola into Namibia, many others being poised to follow.

The following morning, while demonstrations and processions of welcome for UNTAG were occurring throughout the Territory, the

AG told the SRSG that further armed SWAPO personnel had crossed the border overnight and incidents were occurring on a broad front throughout the Ovambo area of northern Namibia. A series of similar reports came in during the day, indicating military action and casualties on a scale not seen for many years in the Namibian conflict. The SRSG sent a team of senior UNTAG officials north to investigate. As already noted, UNTAG was not yet effectively deployed in the Territory. Apart from the military observers and monitors, few personnel, military or civilian, had arrived and their operational capability was severely hampered by the lack of vehicles and communications.

Later on 1 April, the South African Foreign Minister told the Secretary-General that if UNTAG was unable to contain the new situation, it would be necessary for his Government again to deploy its military forces which had, earlier that day, been confined to base under UNTAG monitoring in accordance with the Settlement Proposal; the South West Africa Police were unable to deal with the incursion by heavily armed SWAPO groups. The Secretary-General immediately requested SWAPO representatives to do whatever they could to affect the situation positively.

Given all these circumstances, the Special Representative and the Force Commander sent to the Secretary-General an urgent joint recommendation that they be authorized to accept a strictly limited and temporary suspension of the SADF confinement to base. This recommendation was accepted. The arrangement under which this was to occur was in the following terms:

"Certain specified units, to be agreed, will be released from restriction to base to provide such support as may be needed by the existing police forces, in case they cannot handle the situation by themselves. The situation will be kept under constant review and the movement out of existing bases will throughout be monitored by UNTAG military observers."

The team of UNTAG officials sent to the north held discussions on 2 April with the South African security forces and interviewed two SWAPO prisoners captured the previous day. The latter said that they had been instructed by their commanders in Angola to enter Namibia, avoiding the South African security forces if possible, in order to establish bases in Namibia under United Nations' supervision. Their units were to bring with them all their arms, including rockets and anti-aircraft devices.

In the light of the wide difference between the stated objectives of the captives, who had impressed the UNTAG team with their credibility, and those attributed to them by the South African security forces, who saw their intention as aggressive and hostile, the team immediately requested to see all the general staff of the South African security forces who were then present at Oshakati, together with a senior representative of the South African Foreign Ministry. The team emphasized the immense gravity of the situation and the serious disparity between the two versions of events. They stressed, in unambiguous language, the imperative need for maximum restraint by the security forces, while immediate efforts were made in all quarters to resolve the situation. In Windhoek, the SRSG and Force Commander impressed the same message on the Administrator-General and his senior police and military personnel.

On 2 April, SWAPO emphatically denied that it had violated the cease-fire and stated that it was committed to honouring it in spirit and letter. On the contrary, SWAPO said, South African security forces had attacked its members who had been peacefully celebrating the beginning of the implementation of resolution 435 in northern Namibia and some of whom had been trying to come forward to hand over their weapons to UNTAG. South Africa, for its part, asserted that the incursion of heavily armed and uniformed SWAPO forces was continuing.

The Secretary-General reported on these grave developments to the Security Council in informal consultations on 3 April. He concluded his report as follows:

"The mounting toll of Namibian and South African casualties, at the very moment when the long-delayed independence process has at last commenced, is especially tragic. On the basis of information so far available to it, UNTAG is of the view that SWAPO had infiltrated armed personnel and material into Namibia around the time of the cease-fire. UNTAG, however, feels that this infiltration may not have offensive intent, but instead may be aimed at the establishment of SWAPO camps inside the Territory, which SWAPO would then request UNTAG to monitor. SWAPO, for its part, has emphatically denied any infiltration and has stated that its supporters inside Namibia have been attacked. If the integrity of the Settlement Proposal, which took many years of difficult negotiation to conclude, is not respected by any party, then the people of Namibia will again be the principal sufferers. It is therefore most necessary for all concerned to exercise the maximum restraint at this time, and to advance and reinforce practical arrangements to implement each and every aspect of the Settlement Plan. This is a matter of the greatest political and humanitarian urgency, in view of the grave situation now existing along parts of the northern border of Namibia."

On 4 April,* the South African Foreign Minister wrote to the Secretary-General stating, *inter alia*, that more than 1,000 SWAPO armed forces had now infiltrated Namibia, and that major mechanized, tank and infantry elements of SWAPO had been deployed just north of the Namibian/Angolan border. Unless, he said,

* S/20565.

active and effective measures were taken to stem the rapid deterioration of the situation, the whole peace process in Namibia was in danger of collapse. On 5 April,* he informed the Secretary-General that the South African authorities were appealing by radio to SWAPO forces to return to Angola, and offering them safe conduct to locations north of the 16th parallel where, he said, it had been agreed, in the context of the Joint Commission agreements, that they would be confined.

On 5 April, the Secretary-General put proposals to South Africa and SWAPO for a cease-fire and the establishment of temporary assembly points under UNTAG supervision to which SWAPO armed personnel could report. They could then choose between being escorted across the border and to the north of the 16th parallel, with their arms, or handing over their weapons to UNTAG and returning as unarmed civilians to their homes in Namibia. If these proposals were accepted, South African security units would be required, 48 hours after the restoration of the cease-fire, to return to their bases under United Nations monitoring.

The Secretary-General communicated his proposals also to President Kenneth Kaunda of Zambia, Chairman of the front-line States. Following an emergency summit of the front-line States in Luanda on 6 April, President Kaunda informed the Secretary-General that the summit had accepted his proposals, but wished that the SWAPO forces, having handed over their arms to UNTAG, should remain at the assembly points until the SWAPO leadership returned to Namibia.

On 7 April, the Secretary-General again reported to the Security Council. Fighting was continuing, he said, and well over 200 persons had already been killed. Every effort was being made to expedite the arrival and deployment of UNTAG personnel throughout the Territory; members of the Council had offered fresh transport and logistics support to help to bring UNTAG rapidly up to operational strength. The Secretary-General went on to describe the cease-fire proposals which he had put forward.

On 8 April, South Africa rejected the Secretary-General's proposals, which, it said, would be incompatible with the existing agreements. South Africa stated that it would respect all related agreements and that it would be impossible to complete the peace process unless all other parties did the same.

Also on 8 April, Sam Nujoma, the President of SWAPO, announced that the SWAPO leadership had decided to order its forces

* S/20567.

within Namibia to stop fighting, regroup and report to Angola within 72 hours under the escort of UNTAG.

Meanwhile, the Joint Commission established by the Brazzaville Protocol met in extraordinary session at Mount Etjo, in central Namibia, on 8 and 9 April. Angola, Cuba and South Africa attended, as did the United States and the USSR, as observers. The SRSG and the Administrator-General attended by invitation on 9 April. At the conclusion of the meeting, the parties adopted a Declaration of recommitment to all aspects of the peace process, and urged the Secretary-General urgently to take all necessary measures for the most rapid and complete deployment of UNTAG so that it could fully and effectively carry out its mandate. In an annex to the Declaration, detailed agreement between the parties was recorded on Principles for a withdrawal procedure, and on a sequence of events for the implementation of the Declaration and Principles. These also were signed by the three Governments, having been agreed upon by all others in attendance at the meeting.

The withdrawal procedure was to be conducted under UNTAG supervision. SWAPO forces in Namibia were to present themselves at assembly points for safe passage to locations in Angola north of the sixteenth parallel. There they were to turn their arms over to UNTAG. They were to be informed of this process in local radio broadcasts in which a joint appeal by the Special Representative and the Administrator-General would be made. At the end of the process, and after information provided by SWAPO and joint verification by the Administrator-General and the Special Representative of the exit of all SWAPO forces from Namibian territory, the *status quo ante* 1 April would be deemed to have been reinstated. The parties, in agreeing to these provisions, further stated that they had taken note of the SWAPO announcement of 8 April.

On 9 April, the Secretary-General expressed his welcome for Mr. Nujoma's statement and the Mount Etjo Declaration; he believed that, in the light of these developments, the restoration of the cease-fire in Namibia would be facilitated, together with the process of implementing resolution 435. The next day, the Secretary-General again briefed the Security Council, expressing the hope that there would shortly be an end to the intense suffering and casualties that had scarred the start of UNTAG's work.

The Mount Etjo Declaration was an important step forward but it was not implemented in the manner envisaged. UNTAG found it impossible to persuade the South African security forces to keep their distance from the temporary assembly points. Perhaps as a result of this factor, among others, the SWAPO forces in Namibia chose to avoid them and only a handful, mostly sick or wounded, presented themselves for safe passage back to Angola. The vast majority preferred to make their own way across the border, without UNTAG protection. Unfortunately, a number of clashes occurred during this process. In a further meeting in northern Namibia on 20 April, the Joint Commission decided that in order to facilitate the return of SWAPO forces to Angola, all South African security forces would return to base for a period of 60 hours from 1800 hours local time on 26 April.

There was a further meeting of the Joint Commission in Cape Town, South Africa, from 27 to 29 April, about which the Secretary-General reported to the Security Council on 4 May. He said that he had asked the members of the Commission to ensure that the views of the United Nations were fully heard before the Commission adopted any decisions which would require action by UNTAG or otherwise affect the implementation of resolution 435. However, when the United Nations representatives were invited to join the Commission meetings, it was announced that certain agreements had already been arrived at, the main point being that for a two-week period, ending at 0600 hours local time on 13 May, the South African security forces would be again released from restriction in order to verify that SWAPO armed personnel had returned to Angola and to locate and lift arms caches. The Secretary-General told the Security Council that he would have preferred the outcome to have been a decision requiring that the restriction of South African security forces to their bases should continue without interruption. Regrettably, that had not been the case. He urged all parties to exercise maximum restraint, underlining the imperative need for SWAPO personnel to be given safe passage to the Angolan border.

In a further meeting of the Joint Commission at Cahama, Angola, on 19 May, the members noted the "positive steps" each had taken to fulfil its duties under the Mount Etjo agreement, as well as information provided by UNTAG that SWAPO forces were now confined to base under UNTAG monitoring north of the 16th parallel. The SRSG and the AG confirmed that South African forces also had again been confined to base under UNTAG monitoring, with effect from 13 May, and that a *de facto* cessation of hostilities had been re-established in northern Namibia.

Meanwhile, the returning SWAPO forces and any others present on Angolan territory south of the 16th parallel had concentrated at Chibemba, south of Lubango, where their confinement to base by the Angolan armed forces was monitored by military officers of

UNTAG (Angola). The SWAPO forces were later moved to bases closer to Lubango. These arrangements continued until the personnel concerned returned to Namibia as civilians under the repatriation programme described below.

Implementation of parts of the Settlement Proposal, which allowed a period of only seven months between D-Day and the elections, was now six weeks behind schedule. The intensity of the fighting revived the mistrust and division which had begun to be assuaged during the seven months of *de facto* cease-fire. UNTAG had been criticized in many quarters and its task of establishing its moral and political authority had been made more difficult. Between 300 and 400 combatants, mostly on the SWAPO side, had been killed. The counter-insurgency police, *Koevoet*, had been remobilized, and there would be much pain and tribulation before they were once again neutralized. It had been a nightmare beginning to an operation which had been launched with so much hope.

E. The functions of UNTAG

By mid-May the crisis created by the events of early April had been very largely resolved. UNTAG had also, by then, received most of its personnel, who had been deployed, or were in the process of being deployed, to their nearly 200 duty stations throughout the Territory. UNTAG had also received much, but still not all, of the equipment—vehicles, communications, accommodation—which it so sorely needed. It was thus able to get quickly into its stride in fulfilling the manifold functions assigned to it by the Security Council. These are described in this section.

Creating the political conditions for free and fair elections

As already noted, UNTAG was an essentially political operation whose central function was to create the conditions for free and fair elections to be held in Namibia, a Territory which had endured more than a hundred years of colonial rule and had had no previous experience of such elections. All UNTAG's activities were designed to serve this central function, all were subordinate to it. Implementation of the plan was supposed to begin on D-Day with the formal cease-fire and the confinement to base of South African and SWAPO forces. As described in the previous section, this situation was not, in the event, achieved until mid-May. Once it was achieved, the way was clear for UNTAG to start work on the practical measures which had to be taken, in less than six months, to create the political conditions for free and fair elections.

The South African military structure in Namibia had to be dismantled and the confinement of SWAPO forces to base in Angola monitored. The South West Africa Police had to be brought under effective monitoring. Discriminatory and restrictive legislation had to be repealed, political prisoners and detainees released, an amnesty for returnees proclaimed, and the many thousands of Namibian exiles, including political leaders, had to be enabled to return.

All these matters required negotiations with the South African Administrator-General and sometimes with the South African Government itself. The negotiations were conducted by the SRSG and his various specialist teams, though on important occasions they had to be pursued in New York by the Secretary-General personally. Although satisfactory solutions were always found in the end, the AG's initial positions were rarely acceptable to the Secretary-General and his Special Representative, and in some cases negotiations were protracted and difficult.

It was recognized that if this painful process of negotiation was to be completed with the rapidity demanded by the timetable in the Settlement Plan, the necessary political momentum would have to be created. External interest and pressure had an important part to play but it was also necessary to take full advantage of the enthusiasm and support of the Namibian people for the independence process and for UNTAG's role.

As they completed their deployment throughout the Territory, UNTAG personnel found that the Namibian people were, in many cases, perplexed about what was happening and what UNTAG actually was. As a result of many years of colonialism and *apartheid*, Namibia had a public information system which was geared to maintain this situation, with deeply partisan newspapers and a public broadcasting system prone to disinformation. UNTAG had to neutralize these processes and to provide Namibians with relevant and objective information.

The effort was led by UNTAG's information service which used radio, television, all kinds of visual materials and print, as well as the traditional word-of-mouth. UNTAG's 42 political offices focused initially upon the need to reach out to all the people in their areas to tell them what was happening and what UNTAG was. They targeted local opinion-formers, often the churches, the farmers, the unions or political parties, or made direct contact with the people, often addressing gatherings under trees after church services. Information proved to be one of the key elements in UNTAG's operation; by the end, more than 200 radio broadcasts (usually translated into the country's many languages), 32 television programmes, and more than 590,000 separate information items had been produced.

The return of refugees, which began in mid-June 1989, gave an especial boost to the process of informing the people about the independence process and about UNTAG's role. Quite suddenly, and shown in all the media, thousands of Namibians began to come home. By late June all but 1,500 of the South African troops had left Namibia and the local forces established by South Africa had been demobilized, all under the monitoring of UNTAG. Shortly after that, the law governing registration for the elections received the SRSG's approval, and the process of registration began all over the country.

In late July, the political momentum accelerated further when the Secretary-General visited Namibia and travelled to many parts to see for himself how matters were proceeding. He convened at UNTAG headquarters a meeting of the leaders of all the parties which intended to contest the election. They had never met before in a single room. His message to them was that they should now unite, as Namibians, to build the new nation. He suggested they meet regularly, from then on, under the SRSG's chairmanship, to iron out problems and begin a continuing and effective dialogue.

Thus was planted the seed of a political Code of Conduct which was then negotiated by the SRSG with the party leaders and was followed by the parties during the pre-election campaigning, as well as during and after the elections. It laid down the ground rules for political conduct in a country which had never before enjoyed free and fair elections. It was essentially self-policing and self-enforcing and the parties undertook to publicize it by all available means, as did the SRSG. In his report to the Security Council of 6 October 1989,* the Secretary-General described it as a document of "central importance. It gives reason to hope that the parties will conduct the election campaign in a truly democratic manner, that (despite some recent ugly incidents) they will ensure that their supporters do likewise and that they will all accept the outcome of the election. It is no exaggeration to say that Namibia's ability to make a peaceful and prosperous transition to independence will to a large extent depend upon the manner in which the political parties honour those pledges."

UNTAG made the fullest use of the Code, whose text is annexed to this chapter, utilizing all its information techniques. Regular meetings were held with political leaders at all levels, and at each

* S/20883.

UNTAG regional and district centre, to deal with problems that had arisen and to pre-empt others before they could arise.

The Secretary-General's words became a reality, and the last month of the election campaign, which could have been marked by intimidation and disruption, instead saw an increasing tranquillity, with the elections themselves occurring in conditions of great serenity throughout the Territory.

The election legislation proposed by the AG again required arduous negotiations between teams led by the SRSG and the AG, with frequent interventions from New York by the Secretary-General. Agreement on 6 October led to an intensive preparatory period in which election personnel were trained and a voter education campaign was conducted by UNTAG, by the Administrator-General, and by the political parties. Despite the much-criticized delays in the promulgation of the electoral legislation, the determination of the people of the country to decide their political destiny was made clear during the elections which took place from 7 to 11 November. More than 97 per cent of the registered electorate voted, with only a tiny percentage of spoilt ballots.

Throughout this political process, a helpful role was played by a Joint Working Group on All Aspects of Impartiality, which had been established in May 1989. Delegations from the AG's office and from that of the SRSG dealt with the political problems arising from the day-to-day coexistence of the colonial Power and UNTAG. Allegations of minor misconduct by members of one or the other side, the bias of the broadcasting authorities, limitations on political activities by local public employees, allegations of prejudice in the control of public meetings, etc., were typical agenda items. Meeting weekly under alternating chairmanship, the Group successfully resolved many of the lesser problems that inevitably arose in, especially, the first months of the transition period, and usually managed to prevent them from becoming major bones of contention at the higher political levels.

Monitoring the dismantling of the South African military presence and the confinement of SWAPO forces to base

As already described, the cease-fire and confinement of forces to base which were supposed to come into effect on 1 April were not fully restored until 13 May.

The next step was the dismantling of the South African military presence in Namibia, through the withdrawal of almost all the SADF personnel and their equipment and the demobilization of the local military forces established by South Africa, namely the South West Africa Territorial Force (SWATF, otherwise known as the "ethnic forces"), the "citizen forces" and the "commandos".

Under the Plan, the SADF strength was to be reduced to 1,500 all ranks, confined to base at Grootfontein and Oshivelo, by D-Day plus 12 weeks, i.e., 24 June. In spite of the hostilities of early April, which interrupted the planned SADF withdrawal, the reduction to 1,500 was achieved by 24 June, as required. Throughout the process, UNTAG officers monitored the bases and the withdrawal. The remaining 1,500, known as "the Merlyn Force", were withdrawn one week after the certification of the elections, on 21 November.

A number of other SADF personnel remained in Namibia fulfilling civilian functions. They too were monitored by UNTAG military officers. In early October, they totalled 796, of whom about two thirds were engaged in running airfields, with many of the remainder providing medical services to the population in the north. These arrangements, while in accordance with the Settlement Plan, caused some concern in the Security Council and other quarters because of the numbers of SADF personnel involved. Substantial and successful efforts were accordingly made by the SRSG to find appropriate civilian replacements for these personnel inside Namibia and from other sources in the United Nations system, e.g., the International Civil Aviation Organization and World Health Organization.

Of greater concern to the Security Council was the "civilianization" of other SADF personnel, some of them very senior, who were then assigned to the AG's office as a "Department of Defence Administration". Their functions included making bimonthly payments to former members of SWATF, who remained on the South African payroll until independence. Here, too, UNTAG pressed for, and gradually achieved, a substantial reduction in the numbers involved.

As regards the local forces established by South Africa, the "citizen forces" and "commandos", which were essentially part-time forces numbering 11,578 all ranks, had been demobilized before D-Day and their arms, military equipment and ammunition had been deposited in drill halls which were guarded by personnel from the UNTAG infantry battalions as soon as they arrived in the Territory. Some of the "citizen forces" and "commandos" were reactivated as a result of the events of early April, but by the end of May they had again been demobilized.

The most important element in the local forces, however, was SWATF, which numbered 21,661 all ranks on D-Day, most of the officers being on secondment from the SADF. Their demobilization was completed by 1 June 1989, by which time all their arms, ammunition and military equipment had been deposited in drill halls where they were guarded by UNTAG infantry elements, the whole process having been closely monitored by UNTAG military monitors. However, the majority of the demobilized personnel retained their uniforms and, until after the elections, reported twice monthly to their erstwhile headquarters to receive their pay, in most cases from officers who had previously commanded them. This arrangement caused considerable concern to the Secretary-General and to the Security Council as being inconsistent with the requirement in the Settlement Plan that the command structures of the SWATF should be dismantled. This remained a contentious issue between the SRSG and the AG until after the elections.

Concerns were also expressed over the arrangements for the personnel of the two bushman battalions of the SWATF. Unlike the other ex-members of the SWATF, who could return to their places of origin after demobilization, the bushmen would have had no means of livelihood if sent away from their existing camps in the northern part of the Territory, where they had for many years lived with their families. All concerned sought a viable and humanitarian solution to this problem, but it was not possible to find a solution before UNTAG's mandate ended with the achievement of Namibia's independence.

Under the Settlement Plan, the military component of UNTAG was also required to monitor the cessation of hostile acts by all parties and to keep Namibia's borders under surveillance and prevent infiltration. As regards Namibia's border with South Africa, this task was entrusted to UNTAG's military observers, who established permanently manned check-points at all crossing-points from South Africa and patrolled regularly along the border. Similar arrangements were established around the enclave of Walvis Bay, where South Africa maintained an appreciable military presence after the reduction and eventual withdrawal of the SADF from Namibia. The northern border presented a more difficult problem because of its extent, the presence of dense and closely related populations on both sides of the border and, as described below, repeated allegations of impending infiltration. The Finnish and Malaysian battalions accordingly mounted daily patrols along the border, a task in which they were assisted from time to time by the military monitors and by CIVPOL, who routinely accompanied SWAPOL on their own border patrols. The two infantry battalions, as

well as the Kenyan battalion in the centre and the south, also undertook regular patrols in populated areas in order to advertise UNTAG's
presence and give people the opportunity to raise with UNTAG their
security concerns. This task also was, of course, shared with the
military monitors and with CIVPOL who, as will be described, had
the most important part to play in this context.

Throughout the period leading up to the elections, UNTAG had
to address repeated allegations, mostly deriving from South African
security sources, of imminent invasion of the north by SWAPO forces.
It was asserted, on a number of occasions, that concentrations of
armed SWAPO personnel were present in southern Angola, close
to the Namibian border. These allegations were rejected by Angola
and SWAPO. UNTAG's Angola-based monitors patrolled the areas and
found no evidence to support them. The allegations nevertheless continued, even after almost all SWAPO forces had returned from Angola
to Namibia as civilians to take part in the elections.

The persistence of these allegations caused the Joint Commission, which continued to meet throughout the transition period, to
establish a Joint Intelligence Committee to look into all allegations
of potential breaches of the basic agreements relating to the Angolan-
Namibian border. This Committee, in turn, established a Verification
Mechanism, which was empowered to investigate reports on the
ground. UNTAG participated in these processes, its contribution
being of particular importance because of its presence on the ground
and the communications and other logistics support which it could
provide.

The allegations nevertheless continued and culminated, a few
days before the elections, in a claim by South Africa, on the basis
of supposedly intercepted messages between UNTAG units, that an
imminent incursion into Namibia by SWAPO forces had been verified
by UNTAG military personnel. An investigation by the SRSG of the
transcripts of the alleged messages showed, rapidly and conclusively,
that they were fraudulent and did not come from any UNTAG source.
The South African Foreign Minister publicly withdrew the charges
48 hours later. This was the final episode in what had appeared to
be a campaign by certain quarters to disrupt the independence process through disinformation and other, more direct, means, including
an attack on UNTAG's regional office in Outjo, in which a local
employee was killed, and a political assassination.

Monitoring the South West Africa Police

Following the confinement to base of the South African military forces and their subsequent return to South Africa or demobilization, the only South African–controlled security forces remaining in the Territory were to be the South West Africa Police. The Settlement Plan had recognized that if conditions were to be created for the conduct of free and fair elections, without fear of intimidation from any quarter, it was essential that SWAPOL should fulfil its duty of maintaining law and order in an efficient, professional and non-partisan way. This in practice meant that SWAPOL had to change attitudes and practices which it had developed during the long years of war in the Territory. CIVPOL, as the police element of UNTAG was known, thus had a critical role to perform, a role which, as already indicated, required the Secretary-General, with the consent of the Security Council, to increase its strength from the originally envisaged 360 to a final total of 1,500.

CIVPOL could only carry out its monitoring function with the co-operation of SWAPOL itself. This was not readily provided, though the situation steadily improved during the transitional period. Co-operation was least effective in the north, the scene of former guerrilla warfare, especially in the early months of the mandate. CIVPOL also encountered major problems over the activities of the *Koevoet* counter-insurgency element in SWAPOL and the Security branch of SWAPOL. This problem of limited co-operation was the principal reason for the need to increase the strength of CIVPOL.

In fulfilment of its primary function of monitoring SWAPOL, CIVPOL accompanied SWAPOL on its patrols. Its ability to do so, however, depended on the necessary co-operation from SWAPOL, which was not always forthcoming, and, in the north, on the availability to UNTAG of mine-resistant vehicles, which was a problem at the beginning of the mission for both CIVPOL and the military component. CIVPOL also monitored SWAPOL's conduct of its investigations, its attendance at political rallies, and its presence during the registration and electoral processes. In principle, responsibility for the maintenance of law and order remained with the AG, and CIVPOL had no direct authority in this regard. It had no powers of arrest and could influence the standard of policing only indirectly. As the mission progressed, however, CIVPOL's role became more and more influential. CIVPOL was frequently present, and SWAPOL absent, from political gatherings, and CIVPOL often patrolled on its own, meeting the people and reassuring them by its presence.

The problem of monitoring the security police was never fully resolved. Nor was the SRSG ever fully satisfied with CIVPOL's ability to investigate the many complaints made by the public about SWAPOL's activities, though this did greatly improve during the mission.

The *Koevoet* issue was one of the most difficult UNTAG had to face. This counter-insurgency unit, whose name means "crowbar" in Afrikaans, was formed by South Africa after the adoption of resolution 435, and was not, therefore, mentioned in the Settlement Proposal or related documents. Once *Koevoet*'s role had become clear, the Secretary-General consistently took the position that it was a paramilitary unit and should therefore be disbanded, like other paramilitary units, upon implementation of the Settlement Proposal. About 2,000 of its members had been absorbed into SWAPOL before 1 April 1989, but they reverted to their former role against SWAPO in the events of early April, before once again being incorporated into SWAPOL in mid-May. The ex-*Koevoet* personnel, however, continued to operate as if they were a counter-insurgency unit, travelling around the north in armoured and heavily armed convoys, and habitually behaving in a violent, disruptive and intimidating manner. In June 1989, the Special Representative told the AG that this behaviour was totally inconsistent with the Settlement Proposal, which required the police to be lightly armed. Moreover, the vast majority of the ex-*Koevoet* personnel were quite unsuited for continued employment in the police forces, and this also was incompatible with the Settlement Plan. Unless the problem was dealt with, he would have no option but to halt the transition process.

There ensued a difficult process of negotiation with the South African Government, which continued for two months. The Secretary-General pressed for the removal of all ex-*Koevoet* elements from SWAPOL and the SRSG brought to the AG's attention many complaints of misconduct by them. This was one of the main issues pursued by the Secretary-General during his visit to Namibia in July 1989. The Security Council, in its resolution 640(1989) of 29 August, demanded the disbandment of *Koevoet* and the dismantling of its command structures. The AG, on the other hand, contended that there were repeated indications from his security personnel of imminent armed incursions by SWAPO and that it was necessary for him to maintain a counter-insurgency element in readiness. He also insisted that the *Koevoet* personnel were in fact trained policemen.

After continuing pressure by the United Nations on the South African authorities, the South African Foreign Minister announced on 28 September 1989 that some 1,200 ex-*Koevoet* members of SWAPOL would be demobilized with effect from the following day. A further 400 such personnel were demobilized on 30 October. These demobilizations were supervised by UNTAG military monitors.

This did not entirely eradicate the problem, as the demobilized personnel, fully paid until independence, were free to roam the sensitive and highly populated areas near the northern border. But CIVPOL was gradually able to contain the new situation, and, despite some ugly incidents, the political and electoral process in the northern areas continued with increasing tranquillity. As the United Nations had frequently emphasized, *Koevoet* personnel were a major part of the problem of law and order, rather than making, as was claimed, a contribution to its resolution.

Repeal of discriminatory laws, amnesty, release of prisoners and detainees

Preliminary discussions with South African officials about the repeal of discriminatory or restrictive laws which might abridge or inhibit the holding of free and fair elections in Namibia had begun, before implementation, in New York and Windhoek. Negotiations resumed in Windhoek, and in June 1989 a first tranche of legislation was repealed or substantially amended, followed by a second, more limited repeal. In all, 56 pieces of legislation were affected, amongst them some of the most conspicuous legal instruments of colonial repression and *apartheid*, though various "interim" governments in Namibia had already repealed much of the openly racist legislation that had accumulated there over the years. The first repeal proclamation also made provision for further repeals at the request of the public, although no member of the public in fact took advantage of this provision.

Particular controversy between the United Nations and the South African authorities arose over the law known as AG-8, which provided for a system of ethnic administration. This law was not repealed during the transition period, although its potentially disruptive effects were largely dissipated by other means. The AG took the position that the law fell outside the ambit of the Settlement Plan as it did not abridge or inhibit the holding of free and fair elections. He asserted that its repeal during the transition period would entail a complete reconstruction of local administration, and that there were neither the resources nor the time to do this. In fact, few complaints were received by the SRSG concerning discriminatory or restrictive laws after promulgation of the two repeal proclamations, although SWAPO and many foreign non-governmental organizations continued to emphasize the political unacceptability of AG-8, a position which was also consistently maintained by the Secretary-General and UNTAG.

The grant of a full and unqualified amnesty to all Namibian exiles was an essential prerequisite for their voluntary repatriation under the Settlement Plan. The scope of such an amnesty had been one of the most difficult areas of discussion between the United Nations and South Africa in the years following the adoption of resolution 435. South Africa sought to distinguish between Namibians accused or convicted of political crimes and those accused of common-law crimes. For reasons of principle and practicality, this could not be accepted by the United Nations, and, after implementation began, negotiations continued in Windhoek and New York on the subject. South Africa finally accepted the need for an unqualified amnesty, and the Amnesty Proclamation was promulgated on 6 June 1989, thus permitting implementation of the programme of repatriation, which had been delayed pending a satisfactory outcome. Each returnee received notice of amnesty as he or she re-entered Namibia.

The Settlement Plan required the release of all Namibian political prisoners and detainees. Immediately after implementation had begun, the Special Representative wrote to South Africa, SWAPO, Angola and Zambia, conveying lists of names of persons reported to have been detained or imprisoned. These had been forwarded to him by a number of non-governmental organizations which had been following the course of events in and relating to Namibia. The Special Representative inquired of the various parties whether they might have knowledge of such persons, who were alleged to have been, at one time or another, detained or imprisoned by their authorities or on their territory.

On 24 May 1989, UNTAG military monitors in Angola interviewed about 200 former detainees who had been released by SWAPO. These persons, and a number of others released by SWAPO, were duly repatriated. Meanwhile, discussions had taken place between the SRSG and the AG regarding persons imprisoned or detained by the South African authorities. A number of disputed cases were referred to the Independent Jurist, Professor Nörgaard, and he advised upon them on 19 June 1989. Both the Special Representative and the Administrator-General accepted the Independent Jurist's advice, and 25 former political prisoners were consequently released on 20 July 1989. A number of other disputed cases were referred to the Independent Jurist during the remainder of the mission and, in each instance, his advice was followed and acted upon by UNTAG and South Africa.

However, it was persistently alleged, by both South Africa and SWAPO, that additional prisoners remained in detention and should have been released. In particular, allegations that prisoners remained in SWAPO hands became a major issue in the Namibian electoral campaign. For South Africa, the AG insisted that all persons on the lists submitted to him had either been released or were unknown to the South African authorities. As for SWAPO, it stated that it no longer held any detainees, and invited the international community to investigate allegations to the contrary.

For his part, the SRSG sought to detach fact from allegation, and to produce, as accurately as possible, a verifiable list of Namibians who were missing or otherwise unaccounted for. He decided to send a mission to Angola and Zambia, with the co-operation of those Governments and of SWAPO, to look into the question. The mission spent several weeks during September 1989 visiting sites and seeking to check allegations. It found that no persons were detained at any of the reported locations. As a result of the information it obtained, and subsequently followed up, it was able to reduce an initial list of persons unaccounted for from 1,100 to 315. UNTAG continued to seek and obtain information on this question for the rest of its mandate. Many revisions of detail were made, and the data were subsequently refined, but the overall picture remained the same. The question of missing persons turned out to be one of the most divisive and emotionally charged issues that confronted UNTAG during its time in Namibia.

Return of refugees

The Settlement Plan required that all exiled Namibians be given the opportunity to return to their country in time to participate fully in the political and electoral process. Implementation was entrusted to UNHCR, although the operation formed part of the overall resolution 435 process of transition to independence. A number of other United Nations agencies and programmes contributed to the repatriation programme: the World Food Programme, the World Health Organization, the Food and Agriculture Organization of the United Nations, the United Nations Children's Fund and the United Nations Educational, Scientific and Cultural Organization. In Namibia, the Council of Churches in Namibia was UNHCR's implementing partner.

The great majority of returning Namibians came back from Angola, with smaller but significant numbers from Zambia. Altogether, returnees came from 46 countries, requiring a co-ordinated effort by UNHCR offices world-wide.

A massive airlift began in June, following proclamation of the general amnesty. Three air and three land entry-points, as well as five reception centres, were established in northern and central Namibia to receive and register returnees and provide them with material assistance. Security at the reception centres was provided by the military component of UNTAG. A series of secondary reception centres was also established, but movement by returnees through the centres was, on the whole, brisk, due in large part to the assistance provided and to the resilient Namibian family structure which rapidly reabsorbed the exiles. The process of reintegration and rehabilitation was handled on an inter-agency basis, with special reference to questions of shelter, agriculture, water, health, education, income generation and family support.

The repatriation programme was conducted smoothly. The psychological impact of the return of so many exiles was perceptible throughout the country. Though various political issues were raised regarding one or another aspect of the repatriation process, its size, momentum and effectiveness helped to minimize political controversies. There were some problems in the north when ex-*Koevoet* elements searched villages for SWAPO returnees. This matter was kept under constant surveillance by UNTAG's police monitors, who in this area, as in others, played a valuable role in defusing local tensions and maintaining stability.

By the end of the process, 42,736 Namibians had been brought back from exile.

Registration and electoral supervision

All UNTAG's other functions were focused specifically upon the need to ensure that the whole electoral process, including registration, was transparently free and fair, so that Namibia could move to nationhood and independence through an impeccable act of self-determination. Though the electoral process was to be conducted by the South African Administrator-General, each and every element was to take place under the active supervision and control of the Special Representative and UNTAG. While the United Nations had previously participated as an observer in many final acts of decolonization, its role in Namibia was unique in terms of the degree of the Organization's involvement in the process of political change in the Territory and the central part played by UNTAG in that process.

Planning for the supervision and control of the electoral process had begun in the Special Representative's office immediately after the adoption of resolution 435 in 1978. As already mentioned, it had been decided well before implementation that a system of proportional representation would afford the most equitable and democratic means of ascertaining the popular will in the Namibian context.

As regards registration, a draft proclamation was published by the AG on 24 April 1989 for general information and comment. The SRSG had desired that the fullest possible democratic consultation should take place prior to the finalization of the registration legislation. Many comments, often highly critical, were received on the draft and there ensued intensive negotiations between the SRSG and the AG, which were closely directed by the Secretary-General from New York. On 26 June the SRSG indicated his consent to a much-amended Proclamation which was duly issued.

The SRSG's consent was conditional upon the AG's agreement to an exchange of letters which defined in detail UNTAG's role in the registration process. This contained, *inter alia*, the important provision that no application for registration could be rejected without the concurrence of an UNTAG official. Similar exchanges of letters were concluded between the SRSG and the AG in connection with subsequent legislation concerning the other stages of the electoral process and the Constituent Assembly itself. They provided an important means of ensuring UNTAG's supervision and control of the election, in accordance with the Settlement Plan.

Registration began on 3 July and was originally scheduled to close on 15 September. However, the SRSG requested that the period be extended to 23 September, so that all eligible voters would be given full opportunity to register, and this was done. The Proclamation identified the various categories of persons who would be qualified for registration. Anyone over the age of 18 could vote, if he or she was born in Namibia, or if they had been continuously resident there for four years, or if they were the child of a person born in Namibia. Provision was made for documentary or other proof of age and other qualifications. UNTAG's consent was required before a would-be registrant could be refused, and provision was made for appeals, and for the receipt of objections to registrations.

Seventy registration centres were established, together with 110 mobile registration teams which covered 2,200 points throughout the country. Each registration point was supervised by UNTAG officials, and CIVPOL was present at each location. The central register was also supervised by UNTAG computer experts, and a computerized list of registrants was made available on a weekly basis to all political parties. The number of registrants exceeded by 2.4 per cent the AG's projection of those likely to be qualified to register (701,483, as against 685,276). This confirmed UNTAG's assessment of the vast public enthusiasm for registration and the election generally.

As regards the election Proclamation, a draft was published by the AG on 21 July 1989, with a request for comments by the public within 21 days. The draft again evoked major criticisms from the public and from interested observers. The Secretary-General found it to be seriously deficient, and prolonged and difficult negotiations again ensued between the SRSG and the AG. The SRSG's legal staff was reinforced from New York and the Secretary-General intervened personally at critical moments. The negotiations were not successfully concluded until 6 October. Prior to this, however, an agreed Proclamation was issued on the registration of political parties for the election. Ten parties registered. The electoral arrangements which were finally agreed and incorporated in the proclamation provided for elections on a nation-wide basis (i.e., without constituencies) and for a dual system of ballots—ordinary and "tendered". Voters about whose registration or identity there was agreed to be some doubt would be required to use tendered ballots and to place them in a separate ballot-box, such ballots being subject to a verification system. Voters would be expected to cast their ballots where they had registered; those who did not would be required to vote by tendered ballot.

Practical arrangements for the election were both complex and demanding, not only because of the terrain, but also because of language diversity, the unfamiliarity of many voters with the balloting procedure, the extensive measures taken to preclude fraudulent voting, and UNTAG's intensive supervision of each step. A total of 358 polling stations were established. The total number of United Nations personnel directly involved in the supervisory process was 1,758, including 885 specialist personnel made available by the Governments of 27 States. Three hundred and fifty-eight of the UNTAG personnel, acting as ballot-box supervisors, were drawn from the military component. The remaining electoral supervisors came from UNTAG's civilian component and the rest of the United Nations system. Additionally, 1,023 UNTAG police monitors were assigned to electoral duties.

All UNTAG election supervisory personnel were given specialist training. The process of voter education was inevitably delayed
because of the difficult negotiations over the electoral law, which were
not completed until one month before the elections. Once that had
been agreed, however, a vigorous voter-education programme was
carried out by UNTAG, by the AG and by the political parties. As the
country moved towards elections, the atmosphere became increasingly peaceful, and the last weeks before the election saw a marked
drop in allegations of intimidation.

While there had been many auspicious indications in the last
weeks, and, indeed, UNTAG's whole strategy had aimed at this, few
had anticipated the extraordinary response of the electorate. By the
close of polling on 11 November, more than 97 per cent of the registered voters had voted in conditions of great tranquillity, and with
memorable determination. In the first days, would-be voters formed
peaceful lines, often more than a kilometre in length, sometimes queu-
ing up during the cold nights before the polling stations opened, or
for hours in the sun during the day. Apart from logistical problems
in the north, caused by an unexpected avalanche of voters in the first
days, voting proceeded calmly, and the SRSG had no hesitation in
announcing, shortly after the polls had closed, that he was fully
satisfied that the voting process had been free and fair.

Ballot-counting began on 13 November at the 23 election district
centres and in Windhoek. Final results were declared on the evening of 14 November. They showed that no party had received a two-
thirds majority, but that SWAPO had obtained 41 of the Assembly's
72 seats, that its main opponent, the Democratic Turnhalle Alliance
(DTA), had 21 seats and that five of the remaining eight parties had
also obtained representation. A very small percentage of ballots (1.4
per cent) had been rejected as invalid. A few minutes later, after
informing the Secretary-General, the Special Representative, speak-
ing to the press and public from the steps of UNTAG headquarters
in Windhoek, certified, in fulfilment of his responsibility under the
Settlement Proposal, that the electoral process in Namibia had, at
every stage, been free and fair, and that it had been conducted to
his satisfaction. In his statement, Ahtisaari said: "Its youngest
democracy has given the whole world a shining lesson in democracy,
exemplary as to commitment, restraint and tolerance." In his own
statement, the Secretary-General, after paying tribute to the role
played in the elections by the voters, the political parties, the South
African authorities and UNTAG, said: "Namibia must become a united
nation where the inhabitants of all political persuasions will be able

to enjoy their inalienable rights without fear or favour. These were the aims and objectives of the United Nations when, 43 years ago, the issue of Namibia first came before the General Assembly."

F. Developments from the elections until the end of the mandate

On 21 November 1989, the newly elected Constituent Assembly convened, in accordance with the Settlement Plan and with a Constituent Assembly Proclamation. The latter had been promulgated after the usual difficult negotiations with the SRSG on a draft which, in its first form, was largely unacceptable to the Secretary-General. The Constituent Assembly quickly elected officials and proceeded, initially in committees, to draw up a Constitution. The Constitution was adopted by consensus on 9 February 1990. It provided for independence six weeks later on 21 March 1990. In his report to the Security Council of 16 March 1990,* the Secretary-General reported that the Constitution, which was annexed, was to enter into force on independence, and that it reflected the "Principles concerning the Constituent Assembly and the Constitution for an independent Namibia" adopted by all the parties concerned in 1982. The SRSG had, as considered appropriate by the Assembly, made available his resources, when necessary, to assist in its deliberations and in the drafting of the Constitution.

In the period between the elections and independence, the Administrator-General remained responsible for the administration of the Territory, and his activities continued to be monitored by UNTAG and discussed as necessary with him by the SRSG. After the elections, UNTAG closed some of its centres, and reduced staffing in others, and all were closed at independence. UNTAG's police monitors continued with their tasks until independence and there was no reduction in their strength until just before that time. Indeed, because of reductions in SWAPOL's manpower, after the elections, especially in the north, CIVPOL came to play an increasing role in maintaining calm and stability. Numerous exercises in reconciliation between various elements were undertaken by UNTAG, particularly in the Kavango, Caprivi and Ovambo regions, with no small success.

The military component of UNTAG was gradually wound down in the early months of 1990, with certain logistics elements, and many monitors and observers, leaving during January and February. Mean-

* S/20967/Add.2.

while, however, a Tripartite Military Integration Committee was established, with UNTAG in the chair, to develop a concept for an integrated Namibian army. The Committee was to plan the integration of Namibian armed personnel who had fought on both sides of the war and develop a military structure for a future Namibian army. A team from the Kenyan battalion helped train the integrated nucleus of the new Namibian army, which participated in the independence ceremonies.

The independence ceremony, which took place just after midnight on 21 March, was attended by the Secretary-General, who administered the oath of office to President Sam Nujoma, in accordance with the terms of the Constitution, and by many leaders from around the world. In his final report to the Security Council, on 28 March 1990,* the Secretary-General reported: "Thus was achieved, in dignity and with great rejoicing, the goal of independence for Namibia for which the United Nations and its Member States have striven for so long."

G. **Financial aspects**

In his report of 23 January 1989,† the Secretary-General recommended to the Security Council that the costs of UNTAG should be considered as expenses of the Organization to be borne by Members in accordance with Article 17, paragraph 2, of the Charter. He also expressed his intention to recommend to the General Assembly that the assessments to be levied on Member States be credited to a special account which would be established for this purpose. This recommendation was duly accepted by the General Assembly in resolution 43/232 of 3 March 1989.

As discussed above, the Security Council's request to the Secretary-General in resolution 629(1989) to "identify wherever possible tangible cost-saving measures without prejudice to his ability fully to carry out [UNTAG's] mandate" resulted in a reduction of the overall budget from approximately $700 million to $416 million. Considerable attention to economy during UNTAG's operation, together with voluntary contributions provided by Member States, meant that the total expenditures amounted to approximately $383 million, including the costs arising from UNTAG's liquidation.

---

* S/21215. † S/20412.

H. Conclusions

The UNTAG operation had many novel features and constituted an evolutionary step beyond the United Nations' traditional role of peace-keeping and the monitoring of self-determination processes. This was because of the far-reaching mandate given to the Secretary-General by the Security Council. UNTAG's principal function was to create the conditions for the holding of free and fair elections. This meant that it was required to be, and was, deeply involved in the whole political process of Namibia's transition from illegally occupied colony to sovereign and independent State. UNTAG thus had to play its part in monitoring and implementing a cease-fire, the withdrawal and demobilization of troops, monitoring a local police force, managing a political "normalization" process, supervising and controlling the resultant elections and assisting the transition to independence. Because of the vast international interest in Namibia, a territory with a unique status under international law, each step was taken under a searchlight of public scrutiny and comment. The mandate made it one of the most political of United Nations operations, and the logistical dimensions, together with the strict timetable involved, caused it to be one of the most demanding, in practical terms, to be put in the field.

The internal lessons for the United Nations are far-reaching. The UNTAG experience can be of great value in the planning and execution of United Nations operations in the last decade of the century. The foundation for the success of such operations remains, as ever, the full co-operation of the parties, the continuing support of the Security Council, and the timely provision of the necessary financial resources. If these are forthcoming, UNTAG showed how much the United Nations can achieve by making full use of all its resources, including the diverse skills, and the commitment, of its staff.

Annex

Code of Conduct for political parties during the present election campaign

An essential part of free and fair elections is freedom of political campaigning. Everyone has the right to put forward their political principles and ideas, without threat or fear, to every other person, without exception. But freedom of political campaigning also carries responsibilities, including the duty to accept every other person's freedom to campaign.

The Namibian political parties whose names are subscribed to this document, meeting together in Windhoek under the chairmanship of the Special Representative of the Secretary-General of the United Nations on 12 September 1989, have agreed as follows:

(1) Intimidation, in any form, is unacceptable, and will be expressly forbidden by the parties in directives to their members and supporters.

(2) Party leaders will instruct their members and supporters that no weapon of any kind, including any traditional weapon, may be brought to any political rally, meeting, march or other demonstration.

(3) Parties will notify UNTAG-CIVPOL as well as SWAPOL in advance of their planned meetings and other rallies.

(4) All practical steps will be taken by parties to avoid holding rallies, meetings, marches or demonstrations close to one another at the same time. Party leaders undertake to co-operate in applying this principle in good faith and in a reasonable spirit should any coincidence of time or venue arise.

(5) Speakers at political rallies will at all times avoid using language which threatens or incites violence in any form against any other person or group of persons. Parties will not issue pamphlets, newsletters or posters, whether officially or anonymously, which contain inflammatory language or material.

(6) All parties will consistently emphasize, both to their supporters and also to voters in general, that there will be a secret ballot, and that consequently no one will know how any individual may have voted.

(7) Party members and supporters will not disrupt other parties' rallies, meetings, marches or demonstrations.

(8) Party members and supporters will not seek to obstruct other persons from attending the political rallies of other parties.

(9) Party members and supporters will not plagiarize symbols of other parties, or steal, disfigure or destroy political or campaign materials of other parties.

(10) Party leaders will use their good offices to seek to ensure reasonable freedom of access by all political parties to all potential voters, whether they be at farms, on State-owned properties, in villages, or at secondary reception centres. They will also seek to ensure that such potential voters wishing to

participate in related political activities have freedom to do so. This may, where necessary, take place outside working hours.

(11) Parties will establish effective lines of communication to one another at headquarters, regional and district levels, and will appoint liaison personnel who will be constantly on call to deal with any problems that may arise.

(12) Parties will meet on a fortnightly basis under the chairmanship of UNTAG regional directors or centre heads to discuss all matters of concern relating to the election campaign. A standing committee of party leaders at headquarters will meet on a fortnightly basis under the chairmanship of the Special Representative or his Deputy to deal with such matters on a nation-wide basis. An observer from the Office of the Administrator-General will be invited to attend the meeting of the standing committee. Emergency meetings will be convened as and when necessary.

(13) All allegations of intimidation and other unlawful conduct in the election campaign will be brought to the attention of the nearest UNTAG-CIVPOL and SWAPOL stations or patrols.

(14) Party leaders will issue directives to their members and supporters to observe this Code of Conduct, and take all other necessary steps to ensure compliance.

(15) It is stated in the Settlement Proposal that: "The elections will be under the supervision and control of the United Nations in that, as a condition to the conduct of the electoral process, the elections themselves and the certification of their results, the United Nations Special Representative will have to satisfy himself at each stage as to the fairness and appropriateness of all measures affecting the political process at all levels of administration before such measures take effect." Party leaders undertake to honour the outcome of free and fair elections so certified by the Special Representative of the Secretary-General of the United Nations.

(16) The Special Representative and party leaders undertake to publicize this Code of Conduct throughout Namibia by all means at their disposal.

The Namibian political parties whose names are subscribed below accept and endorse this Code of Conduct as binding upon them. They agree that alleged violations will be brought to and considered by the standing committee referred to in paragraph 12 above.

Name of party	Name of representative	Signature
Action Christian National	J. M. De Wet	*(Signed)*
Democratic Turnhalle Alliance	F. J. Kozonguizi	*(Signed)*
Federal Convention of Namibia	H. Diergaardt	*(Signed)*
Namibia Christian Democratic Party	W. Adam	*(Signed)*
Namibia National Front	I. Uirab	*(Signed)*
National Patriotic Front of Namibia	E. van Zijl	*(Signed)*
South West Africa People's Organization	H.G. Geingob	*(Signed)*
SWAPO-Democrats	for A. Shipanga	*(Signed)*
United Democratic Front	Justus Garoeb	*(Signed)*

In the presence of the Special Representative of the Secretary-General,

(Signed) Martti AHTISAARI
UNTAG headquarters,
Windhoek, 12 September 1989

United Nations Observer Group in Central America

Chapter XVIII

A. Introduction

The United Nations Observer Group in Central America (ONUCA) has played a key part in a peace process designed to bring an end to the protracted conflicts in Central America. It was initially deployed in December 1989 to verify compliance with security commitments undertaken by the Governments of Costa Rica, El Salvador, Guatemala, Honduras and Nicaragua. Its mandate was twice enlarged during the first half of 1990 in response to political and military developments in the region.

B. Background

Years of turmoil in Central America inspired peace initiatives by the Governments of Colombia, Mexico, Panama and Venezuela—known as the Contadora Group—in 1983, and then by the Presidents of Costa Rica, El Salvador, Guatemala, Honduras and Nicaragua. After preliminary consultations in Esquipulas, Guatemala, in 1986, Costa Rican President Oscar Arias Sánchez drafted a comprehensive regional peace plan, based on the principle of solving several interrelated problems simultaneously. The plan, for which President Arias was awarded the 1987 Nobel Peace Prize, was embodied in the final declaration of a summit of the five Central American Presidents held in Guatemala in August 1987.

Esquipulas II Agreement

The "Procedure for the Establishment of a Firm and Lasting Peace in Central America", known both as the Esquipulas II Agreement and the Guatemala Procedure, dealt with issues of national reconciliation; an end to hostilities; democratization; free elections; termination of aid to irregular forces and insurrectionist movements; non-use of the territory of one State to attack other States;

negotiations on security, verification and the control and limitation of weapons; refugees and displaced persons; co-operation, democracy and freedom for peace and development; international verification and follow-up; and a timetable for the fulfilment of commitments.

In conjunction with the Organization of American States (OAS), the United Nations was requested to verify free elections and to participate in an International Verification and Follow-up Commission (CIVS). The Commission would comprise the Secretary-General of the United Nations, the Secretary-General of the OAS, or their representatives, and the Ministers for Foreign Affairs of the Central American countries, the Contadora Group and the Support Group (the Support Group consisting of Argentina, Brazil, Peru and Uruguay). It was to be responsible for verifying and monitoring fulfilment of the commitments contained in the Agreement.*

United Nations endorsement

The subject of peace in Central America had been on the agenda of the General Assembly since 1983 and had been addressed in Security Council resolutions 530(1983) of 19 May 1983 and 562(1985) of 10 May 1985. In the latter, the Council had called upon all States "to refrain from carrying out, supporting or promoting political, economic or military actions of any kind against any State in the region".

On 7 October 1987, in resolution 42/1, the General Assembly expressed its "firmest support" of the Esquipulas II Agreement. It requested the Secretary-General to afford the fullest assistance to the Central American Governments in their effort to achieve peace, especially by responding to the specific requests made of him in the Agreement. Meanwhile, the Secretaries-General of both the United Nations and the OAS had agreed to participate in CIVS, which held its inaugural session in Caracas, Venezuela, on 22 August 1987.

In October 1987 a joint United Nations/OAS mission visited the five Central American countries to evaluate the need for on-site verification of the security commitments in the Esquipulas II Agreement, and in November it undertook a second round of consultations with representatives of the Central American Governments. However, because of lack of agreement among the five Central American Governments, the mission concluded that the conditions did not exist at that time for on-site verification.

* S/19085.

Costa del Sol Declaration

On 8 February 1989, the Ministers for Foreign Affairs of the five Central American countries met the United Nations Secretary-General in New York to prepare for a Presidential summit in El Salvador the following week. The Ministers requested the Secretary-General to appoint a technical group of the Secretariat to elaborate, with representatives of their countries, terms of reference for a mechanism to verify the security aspects of Esquipulas II and to draft a proposal for its establishment. Six days later, the presidential summit issued a Joint Declaration, known as the Costa del Sol Declaration or Tesoro Beach Agreement, which, *inter alia*, announced the decision by the President of Nicaragua to hold elections no later than 25 February 1990. In addition, the Presidents undertook to draw up within 90 days a joint plan for the voluntary demobilization, repatriation or relocation in Nicaragua or third countries of members of the Nicaraguan Resistance and their families. The Executive Commission (which consisted of the Ministers for Foreign Affairs of the five Central American countries) was entrusted with the task of immediately organizing technical meetings to establish, in accordance with the talks held with the Secretary-General of the United Nations, the most appropriate and efficient mechanism for verifying security commitments.*

Technical discussions

Representatives of the Central American Governments held detailed discussions in mid-March with the United Nations Secretariat on the creation of the United Nations verification mechanism. On 31 March 1989, the five Ministers for Foreign Affairs officially requested the Secretary-General to take the necessary steps to set it in motion.† However, it became clear that progress could be made on this aspect of the Central American peace process only when Nicaragua had agreed to postpone a pending legal action against Honduras at the International Court of Justice.

ONUVEN

Meanwhile, however, progress was achieved in another area. The Secretary-General of the United Nations responded positively to a request by the Government of Nicaragua for the United Nations to monitor the elections to be held there. ‡ Several missions

---

* S/20491.   † S/20642.   ‡ A/44/210, A/44/375.

were accordingly sent to Nicaragua to observe the revision of electoral laws and the laws regulating the mass media, as well as to carry
out a study of the new legislation. The foundations were thus laid for
the establishment of the United Nations Observer Mission to Verify
the Electoral Process in Nicaragua (ONUVEN) which became operational on 25 August 1989. As ONUVEN did not involve the use of
military personnel, it is not considered to be a peace-keeping operation and is not further discussed in the present work. It should, however, be recorded that its very successful fulfilment of its mandate
enhanced the role of the United Nations in the Central American
peace process and thus facilitated the work of ONUCA, especially
in Nicaragua.

Tela Accord

On 27 July 1989, in an effort to revive the momentum
of the peace process, the Security Council unanimously adopted
resolution 637(1989). In it the Council, *inter alia*, expressed its firmest
support for the Esquipulas II Agreement and subsequent joint
declarations by the Presidents and called upon them "to continue
their efforts to achieve a firm and lasting peace in Central America".
It also lent the Security Council's full support to the Secretary-General
to continue his mission of good offices.

Considerable progress was made at the summit held at Tela,
Honduras, between 5 and 7 August 1989, when the Presidents issued
a Declaration and a "Joint Plan for the voluntary demobilization,
repatriation or relocation of the members of the Nicaraguan Resistance and their families, as well as assistance in the demobilization
of all those involved in armed actions in the countries of the region
when they voluntarily seek it". The support for this process would
be provided by an International Support and Verification Commission (CIAV), which the Secretaries-General of the United Nations and
the OAS were requested to establish.

Among the functions assigned to CIAV, both those of a
humanitarian nature and those relating to development would be entrusted to the United Nations High Commissioner for Refugees and
the United Nations Development Programme. CIAV was also to be
entrusted with receiving arms, equipment and military supplies from
the members of the Nicaraguan Resistance and storing them until
the five Presidents decided how they should be disposed of.

The Joint Plan also addressed the issue of the voluntary
demobilization of the members of the Salvadoran resistance front,

the Frente Farabundo Martí para la Liberación Nacional (FMLN), but progress in this area is dependent on current efforts to achieve a political solution to the conflict in that country.*

On 25 August, the Secretaries-General of the United Nations and the OAS, meeting at United Nations Headquarters, decided to establish CIAV with effect from 6 September 1989. On 1 September 1989, Secretary-General Pérez de Cuéllar appointed Assistant Secretary-General Alvaro de Soto as his Personal Representative for the peace process in Central America. On 21 September, he informed the President of the Security Council of the establishment of CIAV and expressed the view that the demobilization of the members of the Nicaraguan Resistance was an operation of a clearly military nature, which would have to be launched by the Security Council.†

c. **Establishment of ONUCA**

At the Tela Summit an agreement was also reached between Honduras and Nicaragua regarding the pending litigation between the two countries at the International Court of Justice. With this obstacle out of the way, the Secretary-General was able to send a reconnaissance mission to the region from 3 to 23 September 1989. Brigadier-General Péricles Ferreira Gomes (of Brazil), Chief Military Observer of the United Nations Angola Verification Mission, led the mission, which comprised senior United Nations officials and military personnel provided by Member States. On the basis of the information furnished by the mission, the Secretary-General duly submitted a report to the Security Council on 11 October recommending the deployment of ONUCA. ONUCA's mandate would be to conduct on-site verification of the security undertakings contained in the Esquipulas II Agreement, namely *(a)* the cessation of aid to irregular forces and insurrectionist movements, and *(b)* the non-use of the territory of one State for attacks on other States. The latter undertaking was to include preventing the establishment or use of facilities for radio or television transmissions for the specific purpose of directing or assisting the military operations of irregular forces or insurrectionist movements in any of the five countries.

Because the nature of the terrain in the region would have limited the efficacy of static observation posts, it was judged that the best results would be achieved by establishing mobile teams of at least seven military observers, who would carry out regular patrols by road vehicles with cross-country capability, by helicopter and, in the Gulf

* S/20778. † S/20856.

of Fonseca and certain other coastal areas and rivers, by patrol boats and light speedboats. A small fixed-wing aircraft would be required to transport the Chief Military Observer and his senior staff between the capitals of the five countries and to rotate military observers from one duty station to another.

The mobile teams would also make spot checks on their own initiative and would be instructed to undertake immediate *ad hoc* inspections to investigate allegations of violations of the undertakings. The observers would be grouped in verification centres located as close as possible to sensitive areas where violations of the undertakings on cessation of assistance and non-use of territory would be most likely to occur.

Command of ONUCA in the field would be exercised by a Chief Military Observer, who would be under the command of the United Nations, vested in the Secretary-General, under the authority of the Security Council. The military observers, who would be unarmed, would be provided by Member States, at the request of the Secretary-General.*

In resolution 644(1989) of 7 November 1989, the Security Council approved the Secretary-General's report and decided to set up ONUCA immediately for a period of six months. On 21 November 1989 the Security Council approved the appointment of Major-General Agustín Quesada Gómez, of Spain, who has held this position since then.

Composition

ONUCA's authorized military strength included 260 military observers, as well as crews and support personnel for an air wing and a naval unit. Initially, military observers were contributed by Canada, Colombia, Ireland, Spain and Venezuela. Subsequently, they were joined by military observers from Brazil, Ecuador, India and Sweden. A helicopter unit is contributed by Canada. Argentina provides four fast patrol boats, with crews, for maritime patrolling duties in the Gulf of Fonseca. The Federal Republic of Germany provides a civilian medical unit and a fixed-wing aircraft with civilian crew. The mission also includes international and locally recruited civilian staff. After the enlargement of ONUCA's mandate *(see below)*, Venezuela contributed an infantry battalion to undertake the demobilization of the members of the Nicaraguan Resistance from April to June 1990.

---

* S/20895.

Deployment

ONUCA's initial deployment was carried out in phases over a period of several months. On 3 December 1989, an advance party led by the Chief Military Observer and consisting of approximately 30 military officers and United Nations civilian officials established the Group's headquarters in Tegucigalpa, Honduras. The team made visits to the five countries of the region to set up liaison offices in each capital and make the necessary preparations for the subsequent establishment of verification centres there and elsewhere. In the light of the prevailing security conditions, the El Salvador liaison office could not be established in San Salvador until 17 January 1990. ONUCA reached its full strength on 5 June 1990, at which time, in addition to the liaison offices in the five capitals, it was manning 14 verification centres, five of them in the capitals, and 3 operational posts. In June 1990 the four fast patrol boats joined the mission and began operating from a naval verification centre at San Lorenzo, Honduras.

D. Operations

In fulfilment of ONUCA's original mandate, mobile teams of military observers patrol from the verification centres, each of which is manned by up to 10 observers, and smaller operational posts in forward areas. Patrols are carried out daily by land, by air and occasionally by river. Much of the terrain in the area of operation is rugged and densely forested and road networks are limited. Helicopters are therefore indispensable for observation purposes and for transporting observers and supplies. Monitoring is concentrated in those areas where activities that may be contrary to the security undertakings in the Esquipulas II Agreement are alleged to occur. These have been the areas adjacent to the borders between Costa Rica and Nicaragua, between Honduras and Nicaragua, between Honduras and El Salvador and between Guatemala and El Salvador, together with the north-eastern part of Nicaragua and the south-western part of Honduras. When a complaint is registered with ONUCA it is communicated to the Government complained against, which is asked to extend to ONUCA full co-operation in an investigation. The results of the investigation are then transmitted to both Governments concerned. ONUCA has received very few complaints.

First expansion of the mandate

On 12 December 1989, the five Central American Presidents issued the "Declaration of San Isidro de Coronado" in which, *inter alia*, they requested that ONUCA's mandate be expanded to include verification of any cessation of hostilities and demobilization of irregular forces that might be agreed upon in the region.*

On 15 March, soon after the elections in Nicaragua, the Secretary-General reported to the Security Council that, in consultations between the Nicaraguan Government, the Government-elect and the United Nations, agreement had been reached in principle on modalities for the demobilization of the members of the Nicaraguan Resistance. Those in Honduras would be demobilized at their existing camps and then repatriated without delay. For those in Nicaragua at the time of demobilization, ONUCA would establish temporary assembly points where they would be demobilized and where ONUCA would ensure their security pending their resettlement, which was to be arranged by CIAV without delay. ONUCA would be responsible for taking delivery of their weapons, *matériel* and military equipment, including military uniforms. Armed personnel would be required for these tasks. The Secretary-General accordingly asked the Security Council, on a contingency basis, to enlarge ONUCA's mandate for this purpose and to authorize the addition of armed personnel to its strength. No additional troops would be deployed until agreement existed amongst all concerned on the voluntary demobilization of the Nicaraguan Resistance.†

In resolution 650(1990) of 27 March 1990, the Security Council unanimously approved the Secretary-General's report and decided to authorize, on a contingency basis in accordance with the report, an enlargement of the mandate of ONUCA and the addition of armed personnel to its strength in order to enable it to play a part in the voluntary demobilization of the Nicaraguan Resistance. The Council requested the Secretary-General to keep it fully informed of further developments regarding the implementation of the resolution.

On 2-3 April 1990, the five Central American Presidents agreed to the Secretary-General's proposal that the weapons and other equipment received from the members of the Nicaraguan Resistance should be destroyed *in situ* by ONUCA.‡

---

* S/21019.   † S/21194.   ‡ S/21235.

Demobilization in Honduras

The first company of an armed infantry battalion, contributed by Venezuela, was accordingly deployed to Honduras on 10 April 1990, after agreement had been reached on the demobilization of the two principal groups of the Nicaraguan Resistance remaining in that country. On 16 April 1990, it demobilized 260 members of the Atlantic Front (Yatama) of the Nicaraguan Resistance at La Kiatara in eastern Honduras and destroyed their weapons and military equipment. On 18 April, at the main Nicaraguan Resistance camp at Yamales in Honduras, large quantities of weapons, most of them obsolete and unserviceable, were handed over to ONUCA for destruction. But no personnel were demobilized on this occasion as all active combatants previously located at Yamales had apparently returned to Nicaragua.

Second expansion of the mandate

Before the transfer of political power in Nicaragua on 25 April, intensive negotiations took place between the Nicaraguan Government, representatives of the President-elect and representatives of the Northern, Central and Atlantic Fronts of the Nicaraguan Resistance, with the participation of the Archbishop of Managua, Cardinal Obando y Bravo. The Chief Military Observer of ONUCA and Mr. Iqbal Riza, the Secretary-General's Alternate Personal Representative for the Central American peace process, also took part.

On the night of 18-19 April the Nicaraguan parties signed a complex of agreements relating to the voluntary demobilization of the members of the Nicaraguan Resistance in Nicaragua during the period from 25 April to 10 June 1990. A cease-fire would come into effect at 12 noon local time on 19 April and a separation of forces would take place as a result of the withdrawal of the Nicaraguan Government's forces from certain "security zones" which were to be established in Nicaragua and in which the members of the Nicaraguan Resistance would concentrate for the purposes of demobilization. ONUCA was asked to monitor both the cease-fire and the separation of forces.

On the basis of these agreements, the Secretary-General sought the Security Council's approval of a further expansion of ONUCA's mandate to cover these functions. That approval was granted by resolution 653(1990) of 20 April 1990.*

---

* S/21259.

By resolution 654(1990) of 4 May 1990 the Security Council decided to extend the mandate of ONUCA, as defined in resolutions 644(1989), 650(1990) and 653(1990), for a further period of six months, on the understanding that the additional tasks of monitoring the cease-fire and separation of forces and demobilizing the members of the Nicaraguan Resistance would lapse not later than 10 June 1990.

"Security zones"

Five "security zones" were established on 22 April following the withdrawal of the Nicaraguan Government's forces from the areas in question during the preceding three days. Within each zone, ONUCA personnel—both unarmed observers and armed members of the Venezuelan battalion—were deployed in a "demobilization and logistics support area" where the hand-over of weapons and other activities connected with the demobilization of the members of the Nicaraguan Resistance took place. Each zone was 500-600 square kilometres in area and was surrounded by a demilitarized zone of some 20 kilometres in width. Two additional zones were subsequently established on the Atlantic Coast for the demobilization of the members of the "Yatama" front. These zones covered a total of 2,550 square kilometres.

Progress of demobilization

Although all the necessary arrangements had been made by ONUCA, in co-ordination with leaders of the Nicaraguan Resistance, for demobilization to begin on 25 April at El Amparo in Zone 1, the members of the Resistance who had assembled there declined to lay down their weapons after their commander told them that the minimum conditions for demobilization had not been met. In the ensuing days only a few members of the Resistance demobilized.

On 4 May, after further consultations, the Nicaraguan Government and the leadership of the Nicaraguan Resistance issued the "Managua Declaration", in which, *inter alia*, the Nicaraguan Resistance declared that it would continue its voluntary demobilization and that the process would be completed in all the "security zones" by 10 June at the latest. Demobilization began on 8 May. But during the next two weeks only small numbers came forward for demobilization and it soon became clear that the pace was insufficient to ensure completion by 10 June. The leaders of the Nicaraguan Resistance complained of breaches by the Nicaraguan Army of the agreements relating to the cease-fire and separation of forces.

On 22 and 23 May the Security Council met to discuss this grave situation, and on 23 May the President of the Security Council made a statement expressing the Council's concern at the slow pace of demobilization.*

ONUCA, meanwhile, investigated complaints from both sides relating, on the one hand, to the presence of armed civilians and militia personnel in the "security zones" and demilitarized zones, and, on the other, to the presence outside the "security zones" of armed members of the Nicaraguan Resistance, some of whom had allegedly committed various criminal acts. However, it remained the Secretary-General's assessment that there had been no serious violations of the cease-fire.

This serious situation was resolved on 30 May when a meeting between President Violeta Chamorro of Nicaragua, the leaders of the Nicaraguan Resistance and the Archbishop of Managua resulted in an agreement entitled the "Managua Protocol". Under its terms, the Nicaraguan Government responded to a number of the Resistance's publicly stated concerns, notably through the establishment of "development areas" in which demobilized members of the Resistance would be resettled, and the Resistance reaffirmed its commitment to demobilize by 10 June 1990 at the latest and, to this end, undertook that at least 100 combatants would be demobilized each day in each of the "security zones".†

Completion of demobilization

After 30 May, demobilization generally proceeded rapidly. On 8 June the Secretary-General reported to the Security Council that there had been a marked increase in the rate at which the members of the "Northern Front" and "Central Front", were being demobilized. However, demobilization of the "Atlantic Front", which had begun on 21 May, was proceeding at a less satisfactory pace than that of the main group, largely because of logistic difficulties in concentrating the members at demobilization areas in the large security zones concerned.

In light of the progress of the demobilization, the Secretary-General recommended that the Security Council extend the relevant part of ONUCA's mandate for a brief and clearly defined period. By resolution 656(1990) of 8 June 1990 the Council accordingly decided that ONUCA's tasks of monitoring the cease-fire and separation of

* S/21331. † S/21341, annex.

forces in Nicaragua and demobilizing the Resistance should be extended, on the understanding, as recommended by the Secretary-General, that these tasks would lapse with the completion of the demobilization process not later than 29 June 1990.*

During the following three weeks demobilization proceeded in all zones. The process reached a peak on 10 June, when 1,886 members of the Nicaraguan Resistance were demobilized. On 18 June an eighth "security zone" became operational to facilitate the demobilization of members of the "Southern Front".

On 29 June 1990, the Secretary-General informed the Security Council that at 1900 hours local time on 28 June 1990, demobilization of all armed and unarmed members of the Nicaraguan Resistance had been completed at all locations, except for one in Nicaragua where a handful of members remained to be demobilized. This was soon accomplished, and the final zone was closed on 5 July 1990.†

By the time the process was completed, a total of 19,614 armed and unarmed members of the Nicaraguan Resistance had been demobilized in Nicaragua and 2,759 in Honduras. Weapons handed over to ONUCA by members of the Nicaraguan Resistance included 15,144 small arms (including AK 47s, other assault rifles, rifles and light machine-guns), as well as heavy machine-guns, mortars, grenade launchers, grenades, mines and missiles.

E. Financial aspects

Reporting to the Security Council on 11 October 1989, the Secretary-General recommended that the costs of ONUCA should be considered as expenses of the Organization to be borne by the Members in accordance with Article 17, paragraph 2, of the United Nations Charter. Subsequently, by resolution 44/44 of 7 December 1989, the General Assembly accepted his recommendation that the assessments to be levied on Member States should be credited to a special account which would be established for this purpose.

Upon the expansion of ONUCA's mandate, the Advisory Committee on Administrative and Budgetary Questions authorized the extra expenditures occurring from the addition of armed personnel to ONUCA's strength.

In mid-1990 the cost of ONUCA's operation to the United Nations was approximately $52.7 million. As of 30 June 1990, unpaid assessed contributions to the ONUCA Special Account amounted to $10.7 million.

* S/21349. † S/21379.

F. **Conclusion**

The United Nations' involvement in the Central American peace process vividly illustrates the increasingly complex demands made of the Organization's peace-making and peace-keeping skills.

Although ONUCA was initially established with the limited mandate of verifying only one aspect of the Central American peace process, the tasks entrusted to it have evolved and it has been able to play an important part in assisting the parties concerned to control and resolve the conflicts in the region.

Appendices

Composition and organization

Facts and figures

Maps

Appendix I Composition and organization

Composition

A United Nations peace-keeping operation is considered a subsidiary organ of the United Nations, established pursuant to a resolution of the Security Council or, exceptionally, of the General Assembly.

Military component. A United Nations peace-keeping operation consists of a commander, who is designated Force Commander (or Chief of Staff in the case of UNTSO), and a number of contingents provided by selected Member States of the United Nations upon the request of the Secretary-General. In all peace-keeping operations established since October 1973, the contingents are selected in consultation with the Security Council and with the parties concerned, bearing in mind the principle of equitable geographical representation. The military personnel of an operation, although remaining in their national service, are, during the period of their assignment to the operation, international personnel under the authority of the United Nations and subject to the instructions of the commander, through the chain of command. The functions of the operation are exclusively international, and its members are expected to discharge those functions and regulate their conduct with the interest of the United Nations only in view.

Civilian component. A civilian administrative staff of the operation is provided, as a rule, by the Secretary-General from among existing United Nations staff. These personnel are to follow the rules and regulations of the United Nations Secretariat. Additionally, the commander may recruit such local personnel as the operation requires. The terms and conditions of employment for locally recruited personnel are prescribed by the commander and generally, to the extent possible, follow the practice prevailing in the locality.

In some cases, a peace-keeping operation performs tasks which are of a non-military nature and which require a large civilian component, e.g., civilian police and electoral monitors. In such cases overall command in the field is normally exercised by a civilian official, usually designated Special Representative of the Secretary-General.

Chain of command

United Nations peace-keeping operations are normally established by the Security Council and fall under its authority. The Secretary-General is responsible to the Council for the organization, conduct and direction of the operation, and he alone reports to the Council about it. The Secretary-General keeps the Security Council fully informed of developments relating to the functioning of the operation. All matters which may affect the nature or the continued effective functioning of the operation are referred to the Council for its decision.

The Secretary-General is assisted in this regard by the Office for Special Political Affairs.

Command in the field. Command of the operation in the field is exercised by a Force Commander, Chief Military Observer or Chief of Staff appointed by the Secretary-General with the consent of the Security Council. The commander is responsible to the Secretary-General. The commander exercises full command authority over the operation except for disciplinary questions. The commander has full authority with respect to all assignments of members of his headquarters staff and, through the chain of command, of all members of the operation, including the deployment and movements of all contingents in it and all units assigned to it. The contingents comprising the operation are integral parts of it and take their orders exclusively from the commander. The operation has its own headquarters, whose personnel are representative of the contingents comprising the operation. The commander designates the chain of command for the operation, making use of the offices of his headquarters staff and the commanders of the national contingents made available by troop-contributing Governments. He may delegate his authority through the chain of command. The operation undertakes no functions which are not consistent with the definition of its mandate as set forth in the Security Council resolution establishing the operation. Any doubt about a proposed action of the operation being consistent with such definition must be submitted to the Secretary-General for decision.

Discipline. The commander has general responsibility for the good order and discipline of the operation. He may make investigations, conduct inquiries and require information, reports and consultations for the purpose of discharging this responsibility. Responsibility for disciplinary action in national contingents provided for the operation, however, rests with the commanders of the national contingents. Reports concerning disciplinary action are communicated to the commander who may consult with the commander of the national contingent and, if necessary, through the Secretary-General with the authorities of the troop-contributing Government concerned.

Administration. The Field Operations Division, in general terms, is responsible for organizing the civilian administrative staff to support the operation and, in close collaboration with the Office for Special Political Affairs and the Office of Programme Planning, Budget and Finance, makes arrangements for airlift of the contingents, prepares the final budgetary proposals for the operation and presents those proposals to the General Assembly's Advisory Committee on Administrative and Budgetary Questions and the Assembly's Fifth (Administrative and Budgetary) Committee. Additionally, it arranges for the procurement of the necessary stores for the maintenance of the operation and directs the operations of the civilian administrative staff in the field.

The commander with his civilian Chief Administrative Officer, in accordance with procedures prescribed by him within the limits of the budgetary provisions for the operation and the financial rules and regulations of the United Nations, arranges for: the billeting and provision of food for the military component; the establishment, maintenance and operation of service institutes providing amenities for members of the operation and other United Nations personnel as authorized by the commander; the transportation of personnel and equipment; the procurement, storage and issuance of supplies and equipment which are not directly provided by the participating Governments; maintenance and other services required for the operation; the establishment, operation and maintenance of telecommunication and postal services; and the provision of medical, dental and sanitary services for its personnel. The foregoing is achieved through the co-ordinated effort of the military logistic staff of the operation and the civilian staff. Formulation of provision systems and review of requirements are the responsibility of the military Chief Logistics Officer and his staff, and the responsibility for procurement and timely delivery of provisions rests with the civilian Chief Procurement Officer.

Privileges and immunities. The peace-keeping operation, as a subsidiary organ of the United Nations, enjoys the status, privileges and immunities of the Organization provided in Article 105 of the Charter of the United Nations and the Convention on the Privileges and Immunities of the United Nations. Additionally, the Secretary-General endeavours to conclude a status agreement with the host Government(s) concerning the work of the operation. This agreement covers matters such as the status of the operation and its members, responsibility for criminal and civil jurisdiction over the members of the operation, premises, taxation, customs and fiscal regulation pertaining to the members of the operation, freedom of movement, use of roads, water-ways, port facilities and airfields, water, electricity and other public utilities, locally recruited personnel, settlement of disputes or claims, liaison, etc.

The following charts indicate the standard chain of command of United Nations peace-keeping operations and the organizational structure of current operations. In addition there is a chart showing the organization of UNTAG, an operation which included substantial non-military elements and was commanded by a civilian Special Representative.

The chain of command of United Nations peace-keeping operations

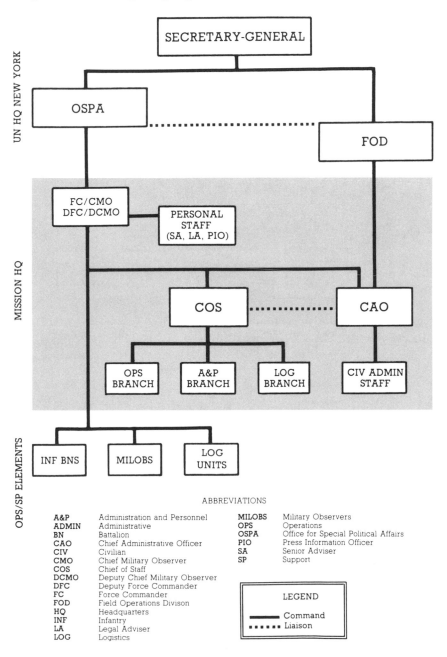

ABBREVIATIONS

A&P	Administration and Personnel	**MILOBS**	Military Observers
ADMIN	Administrative	**OPS**	Operations
BN	Battalion	**OSPA**	Office for Special Political Affairs
CAO	Chief Administrative Officer	**PIO**	Press Information Officer
CIV	Civilian	**SA**	Senior Adviser
CMO	Chief Military Observer	**SP**	Support
COS	Chief of Staff		
DCMO	Deputy Chief Military Observer		
DFC	Deputy Force Commander		
FC	Force Commander		
FOD	Field Operations Division		
HQ	Headquarters		
INF	Infantry		
LA	Legal Adviser		
LOG	Logistics		

LEGEND

——— Command
▪▪▪▪▪▪ Liaison

UNTSO

Organization chart

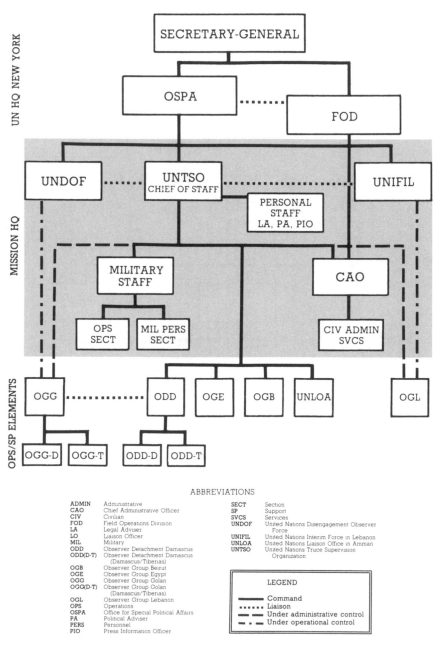

ABBREVIATIONS

ADMIN	Administrative	**SECT**	Section
CAO	Chief Administrative Officer	**SP**	Support
CIV	Civilian	**SVCS**	Services
FOD	Field Operations Division	**UNDOF**	United Nations Disengagement Observer Force
LA	Legal Adviser		
LO	Liaison Officer	**UNIFIL**	United Nations Interim Force in Lebanon
MIL	Military	**UNLOA**	United Nations Liaison Office in Amman
ODD	Observer Detachment Damascus	**UNTSO**	United Nations Truce Supervision Organization
ODD(D-T)	Observer Detachment Damascus (Damascus/Tiberias)		
OGB	Observer Group Beirut		
OGE	Observer Group Egypt		
OGG	Observer Group Golan		
OGG(D-T)	Observer Group Golan (Damascus/Tiberias)		
OGL	Observer Group Lebanon		
OPS	Operations		
OSPA	Office for Special Political Affairs		
PA	Political Adviser		
PERS	Personnel		
PIO	Press Information Officer		

LEGEND

⎯⎯⎯ Command
••••••• Liaison
⎯ ⎯ ⎯ Under administrative control
⎯ • ⎯ • Under operational control

UNDOF
Organization chart

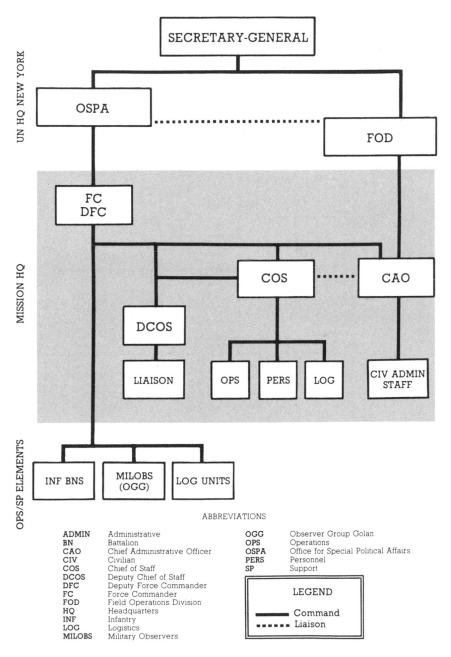

ABBREVIATIONS

ADMIN	Administrative	**OGG**	Observer Group Golan
BN	Battalion	**OPS**	Operations
CAO	Chief Administrative Officer	**OSPA**	Office for Special Political Affairs
CIV	Civilian	**PERS**	Personnel
COS	Chief of Staff	**SP**	Support
DCOS	Deputy Chief of Staff		
DFC	Deputy Force Commander		
FC	Force Commander		
FOD	Field Operations Division		
HQ	Headquarters		
INF	Infantry		
LOG	Logistics		
MILOBS	Military Observers		

LEGEND

—— Command
······ Liaison

UNIFIL
Organization chart

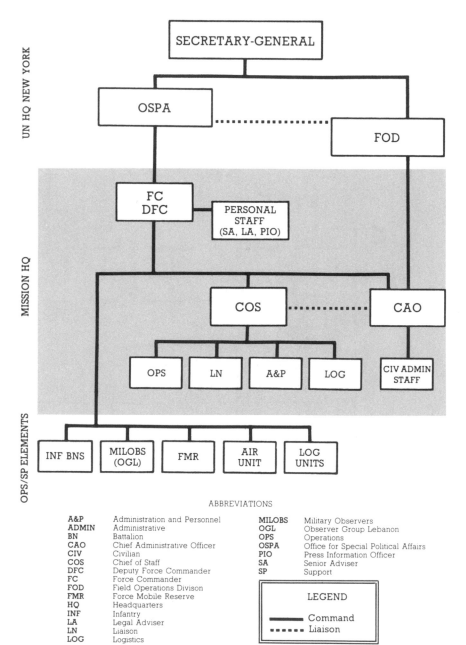

UN HQ NEW YORK

MISSION HQ

OPS/SP ELEMENTS

SECRETARY-GENERAL

OSPA

FOD

FC
DFC

PERSONAL
STAFF
(SA, LA, PIO)

COS

CAO

OPS

LN

A&P

LOG

CIV ADMIN
STAFF

INF BNS

MILOBS
(OGL)

FMR

AIR
UNIT

LOG
UNITS

ABBREVIATIONS

A&P	Administration and Personnel	**MILOBS**	Military Observers
ADMIN	Administrative	**OGL**	Observer Group Lebanon
BN	Battalion	**OPS**	Operations
CAO	Chief Administrative Officer	**OSPA**	Office for Special Political Affairs
CIV	Civilian	**PIO**	Press Information Officer
COS	Chief of Staff	**SA**	Senior Adviser
DFC	Deputy Force Commander	**SP**	Support
FC	Force Commander		
FOD	Field Operations Divison		
FMR	Force Mobile Reserve		
HQ	Headquarters		
INF	Infantry		
LA	Legal Adviser		
LN	Liaison		
LOG	Logistics		

LEGEND

⸻ Command

······ Liaison

UNMOGIP
Organization chart

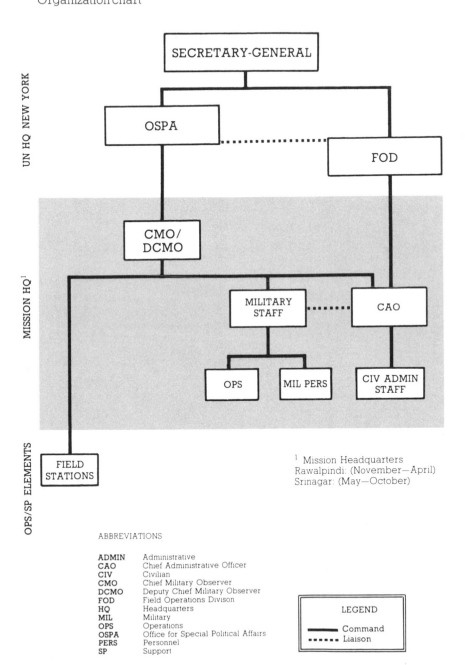

UN HQ NEW YORK

MISSION HQ[1]

OPS/SP ELEMENTS

SECRETARY-GENERAL

OSPA

FOD

CMO/ DCMO

MILITARY STAFF

CAO

OPS

MIL PERS

CIV ADMIN STAFF

FIELD STATIONS

[1] Mission Headquarters
Rawalpindi: (November—April)
Srinagar: (May—October)

ABBREVIATIONS

ADMIN	Administrative
CAO	Chief Administrative Officer
CIV	Civilian
CMO	Chief Military Observer
DCMO	Deputy Chief Military Observer
FOD	Field Operations Divison
HQ	Headquarters
MIL	Military
OPS	Operations
OSPA	Office for Special Political Affairs
PERS	Personnel
SP	Support

LEGEND

—— Command
•••••• Liaison

UNFICYP
Organization chart

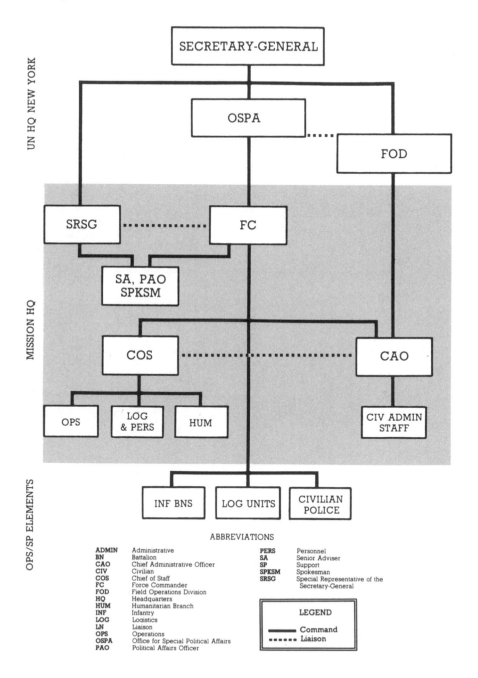

UN HQ NEW YORK

MISSION HQ

OPS/SP ELEMENTS

SECRETARY-GENERAL

OSPA

FOD

SRSG

FC

SA, PAO SPKSM

COS

CAO

OPS

LOG & PERS

HUM

CIV ADMIN STAFF

INF BNS

LOG UNITS

CIVILIAN POLICE

ABBREVIATIONS

ADMIN	Administrative	**PERS**	Personnel
BN	Battalion	**SA**	Senior Adviser
CAO	Chief Administrative Officer	**SP**	Support
CIV	Civilian	**SPKSM**	Spokesman
COS	Chief of Staff	**SRSG**	Special Representative of the
FC	Force Commander		Secretary-General
FOD	Field Operations Division		
HQ	Headquarters		
HUM	Humanitarian Branch		
INF	Infantry		
LOG	Logistics		
LN	Liaison		
OPS	Operations		
OSPA	Office for Special Political Affairs		
PAO	Political Affairs Officer		

LEGEND

——— Command
········· Liaison

UNIIMOG
Organization chart

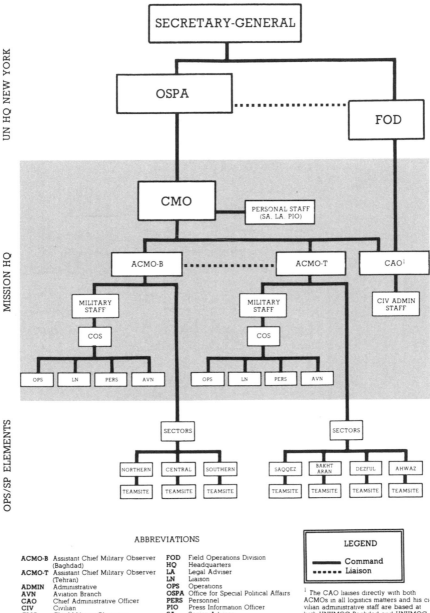

ABBREVIATIONS

ACMO-B	Assistant Chief Military Observer (Baghdad)	**FOD**	Field Operations Division
ACMO-T	Assistant Chief Military Observer (Tehran)	**HQ**	Headquarters
		LA	Legal Adviser
ADMIN	Administrative	**LN**	Liaison
AVN	Aviation Branch	**OPS**	Operations
CAO	Chief Administrative Officer	**OSPA**	Office for Special Political Affairs
CIV	Civilian	**PERS**	Personnel
CMO	Chief Military Observer	**PIO**	Press Information Officer
COS	Chief of Staff	**SA**	Senior Adviser
		SP	Support

LEGEND

———— Command

▪▪▪▪▪▪ Liaison

[1] The CAO liaises directly with both ACMOs in all logistics matters and his civilian administrative staff are based at both UNIIMOG Baghdad and UNIIMOG Tehran.

UNAVEM

Organization chart

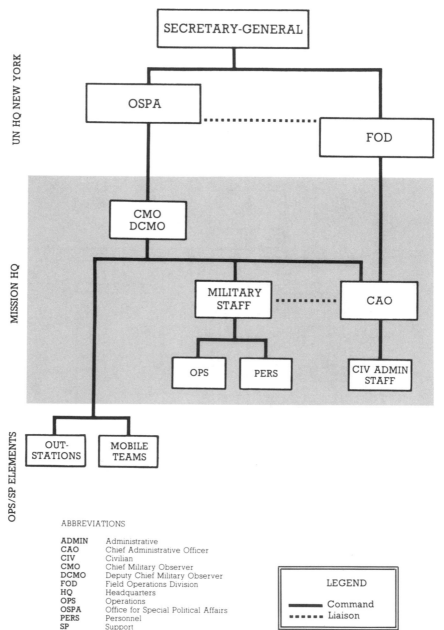

ABBREVIATIONS

ADMIN	Administrative
CAO	Chief Administrative Officer
CIV	Civilian
CMO	Chief Military Observer
DCMO	Deputy Chief Military Observer
FOD	Field Operations Division
HQ	Headquarters
OPS	Operations
OSPA	Office for Special Political Affairs
PERS	Personnel
SP	Support

LEGEND

——— Command

•••••• Liaison

UNTAG
Organization chart

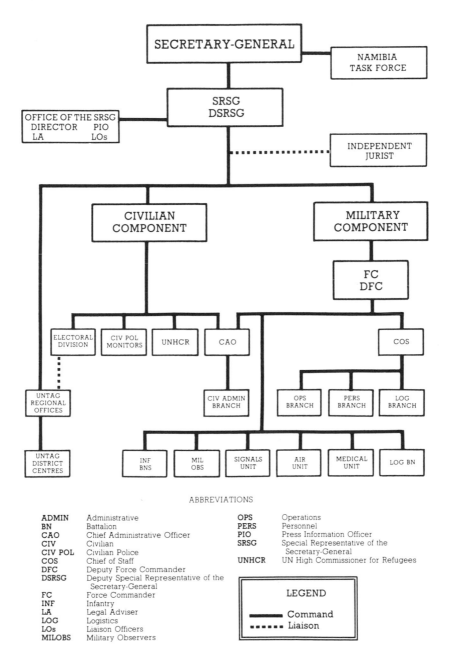

ABBREVIATIONS

ADMIN	Administrative
BN	Battalion
CAO	Chief Administrative Officer
CIV	Civilian
CIV POL	Civilian Police
COS	Chief of Staff
DFC	Deputy Force Commander
DSRSG	Deputy Special Representative of the Secretary-General
FC	Force Commander
INF	Infantry
LA	Legal Adviser
LOG	Logistics
LOs	Liaison Officers
MILOBS	Military Observers

OPS	Operations
PERS	Personnel
PIO	Press Information Officer
SRSG	Special Representative of the Secretary-General
UNHCR	UN High Commissioner for Refugees

LEGEND

_____ Command
■■■■■■ Liaison

ONUCA
Organization chart

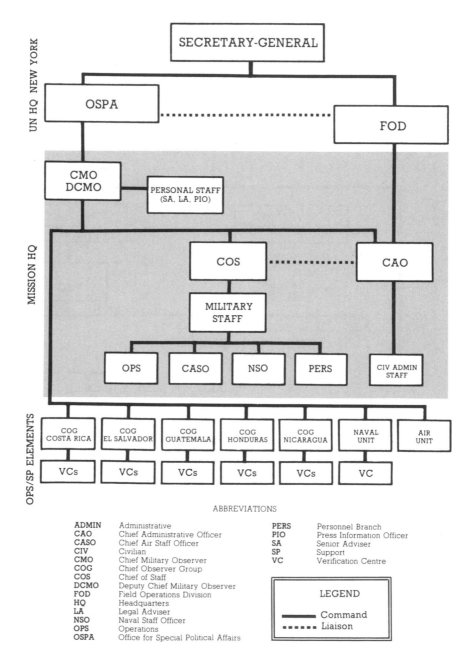

ABBREVIATIONS

ADMIN	Administrative	**PERS**	Personnel Branch
CAO	Chief Administrative Officer	**PIO**	Press Information Officer
CASO	Chief Air Staff Officer	**SA**	Senior Adviser
CIV	Civilian	**SP**	Support
CMO	Chief Military Observer	**VC**	Verification Centre
COG	Chief Observer Group		
COS	Chief of Staff		
DCMO	Deputy Chief Military Observer		
FOD	Field Operations Division		
HQ	Headquarters		
LA	Legal Adviser		
NSO	Naval Staff Officer		
OPS	Operations		
OSPA	Office for Special Political Affairs		

LEGEND

——— Command
▪▪▪▪▪▪ Liaison

Facts and figures

UNTSO
United Nations Truce Supervision Organization

Authorization Security Council resolutions:
50(1948) of 29 May 1948
54(1948) of 15 July 1948
73(1949) of 11 August 1949
101(1953) of 24 November 1953 (to strengthen UNTSO)
114(1956) of 4 June 1956
236(1967) of 11 June 1967
Consensus of 9/10 July 1967 (S/8047) (Suez Canal)
Consensus of 19 April 1972 (S/10611) (Southern Lebanon)
339(1973) of 23 October 1973 (Sinai)

Function Established in June 1948 to assist the Mediator and the Truce Commission in supervising the observance of the truce in Palestine called for by the Security Council. Since then, UNTSO has performed various tasks entrusted to it by the Security Council, including the supervision of the General Armistice Agreements of 1949 and the observation of the cease-fire in the Suez Canal area and the Golan Heights following the Arab–Israeli war of June 1967. At present, UNTSO assists and co-operates with UNDOF and UNIFIL in the performance of their tasks; observer groups are stationed in Beirut and in Sinai.

Headquarters Government House, Jerusalem

Duration 11 June 1948 to date

Maximum strength 572(1948)

Current strength 291 military observers (30 June 1990)

Fatalities 24 (hostile action/accidents)
 4 (other causes)
28 (30 June 1990)

Expenditures From inception of mission to 31 December 1989: $310,521,300

Method of financing Appropriations through the United Nations regular budget

Mediators Count Folke Bernadotte (Sweden)   May–Sep. 1948
Ralph J. Bunche (United States)   Sep. 1948–Aug. 1949
(Acting)

Chiefs of Staff

Lieutenant-General Count Thord Bonde (Sweden)	Jun.–Jul. 1948
Major-General Aage Lundström (Sweden)	Jul.–Sep. 1948
Lieutenant-General William E. Riley (United States)	Sep. 1948–Jun. 1953
Major-General Vagn Bennike (Denmark)	Jun. 1953–Aug. 1954
Lieutenant-General E.L.M. Burns (Canada)	Aug. 1954–Nov. 1956

[continued]

Colonel Byron V. Leary (United States) (Acting)	Nov. 1956–Mar. 1958
Major-General Carl C. von Horn (Sweden)	Mar. 1958–Jul. 1960
Colonel R. W. Rickert (United States) (Acting)	Jul.– Dec. 1960
Lieutenant-General Carl C. von Horn (Sweden)	Jan. 1961– May 1963
Lieutenant-General Odd Bull (Norway)	Jun. 1963– Jul. 1970
Major-General Ensio Siilasvuo (Finland)	Aug. 1970–Oct. 1973
Colonel Richard W. Bunworth (Ireland) (Acting)	Nov. 1973–Mar. 1974
Major-General Bengt Liljestrand (Sweden)	Apr. 1974– Aug. 1975
Colonel K. D. Howard (Australia) (Acting)	Aug.–Dec. 1975
Major-General Emmanuel A. Erskine (Ghana)	Jan. 1976– Apr. 1978
Colonel William Callaghan (Ireland) (Acting)	Apr. 1978– Jun. 1979
Colonel O. Forsgren (Sweden) (Acting)	Jun. 1979– Jan. 1980
Major-General Erkki R. Kaira (Finland)	Feb. 1980– Feb. 1981
Lieutenant-General Emmanuel A. Erskine (Ghana)	Feb. 1981–May 1986
Lieutenant-General William Callaghan (Ireland)	May 1986–Jun. 1987
Lieutenant-General Martin Vadset (Norway)	Jun. 1987 to date

Contributors of military observers	Duration
Argentina	1967 to date
Australia	1956 to date
Austria	1967 to date
Belgium	1948 to date
Burma (now Myanmar)	1967–1969
Canada	1954 to date
Chile	1967 to date
China	1990 to date
Denmark	1954 to date
Finland	1967 to date
France	1948 to date
Ireland	1958 to date
Italy	1958 to date
Netherlands	1956 to date
New Zealand	1954 to date
Norway	1956 to date
Sweden	1948 to date
Switzerland	1990 to date
USSR	1973 to date
United States	1948 to date

Voluntary contributions	Duration	Contribution
United States	1949–Jun. 1967	Aircraft
Netherlands	Jun.–Nov. 1967	Aircraft
Switzerland	Nov. 1967 to date	Chartered commercial aircraft and crew

In 1988 the Government of Switzerland undertook to make available to all peace-keeping and good offices missions an emergency air ambulance service for the repatriation of sick and injured personnel, coding equipment and the expenses arising from training personnel for the maintenance and repair of this equipment.

UNEF I

First United Nations Emergency Force

Authorization	General Assembly resolutions: 998(ES-I) of 4 November 1956 1000(ES-I) of 5 November 1956 1001(ES-I) of 7 November 1956 1125(XI) of 2 February 1957
Function	To secure and to supervise the cessation of hostilities, including the withdrawal of the armed forces of France, Israel and the United Kingdom from Egyptian territory, and after the withdrawal to serve as a buffer between the Egyptian and Israeli forces
Location	First the Suez Canal sector and the Sinai peninsula. Later along the Armistice Demarcation Line in the Gaza area and the international frontier in the Sinai peninsula (on the Egyptian side)
Headquarters	Gaza
Duration	November 1956–June 1967
Maximum strength	6,073 (February 1957)
Strength at withdrawal	3,378 (June 1967)
Fatalities	64 (hostile action/accidents) <u>26</u> (other causes) 90
Expenditures	From inception to end of mission: $214,249,000 (The financial cost was considerably reduced by the absorption by the countries providing contingents of varying amounts of the expenses involved)
Method of financing	Assessments in respect of a Special Account

Commanders

Lieutenant-General E.L.M. Burns (Canada)	Nov. 1956–Dec. 1959
Lieutenant-General P. S. Gyani (India)	Dec. 1959–Jan. 1964
Major-General Carlos F. Paiva Chaves (Brazil)	Jan. 1964–Aug. 1964
Colonel Lazar Musicki (Yugoslavia) (Acting)	Aug. 1964–Jan. 1965
Major-General Syseno Sarmento (Brazil)	Jan. 1965–Jan. 1966
Major-General Indar J. Rikhye (India)	Jan. 1966–Jun. 1967

Contributors	**Duration**	**Contribution**
Brazil	20 Jan. 1957–13 Jun. 1967	Infantry
Canada	24 Nov. 1956–28 Feb. 1959	Medical unit
	24 Nov. 1956–31 May 1967	Signal, engineer, air transport, maintenance and movement control units
Colombia	16 Nov. 1956–28 Oct. 1958	Infantry
Denmark	15 Nov. 1956–9 Jun. 1967	Infantry

(*continued*)

Finland	11 Dec. 1956–5 Dec. 1957	Infantry
India	20 Nov. 1956–13 Jun. 1967	Infantry, and supply, transport and signal units
Indonesia	5 Jan. 1957–12 Sep. 1957	Infantry
Norway	15 Nov. 1956–9 Jun. 1967	Infantry
	1 Mar. 1959–9 Jun. 1967	Medical unit
Sweden	21 Nov. 1956–9 Jun. 1967	Infantry
Yugoslavia	17 Nov. 1956–11 Jun. 1967	Infantry

Voluntary contributions	**Duration**	**Contribution**
Canada	Nov. 1956	Airlift
Italy	Nov. 1956	Airlift, logistic support
Switzerland	Nov. 1956	Airlift
United States	Nov. 1956	Airlift

UNEF II
Second United Nations Emergency Force

Authorization	Security Council resolutions:
	340(1973) of 25 October 1973
	341(1973) of 27 October 1973
	346(1974) of 8 April 1974
	362(1974) of 23 October 1974
	368(1975) of 17 April 1975
	371(1975) of 24 July 1975
	378(1975) of 23 October 1975
	396(1976) of 22 October 1976
	416(1977) of 21 October 1977
	438(1978) of 23 October 1978

Function   To supervise the cease-fire between Egyptian and Israeli forces and, following the conclusion of the agreements of 18 January 1974 and 4 September 1975, to supervise the redeployment of Egyptian and Israeli forces and to man and control the buffer zones established under those agreements

Location   Suez Canal sector and later the Sinai peninsula

Headquarters   Ismailia

Duration   25 October 1973–24 July 1979

Maximum strength   6,973 (February 1974)

Strength at withdrawal   4,031 (July 1979)

Fatalities   30 (hostile action/accidents)
13 (other causes)
 9 (killed in a UNEF aircraft crash in Syria, as a result of anti-aircraft fire, during a flight in support of UNDOF on 9 August 1974)
52

Expenditures   From inception to end of mission: $446,487,000

Method of financing   Assessments in respect of a Special Account

Commanders

Lieutenant-General Ensio P. H. Siilasvuo (Finland)	
Interim Commander:	25 Oct. 1973–11 Nov. 1973
Commander:	12 Nov. 1973–19 Aug. 1975
Lieutenant-General Bengt Liljestrand (Sweden)	20 Aug. 1975–30 Nov. 1976
Major-General Rais Abin (Indonesia)	1 Dec. 1976–6 Sep. 1979

Contributors	**Duration**	**Contribution**
Australia	Jul. 1976–Oct. 1979	Air unit (helicopters and personnel)
Austria	26 Oct. 1973–3 Jun. 1974	Infantry
Canada	10 Nov. 1973–30 Oct. 1979	Logistics: signals, air and service units
Finland	26 Oct. 1973–Aug. 1979	Infantry
Ghana	22 Jan. 1974–Sep. 1979	Infantry
Indonesia	21 Dec. 1973–Sep. 1979	Infantry

(continued)

Ireland	30 Oct. 1973–22 May 1974	Infantry
Nepal	3 Feb. 1974–4 Sep. 1974	Infantry
Panama	11 Dec. 1973–25 Nov. 1974	Infantry
Peru	25 Nov. 1973–3 Jun. 1974	Infantry
Poland	15 Nov. 1973–20 Jan. 1980	Logistics: engineering, medical and transport units
Senegal	18 Jan. 1974–Jun. 1976	Infantry
Sweden	26 Oct. 1973–30 Apr. 1980	Infantry

Voluntary contributions	**Duration**	**Contribution**
Australia	Feb. 1974	Airlift: Nepalese troops, Calcutta—Cairo
Canada	Nov. 1973	Airlift: Canadian troops
Germany, Federal Republic of	Jan. 1974	Airlift: Ghanaian and Senegalese troops
Japan	Feb. 1974	Cash contribution for airlift of Nepalese troops Kathmandu–Calcutta, and transport of its equipment to UNEF
Norway	Oct. 1973	Airlift: Swedish troops, Sweden–UNEF
Poland	Nov. 1973	Airlift: Polish troops
Sweden	Oct. 1973	Airlift: Swedish troops
Switzerland		Aircraft placed at disposal of UNTSO was available to UNEF as required
United Kingdom	Oct. 1973	Airlift: Austrian, Finnish, Irish and Swedish troops and vehicles, Cyprus–UNEF
USSR	Nov. 1973	Airlift: Austrian troops, Austria–UNEF, Finnish troops and heavy equipment Finland–UNEF
United States	Nov. 1973	Airlift: Irish troops, Ireland–UNEF
	Nov. 1973	Finnish troops, Finland–UNEF
	Nov. 1973	Peruvian troops, Peru–UNEF
	Dec. 1973	Austrian troops, Austria–UNEF
	Dec. 1973	Indonesian troops, Indonesia–UNEF
	Dec. 1973	Panamanian troops, Panama–UNEF
	Oct. 1976	$10 million in goods and services

UNDOF
United Nations Disengagement Observer Force

Authorization	Security Council resolutions:	
	350(1974) of 31 May 1974	524(1982) of 29 November 1982
	363(1974) of 29 November 1974	531(1983) of 26 May 1983
	369(1975) of 28 May 1975	543(1983) of 29 November 1983
	381(1975) of 30 November 1975	551(1984) of 30 May 1984
	390(1976) of 28 May 1976	557(1984) of 28 November 1984
	398(1976) of 30 November 1976	563(1985) of 21 May 1985
	408(1977) of 26 May 1977	576(1985) of 21 November 1985
	420(1977) of 30 November 1977	584(1986) of 29 May 1986
	429(1978) of 31 May 1978	590(1986) of 26 November 1986
	441(1978) of 30 November 1978	596(1987) of 29 May 1987
	449(1979) of 30 May 1979	603(1987) of 25 November 1987
	456(1979) of 30 November 1979	613(1988) of 31 May 1988
	470(1980) of 30 May 1980	624(1988) of 30 November 1988
	481(1980) of 26 November 1980	633(1989) of 30 May 1989
	485(1981) of 22 May 1981	645(1989) of 29 November 1989
	493(1981) of 23 November 1981	655(1990) of 31 May 1990
	506(1982) of 26 May 1982	

Function To supervise the cease-fire between Israel and Syria; to supervise the redeployment of Syrian and Israeli forces; and to establish a buffer zone, as provided in the Agreement on Disengagement between Israeli and Syrian forces of 31 May 1974

Location Syrian Golan Heights

Headquarters Damascus

Duration 3 June 1974 to date

Authorized strength 1,450

Current strength 1,338 (30 June 1990)

Fatalities 14 (hostile action/accidents)
<u>10</u> (other causes)
24 (30 June 1990)

Amount apportioned From inception of mission to 30 November 1990: $452.4 million

Method of financing Assessments in respect of a Special Account

Commanders

Brigadier-General Gonzalo Briceño Zevallos (Peru), Interim Commander	3 June–14 Dec. 1974
Colonel Hannes Philipp (Austria), Officer-in-Charge	15 Dec. 1974–7 July 1975
Major-General Hannes Philipp (Austria)	8 July 1975–21 Apr. 1979
Colonel Günther G. Greindl (Austria)	22 Apr.–30 Nov. 1979
Major-General Günther G. Greindl (Austria)	1 Dec. 1979–25 Feb. 1981
Major-General Erkki R. Kaira (Finland)	26 Feb. 1981–31 May 1982
Major-General Carl-Gustaf Stahl (Sweden)	1 Jun. 1982–31 May 1985
Major-General Gustav Hägglund (Finland)	1 Jun. 1985–31 May 1986
Brigadier-General W. A. Douglas Yuill (Canada) (Acting)	1 Jun.–30 Jun. 1986
Major-General N. Gustaf A. Welin (Sweden)	1 Jul. 1986–9 Sep. 1988
Major-General Adolf Radauer (Austria)	10 Sep. 1988 to date

Contributors	Duration	Contribution
Austria	Jun. 1974 to date	Infantry
Canada	Jun. 1974 to date	Logistics: signals, supply and transport units
Finland	Mar. 1979 to date	Infantry
Iran	Aug. 1975–Mar. 1979	Infantry
Peru	Jun. 1974–Jul. 1975	Infantry
Poland	Jun. 1974 to date	Logistics: engineers and transport service

UNIFIL
United Nations Interim Force in Lebanon

Authorization	Security Council resolutions:	536(1983) of 18 July 1983
	425(1978) of 19 March 1978	538(1983) of 18 October 1983
	426(1978) of 19 March 1978	549(1984) of 19 April 1984
	434(1978) of 18 September 1978	555(1984) of 12 October 1984
	444(1979) of 19 January 1979	561(1985) of 17 April 1985
	450(1979) of 14 June 1979	575(1985) of 17 October 1985
	459(1979) of 19 December 1979	583(1986) of 18 April 1986
	474(1980) of 17 June 1980	586(1986) of 18 July 1986
	483(1980) of 17 December 1980	594(1987) of 15 January 1987
	488(1981) of 19 June 1981	599(1987) of 31 July 1987
	498(1981) of 18 December 1981	609(1988) of 29 January 1988
	511(1982) of 18 June 1982	617(1988) of 29 July 1988
	519(1982) of 17 August 1982	630(1989) of 30 January 1989
	523(1982) of 18 October 1982	639(1989) of 31 July 1989
	529(1983) of 18 January 1983	648(1990) of 31 January 1990

Function To confirm the withdrawal of Israeli forces from southern Lebanon, to restore international peace and security and to assist the Government of Lebanon in ensuring the return of its effective authority in the area

Location Southern Lebanon

Headquarters Naqoura

Duration 19 March 1978 to date

Authorized strength 7,000

Current strength 5,904 (30 June 1990)

Fatalities 130 (hostile action/accidents)
  40 (other causes)
170 (30 June 1990)

Amount apportioned From inception of mission to 31 July 1990: $1,762.9 million

Method of financing Assessments in respect of a Special Account

Commanders

Lieutenant-General Emmanuel A. Erskine (Ghana)	19 Mar. 1978–14 Feb. 1981
Lieutenant-General William Callaghan (Ireland)	15 Feb. 1981–31 May 1986
Major-General Gustav Hägglund (Finland)	1 Jun. 1986–30 Jun. 1988
Lieutenant-General Lars-Eric Wahlgren (Sweden)	1 Jul. 1988 to date

Contributors	**Duration**	**Contribution**
Canada	Mar.–Oct. 1978	Signals and movement control units
Fiji	May 1978 to date	Infantry battalion
Finland	Nov. 1982 to date	Infantry battalion
France	Mar. 1978–Mar. 1979, May 1982–Dec. 1986	Infantry battalion

(continued)	Mar. 1978 to Dec. 1986	Logistics: engineering, supply, transport and maintenance units
	Dec. 1986 to date	Composite battalion (maintenance and defence company)
Ghana	Sep. 1979 to date	Infantry battalion
	Sep. 1979 to date	Integrated headquarters camp command (defence platoon and engineering platoon)
Iran	Mar. 1978–Mar. 1979	Infantry battalion
Ireland	May 1978 to date	Infantry battalion
	Oct. 1978–Sep. 1979	Headquarters camp command (defence platoon and administrative personnel)
	Oct. 1978 to date	Integrated headquarters camp command (administrative personnel)
Italy	Jul. 1979 to date	Air unit: helicopters, ground and air crews
Nepal	Apr. 1978–May 1980, Jun. 1981–Nov. 1982, Jan. 1985 to date	Infantry battalion
Netherlands	Feb. 1979–Oct. 1985	Infantry battalion
Nigeria	May 1978–Feb. 1983	Infantry battalion
Norway	Mar. 1978 to date	Infantry battalion
	Mar. 1978–Jul. 1979	Logistics: air unit
	Mar. 1978–Aug. 1980	Medical unit
	Mar. 1978 to date	Maintenance company
	Mar. 1978 to date	Movement control unit
Senegal	Apr. 1978–Nov. 1984	Infantry battalion
Sweden	Mar.–May 1978	Infantry company
	Aug. 1980–Dec. 1986	Logistics: medical unit
	Dec. 1986 to date	Logistics battalion

In January 1987, a composite mechanized company became operational as the Force Mobile Reserve. In June 1990 its personnel were contributed by Fiji, Finland, Ghana, Ireland, Nepal, Norway and Sweden.

Voluntary contributions	**Duration**	**Contribution**
Australia	Jun. 1978	Arms and ammunition for Fijian contingent
Germany, Federal Republic of	Mar. 1978	Airlift: Norwegian troops
	Apr. 1978	Provided substantial part of vehicles and equipment for Nepalese contingent
Japan	Mar. 1988	Financial
United Kingdom	Jun. 1978	Airlift: Fijian troops
United States	Mar.–Jun. 1978	Airlift: Norwegian, Nepalese, Senegalese and Irish troops
		Airlift: equipment for Fijian troops

UNMOGIP
United Nations Military Observer Group in India and Pakistan

Authorization Security Council resolutions:
47(1948) of 21 April 1948
91(1951) of 30 March 1951
201(1965) of 6 September 1965
(to strengthen UNMOGIP)

Function To supervise, in the State of Jammu and Kashmir, the cease-fire between India and Pakistan

Location The State of Jammu and Kashmir and the border between that State and Pakistan

Headquarters Rawalpindi (November-April)
Srinagar (May-October)

Duration 24 January 1949 to date

Maximum strength 102 (October 1965)

Current strength 36 military observers (30 June 1990)

Fatalities 4 (hostile action/accidents)
1 (other causes)
5 (30 June 1990)

Expenditures From inception of mission to 31 December 1989: $67,709,300

Method of financing Appropriations through the United Nations regular budget

Chief Military Observers	Duration
Brigadier H. H. Angle (Canada)	1 Nov. 1949–Jul. 1950
Colonel Siegfried Coblentz (United States) (Acting)	Jul. 1950–27 Oct. 1950
Lieutenant-General R. H. Nimmo (Australia)	28 Oct. 1950–3 Jan. 1966
Colonel J. H. J. Gauthier (Canada) (Acting)	4 Jan. 1966– 7 Jul. 1966
Lieutenant-General Luis Tassara-Gonzalez (Chile)	8 Jul. 1966–18 Jun. 1977
Lieutenant-Colonel P. Bergevin (Canada) (Acting)	19 Jun. 1977–8 Apr. 1978
Colonel P. P. Pospisil (Canada) (Acting)	9 Apr. 1978–3 Jun. 1978
Brigadier-General Stig Waldenstrom (Sweden)	4 Jun. 1978–7 Jun. 1982
Brigadier-General Thor Johnsen (Norway)	8 Jun. 1982–30 May 1986
Lieutenant-Colonel G. Beltracchi (Italy) (Acting)	31 May 1986–31 July 1986
Brigadier-General Alf Hammer (Norway)	1 Aug. 1986–4 Aug. 1987
Lieutenant-Colonel G. Beltracchi (Italy) (Acting)	5 Aug. 1987–27 Sep. 1987
Brigadier-General James Parker (Ireland)	28 Sep. 1987–19 May 1989
Lieutenant-Colonel Mario Fiorese (Italy) (Acting)	20 May 1989–27 Jun. 1989
Brigadier-General Jeremiah Enright (Ireland)	28 Jun. 1989 to date

Contributors of military observers	Duration
Australia	1952–1985
Belgium	1949 to date
Canada	1949–1979
Chile	1950 to date
Denmark	1950 to date
Ecuador	1952
Finland	1963 to date
Italy	1961 to date
Mexico	1949
New Zealand	1952–1977
Norway	1949–1952
	1957 to date
Sweden	1950 to date
Uruguay	1952 to date
United States	1949–1954

Voluntary contributions	Duration	Contribution
Australia	1975–1978	Aircraft
Canada	1974–1975	Aircraft
Italy	1957–1963	Aircraft
United States	1949–1954	Aircraft

UNIPOM
United Nations India-Pakistan Observation Mission

Authorization: Security Council resolution 211(1965) of 20 September 1965

Function To supervise the cease-fire along the India/Pakistan border except the State of Jammu and Kashmir where UNMOGIP operated, and the withdrawal of all armed personnel to the positions held by them before 5 August 1965

Location Along the India/Pakistan border between Kashmir and the Arabian Sea

Headquarters Lahore (Pakistan)/Amritsar (India)

Duration 23 September 1965–22 March 1966

Maximum strength 96 military observers (October 1965)

Strength at withdrawal 78 military observers

Fatalities None

Expenditures From inception to end of Mission: $1,713,280

Method of financing Appropriations through the United Nations regular budget

Chief Officer Major-General B. F. Macdonald
(Canada)   Sep. 1965–Mar. 1966

Contributors **In its initial stage**
(from UNTSO and UNMOGIP)   **28 Sep. 1965–22 Mar. 1966**
Australia   Brazil
Belgium   Burma (now Myanmar)
Canada   Canada (also air unit, Oct. 1965–Mar.
Chile   1966)
Denmark   Ceylon (now Sri Lanka)
Finland   Ethiopia
Ireland   Ireland
Italy   Nepal
Netherlands   Netherlands
New Zealand   Nigeria
Norway   Venezuela
Sweden

UNOGIL
United Nations Observation Group in Lebanon

Authorization Security Council resolution 128(1958) of 11 June 1958

Function To ensure that there was no illegal infiltration of personnel or supply of arms or other *matériel* across the Lebanese borders

Location Lebanese-Syrian border areas and vicinity of zones held by opposing forces

Headquarters Beirut

Duration 12 June–9 December 1958

Maximum strength 591 military observers (November 1958)

Strength at withdrawal 375 military observers

Fatalities None

Expenditures From inception to end of mission: $3,697,742

Method of financing Appropriations through the United Nations regular budget

Members of Observation Group

Galo Plaza Lasso (Ecuador)	Chairman
Rajeshwar Dayal (India)	Member
Major-General Odd Bull (Norway)	Executive member in charge of military observers

Contributors of military observers

Afghanistan	Indonesia
Argentina	Ireland
Burma (now Myanmar)	Italy
Canada	Nepal
Ceylon (now Sri Lanka)	Netherlands
Chile	New Zealand
Denmark	Norway
Ecuador	Peru
Finland	Portugal
India	Thailand

UNYOM
United Nations Yemen Observation Mission

Authorization	Security Council resolution 179(1963) of 11 June 1963
Function	To observe and certify the implementation of the disengagement agreement between Saudi Arabia and the United Arab Republic
Location	Yemen
Headquarters	San'a
Duration	4 July 1963–4 September 1964
Maximum strength	25 military observers 114 officers and other ranks of reconnaissance unit (Yugoslavia) 50 officers and other ranks of air unit (Canada) 189
Strength at withdrawal	25 military observers and supporting air unit (Canada)
Fatalities	None
Expenditures	From inception to end of mission: $1,840,450
Method of financing	Contributions from Saudi Arabia and Egypt in equal parts

Commanders

Lieutenant-General Carl C. von Horn (Sweden)	Jul.–25 Aug. 1963
Colonel Branko Pavlović (Yugoslavia) (Acting)	26 Aug.–11 Sep. 1963
Lieutenant-General P. S. Gyani (India)	12 Sep.–7 Nov. 1963

Special Representative P. P. Spinelli (Italy) **of Secretary-General** **and Head of Mission**	4 Nov. 1963–4 Sep. 1964

Chiefs-of-Staff

Colonel Branko Pavlović (Yugoslavia)	8–25 Nov. 1963
Colonel S. C. Sabharwal (India)	26 Nov. 1963–4 Sep. 1964

Contributors	**Duration**	**Contribution**
Australia	Jul. 1963–Nov. 1963	Military observers
Canada	Jul. 1963–Sep. 1964	Air unit (aircraft and helicopters)
Denmark	Jul. 1963–Sep. 1964	Military observers
Ghana	Jul. 1963–Sep. 1964	Military observers
India	Jan. 1964–Sep. 1964	Military observers
Italy	Jan. 1964–Sep. 1964	Military observers
Netherlands	Jan. 1964–Sep. 1964	Military observers
Norway	Jul. 1963–Sep. 1964	Military observers
Pakistan	Jan. 1964–Sep. 1964	Military observers
Sweden	Jul. 1963–Sep. 1964	Military observers
Yugoslavia	Jul. 1963–Nov. 1963	Reconnaissance unit
	Jul. 1963–Sep. 1964	Military observers

DOMREP
Mission of the Representative of the Secretary-General
in the Dominican Republic

Authorization Security Council resolution 203(1965) of 14 May 1965

Function To observe the situation and to report on breaches of the cease-fire between the two *de facto* authorities

Location Dominican Republic

Headquarters Santo Domingo

Duration 15 May 1965–22 October 1966

Strength 2 military observers

Fatalities None

Expenditures From inception to end of mission: $275,831

Method of financing Appropriations through the United Nations regular budget

Representative of the Secretary-General José Antonio Mayobre (Venezuela)

Military Adviser Major-General Indar J. Rikhye (India)
(The Military Adviser was provided with a staff of 2 military observers at any one time. These observers were provided, one each, by Brazil, Canada and Ecuador)

ONUC
United Nations Operation in the Congo

Authorization	Security Council resolutions:
	143(1960) of 14 July 1960
	145(1960) of 22 July 1960
	146(1960) of 9 August 1960
	161(1961) of 21 February 1961
	169(1961) of 24 November 1961
Function	Initially, to ensure withdrawal of Belgian forces, to assist the Government in maintaining law and order and to provide technical assistance. The function of ONUC was subsequently modified to include maintaining the territorial integrity and the political independence of the Congo, preventing the occurrence of civil war, and securing the removal from the Congo of all foreign military, paramilitary and advisory personnel not under the United Nations Command, and all mercenaries
Location	Republic of the Congo (now Zaire)
Headquarters	Leopoldville (now Kinshasa)
Duration	15 July 1960–30 June 1964
Maximum strength	19,828 (July 1961)
Strength at withdrawal	5,871 (30 December 1963)
Fatalities	195 (hostile action/accidents)
	39 (other causes)
	234
Expenditures	From inception to end of mission: $400,130,793
Method of financing	Assessments in respect of a Special Account

Special Representatives

Ralph J. Bunche (United States)	Jul. –Aug. 1960
Andrew W. Cordier (United States)	Aug.–Sep. 1960
Rajeshwar Dayal (India)	Sep. 1960–May 1961
Mekki Abbas (Sudan) (Acting)	Mar.–May 1961

Officers-in-Charge

Sture Linner (Sweden)	May 1961–Jan. 1962
Robert K. A. Gardiner (Ghana)	Feb. 1962–May 1963
Max H. Dorsinville (Haiti)	May 1963–Apr. 1964
Bibiano F. Osorio-Tafall (Mexico)	Apr.–Jun.1964

Commanders

Lieutenant-General Carl C. von Horn (Sweden)	18 Jul.–Dec. 1960
Lieutenant-General Sean MacEoin (Ireland)	Jan. 1961–Mar. 1962
Lieutenant-General Kebbede Guebre (Ethiopia)	Apr. 1962–Jul. 1963
Major-General Christian Kaldager (Norway)	Aug.–Dec. 1963
Major-General Aguiyu Ironsi (Nigeria)	Jan.–Jun. 1964

Contributors	Duration	Contribution
Argentina	Jul. 1960–Feb. 1963	Aircraft personnel (air and ground)
Austria	14 Dec. 1960–Aug. 1963	Aircraft personnel (air and ground), field hospital and personnel, staff personnel
Brazil	Jul. 1960–Jun. 1964	Aircraft personnel (air and ground) staff personnel
Burma (now Myanmar)	Aug. 1960–Jun. 1964	Staff personnel
Canada	Jul. 1960–Jun. 1964	Aircraft personnel (air and ground), staff personnel, signals
Ceylon (now Sri Lanka)	Aug. 1960–Apr. 1962	Staff personnel
Denmark	Aug. 1960–Jun. 1964	Aircraft personnel (air and ground), staff personnel, workshop control, transport company
Ethiopia	15 Jul. 1960–16 Jun. 1964	Infantry, aircraft personnel (air and ground), staff personnel
Ghana	15 Jul. 1960–25 Sep. 1963	Infantry, 2 medical units, staff personnel, police companies
Guinea	25 Jul. 1960–Jan. 1961	Infantry
India	Jul. 1960–Jun. 1964	Infantry, aircraft personnel (air and ground), field hospital and personnel, staff personnel, supply unit, signal company, air dispatch team, postal unit
Indonesia	4 Oct. 1960–Apr. 1964	Infantry
Iran	Dec. 1962–Jul. 1963	Aircraft and air and ground personnel
Ireland	28 Jul. 1960–11 May 1964	Infantry, staff personnel
Italy	Oct. 1960–Jun. 1964	Aircraft personnel (air and ground), field hospital, staff personnel
Liberia	25 Jul. 1960–May 1963	Infantry, movement control, staff personnel
Malaya	30 Oct. 1960–Apr. 1963	Infantry, staff personnel
Federation of Mali (now Mali and Senegal)	1 Aug. 1960–Nov. 1960	Infantry
Morocco	15 Jul. 1960–31 Jan. 1961	Infantry, parachute company
Netherlands	Aug. 1960–Oct. 1963	Hygiene teams, staff personnel
Nigeria	10 Nov. 1960–30 Jun. 1964	Infantry, police unit, staff personnel
Norway	Jul. 1960–Mar. 1964	Aircraft personnel (air and ground), staff personnel, workshop control
Pakistan	31 Aug. 1960–May 1964	Ordnance and transport units, staff personnel
Philippines	Feb. 1963–Jun. 1963	Aircraft personnel (air and ground), staff personnel
Sierra Leone	Jan. 1962–Mar. 1963	Infantry
Sudan	Aug. 1960–Apr.–Dec. 1961	Infantry
Sweden	20 Jul. 1960–15 May 1964	Infantry, aircraft personnel (air and ground), movement control, engineering personnel, workshop unit, signal detachment, staff personnel
Tunisia	15 Jul. 1960–May 1963	Infantry
United Arab Republic	20 Aug. 1960–1 Feb. 1961	Infantry, parachute battalion
Yugoslavia	Jul. 1960–Dec. 1960	Aircraft personnel (air and ground)

From February 1963 to the end of the United Nations Operation in the Congo, a battalion of the Congolese National Army was incorporated in ONUC

Voluntary contributions	Duration	Contribution
Canada	Beginning of operation	Airlift of food
Switzerland	Beginning of operation	Airlift of food and other supplies
USSR	Beginning of operation	Airlift of food
United Kingdom	Beginning of operation	Airlift of food and Ghanaian troops
United States	Beginning of operation	Airlift of food supplies and equipment
		Aircraft
		Airlift of Ghanaian, Guinean, Moroccan, Swedish and Tunisian troops
		Sealift of Malayan troops

UNSF
United Nations Security Force in West New Guinea (West Irian)

Authorization	General Assembly resolution 1752(XVII) of 21 September 1962
Function	To maintain peace and security in the territory under the United Nations Temporary Executive Authority (UNTEA) established by agreement between Indonesia and the Netherlands
Location	West New Guinea (West Irian)
Headquarters	Hollandia (now Jayaphra)
Duration	3 October 1962–30 April 1963
Maximum strength	1,500 infantry personnel and 76 aircraft personnel
Strength at withdrawal	1,500 infantry personnel and 76 aircraft personnel
Fatalities	None
Method of financing	The Governments of Indonesia and the Netherlands paid full costs in equal amounts
Commander	Major-General Said Uddin Khan (Pakistan)

Contributors	Duration	Contribution
Pakistan	3 Oct. 1962–30 Apr. 1963	Infantry
Canada	3 Oct. 1962–30 Apr. 1963	Supporting aircraft and crews
United States	3 Oct. 1962–30 Apr. 1963	Supporting aircraft and crews

(From 18 August to 21 September 1962, the Secretary-General's Military Adviser, Brigadier-General Indar Jit Rikhye (India), and a group of 21 military observers assisted in the implementation of the agreement of 15 August 1962 between Indonesia and the Netherlands on cessation of hostilities. The military observers were provided by Brazil, Ceylon (now Sri Lanka), India, Ireland, Nigeria and Sweden.)

UNFICYP
United Nations Peace-keeping Force in Cyprus

Authorization Security Council resolutions:

186(1964) of 4 March 1964	391(1976) of 15 June 1976
187(1964) of 13 March 1964	401(1976) of 14 December 1976
192(1964) of 20 June 1964	410(1977) of 15 June 1977
Consensus of 11 August 1964	422(1977) of 15 December 1977
194(1964) of 25 September 1964	430(1978) of 16 June 1978
198(1964) of 18 December 1964	443(1978) of 14 December 1978
201(1965) of 19 March 1965	451(1979) of 15 June 1979
206(1965) of 16 June 1965	458(1979) of 14 December 1979
219(1965) of 17 December 1965	472(1980) of 13 June 1980
220(1966) of 16 March 1966	482(1980) of 11 December 1980
222(1966) of 16 June 1966	486(1981) of 4 June 1981
231(1966) of 15 December 1966	495(1981) of 14 December 1981
238(1967) of 19 June 1967	510(1982) of 15 June 1982
244(1967) of 22 December 1967	526(1982) of 14 December 1982
247(1968) of 18 March 1968	534(1983) of 15 June 1983
254(1968) of 18 June 1968	541(1983) of 18 November 1983
261(1968) of 10 December 1968	544(1983) of 15 December 1983
266(1969) of 10 June 1969	553(1984) of 15 June 1984
274(1969) of 11 December 1969	559(1984) of 14 December 1984
281(1970) of 9 June 1970	565(1985) of 14 June 1985
291(1970) of 10 December 1970	578(1985) of 12 December 1985
293(1971) of 26 May 1971	585(1986) of 13 June 1986
305(1971) of 13 December 1971	593(1986) of 11 December 1986
315(1972) of 15 June 1972	597(1987) of 12 June 1987
324(1972) of 12 December 1972	604(1987) of 14 December 1987
334(1973) of 5 June 1973	614(1988) of 15 June 1988
343(1973) of 14 December 1973	625(1988) of 15 December 1988
349(1974) of 29 May 1974	634(1989) of 9 June 1989
364(1974) of 13 December 1974	646(1989) of 14 December 1989
370(1975) of 13 June 1975	657(1990) of 15 June 1990
383(1975) of 13 December 1975	

Function "In the interest of preserving international peace and security, to use its best efforts to prevent the recurrence of fighting and, as necessary, to contribute to the maintenance and restoration of law and order and a return to normal conditions." Since the hostilities of 1974, this has included supervising the cease-fire and maintaining a buffer zone between the lines of the Cyprus National Guard and of the Turkish and Turkish Cypriot forces

Location Cyprus

Headquarters Nicosia

Duration 27 March 1964 to date

Maximum strength 6,411 (June 1964)

Current strength 2,137 + 39 civil police (30 June 1990)

Fatalities 86 (hostile action/accidents)
63 (other causes)
149 (30 June 1990)

Estimated cost From inception of mission to 15 December 1990: $635.7 million*

*Projected expenditures financed entirely from voluntary contributions.

Method of financing   Voluntary contributions

Mediators
Sakari S. Tuomioja (Finland)   Mar.–Sep. 1964
Galo Plaza Lasso (Ecuador)   Sep. 1964–Dec. 1965

Special Representatives
Galo Plaza Lasso (Ecuador)   May–Sep. 1964
Carlos A. Bernardes (Brazil)   Sep. 1964–Jan. 1967
P. P. Spinelli (Italy) (Acting)   Jan.–Feb. 1967
Bibiano F. Osorio-Tafall (Mexico)   Feb. 1967–Jun. 1964
Luis Weckmann-Muñoz (Mexico)   Jul. 1974–Oct. 1975
Javier Pérez de Cuéllar (Peru)   Oct. 1975–Dec. 1977
Rémy Gorgé (Switzerland) (Acting)   Dec. 1977–Apr. 1978
Reynaldo Galindo-Pohl (El Salvador)   May 1978–Apr. 1980
Hugo Juan Gobbi (Argentina)   May 1980–Dec. 1984
James Holger (Chile) (Acting)   Jan. 1985–Feb. 1988
Oscar Camilión (Argentina)   Feb. 1988 to date

Commanders
Lieutenant-General P.S. Gyani (India)   Mar.–Jun. 1964
General K. S. Thimayya (India)   Jun. 1964–Dec. 1965
Brigadier A. J. Wilson (United Kingdom) (Acting)   Dec. 1965–May 1966
Lieutenant-General I. A. E. Martola (Finland)   May 1966–Dec. 1969
Lieutenant-General Dewan Prem Chand (India)   Dec. 1969–Dec. 1976
Major-General James J. Quinn (Ireland)   Dec. 1976–Feb. 1981
Major-General Günther G. Greindl (Austria)   Mar. 1981–Apr. 1989
Major-General Clive Milner (Canada)   Apr. 1989 to date

Contributors	Duration	Contribution
Australia	May 1964 to date	Civilian police
Austria	Apr. 1964–Jul. 1977	Civilian police
	May 1964–Oct. 1973	Field hospital and personnel
	Oct. 1973–Apr. 1976	Medical centre
	Apr. 1972 to date	Infantry
Canada	Mar. 1964 to date	Infantry
	Apr. 1976 to date	Medical centre
Denmark	May 1964 to date	Infantry
	May 1964–Jun. 1975	Civilian police
Finland	Mar. 1964–Oct. 1977	Infantry
	Oct. 1977 to date	Staff officers
Ireland	Mar. 1964–Oct. 1973	Infantry
	Oct. 1973 to date	Staff officers
New Zealand	May 1964–Jun. 1967	Civilian police
Sweden	Mar. 1964–Dec. 1987	Infantry
	Jan. 1988 to date	Staff officers
	May 1964 to date	Civilian police
United Kingdom	Mar. 1964 to date	Infantry, force reserve, air unit, logistics
	Apr. 1976 to date	Medical centre

Voluntary contributions The contributors listed above provide their personnel without cost to the United Nations except in those cases where they request reimbursement for certain extra and extraordinary expenses

Italy   Airlift
United States   Airlift

UNGOMAP
United Nations Good Offices Mission in Afghanistan and Pakistan

Authorization	Letter of 25 April 1988 from the President of the Security Council addressed to the Secretary-General (S/19836) Security Council resolutions: 622(1988) of 31 October 1988 647(1990) of 11 January 1990
Function	To assist the Representative of the Secretary-General to lend his good offices to the parties in ensuring the implementation of the Agreements on the Settlement of the Situation Relating to Afghanistan and in this context to investigate and report possible violations of any of the provisions of the Agreements
Location	Afghanistan and Pakistan
Headquarters	Kabul and Islamabad
Duration	15 May 1988–15 March 1990
Maximum strength	50 (May 1988). UNGOMAP comprised officers temporarily detached from existing operations (UNTSO, UNDOF, UNIFIL)
Strength at withdrawal	35 (March 1990)
Fatalities	None
Expenditures	$14,029,010 (from inception until end of mission)
Method of financing	Appropriations from the regular budget of the United Nations

Representative of the Secretary-General on the Settlement of the Situation Relating to Afghanistan	Diego Cordovez (Ecuador) Benon Sevan (Cyprus)	26 Apr. 1988-15 Jan. 1990 19 Jan. 1990 to date
Deputy Representative	Major-General Rauli Helminen (Finland) Colonel Heikki Happonen (Finland)	26 Apr. 1988–9 May 1989 19 May 1989–15 Mar. 1990
Contributors	Austria Canada Denmark Fiji Finland Ghana Ireland Nepal Poland Sweden	
Voluntary contribution	Japan	Financial contribution

UNIIMOG
United Nations Iran-Iraq Military Observer Group

Authorization	Security Council resolutions: 598(1987) of 20 July 1987 619(1988) of 9 August 1988 631(1989) of 8 February 1989 642(1989) of 29 September 1989 651(1990) of 29 March 1990	
Function	To verify, confirm and supervise the cease-fire and the withdrawal of all forces to the internationally recognized boundaries, pending a comprehensive settlement	
Location	Iran and Iraq	
Headquarters	Tehran and Baghdad	
Duration	20 August 1988 to date	
Current strength	399 (30 June 1990)	
Fatalities	1 (hostile action/accidents) <u>0</u> (other causes) 1 (30 June 1990)	
Amount apportioned	From inception of mission to 30 September 1990: $172.9 million	
Method of financing	Assessments in respect of a Special Account	
Personal Representative of the Secretary-General	Jan K. Eliasson (Sweden)	1 September 1988 to date
Chief Military Observer	Major-General Slavko Jović (Yugoslavia)	12 August 1988 to date

Contributors of military observers	**Duration**
Argentina	Aug. 1988 to date
Australia	Aug. 1988 to date
Austria	Aug. 1988 to date
Bangladesh	Aug. 1988 to date
Canada	Aug. 1988 to date
Denmark	Aug. 1988 to date
Finland	Aug. 1988 to date
Ghana	Aug. 1988 to date
Hungary	Aug. 1988 to date
India	Aug. 1988 to date
Indonesia	Aug. 1988 to date
Ireland	Aug. 1988 to date
Italy	Aug. 1988 to date
Kenya	Aug. 1988 to date
Malaysia	Aug. 1988 to date
New Zealand	Aug. 1988 to date
Nigeria	Aug. 1988 to date
Norway	Aug. 1988 to date
Peru	Sep. 1988 to Oct. 1989

(continued)

Poland	Aug. 1988 to date
Senegal	Aug. 1988 to date
Sweden	Aug. 1988 to date
Turkey	Aug. 1988 to date
Uruguay	Sep. 1988 to date
Yugoslavia	Aug. 1988 to date
Zambia	Aug. 1988 to date

Other contributions	**Duration**	**Contribution**
Austria	Dec. 1988 to date	Medical section
Canada	Aug. to Dec. 1988	Signals unit
Ireland	Oct. 1988 to date	Military police unit
New Zealand	Oct. 1988 to date	Air unit

Voluntary contributions

Italy	Airlift: equipment
Japan	Financial
Kuwait	Trucks, vehicle workshop equipment, office, electrical, and communications supplies
Morocco	Financial
New Zealand	Contribution towards preparing and positioning one aircraft in the mission area
Republic of Korea	Forklifts, office equipment
Switzerland	One fixed-wing aircraft
USSR	Airlift: Canadian military personnel

UNAVEM
United Nations Angola Verification Mission

Authorization	Security Council resolution: 626(1988) of 20 December 1988
Function	To verify the redeployment northwards and the phased and total withdrawal of Cuban troops from the territory of Angola in accordance with the timetable agreed between Angola and Cuba
Location	Angola
Headquarters	Luanda
Duration	3 January 1989–to date
Maximum strength	70 (April-December 1989)
Current strength	60 (30 June 1990)
Fatalities	None (30 June 1990)
Amount apportioned	From inception of mission to 2 January 1991: $14.7 million
Method of financing	Assessments in respect of a Special Account
Chief Military Observer	Brigadier-General Péricles Ferreira Gomes (Brazil) 23 Dec. 1988 to date

Contributors

Algeria	Jan. 1989 to date
Argentina	Jan. 1989 to date
Brazil	Jan. 1989 to date
Congo	Jan. 1989 to date
Czechoslovakia	Jan. 1989 to date
India	Jan. 1989 to date
Jordan	Jan. 1989 to date
Norway	Jan. 1989 to date
Spain	Jan. 1989 to date
Yugoslavia	Jan. 1989 to date

UNTAG

United Nations Transition Assistance Group in Namibia

Authorization	Security Council resolutions: 435(1978) of 29 September 1978 632(1989) of 16 February 1989	
Function	To assist the Special Representative of the Secretary-General to ensure the early independence of Namibia through free and fair elections under the supervision and control of the United Nations	
Location	Namibia and Angola	
Headquarters	Windhoek	
Duration	1 April 1989–21 March 1990	
Authorized upper limit of military component	7,500	
Maximum strength of military component	4,493 (November 1989)	
Fatalities	4 civilian personnel 4 civilian police 11 military personnel 19 (hostile action/accidents/other causes)	
Expenditures	$383.5 million*	
Method of financing	Assessments in respect of a Special Account	

Special Representative of the Secretary-General Mr. Martti Ahtisaari (Finland) 27 Jul. 1978–21 Mar. 1990

Force Commanders

Major-General Hannes Philipp (Austria), Commander designate	7 Sep. 1978–11 Jan. 1980
Lieutenant-General Dewan Prem Chand (India), Commander designate Force Commander	12 Jan. 1980–31 Mar. 1989 1 Apr. 1989–21 Mar. 1990

Contributors

Australia	Military engineers Electoral supervisors
Austria	Police monitors
Bangladesh	Military observers Police monitors
Barbados	Police monitors
Belgium	Police monitors

*Estimated expenditures, including liquidation costs and voluntary contributions in kind amounting to $10.1 million

(continued)

Canada	Logistics
	Police monitors
	Electoral supervisors
China	Electoral supervisors
Congo	Electoral supervisors
Costa Rica	Electoral supervisors
Czechoslovakia	Military observers
Denmark	Movement control
	Electoral supervisors
Egypt	Police monitors
Fiji	Police monitors
Finland	Military observers
	Infantry battalion
	Electoral supervisors
France	Electoral supervisors
German Democratic Republic	Police monitors
	Electoral supervisors
Germany, Federal Republic of	Police monitors
	Electoral supervisors
	Civilian mechanics
Ghana	Police monitors
	Electoral supervisors
Greece	Electoral supervisors
Guyana	Police monitors
Hungary	Police monitors
India	Military observers
	Police monitors
	Electoral supervisors
Indonesia	Police monitors
Ireland	Military observers
	Police monitors
	Electoral supervisors
Italy	Helicopter unit
Jamaica	Police monitors
Japan	Electoral supervisors
Kenya	Infantry battalion
	Military observers
	Police monitors
	Electoral supervisors
Malaysia	Infantry battalion
	Military observers
Netherlands	Police monitors
New Zealand	Police monitors
Nigeria	Police monitors
	Electoral supervisors
Norway	Police monitors
	Electoral supervisors
Pakistan	Military observers
	Police monitors
	Electoral supervisors
Panama	Military observers
Peru	Military observers
Poland	Logistic battalion
	Military observers
	Electoral supervisors
Portugal	Electoral supervisors
Singapore	Police monitors
	Electoral supervisors

(continued)

	Spain	Light aircraft personnel
	Sudan	Military observers
	Sweden	Police monitors
		Electoral supervisors
	Switzerland	Civilian medical unit
		Electoral supervisors
	Thailand	Electoral supervisors
	Togo	Military observers
	Trinidad and Tobago	Electoral supervisors
	Tunisia	Police monitors
	USSR	Electoral supervisors
	United Kingdom	Signals squadron
		Electoral supervisors
	Yugoslavia	Military observers
Voluntary contributions	Germany, Federal Republic of	Light vehicles, minibuses, mobile workshops, ambulances, spare parts; secondment of technical staff; transportation of police monitors
	Greece	Various logistics equipment
	Japan	Financial
	Switzerland	Three aircraft and crew
	United States	Airlift services

ONUCA
United Nations Observer Group in Central America

Authorization Security Council resolutions:
644(1989) of 7 November 1989
650(1989) of 27 March 1989 (first expansion of mandate)
653(1990) of 20 April 1990 (second expansion of mandate)
654(1990) of 4 May 1990

Function In accordance with the original mandate: to verify compliance by the Governments of Costa Rica, El Salvador, Guatemala, Honduras and Nicaragua with the undertakings in respect of security contained in the Esquipulas II Agreement, namely the cessation of aid to irregular forces and insurrectionist movements operating in the region and the non-use of the territory of one State for attacks on others. The mandate was subsequently twice expanded: first, to enable ONUCA to play a part in the voluntary demobilization of the members of the Nicaraguan Resistance; and second, to enable ONUCA to monitor a cease-fire and the separation of forces agreed by the Nicaraguan parties as part of the demobilization process

Location Costa Rica, El Salvador, Guatemala, Honduras and Nicaragua

Headquarters Tegucigalpa, Honduras

Duration 7 December 1989 to date

Maximum strength 1,098 (31 May 1990)

Current strength 545 (30 June 1990)

Fatalities None (30 June 1990)

Amount apportioned From inception of mission to 7 November 1990: $56.9 million

Method of financing Assessments in respect of a Special Account

Chief Military Observer Major-General Agustín Quesada
Gómez (Spain)   21 November 1989 to date

Contributors	Duration	Contribution
Argentina	Jun. 1990 to date	Naval crew and four fast patrol boats
Brazil	Apr. 1990 to date	Military observers
Canada	Dec. 1989 to date	Military observers, helicopter unit
Colombia	Dec. 1989 to date	Military observers
Ecuador	Apr. 1990 to date	Military observers
Federal Republic of Germany	Dec. 1989 to date	Civilian medical personnel, air crew
India	May 1990 to date	Military observers
Ireland	Dec. 1989 to date	Military observers
Spain	Dec. 1989 to date	Military observers
Sweden	May 1990 to date	Military observers
Venezuela	Dec. 1989 to date	Military observers, logistics unit
	Apr.–Jul. 1990	Infantry battalion

Voluntary contributions

| Federal Republic of Germany | Dec. 1989 to date | Rental, equipment and maintenance of a fixed wing aircraft; basic salary of air crew and of civilian medical personnel |

Appendix III **Maps**

PEACE-KEEPING FORCES AND OBSERVER MISSIONS

UNEF I
1956-1967

UNOGIL
1958

UNIFIL
1978-

UNEF II
1973-1979

UNFICYP
1964-

UNTSO
1948-

UNDOF
1974-

UNIIMOG
1988-

UNGOMAP
1988-1990

UNMOGIP
1949-

UNIPOM
1965-1966

ONUCA
1989-

UNSF
1962-1963

DOMREP
1965-1966

ONUC
1960-1964

UNYOM
1963-1964

UNAVEM
1989-

UNTAG
1989-1990

UNDOF	Peace-keeping forces
UNTSO	Observer missions
•	Headquarters

MAP NO. 3574 Rev. 1   UNITED NATIONS
JUNE 1990

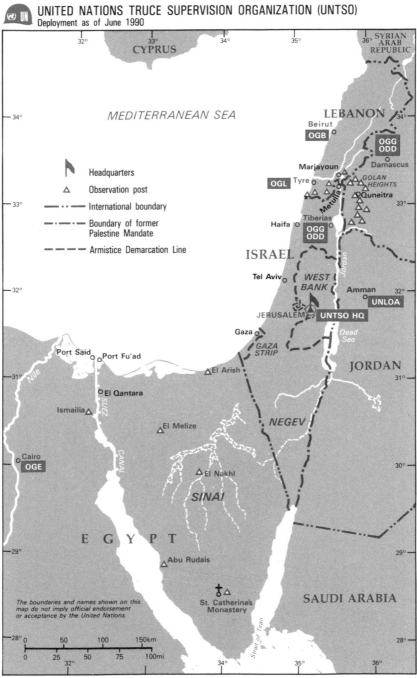

UNITED NATIONS TRUCE SUPERVISION ORGANIZATION (UNTSO)
Deployment as of June 1990

Headquarters

Observation post

International boundary

Boundary of former Palestine Mandate

Armistice Demarcation Line

CYPRUS

MEDITERRANEAN SEA

SYRIAN ARAB REPUBLIC

LEBANON

Beirut
OGB

OGG ODD

Damascus

Marjayoun

OGL Tyre
GOLAN HEIGHTS

Metulla
Quneitra

Haifa
Tiberias
OGG ODD

ISRAEL

Tel Aviv
WEST BANK

Amman
UNLOA

JERUSALEM
UNTSO HQ

Gaza
GAZA STRIP

Dead Sea

JORDAN

Port Said
Port Fu'ad
El Arish

El Qantara

Ismailia

El Melize

NEGEV

Cairo
OGE

El Nakhl

SINAI

EGYPT

Abu Rudais

St. Catherine's Monastery

SAUDI ARABIA

Strait of Tiran

The boundaries and names shown on this map do not imply official endorsement or acceptance by the United Nations.

0 50 100 150km
0 25 50 75 100mi

MAP NO. 3329.1 Rev. 1   UNITED NATIONS
JUNE 1990

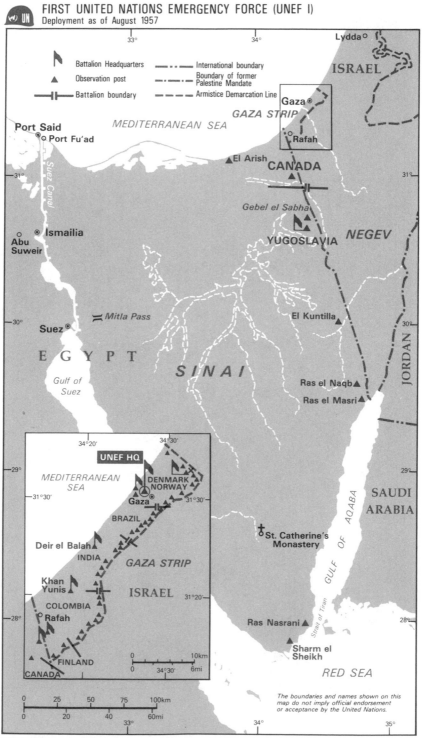

FIRST UNITED NATIONS EMERGENCY FORCE (UNEF I)
Deployment as of August 1957

Battalion Headquarters
Observation post
Battalion boundary

International boundary
Boundary of former Palestine Mandate
Armistice Demarcation Line

ISRAEL
Lydda
Gaza
GAZA STRIP
Rafah
El Arish
CANADA
Gebel el Sabha
YUGOSLAVIA
NEGEV
Port Said
Port Fu'ad
MEDITERRANEAN SEA
Ismailia
Abu Suweir
Suez
Mitla Pass
Gulf of Suez
E G Y P T
S I N A I
El Kuntilla
JORDAN
Ras el Naqb
Ras el Masri

UNEF HQ
MEDITERRANEAN SEA
DENMARK
NORWAY
Gaza
BRAZIL
Deir el Balah
INDIA
GAZA STRIP
Khan Yunis
ISRAEL
COLOMBIA
Rafah
FINLAND
CANADA

St. Catherine's Monastery
SAUDI ARABIA
GULF OF AQABA
Strait of Tiran
Ras Nasrani
Sharm el Sheikh
RED SEA

The boundaries and names shown on this map do not imply official endorsement or acceptance by the United Nations.

0 25 50 75 100km
0 20 40 60mi

0 10km
0 6mi

MAP NO. 3329.2 Rev. 1 UNITED NATIONS
JUNE 1990

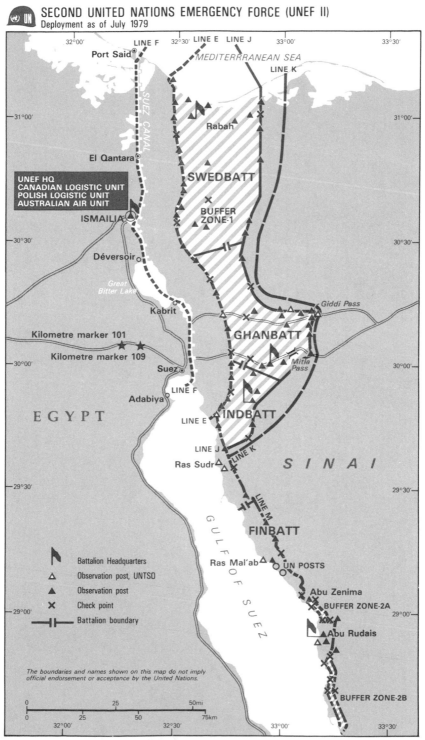

SECOND UNITED NATIONS EMERGENCY FORCE (UNEF II)
Deployment as of July 1979

LINE F LINE E LINE J
32°00'   32°30'   33°00'   33°30'

Port Said

MEDITERRRANEAN SEA

LINE K

31°00'

Rabah

El Qantara

UNEF HQ
CANADIAN LOGISTIC UNIT
POLISH LOGISTIC UNIT
AUSTRALIAN AIR UNIT

SWEDBATT

×
BUFFER
ZONE-1

ISMAILIA

30°30'

Déversoir

*Great
Bitter Lake*

Giddi Pass

Kabrit

GHANBATT

Kilometre marker 101

*Mitla
Pass*

Kilometre marker 109

30°00'

Suez

LINE F

Adabiya

LINE E   INDBATT

E G Y P T

LINE J

LINE K

Ras Sudr

S I N A I

29°30'

Line M

FINBATT

Battalion Headquarters

Ras Mal'ab   UN POSTS

△ Observation post, UNTSO

Abu Zenima

▲ Observation post

BUFFER ZONE-2A

× Check point

29°00'

⊢⊩⊣ Battalion boundary

Abu Rudais

*The boundaries and names shown on this map do not imply
official endorsement or acceptance by the United Nations.*

0   25   50mi
0   25   50   75km

BUFFER ZONE-2B

32°00'   32°30'   33°00'   33°30'

MAP NO. 3329.3 Rev. 1 UNITED NATIONS
JUNE 1990

UNITED NATIONS DISENGAGEMENT OBSERVER FORCE (UNDOF)
Deployment as of June 1990

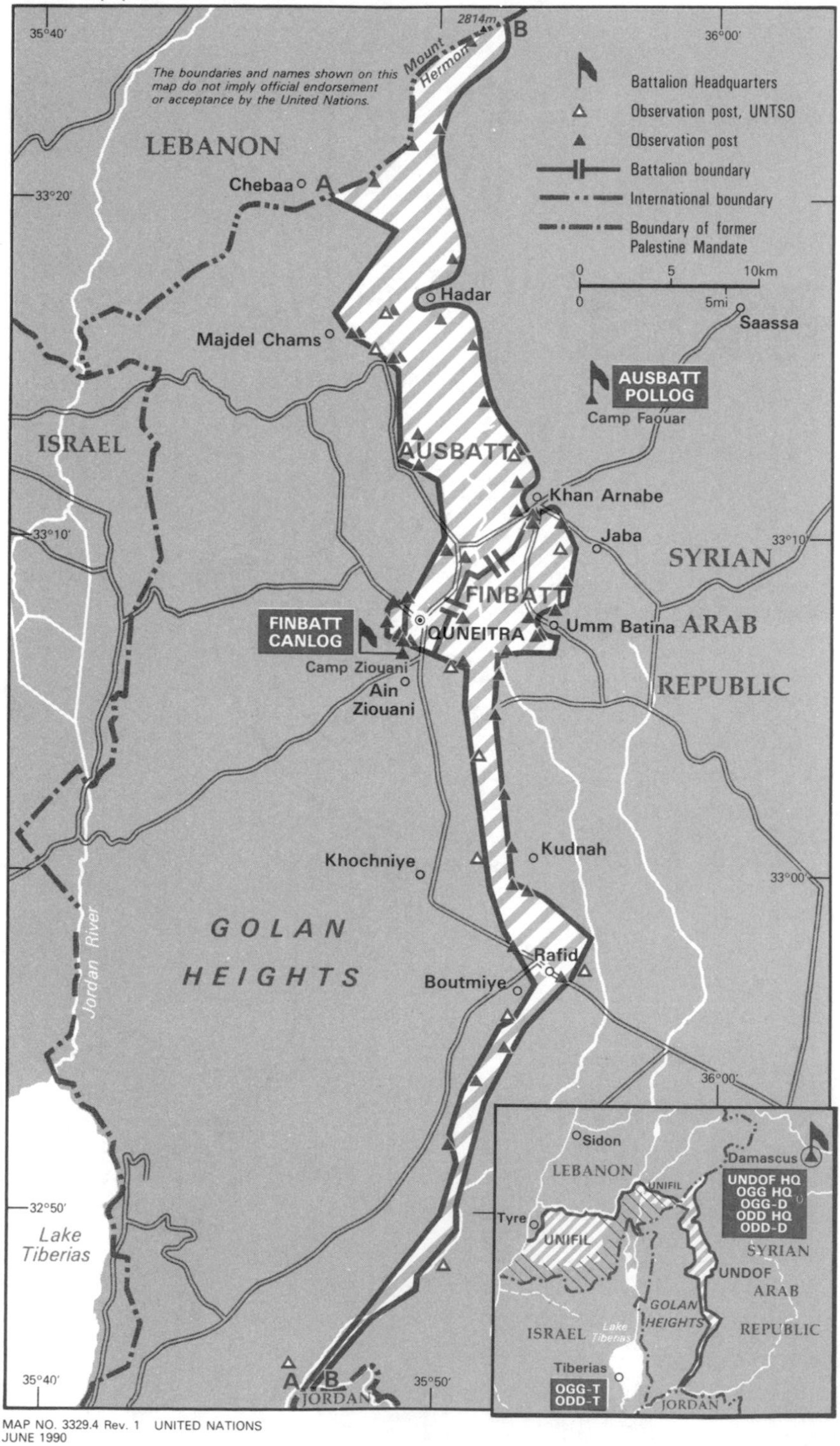

The boundaries and names shown on this map do not imply official endorsement or acceptance by the United Nations.
Battalion Headquarters
Observation post, UNTSO
Observation post
Battalion boundary
International boundary
Boundary of former Palestine Mandate
0
5
10km
0
5mi
35°40′
36°00′
33°20′
33°10′
33°00′
32°50′
35°50′
2814m
Mount Hermon
A
B
LEBANON
ISRAEL
SYRIAN ARAB REPUBLIC
GOLAN HEIGHTS
JORDAN
Jordan River
Lake Tiberias
Chebaa
Hadar
Majdel Chams
Saassa
AUSBATT POLLOG
Camp Faouar
AUSBATT
Khan Arnabe
Jaba
FINBATT
FINBATT CANLOG
QUNEITRA
Umm Batina
Camp Ziouani
Ain Ziouani
Kudnah
Khochniye
Rafid
Boutmiye
Sidon
Damascus
UNIFIL
Tyre
UNDOF HQ
OGG HQ
OGG-D
ODD HQ
ODD-D
UNDOF
Tiberias
OGG-T
ODD-T

MAP NO. 3329.4 Rev. 1 UNITED NATIONS
JUNE 1990

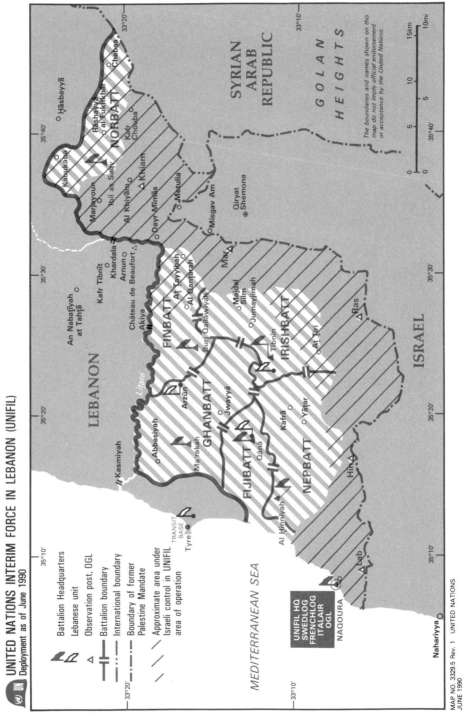

UNITED NATIONS INTERIM FORCE IN LEBANON (UNIFIL)
Deployment as of June 1990

Battalion Headquarters
Lebanese unit
△ Observation post, OGL
Battalion boundary
International boundary
Boundary of former Palestine Mandate
Approximate area under Israeli control in UNIFIL area of operation

UNIFIL HQ
SWEDLOG
FRENCHLOG
ITALAIR
OGL
NAQOURA

The boundaries and names shown on this map do not imply official endorsement or acceptance by the United Nations.

0 5 10 15km
0 5 10mi

MEDITERRANEAN SEA

LEBANON

SYRIAN ARAB REPUBLIC

GOLAN HEIGHTS

ISRAEL

NORBATT
FINBATT
GHANBATT
FIJIBATT
NEPBATT
IRISHBATT

Nahariyya

MAP NO. 3329.5 Rev. 1   UNITED NATIONS
JUNE 1990

UNITED NATIONS MILITARY OBSERVER GROUP IN INDIA AND PAKISTAN
Deployment as of June 1990 (UNMOGIP)

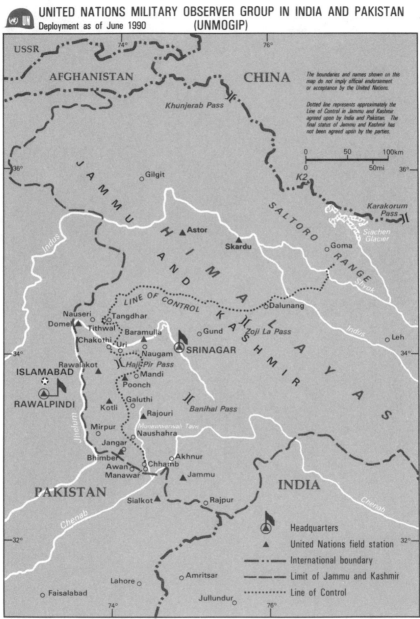

The boundaries and names shown on this map do not imply official endorsement or acceptance by the United Nations.

Dotted line represents approximately the Line of Control in Jammu and Kashmir agreed upon by India and Pakistan. The final status of Jammu and Kashmir has not been agreed upon by the parties.

0	50	100km
0		50mi

USSR
AFGHANISTAN
CHINA
Khunjerab Pass
K2
Karakorum Pass
Gilgit
SALTORO RANGE
Siachen Glacier
Astor
Skardu
Goma
Shyok
JAMMU
HIMALAYAS
AND
KASHMIR
LINE OF CONTROL
Dalunang
Nauseri
Tangdhar
Domel
Tithwal
Baramulla
Gund
Zoji La Pass
Chakothi
Uri
Naugam
SRINAGAR
Leh
Indus
Rawalakot
Haji Pir Pass
ISLAMABAD
Mandi
Poonch
RAWALPINDI
Galuthi
Kotli
Rajouri
Banihal Pass
Mirpur
Munawwarwah Tawi
Jangar
Naushahra
Bhimber
Akhnur
Awan
Chhamb
Manawar
Jammu
PAKISTAN
INDIA
Sialkot
Rajpur
Chenab
Jhelum
Chenab
Lahore
Amritsar
Faisalabad
Jullundur

Headquarters
▲ United Nations field station
─·─·─ International boundary
─ ─ ─ Limit of Jammu and Kashmir
··········· Line of Control

UNITED NATIONS OBSERVATION GROUP IN LEBANON (UNOGIL)
Deployment as of July 1958

The boundaries and names shown on this
map do not imply official endorsement
or acceptance by the United Nations.

35°30'   36°   36°30'

Arida   Chadra
Azizïyé   Notre-Dame
du-Fort
Halba   Beino
34°30'   34°30'
Munié   Koussair
Tripoli   Hermel
Sir Danié
El Kah
Amioun   Ehden

MEDITERRANEAN SEA
Hadeth Jobbé   Zabboud   Râs Baalbek
El Laboué   Arsal
Aïnata
Yammouné
Btedaï
LEBANON
Baalbek
34°   34°
UNOGIL HQ   Dhour Choueir   A.U.E.F.
BEIRUT   Rayak   Maarboûn
Chtaura   Zahlé   Jennta
Deir el   Masnaa   UNITED ARAB
Kamar   Barouk   REPUBLIC
Aïn Zebdé   Aïta el Foukhar   (SYRIA)
Aïn Arab
Deir el
Kfar   Aachayer
Sidon   Mechki
Jezzine
33°30'   33°30'

Station
El Haouch
Hasbaya   Sub-station
Marjayoûn   Chebaa
Observation post and
Deir Mimass   Traffic check post
Kherouia   Station boundary
Tyre
International boundary
Boundary of former
Palestine Mandate

0   10   20   30   40   50km

0   10   20   30mi

ISRAEL   35°30'   36°

MAP NO. 3329.7 Rev. 1 UNITED NATIONS
JUNE 1990

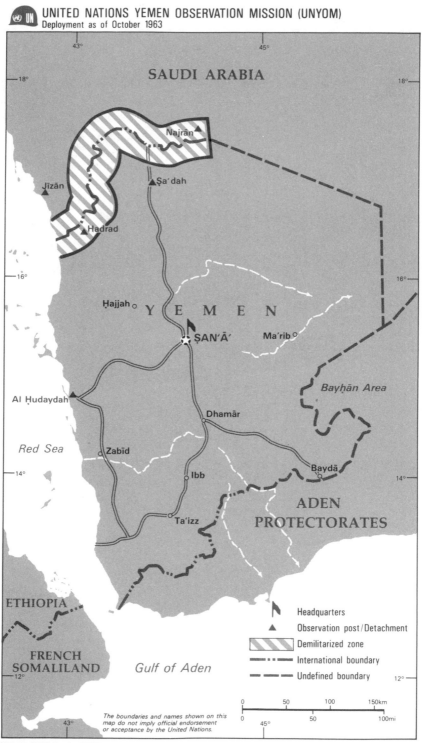

UNITED NATIONS YEMEN OBSERVATION MISSION (UNYOM)
Deployment as of October 1963

SAUDI ARABIA

18°

Najrān

Jīzān

Ṣa'dah

Hadrad

16°

Ḥajjah

Y E M E N

ŞAN'Ā'

Ma'rib

Bayḥān Area

Al Ḥudaydah

Dhamār

Red Sea

Zabīd

14°

Ibb

Baydā

Ta'izz

ADEN
PROTECTORATES

ETHIOPIA

Headquarters

Observation post / Detachment

Demilitarized zone

International boundary

FRENCH
SOMALILAND

Gulf of Aden

Undefined boundary

12°

| 0 | 50 | 100 | 150km |
| 0 | 50 | | 100mi |

43°

45°

The boundaries and names shown on this
map do not imply official endorsement
or acceptance by the United Nations.

MAP NO. 3329.8 Rev. 1   UNITED NATIONS
JUNE 1990

UNITED NATIONS OPERATION IN THE CONGO (ONUC)
Deployment as of June 1961

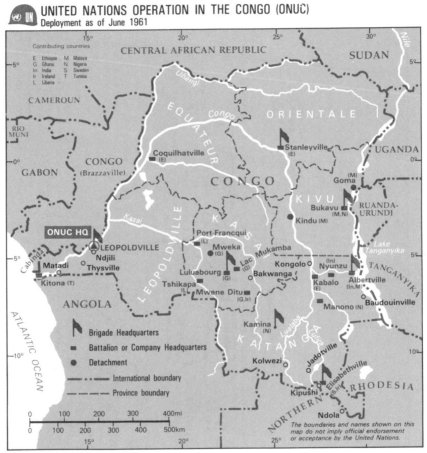

Contributing countries

E	Ethiopia	M	Malaya
G	Ghana	N	Nigeria
In	India	S	Sweden
Ir	Ireland	T	Tunisia
L	Liberia		

CENTRAL AFRICAN REPUBLIC

SUDAN

CAMEROUN

RIO MUNI

GABON

CONGO (Brazzaville)

EQUATEUR

ORIENTALE

Coquilhatville (E)

Stanleyville (E)

UGANDA

CONGO

Goma (M)

KIVU

Bukavu (M,N)

RUANDA-URUNDI

Kindu (M)

ONUC HQ

LEOPOLDVILLE

Ndjili

Thysville

Matadi

Kitona (T)

Port-Francqui (L)

Mweka (G)

Mukamba

Kongolo

Nyunzu (In)

TANGANYIKA

Luluabourg (G)

Bakwanga

Kabalo (E)

Albertville (In,M)

Lake Tanganyika

Tshikapa

Mwene Ditu (G,Ir)

Manono (N)

Baudouinville

ANGOLA

Kamina (N)

KATANGA

ATLANTIC OCEAN

Brigade Headquarters

Battalion or Company Headquarters

Detachment

International boundary

Province boundary

Kolwezi

Jadotville

Kipushi

Elisabethville (S,In)

RHODESIA

NORTHERN

Ndola

0	100	200	300	400mi
0	100	200	300	400	500km

The boundaries and names shown on this map do not imply official endorsement or acceptance by the United Nations.

MAP NO. 3329.9 Rev. 1   UNITED NATIONS
JUNE 1990

UNITED NATIONS PEACE-KEEPING FORCE IN CYPRUS (UNFICYP)
Deployment as of December 1965

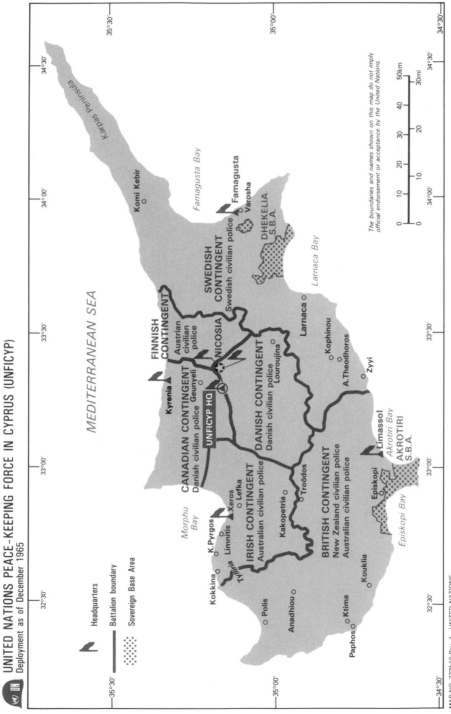

Headquarters

Battalion boundary

Sovereign Base Area

MEDITERRANEAN SEA

Karpas Peninsula

Komi Kebir

Famagusta Bay

Famagusta
Varosha

DHEKELIA
S.B.A.

SWEDISH
CONTINGENT
Swedish civilian police

Larnaca Bay

Larnaca

FINNISH
CONTINGENT

Austrian
civilian
police

NICOSIA

Kophinou

Kyrenia

CANADIAN CONTINGENT
Danish civilian police   Geunyeli

UNFICYP HQ

DANISH CONTINGENT
Danish civilian police
Louroujina

A.Theodhoros

Zyyi

Morphu
Bay

Xeros
Lefka

IRISH CONTINGENT
Australian civilian police

Kakopetria

Troodos

Limassol

Akrotiri Bay

AKROTIRI
S.B.A.

K.Pyrgos
Limnitis
Tylliria

BRITISH CONTINGENT
New Zealand civilian police
Australian civilian police

Episkopi

Episkopi Bay

Kokkina

Polis

Anadhiou

Kakopetria

Kouklia

Paphos
Ktima

34°30'
34°00'
33°30'
33°00'
32°30'

35°30'
35°00'
34°30'

The boundaries and names shown on this map do not imply
official endorsement or acceptance by the United Nations.

0   10 20 30 40 50km
0   10 20   30mi

MAP NO. 3329.10 Rev. 1   UNITED NATIONS
JUNE 1990

UNITED NATIONS PEACE-KEEPING FORCE IN CYPRUS (UNFICYP)
Deployment as of June 1990

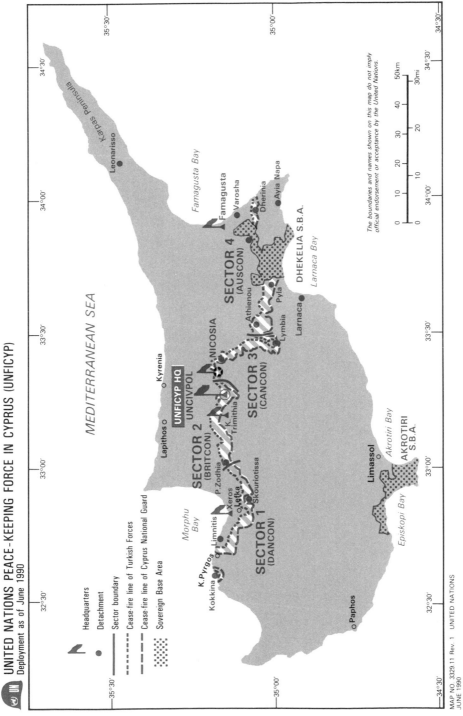

Headquarters

Detachment

Sector boundary

Cease-fire line of Turkish Forces

Cease-fire line of Cyprus National Guard

Sovereign Base Area

MEDITERRANEAN SEA

Karpas Peninsula

Leonarisso

Famagusta Bay

Famagusta

Varosha

Dherinia

Ayia Napa

SECTOR 4
(AUSCON)

DHEKELIA S.B.A.

Larnaca Bay

Athienou

Pyla

Larnaca

Lymbia

SECTOR 3
(CANCON)

Kyrenia

Lapithos

NICOSIA

UNFICYP HQ

UNCIVPOL

K.
Trimithia

SECTOR 2
(BRITCON)

P.Zodhia

Lefka

Skouriotissa

Xeros

Limnitis

K.Pyrgos

Kokkina

SECTOR 1
(DANCON)

Morphu
Bay

Limassol

Akrotiri Bay

AKROTIRI
S.B.A.

Episkopi Bay

Paphos

The boundaries and names shown on this map do not imply
official endorsement or acceptance by the United Nations.

0   10   20   30   40   50km

0   10   20   30mi

35°30'

34°30'

34°00'

33°30'

33°00'

32°30'

35°30'

35°00'

34°30'

34°00'

33°30'

33°00'

32°30'

34°30'

35°00'

34°30'

34°00'

MAP NO. 3329.11 Rev. 1   UNITED NATIONS
JUNE 1990

UNITED NATIONS GOOD OFFICES MISSION IN AFGHANISTAN AND PAKISTAN (UNGOMAP)
Deployment as of February 1989

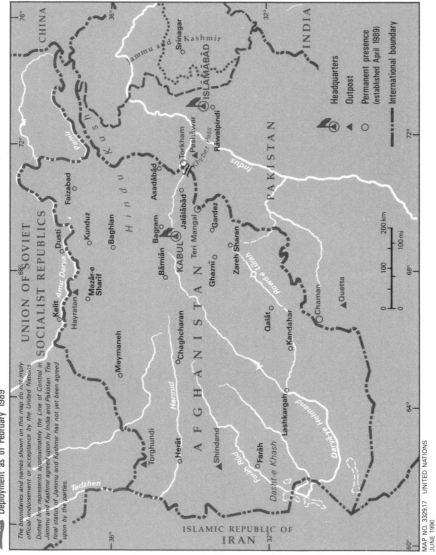

The boundaries and names shown on this map do not imply official endorsement or acceptance by the United Nations.

Dotted line represents approximately the Line of Control in Jammu and Kashmir agreed upon by India and Pakistan. The final status of Jammu and Kashmir has not yet been agreed upon by the parties.

Legend:
- Headquarters
- Outpost
- Permanent presence (established April 1989)
- International boundary

MAP NO. 3329.17   UNITED NATIONS
JUNE 1990

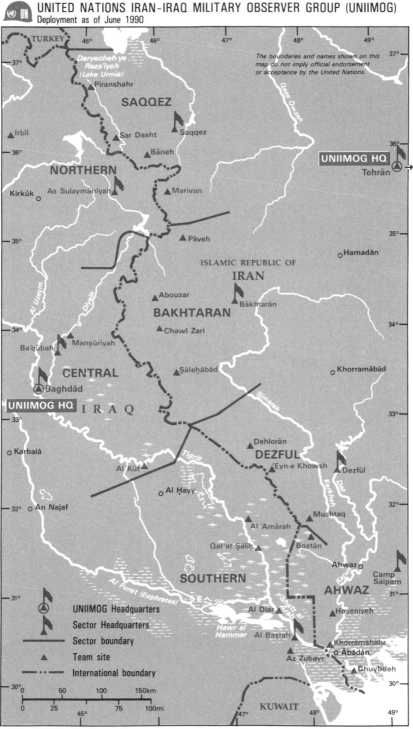

UNITED NATIONS IRAN-IRAQ MILITARY OBSERVER GROUP (UNIIMOG)
Deployment as of June 1990

The boundaries and names shown on this map do not imply official endorsement or acceptance by the United Nations.

TURKEY

Daryacheh-ye Reza'iyeh (Lake Urmia)

Piranshahr

SAQQEZ

Irbīl

Sar Dasht

Saqqez

Bāneh

NORTHERN

Kirkūk

As Sulaymānīyah

Marivan

Pāveh

UNIIMOG HQ
Tehrān

Hamadān

ISLAMIC REPUBLIC OF

IRAN

Abouzar

Bākhtarān

BAKHTARAN

Chawl Zari

Ba'qūbah

Manşūriyah

CENTRAL

Şālehābād

Khorramābād

Baghdād

UNIIMOG HQ

IRAQ

Karbalā

Dehlorān

Al Kūt

DEZFUL

'Eyn-e Khowsh

Dezfūl

Al Hayy

An Najaf

Mushtaq

Al 'Amārah

Qal'at Şālih

Bostān

Ahwaz

Camp Saipam

Al Furāt (Euphrates)

SOUTHERN

AHWAZ

Hoseniyeh

Al Diar

Hawr al Hammar

Al Başrah

Khorramshahr

Ābādān

Az Zubayr

Chuybdeh

△ UNIIMOG Headquarters
Sector Headquarters
—— Sector boundary
▲ Team site
—·—·— International boundary

| 50 | 100 | 150km |
| 25 | 75 | 100mi |

KUWAIT

MAP NO. 3329.12   UNITED NATIONS
JUNE 1990

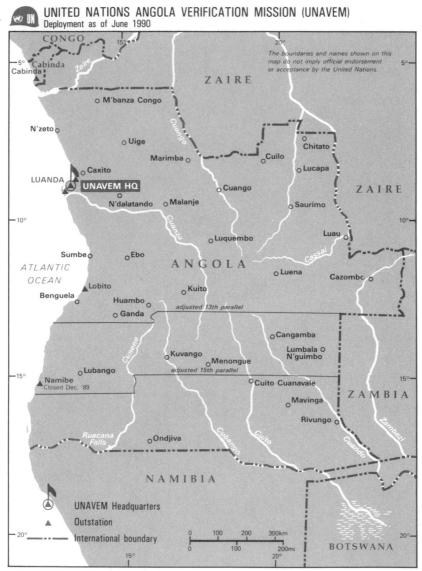

UNITED NATIONS ANGOLA VERIFICATION MISSION (UNAVEM)
Deployment as of June 1990

The boundaries and names shown on this map do not imply official endorsement or acceptance by the United Nations.

CONGO

ZAIRE

Cabinda
Cabinda
Zaire

M'banza Congo

N'zeto

Uige

Marimba

Cuango

Cuilo

Chitato

Lucapa

Caxito

LUANDA
UNAVEM HQ

Cuango

ZAIRE

N'dalatando
Malanje

Saurimo

Cuanza

Luquembo

Luau

Sumbe
Ebo

ANGOLA

Cassai

Luena

Cazombo

ATLANTIC
OCEAN

Lobito

Kuito

Benguela

Huambo

adjusted 13th parallel

Ganda

Cangamba

Lumbala
N'guimbo

Cunene

Kuvango
Menongue

adjusted 15th parallel

Lubango

Namibe
Closed Dec. '89

Cuito Cuanavale

ZAMBIA

Mavinga

Cubango

Cuito

Rivungo

Zambezi

Ruacana
Falls

Ondjiva

Cuando

NAMIBIA

UNAVEM Headquarters
Outstation
International boundary

0   100   200   300km
0   100   200mi

BOTSWANA

MAP NO. 3329.15 UNITED NATIONS
JUNE 1990

UNITED NATIONS TRANSITION ASSISTANCE GROUP (UNTAG)
Civilian Deployment as of November 1989

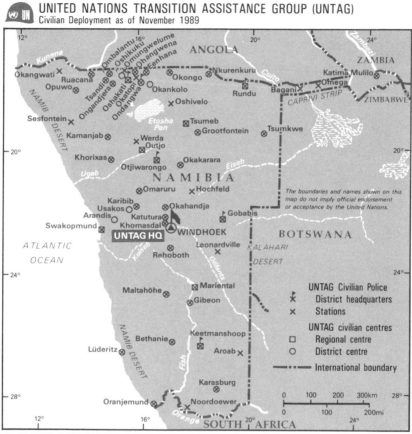

UNITED NATIONS TRANSITION ASSISTANCE GROUP (UNTAG)
Military Deployment as of November 1989

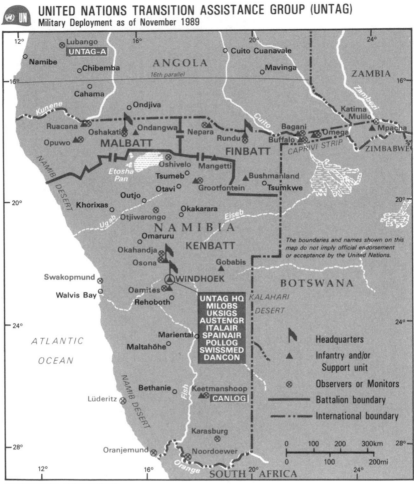

ANGOLA

12°   16°   20°   24°

Lubango
UNTAG-A
Namibe
Chibemba
16th parallel
Cuito Cuanavale
Mavinga
ZAMBIA

16°   16°

Cahama

Ondjiva
Katima
Mulilo
Kunene
Ruacana   Bagani
Oshakati   Ondangwa   Nepara   Rundu   Buffalo   Omega   Mpacha
Opuwo   MALBATT   FINBATT   CAPRIVI STRIP   ZIMBABWE

Oshivelo   Mangetti
Etosha   Tsumeb   Bushmanland
Pan   Otavi   Grootfontein   Tsumkwe
Outjo

20°   20°
Khorixas

Otjiwarongo   Okakarara
Ugab   Eiseb

NAMIBIA
Omaruru
KENBATT
Okahandja
Osona   Gobabis   The boundaries and names shown on this
map do not imply official endorsement
or acceptance by the United Nations.

Swakopmund   WINDHOEK   BOTSWANA
Oamites   KALAHARI
Walvis Bay   Rehoboth   DESERT

UNTAG HQ
MILOBS
UKSIGS
AUSTENGR   Headquarters
Marienta   ITALAIR
ATLANTIC   SPAINAIR
Maltahöhe   POLLOG   Infantry and/or
OCEAN   SWISSMED   Support unit
DANCON

Observers or Monitors

Bethanie   Keetmanshoop
Lüderitz   Fish   CANLOG   Battalion boundary

International boundary

Karasburg

0   100   200   300km   28°
Oranjemund   Noordoewer   0   100   200mi
Orange
12°   16°   SOUTH   AFRICA   24°

24°   24°

28°

MAP NO. 3329.13   UNITED NATIONS
JUNE 1990

UNITED NATIONS OBSERVER GROUP IN CENTRAL AMERICA (ONUCA)
Deployment as of June 1990

MEXICO

Bahia de Campeche

90° 88° 86° 84°

18° 18°

o Belize City

CARIBBEAN SEA

o Belmopan

BELIZE

Hondo

o Comitán

16° 16°

Gulf of Honduras

o Puerto Barrios

Islas de la Bahia

L. de Izabal

o Puerto Cortés

GUATEMALA

o San Pedro Sula

Usumacinta

Quezaltenango   Zacapa

HONDURAS

GUATEMALA CITY   Esquipulas   Santa Rosa de Copán

Ulúa

Patuca

ONUCA HQ

Mazatenango   La Esperanza   TEGUCIGALPA

Coco

Cuilapa   Guarita

Jutiapa   Las Trojes   6

Alvarado   Erandique

14°   Puerto Cabezas   14°

Santa Ana   San Lorenzo   Danlí

SAN SALVADOR   Ocotal   San José de Bocay

EL SALVADOR   Choluteca   1   2

Zacatecoluca   3

San Miguel   Jinotega

Golfo de Fonseca   El Tanque   Estelí   7

Chinandega   León   Matagalpa

12°   4   12°

NICARAGUA

PACIFIC OCEAN   MANAGUA   o Granada   o Bluefields

Lago de Nicaragua   5   8

ONUCA Headquarters

Liaison office

Verification centre   Liberia

10°   El Platanar   10°

Operational post   Puntarenas   SAN JOSÉ   Limón

Security zone   COSTA RICA

International boundary   Golfo de Nicoya

PANAMA

0   100   200   300km

0   100   200mi

The boundaries and names shown on this map do not imply
official endorsement or acceptance by the United Nations.

88°   86°   84°   8°

MAP NO. 3329.16   UNITED NATIONS
JUNE 1990

NOTES

NOTES

NOTES